Security and
Loss Prevention

Security and Loss Prevention

An Introduction
Third Edition

Philip P. Purpura, CPP

Butterworth–Heinemann
Boston   Oxford   Johannesburg   Melbourne   New Delhi   Singapore

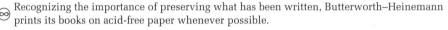 Butterworth–Heinemann supports the efforts of American Forests and the Global ReLeaf program in its campaign for the betterment of trees, forests, and our environment.

Library of Congress Cataloging-in-Publication Data
Purpura, Philip P., 1950–
    Security and loss prevention : an introduction / Philip P.
Purpura.—3d ed.
        p.   cm.
    Includes bibliographical references and index.
    ISBN 0-7506-9642-7 (alk. paper)
    1. Private security services.   2. Burglary protection.
3. Employee theft—Prevention.   4. Fire prevention.   5. Shoplifting—
Prevention.   6. Security systems.   I. Title.
HV8290.P87   1998
658.4'73—dc21   97-38810
                                                                                                        CIP

British Library Cataloguing-in-Publication Data
A catalogue record for this book is available from the British Library.

The publisher offers special discounts on bulk orders of this book.
For information, please contact:
Manager of Special Sales
Butterworth–Heinemann
225 Wildwood Avenue
Woburn, MA 01801-2041
Tel: 781-904-2500
Fax: 781-904-2620

For information on all Butterworth–Heinemann books available,
contact our World Wide Web home page at: http://www.bh.com

10 9 8 7 6 5 4 3 2 1

Printed in the United States of America

This edition is dedicated
to the hundreds of thousands
of security professionals whose efforts create
a secure environment for millions of people.

Contents

About the Author

Philip P. Purpura, CPP, is a college educator, consultant, expert witness, and writer. He began his security career in New York City and held management and proprietary and contract investigative positions. He also worked with a public police agency. Mr. Purpura is the author of three other security textbooks: *Retail Security and Shrinkage Protection* (Butterworth–Heinemann, 1993), *Modern Security and Loss Prevention Management* (Butterworth–Heinemann, 1989), and *The Security Handbook* (Delmar, 1991). He has also written *Criminal Justice: An Introduction* (Butterworth–Heinemann, 1997), and numerous articles in journals, magazines, and newsletters. He served as a contributing editor to three security periodicals. Mr. Purpura holds bachelor's and master's degrees in criminal justice from the University of Dayton and Eastern Kentucky University, respectively. He also studied in several foreign countries. He serves on the American Society for Industrial Security Standing Committee on Academic Programs. Presently, he is Director of the Security Training Institute and Resource Center and coordinator of the Church Security Project in South Carolina.

Preface

The third edition of *Security and Loss Prevention: An Introduction* continues to focus on loss problems and those countermeasures that protect against crimes, fires, and accidents. Because many fields of study hold answers to protection problems, the foundation of this text is interdisciplinary and draws on such disciplines as law, criminal justice, business, accounting, risk management, fire protection, safety, sociology, and psychology. The traditional focus of security—guards, fences, and alarms—is too narrow to deal with an increasingly complex world. Practitioners are being asked to do more with less resources and prove that the money spent on protection has a return on investment. In a world of rapid change, management expects protection personnel to produce answers quickly. The true professional maintains a positive attitude and sees problems as challenges that have solutions. An interdisciplinary approach can be an immense aid to the practitioner.

This third edition has been updated to reflect new laws, technology, security strategies, and statistics. Many new sources were added to support the contents of each chapter. This new edition also serves as a helpful directory; professional organizations that enhance protection programs are included with updated addresses and telephone numbers. The first five chapters provide an introduction and foundation for protection strategies. Chapter 1 defines security and loss prevention and presents a historical evolution of protection. The second chapter concentrates on the growth of the security industry and its problems. The next three chapters provide a foundation from which protection programs can become more efficient and effective: Chapter 3 focuses on risk analysis, planning, evaluation, research, performance measures, and security standards; Chapter 4 provides an overview of civil and criminal law and includes discussions of premise protection and negligence and arrest law; and Chapter 5, "Internal and External Relations," explains the why and how of recruiting people and organizations to assist with loss prevention efforts. Chapters 6, 7, and 8 emphasize strategies for curbing internal and external crime threats. These include job applicant screening, policies, procedures, and physical security. Chapter 9, on purchasing security services and devices, is vital because not all security specialists are wise consumers, and the best plans are useless when followed by poor purchasing decisions. Chapter 10 provides practical information on investigations. The strategies of accountability, accounting, and auditing described in Chapter 11 provide an understanding as to why these areas are essential for survival. Chapters 12, 13, and 14 cover fire and other disasters, safety, and risk management. Specialized security programs are explained in the next three chapters. These include such industries as retail, computer, nuclear, Department of Defense contractors, education, health-care, finance, and the government. Chapter 18 concentrates on six topics of concern: protection of sensitive information, communications security, terrorism, executive protection, substance abuse, and workplace violence. The final chapter covers the future, research directions, and employment opportunities. Topics that have been expanded and added are listed here:

Topics Expanded	Topics Added
Ethics	Privatization
Value-added security	Industry standards
Premise protection and negligent security	Maxims and models of security
Employee privacy	Performance measures
Employment law	Compliance auditing
Access cards	Environmental compliance
Interior and exterior intrusion sensors	Due diligence
Integrated systems	Federal sentencing guidelines
Illumination and lamps	"Inspections, not search and seizure"
Legal restrictions of investigations	Marketing security
Polygraph testing procedures	Cultural diversity
Bomb threats and explosions	Sexual harassment
Emergency planning and disaster recovery	Overseas investigations
Terrorism and countermeasures	OSHA and security
Trends affecting security and loss	Security for government institutions
prevention	Corporate intelligence gathering and
Career opportunities and advice	countermeasures
	Communications security
	Workplace violence

The student or practitioner will find this book to be user-friendly and interactive. Several features will assist the reader in understanding not only the basics but also the "reality" of the field. Within each chapter the loss problems are described and are followed by a discussion of the nuts-and-bolts countermeasures. New to the third edition are sidebars in each chapter that emphasize significant points and facilitate critical thinking about security issues. Cases titled "You Be the Judge" appear throughout the text. These are fictional accounts of actual cases that deal with security-related legal problems. The reader is asked for a verdict based on the material at hand and then is directed to the end of the chapter for the court's ruling. Additional boxed cases appear in most chapters and offer bits of interesting information or analyze a loss problem relevant to the subject matter of the chapter. An "international perspective" has been added to the text through boxed discussions of security problems and strategies facing other countries. Case problems at the end of most chapters have been increased in this third edition. These applications bridge theory to practice and ask the reader to apply the general concepts of the chapter to real-world situations. This activity enables the reader to consider alternate strategies, helps to stimulate controversy in group discussions, and allows the reader to make mistakes and receive feedback, thereby acquiring the skills for problem solving.

This book also helps applicants prepare for the Certified Protection Professional examination, which is sponsored by the American Society for Industrial Security. Numerous topics included in the examination are covered in this textbook.

The tremendous growth of the security and loss prevention field provides fertile ground to advance in a rewarding career. In such a competitive world, the survival and protection of businesses, technological innovations, and even the national interest will depend greatly on security and loss prevention programs. This book should inspire and motivate students and practitioners to fulfill these vital protection needs.

Acknowledgments

I would like to thank the many people who contributed to this third edition. Gratitude goes to my wife, Amyie, for her superb typing and editorial assistance, and to my family for their patience. I am thankful to the many security practitioners and librarians who helped to provide a wealth of information to support the contents of this book. The hardworking editorial team at Butterworth–Heinemann, including Laurel DeWolf, Stephanie Gelman, and Jodie Allen are to be recognized for their talents and skills in publishing this book. I am grateful for the team effort, among so many people, for without it this book could not be published.

INTRODUCTION TO SECURITY AND LOSS PREVENTION

1

History of Security and Loss Prevention

OBJECTIVES

After studying this chapter the reader will be able to

1. Define security and loss prevention;
2. Trace the early development of security and policing;
3. Describe the growth of security companies in the United States.

SECURITY AND *LOSS PREVENTION* DEFINED

A review of the literature defining *security* and *loss prevention* reveals a mixture of statements. Each definition reflects the broadness of this field and the definer's background and subjectivity. A concise, all-encompassing, and mutually agreeable definition is difficult to construct.

Webster's New Collegiate Dictionary defines security as "the quality or state of being secure . . . freedom from danger . . . safety . . . freedom from fear or anxiety . . . protection . . . measures taken to guard against espionage or sabotage, crime, attack, escape . . . an organization or department whose task is security." Green, author of *Introduction to Security*, points out that "security in its semantic and philosophical sense, implies a stable, relatively predictable environment in which an individual or group may pursue its ends without disruption or harm, and without fear of such disturbance or injury."[1] In *Security Administration: An Introduction*, Post and Kingsbury define security as "those means, active or passive, which serve to protect and preserve an environment which allows for the conduct of activities within the organization or society without disruption."[2] These definitions imply that security provides a tranquil environment whereby individual or organizational objectives can be attained.

Within our organized society, security can be provided primarily by our armed forces, public safety agencies (e.g., police and fire departments), and private security. This text focuses on the private sector.

3

The methods of private security have increased in terms of specialization and diversification. Methods not previously associated with security have emerged and become important components of the total security effort. Guards, fences, and alarms have been the hallmark of traditional security functions. Today, with industrialized society becoming increasingly complex, additional specialization—accounting, auditing, OSHA* (Occupational Safety and Health Administration) standards, fire protection, safeguarding hazardous materials, insurance, environmental design, to name a few—continuously are being added to the security function.

Because of the increase in diverse specialization within the security function, many practitioners favor a broader term for all of these functions, known as *loss prevention*. Post and Kingsbury write,

> Over the last several years, security has become synonymous with loss prevention. The concept of total loss control or protection from all forms and classes of hazards has thus provided a broad framework for the provision of asset protection.[3]
>
> It [loss prevention] serves to provide an "umbrella" under which all the subsystems of societal and corporate protection are provided. They include insurance, architecture and design, police and fire protection, and safety programs. These subsystems are the components of a "total loss control program."[4]

Another reason for the growing shift in terminology from *security* to *loss prevention* involves the negative connotations of security. Saul Astor points out:

> In the minds of many, the very word "security" is its own impediment.
> . . . Security carries a stigma; the very word suggests police, badges, alarms, thieves, burglars, and some generally negative and even repellent mental images. . . . Simply using the term "loss prevention" instead of the word "security" can be a giant step toward improving the security image, broadening the scope of the security function, and attracting able people.[5]

Post and Kingsbury add

> the term "security" is quickly being replaced in the corporate environment by terminology such as loss prevention, asset protection, or total loss control. The reliance on a negatively described, defensively oriented managerial subsystem is being replaced by a "system concept" embracing all aspects of corporate activity. Totally integrated subsystems of protection now include "security" within them rather than viewing it as a separate and distinct operational system.[6]

---

* OSHA is an administration, established by congressional act, requiring employers to provide a safe and healthy work environment for employees.

Because of additional specialization included in the security function and the frequently negative connotations associated with the term *security*, the all-encompassing term for describing the contents of this text is *loss prevention*. The security function and other specialized fields (safety, auditing, insurance, etc.) are subsumed in loss prevention.

Security is narrowly defined as traditional methods (security officers, fences, alarms) used to increase the likelihood of a crime-controlled, tranquil, and uninterrupted environment for an individual or organization in pursuit of objectives.

Loss prevention is broadly defined as any method (e.g., security officers, safety, auditing, insurance) used by an individual or organization to increase the likelihood of preventing and controlling loss (e.g., people, money, productivity, materials) resulting from a host of adverse occurrences (e.g., crime, fire, accident, error, poor supervision or management, bad investment). This broad definition provides a foundation for the loss prevention practitioner whose innovations are limited only by his or her imagination. It is hoped that these concepts not only will guide the reader through this text but also reinforce a trend in the use of these definitions.

Security is narrowly defined; *loss prevention* is broadly defined.

EARLY CIVILIZATIONS

Prehistoric human beings depended on nature for protection, because they had not learned how to build strong houses and fortifications. In cold climates, caves provided protection and shelter, whereas in the tropics, trees and thickets were used. Caves were particularly secure because rocky walls guarded tribes on all sides except at the cave mouth. To protect the entrance, redundant (i.e., duplicating to prevent failure) security was employed: large rocks acted as barriers when they were rolled in front of entrances; dogs, with their keen sense of smell, served to alarm and attack; and fires added additional defense. By living on the side of a mountain with access via a narrow, rocky ledge, cave dwellers were relatively safe from enemies and beasts. Early Pueblo Indians, living in present-day New Mexico and Arizona, ensured greater protection for themselves in their dwellings by constructing ladders that could be pulled in, and this defense proved useful until enemies attacked with their own ladders. In fact, since early civilizations, as today, security measures have never been foolproof, and adversaries typically strive to circumvent (i.e., to go around) defenses.

> Through history, redundant security has been used to block adversaries attempting to circumvent defenses.

The Great Wall of China is the longest structure ever built. It was constructed over hundreds of years beginning in the 400s B.C. Hundreds of thousands of workers lived their lives near the wall and participated in this huge project that stretched 4000 miles and reached heights of 25 feet. Unfortunately, the wall provided protection only from minor attacks; when a major invasion force struck, the defense could not withstand the onslaught. The army of Mongol leader Genghis Khan swept across the wall during the 1200s A.D. and conquered much of China. (Since 1949, the Chinese government has restored some sections of the mostly collapsed wall, which is a major tourist attraction.)[7]

It is interesting to note the changing character of security through history. In earlier years, huge fortifications could be built with cheap labor. Today, physical barriers such as fences and walls are expensive, as is the posting of security forces at physical barriers; a king could secure a perimeter with many inexpensive guards. Today, one 24-hour post costs tens of thousands of dollars a year.

As societies became more complex, the concepts of leadership, authority, and organization began to evolve. Mutual association created social and economic advantages but also inequities, so people and assets required increased protection. Intergroup and intragroup conflicts created problems whose "solutions" often took the form of gruesome punishments, including stoning, flaying, burning, and crucifying. A person's criminal record was carried right on his or her body, through branding and mutilation. By 1750 B.C. the laws of *Hammurabi, king of Babylon,* not only codified the responsibilities of the individual to the group and the rules for private dealings between individuals but discussed retributive penalties.[8]

Ancient Greece

Between the ninth and the third centuries B.C. ancient Greece blossomed as an advanced commercial and culturally rich civilization. The Greeks protected their advancing civilization through the use of the *polis,* or city-state, which consisted of a city and the surrounding land protected by a centrally built fortress overlooking the countryside. A stratified society brought the ruling classes constant fear of revolution from below. Spartans, for example, kept their secret agents planted among the lower classes and subversives. *During the time of the Greek city-states, the first police force evolved to protect local communities, although citizens were responsible for this function.*

The Greek rulers did not view local policing as a state responsibility, and when internal conflicts arose, they used the army. During this era, the Greek philosopher Plato introduced an advanced concept of justice, in which an offender not only would be forced to pay a sort of retribution but also would be forced into a method of reform or rehabilitation.

Ancient Rome

The civilization of ancient Rome also developed both commercially and culturally before the birth of Christ. Rome was located only 15 miles from the sea and could easily share in the trade of the Mediterranean. This city sat on seven hills overlooking the Tiber River, which permitted ease in fortification and defense. A primitive but effective alarm system was used by placing geese at strategic locations so their very sensitive hearing would trigger squawking at the sound of an approaching army.

The Roman regime was well designed to carry on the chief business of the Roman state, which was war. A phalanx of 8000 foot soldiers became the basic unit of a Roman army equipped with helmets, shields, lances, and swords. Later, a more maneuverable legion of 3600 men armed in addition with iron-tipped javelins was used. These legions also were employed to maintain law and order. The first emperor of Rome, Augustus (27 B.C.–14 A.D.), created the *Praetorian Guard* to provide security for his life and property. These urban cohorts of 500 to 600 men were deployed to keep the peace in the city. Some believe that after about 6 A.D. this was the most effective police force until recent developments in law enforcement. Modern-day coordinated patrolling and preventive security began with the subsequent nonmilitary *vigiles*, night watchmen who were active in both policing and fire fighting.[9]

The Romans have an interesting history in fire protection. During the 300s B.C., slaves were assigned firefighting duties. Later, improved organization established divisions encompassing hundreds of people, who carried water in jars to fires or brought large pillows so victims trapped in taller structures could jump with improved chances for survival. The completion of the aqueducts to Rome aided firefighting by making water easier to obtain. Hand pumps and leather hoses were other innovations.

The Middle Ages in Europe

During the Dark Ages, the period in history after the destruction of the ancient Greek and Roman empires, *feudalism* gradually developed in Europe. Overlords supplied food and security to those who farmed and provided protection around castles fortified by walls, towers, and a drawbridge that could be raised from its position across a moat. Even then, security required registration, licensing, and a fee—Henry II of England (reigned

1154–1189 A.D.) destroyed more than 1100 unlicensed castles that had been constructed during a civil war![10]

Another mutual arrangement was the war band of the early Germans, the *comitatus*, by which a leader commanded the loyalty of followers, who banded together to fight and win booty. (Today, the term *posse comitatus* denotes a body of citizens that authority can call on for assistance against offenders.) To defend against these bands of German barbarians, many landowners throughout Europe built their own private armies.

Much of the United States' customs, language, laws, and police and security methods can be traced to its English heritage. For this reason, England's history of protection is examined here.

Between the seventh and tenth centuries, the frankpledge system and the concept of tithing fostered increased protection. The *frankpledge system,* which originated in France and spread to England, emphasized communal responsibility for justice and protection. The *tithing*, or group of ten families, shared the duties of maintaining the peace and protecting the community.

In 1066, William, Duke of Normandy (in present-day France), crossed the English Channel and defeated the Anglo-Saxons at Hastings. A highly repressive police system developed under martial law as the state appropriated responsibility for peace and protection. Community authority and the tithing system were weakened. William divided England into 55 districts, or *shires*. A *reeve*, drawn from the military, was assigned to each district. (Today, we use the word *sheriff*, derived from *shire-reeve*.) William is credited with changing the law to make a crime an offense against the state rather than against the individual and was instrumental in separating police from judicial functions. A traveling judge tried the cases of those arrested by the shire-reeves.

In 1215 King John signed the *Magna Carta*, which guaranteed civil and political liberties. Local government power increased at the expense of the national government, and community protection increased at the local level.

Another security milestone was the *Statute of Westminster* (1285) issued by King Edward I to organize a police and justice system. A *watch and ward* was established to keep the peace. Every town was required to deploy men all night, to close the gates of walled towns at night, and to enforce a curfew.

MORE CONTEMPORARY TIMES

Modern England

For the next 500 years, repeated attempts were made to improve protection and justice in England. Each king was confronted with increasingly serious crime problems and cries from the citizenry for solutions. As England colonized many parts of the world and as trade and commercial pursuits brought many people into the cities, urban problems and high crime rates persisted. Merchants, dissatisfied with the protection afforded by the government, hired private security forces to protect their businesses.

By the 18th century, the Industrial Revolution compounded urban problems. Many citizens were forced to carry arms for their own protection, because a strong government policing system was absent. Various police and private security organizations did strive to reduce crime; *Henry Fielding,* in 1748, was appointed magistrate; and he devised the strategy of preventing crime through police action by helping to form the famous *Bow Street Runners,* the first detective unit. The merchant police were formed to protect businesses, and the Thames River police provided protection at the docks. During this period, over 160 crimes, including stealing food, were punishable by death. Policing and justice were impotent—as pickpockets were being hanged, others moved among the spectators, picking pockets.

Peel's Reforms

In 1829, *Sir Robert Peel's* efforts produced the *Metropolitan Police Act,* a revolution in law enforcement. Modern policing was born. Peel's innovative ideas were accepted by Parliament, and he was selected to implement an act that established a full-time, unarmed police force with the major purpose of patrolling London. Peel is credited also with reforming the criminal law by limiting its scope and abolishing the death penalty for more than 100 offenses. It was hoped that such a strategy would gain public support and respect for the police. Peel was very selective in hiring his personnel, and training was an essential part of developing a professional police force. Peel's reforms are applicable today and include crime prevention, the strategic deployment of police according to time and location, a command of temper rather than violent action, record keeping, and crime news distribution.

Although Sir Robert Peel produced a revolution in law enforcement in 1829, crime and the private security industry continued to grow.

Early America

The Europeans who colonized North America had brought with them the heritage of their mother countries, including various customs of protection. The watchman system and collective responses remained popular. A central fortification in populated areas provided increased security from hostile threats. As communities expanded in size, the office of sheriff took hold in the South, whereas the functions of constable and watchman were the norm in the Northeast. The sheriff's duties involved apprehending offenders, serving subpoenas, and collecting taxes. Because a sheriff was paid a higher fee for collecting taxes, policing became a lower priority. Constables performed a variety of tasks such as keeping the peace, bringing suspects and witnesses to court, and eliminating health hazards. As in England, the watch system had its share of inefficiency, and to make matters worse, those convicted of minor crimes were sentenced to serve time on the watch.

The watch also warned citizens of fire. In colonial towns, each home had to have two fire buckets, and homeowners were subject to a fine if they did not respond to a fire, buckets in hand. A large fire in Boston in 1679 prompted the establishment of the first paid fire department in North America.[11]

The Growth of Policing

The period of the middle 1800s was a turning point for both law enforcement and private security in America, as it had been in England. Several major cities (e.g., New York, Philadelphia, San Francisco) organized police forces, often modeled after the London Metropolitan Police. However, corruption was widespread. Numerous urban police agencies in the Northeast received large boosts in personnel and resources to combat the growing militancy of the labor unions in the late 1800s and early 1900s. According to Richard Holden, to a large extent, many of the large urban police departments originally were formed as strikebreakers.[12] Federal policing also experienced growth during this period. The U.S. Treasury had already established an investigative unit in 1864. As in England, an increase in public police did not quell the need for private security.

The History of Loss Prevention in a Nutshell

Loss prevention has its origin in the insurance industry. Before the Civil War, insurers gave minimal attention to the benefits of loss prevention. For instance, in the fire insurance business, executives generally viewed fires as good for business. Insurance rates were based on past loss experience, premiums were paid by customers, losses were paid to unfortunate customers, and a profit was expected by the insurer. When excessive fire losses resulted in spiraling premiums, the changing nature of the fire insurance business created a hardship for both the insurer and the insured. Insurance executives were forced to raise premiums to cover losses and customers complained about high rates. The predominance of wooden construction (even wooden chimneys) in dense urban areas made fire insurance unaffordable for many. A serious fire peril persisted.

After the Civil War, loss prevention began to gain momentum as a way to reduce losses and premiums. Fire insurance companies formed the National Board of Fire Underwriters, which, through the use of engineers, investigation, research, and education, was credited with preventing losses. In 1965, the board was merged into the American Insurance Association (AIA). AIA activities have brought about the development of the National Building Code, a model code adopted by many municipalities to reduce fire losses.

Today, executives throughout the insurance industry view loss prevention as essential. Many insurers have loss prevention departments to aid themselves and customers. Furthermore, customers (i.e., the insured), to reduce premiums, have become increasingly concerned about preventing losses. Management in many businesses instituted loss prevention strategies (e.g., fire protection). These strategies repeatedly are handled by the security departments within businesses, which results in an expanded role for security. Expansion of the security function to such fields as fire protection and safety has led to the use of the broader term *loss prevention* rather than *security*.

Some practitioners employ the less popular terms *loss protection* or *loss control*. These terms refer to minimizing loss if or when a peril (e.g., accident) occurs. To illustrate, by installing a traffic signal at the intersection of two heavily traveled roads, accidents may be prevented. Because traffic signals usually cause vehicles to slow down, the severity of accidents may be reduced (i.e., loss protection or loss control).

The Growth of Security Companies

In 1850, *Allan Pinkerton*, a cooper, opened a detective agency in the United States after becoming the Chicago Police Department's first detective. Because public police were limited by geographic jurisdiction, they were handicapped when investigating and apprehending fleeing offenders. This limitation facilitated the growth of private security. Pinkerton (see Figure 1–1) and others became famous as they pursued criminals across state boundaries throughout the country. Today, Pinkerton Service Corporation, with headquarters in Encino, California, is one of the largest security companies in the United States (Pinkerton Service Corporation, 15910 Ventura Blvd., Suite 900, Encino, CA 91436; Tel.: 1-800-232-7465).

During the 1800s, because public police were limited by geographic jurisdiction and restrained from chasing fleeing offenders, private security filled this need and became a growth industry.

To accompany Americans' expansion westward during the 19th century and to ensure the safe transportation of valuables, *Henry Wells* and *William Fargo* supplied a wide-open market by forming Wells, Fargo & Company in 1852, opening the era of bandits accosting stagecoaches and their shotgun riders. Today, Wells Fargo Alarm, Armored Truck, and Guard Services are subsidiaries of Borg-Warner Security Corporation, the largest security company in the United States (Borg-Warner Security Corporation, 200 South Michigan Ave., Chicago, IL 60604; Tel.: 1-800-80-SECURE).

Figure 1–1   Major Allan Pinkerton, President Lincoln, and General John A. McClellan, Antietam, MD, October 1862. Courtesy: National Archives.

Another security entrepreneur, *William Burns*, first was a Secret Service agent who directed the Bureau of Investigation that preceded the FBI. In 1909, this experienced investigator opened the William J. Burns Detective Agency (see Figure 1–2), which became the investigative arm of the American Bankers Association. Today, Burns International is involved in guard and investigative services and is a subsidiary of Borg-Warner Security Corporation.

Washington Perry Brink, in 1859, also took advantage of the need for the safe transportation of valuables. From freight and package delivery to the transportation of payrolls, his service required increased protection through the years as cargo became more valuable and more vulnerable. Following the killing of two Brink's guards during a robbery, the armored truck was initiated in 1917. Today, Brink's, Inc., a subsidiary of the Pittston Co., does business in 40 countries (Brink's, Inc., One Thorndal Circle, P.O. Box 1225, Darien, CT 06820; Tel.: 203-662-7800).

Edwin Holmes is another historical figure in the development of private security in the United States. He pioneered the electronic security alarm business. During 1858, Holmes had a difficult time convincing people that an alarm would sound on the second floor of a home when a door or

Figure 1–2   In 1910, William J. Burns, the foremost American investigator of his day and the first director of the government agency that became the FBI, formed the William J. Burns Detective Agency. Courtesy: Borg-Warner Security Corp.

window was opened on the first floor. His sales strategy was to carry door-to-door a small model of a home containing his electric alarm system. Soon sales soared, and the first central office burglar alarm monitoring operation began. Today, Holmes Protection Group, Inc., with headquarters in New York City, provides a variety of clients with intrusion and fire detection systems (Holmes Protection Group, Inc., 440 Ninth Ave., New York, NY 10001; Tel.: 1-800-4HOLMES).

Railroads and Labor Unions

The history of private security businesses in the United States must include two important events of the nineteenth century: the growth of railroads and labor unions.

Although railroads were valuable in providing the vital East-West link that enabled the settling of the American frontier, these powerful businesses used their domination of transportation to control several industries, such as coal and kerosene. Farmers were especially hurt in economic terms, because they had no alternative but to pay high fees to transport their products via the railroads. The monopolistic practices of railroads created considerable hostility; when Jesse James and other criminals robbed trains, citizens applauded. Railroads could not rely on public police protection because of jurisdictional boundaries. Consequently, numerous states passed laws enabling railroads to organize proprietary security forces with full arrest powers and the authority to apprehend criminals transcending multiple jurisdictions. Railroad police numbered 14,000 by 1914. During World War I, they were deputized by the federal government to ensure protection of this vital transportation network.

The growth of labor unions at the end of the nineteenth century resulted in increased business for security firms who acted as strikebreakers for large corporations. However, this venture proved costly. A bloody confrontation between Pinkerton men and workers at the Carnegie steel plant in Homestead, Pennsylvania, resulted in eight deaths (three security men and five workers). Pinkerton's security force surrendered. The plant then was occupied by federal troops. Later, the Ford Motor Company and other businesses were involved in bloody confrontations, and the negative image brought to the public eye by newspaper coverage tarnished many businesses and security firms.

The Great Wars

World Wars I and II brought about an increased need for protection in the United States. Sabotage and espionage were serious threats. Key industries and transportation systems required expanded and improved security. The social and political climate in the early 20th century reflected urban problems, labor unrest, and worldwide nationalism. World War I compounded these turbulent times and people's fears. Security became a primary concern. A combination of the "war to end all wars," Prohibition, intense labor unrest, and the Great Depression all overtaxed public police. Private security companies helped fill the void.

By the late 1930s, Europe was at war again, and the Japanese were expanding in the Far East. A surprise Japanese bombing of the Pacific fleet at Pearl Harbor in 1941 jolted the United States into World War II, and security concerns appeared again. The United States went into full production, and protection of vital industries became crucial, leading the federal government to bring plant security personnel into the army as an auxiliary to military police. By the end of the war, more than 200,000 of these security workers had been sworn in.

The Third Wave

In the decades following World War II private security expanded even more; during the 1950s, the Korean war and the unrelenting "cold war" created worldwide tension and competition between the democracies and communist regimes. The Department of Defense, in 1952, strengthened the security requirements of defense industries to protect classified information and materials. When the Soviets successfully launched the first earth satellite (Sputnik, in 1957) and first reached the moon with an unmanned rocket (1959), Americans were stunned. The technological race became more intense and information protection became more important.

The turbulent 1960s created massive social and political upheaval in the United States, and public police forces were overwhelmed by responses to the unpopular Vietnam war; protests over the denial of civil rights to minority groups; the assassinations of President John F. Kennedy, Senator Robert Kennedy, and the Reverend Martin Luther King, Jr.; and rising crime and drug problems. Private security boomed.

Protests, crime, terrorism, and limited public police resources marked the 1970s, 1980s, and 1990s. By this time the advanced nations of the world had developed into what Alvin Toffler's *The Third Wave*[13] and John Naisbitt's *Megatrends* [14] call *third wave* societies: societies based on information and technology. ("First wave" societies had agriculture as a foundation, and these dominated the world for thousands of years, deriving energy from human and animal power. Offenders stole cattle, gold, and other valuables. The "second wave" occurred during the Industrial Revolution when production was powered by irreplaceable energy sources such as coal and oil. Criminals focused on money and booming economic conditions.) With the depletion of world resources, the world is becoming more dependent on technology and information; and "third wave" criminals exploit technology to commit their crimes, the extent of which is limited only by technological innovation and the offenders' imaginations.

> Today a thief can steal without physically trespassing, by using a computer and modem from the comfort of his or her own home.

NOTES

1. Gion Green, *Introduction to Security*, 4th ed., revised by Robert J. Fischer (Boston: Butterworth–Heinemann, 1987), p. 3.
2. Richard S. Post and Arthur A. Kingsbury, *Security Administration: An Introduction*, 3rd ed. (Springfield, IL: Charles C Thomas, 1977), p. 14.
3. Ibid., p. 16.
4. Ibid., p. 16.
5. Saul D. Astor, *Loss Prevention: Controls and Concepts* (Stoneham, MA: Butterworths, 1978), p. 27.
6. Post and Kingsbury, *Security Administration*, p. 17.
7. *World Book Encyclopedia* (Chicago: World Book, 1986), p. 348.
8. A. C. Germann et al., *Introduction to Law Enforcement and Criminal Justice* (Springfield, IL: Charles C Thomas, 1973), p. 43.
9. See Post and Kingsbury, *Security Administration*; and Henry S. Ursic and Leroy E. Pagano, *Security Management Systems* (Springfield, IL: Charles C Thomas, 1974).
10. Crane Brinton et al., *Civilization in the West* (Englewood Cliffs, NJ: Prentice-Hall, 1973), p. 167.
11. Percy Bugbee, *Principles of Fire Protection* (Boston: National Fire Protection Assoc., 1978), p. 5.
12. Richard N. Holden, *Modern Police Management* (Englewood Cliffs, NJ: Prentice-Hall, 1986), p. 23.
13. Alvin Toffler, *The Third Wave* (New York: Morrow, 1980).
14. John Naisbitt, *Megatrends* (New York: Warren Books, 1982).

2

The Business of Security and Loss Prevention

OBJECTIVES

After studying this chapter the reader will be able to

1. Describe the variety and extent of losses facing our society;
2. Discuss the security industry and its services and devices;
3. List and explain the basic differences between public and private police;
4. Explain the limitations of the criminal justice system;
5. List and discuss the problems of the security industry and include the issue of privatization.

> The basic purpose of security and loss prevention is to protect people and assets.

THE EXTENT OF LOSSES

The variety of loss-provoking occurrences detrimental to businesses, institutions, and organizations is innumerable. Furthermore, the frequency and cost of each loss varies. Table 2–1 depicts several occurrences that can cause losses.

Each type of loss-provoking occurrence may have its own type of specialist to work toward solutions. For instance, a rash of robberies in a liquor store may require additional public law enforcement assistance and the installation of a more sophisticated alarm system from the private sector. Numerous injuries at a manufacturing plant may require assistance from a safety specialist. A building may require civil engineers to design an

Table 2–1   Loss-Provoking Occurrences

Criminal Acts	Natural Disasters	Miscellaneous
Larceny/theft	Floods/excessive rain	Poor supervision
Burglary	Excessive snow/ice	Error
Robbery	Lightning	Waste
Embezzlement	Pestilence	Bad investment
Fraud	Earthquake	Poor safety
Shoplifting	Landslide	Equipment failure
Murder	Tornado	Fire
Terrorism	Hurricane	Explosion
Computer crime	Volcanic eruption	Pollution
Product tampering	Tidal wave	Power outage
Counterfeiting		Strike
Arson		Mine disaster
Vandalism		Oil spill
Riot		Sonic boom
Extortion		Nuclear accident
Kidnapping		War
Espionage		
Strike		
Sabotage		

improved drainage system to prevent loss caused by excessive rain and snow. Thus, the loss prevention manager—a specialist in his or her own right or with the assistance of a specialist—must plan, implement, and monitor programs to anticipate, prevent, and reduce loss.

What are the losses to businesses, institutions, and organizations in terms of lives, money, and property damage? To begin, completely accurate data are difficult to obtain, and some types of loss-provoking activities are almost impossible to measure. Losses attributed to human error are mind-boggling if one considers only manufacturing, hospitals, and criminal justice. The following statistics reveal only a partial list of the massive losses that are pervasive in modern society:

1.   According to the National Safety Council, in 1995 (U.S.), 5,300 people were killed unintentionally at work and 3.6 million people had disabling injuries. Work-related accidents cost $119.4 billion in 1995; this included wage loss, medical expense, health insurance administration cost, and fire loss.[1]
2.   The National Fire Protection Association reported that, in 1995, public fire departments responded to 1,965,500 fires, civilian fire deaths totaled 4,585, civilian fire injuries totaled 25,775, and property damage was estimated at $8.9 billion.[2]

3. The FBI's *Uniform Crime Report* (UCR) for 1995 showed a downward trend in crime; however, in that year there were 1,099,179 aggravated assaults, 2,594,995 burglaries, and 8,000,631 larcenies or thefts.[3] Crime is a significant threat, and according to the National Institute of Justice, it costs the United States $450 billion annually, when counting tangibles such as property loss, lost wages, and medical expenses and intangibles such as pain and suffering (calculated by using methods employed in civil damage lawsuits).[4]

> The extent of losses exemplifies the magnitude of the loss problem and the complex task for the loss prevention practitioner.

Direct and Indirect Losses

Businesses, institutions, and organizations can suffer extensive direct losses from loss-provoking occurrences. Additionally, indirect losses can be devastating and often surpass direct losses. *Direct losses* are immediate, obvious losses, whereas *indirect losses* are prolonged and often hidden. A burglary at a business, for example, may show the loss of, say, $300 from a safe. However, on close inspection of indirect losses, total losses may include the following: damage to the door or window where the break-in occurred, replacement of the destroyed safe, insurance policy deductible, loss of sales from a delay in opening the business, and employee time required to speak with police, insurance representatives, and repair people. *Security practitioners can help justify their position and their value to the business community by demonstrating total losses resulting from each incident.* The Wilson case shows the role of security in a costly strike and the extent of direct and indirect losses.

Strike at Wilson Manufacturing Plant[a]

During the last six months, union leaders and company executives spent hundreds of hours discussing various issues pertaining to employee pay, benefits, and working conditions at the Wilson Manufacturing Plant. Finally, on June 25, "talks broke down" and a strike became a reality.

Three months later, the strike was settled and employees returned to work. At this time, management began to realize the full impact of the strike. The direct losses amounted to approximately $500,000 in sales. The weekly management meeting revealed the indirect losses from various departments.

continued

The plant manager showed that productivity declined by 8 percent during the two months preceding the strike. The accounting department head pointed to losses from lost productivity and the cost of idled equipment. The head of marketing reported that three of Wilson's customers switched to a competitor. This indirect loss would be felt for many months until additional customers could be generated. The personnel manager reported that thousands of dollars were spent to carry the cost of strikers' hospital, medical, and life insurance. Several managers and supervisors were needed to work in production to fulfill select customer orders. This caused a strain on managerial productivity and lowered morale. During the strike 27 employees sought employment elsewhere and subsequently never returned. The company lost employees with valuable training and experience. The loss prevention manager revealed that *shrinkage*[b] increased from 2 to 5 percent during the three months preceding the strike. Also, 11 cases of theft were uncovered, totaling $4,000; vandalism cost $12,000; and various cases of sabotage were discovered. The loss prevention manager pointed out that these statistics were only the tip of the iceberg, because his subordinates were discovering criminal acts each day. Additional private security officers were needed during the three-month strike, which cost $60,000. Furthermore, at the present time, negotiations were continuing over the reemployment of 14 strikers who were caught in acts of theft, vandalism, and sabotage. These negotiations added to indirect costs for the company legal counsel, the plant and loss prevention managers, and the criminal justice system.

[a] This case was formulated with the assistance of an article by Woodruff Imberman, "Strikes Cost More Than You Think," *Harvard Business Review* 57, no. 3 (May–June 1979), pp. 133–138.
[b] *Shrinkage* is a common term used in the loss prevention field. It refers to the amount of inventory lost through internal theft, shoplifting, damage, and paperwork errors.

THE SECURITY INDUSTRY

The security industry is a multibillion-dollar business. Every decade seems to bring an increased need for security services. Street crime, terrorism, third wave crime, and so on, bring greater demands for the protection of people and assets.

Research on the private security industry sponsored by the National Institute of Justice, U.S. Department of Justice, showed the following:

- Private security is clearly the nation's primary protective resource, outspending public law enforcement by 73 percent and employing $2^{1}/_{2}$ times the workforce (see Figure 2–1).
- Annual spending for private security is $52 billion, and private agencies employ 1.5 million persons. Public law enforcement spends $30 billion a year and has a workforce of about 600,000 (see Figure 2–1).

Private Security and Law Enforcement Employment

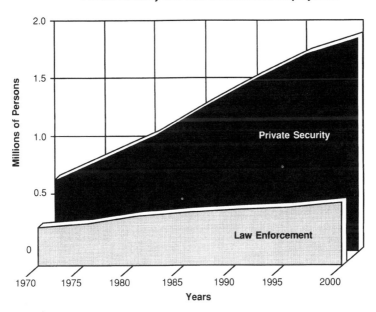

Private Security and Law Enforcement Spending

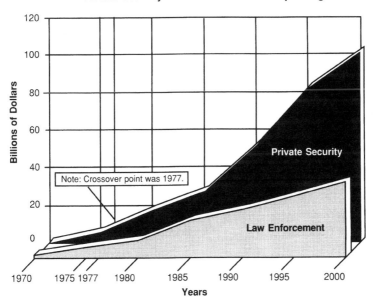

Figure 2–1 Private security and law enforcement employment and spending. Source: William C. Cunningham et al., *Private Security: Patterns and Trends* (Washington, DC: National Institute of Justice, August 1991), p. 3.

- These trends will continue through the year 2000.
- Public expenditures for law enforcement will reach $44 billion by the year 2000; and they will be dwarfed by private security expenditures, which will reach $104 billion.
- The average annual rate of growth in private security will be 8 percent, double that of public law enforcement.
- The rapid growth of security technology will not necessarily mean a reduction in the number of security personnel but may change the functions they perform. By the year 2000, there will be an estimated 750,000 contract security officers and 410,000 proprietary security personnel (280,000 will be security officers).[5]

Research by The Freedonia Group, Inc. (Tel.: 216-921-6800), of the worldwide security market, showed that *security services* revenues in the United States are expected to rise from $18 billion in 1995 to $25 billion by the year 2000, growing at 7.0 percent annually. Worldwide, such revenues are expected to rise from $42 billion (U.S.$) to $62 billion (U.S.$) during the same years, growing 7.9 percent annually. *Security equipment* revenues in North America are expected to rise from $8 billion in 1994 to $13 billion by the year 2000, growing at 8.1 percent annually. Worldwide, this market should rise from $26 billion (U.S.$) to $44 billion (U.S.$) during the same years, at an annual rate of 9.2 percent.[6]

Research by *Security Letter* showed low profits for the top three contract guard firms between 1990 and 1996; none of the three earned above 1 percent after taxes. Entrepreneurs who operate high-quality local or regional firms say the security guard industry is a profitable business.[7]

Most security companies are small. The United States has about 10,000 contract security firms (security officers), 26,000 investigative firms, and 10,000 alarm installation firms.[8]

Contract versus Proprietary Security Officers

The figures cited in Table 2–2 for the security industry focus on contract security firms that provide a service to the business community (see Figure 2–2). Depending on its unique needs and weighing several factors, an organization needing security may prefer to establish a proprietary (in-house) security force, of which there are thousands. Also, an organization may use both contract and proprietary security.

The *Report of the Task Force on Private Security* lists several factors to consider concerning contract versus proprietary security.[10] Contract security generally is less expensive, although there are exceptions. The service company typically handles recruitment, selection, training, and supervision. Hiring unqualified security officers and rapid turnover are two primary disadvantages of a contract service. Many contract officers are "moonlighting"

Table 2–2   Ten largest U.S. security guard, patrol, and investigative companies[9]

Company, Head Office	Employees	1996 Revenues
Borg-Warner Security Corp., Chicago, IL	88,450	$1.2 billion
Pinkerton's, Inc., Encino, CA	45,000	747 million
The Wackenhut Corp., Palm Beach Gardens, FL	22,000	580 million
American Protective Services, Oakland, CA	16,500	354 million
Guardsmark, Inc., Memphis, TN	11,500	212 million
ITS Security Officers, Cleveland	13,000	158 million
Allied Security, Inc., Pittsburgh, PA	8,000	154 million
US Security Associates, Atlanta, GA	10,000	146 million
Stanley Smith Security, Inc., San Antonio, TX	8,200	143 million
Argenbright Holdings, Ltd., Atlanta	10,000	140 million

Figure 2–2   Security officers. Courtesy: Borg-Warner Security Corp.

and subject to fatigue. Questions concerning insurance and liability between the security company and the client often are hazy.

A major advantage of a proprietary force is that greater control is maintained over personnel, including selection, training, and supervision, and of course, such a force is more familiar with the unique needs of the company.

Salaries and benefits, however, often make establishment of a proprietary force more expensive.

LOSS PREVENTION SERVICES AND SPECIALISTS

Many services and specialists from the private sector can help the loss prevention practitioner develop an effective loss prevention program. These services and specialists can be in-house or attainable through outside sources. Tables 2–3, 2–4, and 2–5 point out various facilities requiring loss prevention programs, security services and equipment from the private sector, and specialists and consultants who can aid in loss prevention efforts. These tables are not conclusive, because loss prevention programs are becoming increasingly specialized and diversified. Therefore, additional specialization will evolve to aid these programs.

Table 2–3 Facilities Requiring Loss Prevention Programs

Industrial	Hospital
Retail	Campus
Cargo	School
Railroad	Museum
Airport/airline	Library
Financial institution	Park and recreation
Office building	Hotel/motel/restaurant
Nuclear plant	Sporting event
Computer	Others
Housing	

Table 2–4 Security services and equipment from the private sector

Services	Equipment
Security officer protection	Access control systems
Investigation	Locks and keys
Undercover investigation	Intrusion alarm systems
Central alarm station (see Figure 2–3)	Closed-circuit television
Armored truck (see Figure 2–4)	Fire alarm systems
Security survey	Barriers
Guard dog (canine)	Glazing
Deception detection	Doors
Honesty shopping service	Lighting
Bodyguard/executive protection	Safes and vaults
Sweeps for bugging devices	Security vehicles
Others	Weapons
	Others

Table 2–5   Specialists and consultants who can aid loss prevention efforts

Manufacturing loss prevention specialist	General loss prevention specialist
Institutional loss prevention specialist	Architect
Locksmith	Computer scientist
Electronic surveillance specialist (CCTV, photography)	Criminologist
	Forensic scientist
Lighting specialist	Industrial engineer
Audio surveillance countermeasures specialist (debugging)	Electrical engineer
	Civil engineer
Fire and safety specialist	Nuclear engineer
Training specialist	Nuclear safety specialist
Legal specialist/attorney	Others
Insurance/bonding specialist	
Accountant	
Auditor	

Figure 2–3   Alarm services technology links intrusion and fire detection, sprinkler, CCTV, and access control. Courtesy: Wells Fargo Alarm Services, Inc.

The Basic Differences Between Public and Private Police

The primary differences pertain to the *employer*, the *interests served*, *basic strategies*, and *legal authority*. Public police are employed by governments and serve the general public. Tax dollars support public police activities. On the other hand, private police are employed by and serve private concerns (e.g., businesses) that provide the funds for this type of protection. There are exceptions to these general statements. For instance, government agencies sometimes contract protection needs to private security agencies to cut costs. Also, public police often are involved in efforts to assist business owners in preventing crimes through security surveys and public education.

Another difference involves basic strategies. Public police devote considerable resources to *reacting* to crimes. This entails detection, investigation, and apprehension of offenders. Law enforcement is a key objective. In contrast, private police stress the *prevention* of crimes; arrests are often deemphasized. But, here again, there are exceptions to these generalities. In the last decade public police agencies have increased expenditures to improve community crime prevention, even though law enforcement is a dominant objective. Some entities in the private sector place a heavy reliance on the deterrent effects of arrests while also adhering to a prevention philosophy.

The degree of police powers among public and private police is another distinguishing characteristic. Public police derive their authority from statutes and ordinances, whereas private police function commonly as private citizens. Public police have greater arrest, search, and interrogation powers. Depending on jurisdiction and state laws, private police may be deputized or given special commissions that increase powers. Certain state laws also stipulate that private police have greater arrest powers only on the protected premises. Those with greater arrest powers are subject to constitutional limitations that thus far generally have not been applied to private police possessing citizen arrest powers.

Which security career interests you?

Tables 2–3 through 2–5 also can serve as a source of employment opportunities. In subsequent chapters, some of these facilities, security services, and specialists are discussed in greater detail.

Obviously, a loss prevention practitioner cannot possess expertise in all of these fields. Most loss prevention managers are generalists, which means that they have a broad knowledge of the field plus a specialized knowledge of their particular loss prevention problems. When feasible, a

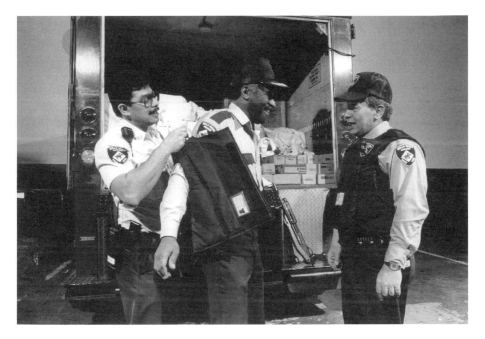

Figure 2–4   Employees wear bullet-resistant vests and personal hold-up alarms to help protect them as they pick up and deliver valuable shipments. Courtesy: Wells Fargo Alarm Services, Inc.

loss prevention manager should develop an interdisciplinary staff to assist in loss prevention objectives. The staff should represent various specializations as appropriate, such as security, safety, and auditing. Although loss prevention programs and the private security industry are tremendous aids in reducing loss in our society, these vital areas are not immune to problems and deficiencies. A knowledge of these problems and deficiencies can aid the practitioner in working toward solutions and ultimately lower losses.

THE LIMITATIONS OF THE CRIMINAL JUSTICE SYSTEM: IMPLICATIONS FOR LOSS PREVENTION PRACTITIONERS

Although the criminal justice system in the United States maintains a budget of over $93 billion a year for police, courts, and corrections and employs over 1.7 million personnel, its overall success rate has met with considerable criticism.[11]

Many theories underpinning crime prevention and law enforcement measures have come under increased scrutiny. As an example, numerous offenders simply find that "crime pays,"[12] because the certainty of punishment is a

myth. The common denominator for many law violators is that certain punishment is not a reality (in preventing and reducing crime) and, consequently, the odds are in the offender's favor. Whether sanctions on criminal
activity, such as isolating an offender from society, serve as deterrents and
reduce crime is not known for certain, according to members of an eminent
panel of social scientists such as James Q. Wilson and Marvin Wolfgang.[13]
Furthermore, research on the percentage of offenders who actually serve
time in prison shows a consistent 1 percent.[14]

Research by the American Bar Association (ABA) shows a criminal
justice system faced with a staggering number of cases, too many of which
involve drugs, and starved for resources to meet its obligations.[15] National
Institute of Justice research revealed results similar to the ABA. Criminal
justice practitioners reported the need for more drug education, prevention,
and treatment programs and expressed concern that arrest and incarceration
alone were insufficient to deter drug-dependent offenders.[16]

Tight budgets and reduced resources and personnel are the main reasons why public safety agencies play a very minor role in private loss prevention programs. Public police agencies cannot afford to assign personnel
to patrol inside business establishments or watch for employee theft. An
occasional (public) police patrol and a response to a crime are the primary
forms of assistance that public police can provide to businesses. Prosecutors
are unwilling to prosecute certain crimes against businesses because of
heavy caseloads. Consequently, public protection is being supplemented or
replaced by private security and volunteer efforts in many locales.

The U.S. law enforcement community employs an average of 2.3
full-time officers for every 1,000 inhabitants.[17]

Despite tight budgets for the criminal justice system and citizen aversion to
tax increases, sources of funding include the *Violent Crime Control and Law
Enforcement Act of 1994*, which is the largest crime bill in the history of our
country. It focuses on violent crime, hiring additional police officers, community policing, and building more prisons. *Asset forfeiture* is another
source of funds for law enforcement; this involves government seizure of
property derived from or used in criminal activity.

What are the most serious problems of the criminal justice system,
and what are your solutions?

PROBLEMS IN THE SECURITY INDUSTRY

In the remainder of this chapter, and in subsequent chapters, the following industry problems are covered: cooperation between public and private police, regulation of the industry, training, ethics, management problems, false alarms, privatization, private justice (Chapter 5), and moonlighting (Chapter 9).

Business and government leaders have realized that the growing private security industry is a great ally of the criminal justice system. Both crime-fighting sectors have mutual and overlapping functions in controlling crime. With this thinking in mind, the U.S. Department of Justice provided financial support for the production of important research reports. *The Rand Report* (1972) focused national attention on the problems and needs of the private security industry. This report stated that "the typical private guard is an aging white male, poorly educated, usually untrained, and very poorly paid."[18] This conclusion has met with criticism because the research sample was small and thus did not represent the entire security industry. However, with the assistance of this report and its recommendations, the professionalism of private security improved.

The Rand Report was a great aid (because of limited literature in the field) to the *Report of the Task Force on Private Security* (1976). This report of the National Advisory Committee on Criminal Justice Standards and Goals represented the first national effort to set realistic and viable standards and goals designed to maximize the ability, competency, and effectiveness of the private security industry for its role in the prevention and reduction of crime.[19] A major emphasis of the report was that all businesses that sell security services should be licensed and all personnel in private security work should be registered.

The task force's urging of stricter standards for the security industry reflected a need to reduce ineptitude and industry abuses, while striving toward professionalism. For example, in the private police industry, minimal hiring, training, and salary standards are pervasive. These minimal standards enable companies to reduce costs and provide potential clients with low bids for contract service. Thus, professionalism is sacrificed to keep up with competition. The task force recommended improved hiring criteria, higher salaries (especially to reduce turnover), and better training, among other improvements. Both studies recommended state level regulation for the security industry in general as a means of creating more uniformity.

Another major study of the security industry funded by the U.S. Department of Justice was published in 1985. *Private Security and Police in America: The Hallcrest Report*, prepared by Hallcrest Systems, Inc., focused research on three major areas: (1) the contributions of both public police and private police to crime control, (2) the interaction of these two forces and their level of cooperation, and (3) the characteristics of the private security industry.[20] Several industry problems and preferred solutions were discussed in this report, as covered in subsequent pages.

The U.S. Department of Justice funded a second Hallcrest Report, entitled *Private Security Trends: 1970–2000, The Hallcrest Report II*. This report provides a study of security trends to the 21st century. Some of its findings follow:

- Crime against business in the United States cost $67 billion in 1980, $114 billion in 1990, and will cost $200 billion by the year 2000.
- Since the middle 1980s, companies have been less inclined to hire security managers with police and military backgrounds and more inclined to hire those with a business background.
- During the 1990s, in-house security staffs will diminish with an increase reliance on contract services and equipment.
- The negative stereotypical security personnel are being replaced with younger, better educated officers with greater numbers of women and minority group members. However, the problems of quality, training, and compensation remain.
- The false-alarm problem is continuing. There is a massive waste of public funds when police and fire agencies must respond to current levels of false alarms. Between 97 and 99 percent of all alarms are false.[21]

Cooperation Between Public and Private Police

A persistent problem noted by several research reports involves disrespect and even conflict between public and private police.

> Some law enforcement officers believe that being a "public servant" is of a higher moral order than serving private interests. . . . They then relegate private security to an inferior status. . . . This perceived status differential by law enforcement personnel manifests itself in lack of respect and communication, which precludes effective cooperation.[22]

To reduce conflict, the Task Force Report and the Hallcrest Reports recommended liaison be implemented between public and private police. During the 1980s, the International Association of Chiefs of Police, the National Sheriffs' Association, and the American Society for Industrial Security (ASIS) began joint meetings to foster better cooperation between the public and private sectors.[23] This effort continued into the 1990s. In 1996, ASIS members testified before Congress in support of legislation to increase cooperation between private security and public law enforcement.[24] Avenues of increased cooperation include appointing high-ranking practitioners from both sectors to increase communication and instituting short training lessons in established training programs. The greater the cooperation, the more each sector will enhance its capabilities and resources to control crime.

Regulation of the Industry

The security field has its share of charlatans, who tarnish the industry, and as with many types of services offered the public, government intervention has taken the form of licensing and registration. State agencies screen applications of those interested in security work (e.g., check criminal records). The Task Force Report and Hallcrest Reports recommend regulation of the security industry by all states. The majority of states have such legislation, but it is varied. Although government regulation does not guarantee that all security practitioners will perform in a satisfactory manner, it does prevent people who have criminal records from entering the profession.

Attempts have been made through Congress to pass a national law to regulate the security industry. H.R. 2092, *The Private Security Officers Quality Assurance Act of 1995* was introduced by Rep. Bob Barr (R-GA). It languished in Congress in various forms since 1993 when Rep. Matthew Martinez (D-CA) introduced a similar bill. Known as the Barr-Martinez Bill, if passed, it would provide state regulators with expedited FBI criminal background checks of prospective and newly hired security officers. The minimal training standards of the bill were stricken, which would have required 8 hours of training and 4 hours of on-the-job training for unarmed officers and an additional 15 hours for armed officers. Critics argue that states are against such a national law and state regulations are sufficient.[25]

Which government agency in your state regulates the private security industry?

The Issue of Privatization

Privatization is the contracting out of government programs, either wholly or in part, to for-profit and not-for-profit organizations. There is a growing interdependence of the public and private sectors. The Hallcrest Report II noted that, during the late 1980s, state and local spending for private sector services increased dramatically to an estimated $100 billion, with federal spending for such services at twice that amount.[26] A broad array of services are provided to government agencies by the private sector today, from consulting services to janitorial services. Hospitals, schools, and other institutions formerly dominated by the government are being operated by both the public and private sectors. For crime control efforts, we see private security

continued

patrols in residential areas, private security officers in courts, and private prisons. Business people make themselves attractive to governments when they claim that they can perform services more efficiently and at a lower cost than the public sector.

Privatization is not a new concept. In the late 1600s, much security and incarceration for early urban areas was supplied by the private sector. By the 1700s, government dominated these services. Today, privatization can be viewed as a movement to demonopolize and decentralize services dominated by government. This movement to privatize criminal justice services encourages shared responsibility for public safety.[27]

Another factor fueling the privatization movement is victim and citizen dissatisfaction with the way in which government is handling crime. Increasing numbers of citizens are confronting crime through neighborhood watches, citizen patrols, crime stoppers, hiring private attorneys to assist prosecutors, and dispute resolution.[28]

Critics of privatization argue that crime control by government is rooted in constitutional safeguards and crime control should not be contracted to the private sector. Use of force and searches by the private sector, punishment in private prisons, and liabilities of governments and contractors are examples of the thorny issues that face privatization.

What are your views on privatization? Do you view it as a wise choice to improve crime control strategies?

The Need for Training

Numerous research reports and other publications have pointed to the need for more training of personnel in the security industry. Training of all security officers should be required by law prior to assignment. The harsh realities of the contract security business make this objective difficult to reach. Low pay and the enormous turnover of officers lead many security executives to consider costly training difficult to justify. With liability a constant threat and with insurance often unaffordable, many security firms are simply gambling by not adequately preparing their officers for the job. The Task Force Report and the Hallcrest Reports stress the need for improved recruitment, selection, pay, and training within the security industry.

The Hallcrest Report II noted that the typical uniformed security officer receives an estimated four to six hours of training before assignment. Seventeen states require minimum training for unarmed officers, 32 states mandate some firearms training for armed officers, and amazingly, 14 states require not even a minimal background check for armed officers. The Task Force on Private Security recommended 24 hours of training for armed security officers. Because of potential liability and the rise in insurance premiums, it is estimated that by the year 2000, only 5 percent of officers will be armed.[29]

Ethics

A code of ethics is a partial solution to strengthen the professionalism of security practitioners. Such a code helps to guide behavior by establishing standards of ethical conduct. Having a code makes good business sense because consumers make purchasing decisions based on past experience or the experiences of others. The Task Force Report provides a comprehensive code of ethics that can be a model. Another way to promote professional standards of ethics is to adhere to the certification standards set down by professional associations in the industry (see the box at the end of this chapter). For businesses in general, the Ethics Resource Center is a private, non-profit educational organization that has assisted hundreds of companies through its educational materials, videotapes, and newsletter (1120 G Street, NW, Suite 200, Washington, DC 20005; Tel.: 202-737-2258).

Management Problems

One management problem involves the hierarchical level of security and loss prevention within businesses, institutions, and organizations. Many security and loss prevention departments are on such a low level within the organization that their efforts are considerably hampered and their budget and personnel may be among the first to be cut. The benefits of such a service usually are not realized until a traumatic event boosts the status and initiates greater utilization of the loss prevention program.

Another management problem is associated with the decision to fire and prosecute dishonest employees. Many loss prevention managers are ardent supporters of strict prosecution practices as a deterrent to future crimes, whereas human resources managers may favor a more relaxed policy because of invested training and experience. Also, a public relations manager would be inclined to think of the adverse publicity stemming from prosecution.

The False Alarm Problem

Another persistent problem that causes friction between public police and the private sector is false alarms. It is generally agreed that over 95 percent of all alarm response calls received by public police are false alarms. However, the definition of *false alarm* is subject to debate. It often is assumed that, if a burglar is not caught on the premises, the alarm was false. Police do not always consider that the alarm or the approaching police could have frightened away a burglar.

The Hallcrest Reports noted that 10 to 12 percent of all public police calls-for-service were false alarms. In 1995, Metropolitan Dade County, Florida, police responded to 121,717 alarm calls, each costing $23.90, for a total of $2,909,036. In the same year the Reno, Nevada, police responded to 11,185 alarm calls, each costing $71.70, for a total of $801,964. Because of pressure on police resources and the high proportion of alarm calls that are false, some cities such as Chicago and Los Angeles are delaying response, not responding, or selectively responding.[30]

One view of public police responses to alarms is that it is a free service for the alarm companies, who profit at police expense. Hallcrest research showed eight out of ten local managers of security officer and patrol services reporting that they would be willing to take over alarm response on a contractual basis.[31]

The Task Force and Hallcrest Reports emphasized improved training of alarm service technicians and cooperation among those involved in the manufacturing, use, and alarm response process. The reports also placed emphasis on local government false alarm control ordinances as a means of reducing the problem. These ordinances require alarm system permits and impose fines for excessive false alarms.

What are the most serious problems of the private security industry, and what are your solutions?

Associations of Security Practitioners

Several security associations exist to promote professionalism and improve the security field. Two of these are

- *American Society for Industrial Security* (ASIS), 1625 Prince Street, Alexandria, VA 22314; Tel.: 703-519-6200. With a membership at almost 30,000, the ASIS is the leading general organization of protection executives and specialists. Its monthly magazine, *Security Management*, is an excellent source of information. Courses, seminars, and a certification program for the certified protection professional (CPP) also are available.
- *International Foundation for Protection Officers* (IFPO), Bellingham Business Park, 4200 Meridian, Suite 200, Bellingham, WA 98226; Tel.: 360-733-1571. This organization publishes *The Protection Officer* magazine and offers the certified protection officer (CPO) and certified security supervisor (CSS) programs.

NOTES

1. *Accident Facts, 1996 Edition*, National Safety Council (444 N. Michigan Ave., Chicago, IL 60611), p. 48.
2. Michael Karter, Jr., "NFPA's Latest Fire Loss Figures," *NFPA Journal* (September–October 1996): 53.
3. U.S. Department of Justice, Federal Bureau of Investigation, *Uniform Crime Reports, 1995, Crime in the United States* (Washington, DC: U.S. Government Printing Office, 1996), pp. 31, 38, and 43.
4. "Crime Costs Victims $450 Billion Annually," *Security* (May 1996): 84.
5. William C. Cunningham et al., *Private Security: Patterns and Trends* (Washington, DC: National Institute of Justice, August 1991).
6. "Security Business," *Security Letter*, Part III (September 1995 and September 1996).
7. "Largest US Security Guard, Patrol and Investigative Companies," *Security Letter* (April 1, 1997), Part III.
8. Sources: U.S. Department of Justice, National Institute of Justice, *Crime and Protection in America: Executive Summary of the Hallcrest Report* (Washington, DC: U.S. Government Printing Office, 1985), pp. 19–21; "Exploring Security Trends," *Security* [Cahners Publishing Co.] (1989); and *Security Letter* 19 (September 1, 1989).
9. "Largest US Security," Part II.
10. U.S. Department of Justice, *Report of the Task Force on Private Security* (Washington, DC: U.S. Government Printing Office, 1976), pp. 146–147 and 249–257.
11. Bureau of Justice Statistics, *Sourcebook of Criminal Justice Statistics—1994* (Washington, DC: BJS, 1995), pp. 4 and 26.
12. Thomas Plate, "Crime Pays," *Readings in Criminology* (Lexington, MA: D.C. Heath & Co., 1978), pp. 37–43.
13. "Deterrence Research Still Inconclusive," *Criminal Justice Newsletter* 9 (February 27, 1978), p. 3.
14. Samuel Walker, *Sense and Nonsense About Crime: A Policy Guide* (Monterey, CA: Brooks/Cole Pub., 1985), p. 25; Philip Purpura, *Criminal Justice: An Introduction* (Boston: Butterworth–Heinemann, 1997), p. 105.
15. "Drug Cases Swamping CJ System," *Law Enforcement News* 19 (February 28, 1993), p. 3.
16. U.S. Department of Justice, *Assessing Criminal Justice Needs* (Washington, DC: National Institute of Justice, August 1992), pp. 1–8.
17. U.S. Department of Justice, *Crime in the United States, 1993, Uniform Crime Reports* (Washington, DC: U.S. Government Printing Office, 1994), p. 288.
18. U.S. Department of Justice, *Private Police in the United States: Findings and Recommendations* 1 (Washington, DC: U.S. Government Printing Office, 1972), p. 30.
19. U.S. Department of Justice, National Criminal Justice Reference Service, Abstract for the *Report of the Task Force on Private Security* (1976).
20. William C. Cunningham and Todd H. Taylor, *Private Security and Police in America: The Hallcrest Report* (Portland, OR: Chancellor Press, 1985).
21. William C. Cunningham et al., *Private Security Trends: 1970–2000, The Hallcrest Report II* (Boston: Butterworth–Heinemann, 1990).

22. U.S. Department of Justice, *Law Enforcement and Private Security: Sources and Areas of Conflict* (Washington, DC: U.S. Government Printing Office, 1976), p. 6.
23. William C. Cunningham et al., *Private Security: Patterns and Trends* (Washington, DC: National Institute of Justice, August 1991), p. 2.
24. Kate Doherty, "Public/Private Cooperation Needed, ASIS Tells Congress," *Access Control* (October 1996): 6.
25. Robert King, "Security Guard Bill Referred out of Committee," *Security Concepts* (October 1996): 1.
26. Cunningham et al., *Private Security*, p. 2.
27. Gary Bowman et al., *Privatizing the United States Justice System* (Jefferson, NC: McFarland Pub., 1992), pp. 15–57.
28. Purpura, *Criminal Justice*, p. 13.
29. King, "Security Guard Bill," p. 16; Cunningham et al., *Private Security*, p. 4.
30. Simon Hakim and Erwin Blackstone, "Keeping a Watchful Eye on the Cost of Response to False Alarms," *Security Dealer* (August 1996): 102–108.
31. Cunningham et al., *Private Security*, p. 3.

II

REDUCING THE PROBLEM OF LOSS

3

Foundations of Security and Loss Prevention

OBJECTIVES

After studying this chapter the reader will be able to

1. List and explain the three-step risk analysis process;
2. Discuss planning and its importance;
3. Explain and illustrate how to evaluate security and loss prevention programs;
4. Discuss standards for protection;
5. Describe the characteristics of proprietary security programs.

Before a program of security and loss prevention can be implemented, careful planning is absolutely necessary. Such planning should begin by identifying the threats that face the organization requesting security. A retailer, for example, typically incurs losses from internal theft and shoplifting, and fire and accidents also are serious threats. Once the security planner has pinpointed the organization's vulnerabilities, the next step is to use this information to plan and implement countermeasures. In the absence of a careful and thorough appraisal of threats facing an organization, the foundation of any protection program is weak, no matter how cleverly it has been designed.

This chapter focuses on five tools that help to strengthen the foundation of a protection program: risk analysis, planning, evaluation, research, and standards.

The chapter also provides an overview of the proprietary security organization that implements the protection plans. Sound plans and a sound security organization are the best foundation for a successful security and loss prevention effort.

RISK ANALYSIS

The term *risk analysis* is used interchangeably with *risk assessment* and *risk evaluation*. This chapter uses *risk analysis*, defining it as a tool to estimate the expected loss from specific threats using the following three-step process: (1) the loss prevention survey, (2) identifying vulnerabilities, and (3) determining probability, frequency, and cost.

The Loss Prevention Survey

The purpose of a loss prevention survey is to pinpoint vulnerabilities (e.g., poor locks, unsafe conditions) and develop plans for improved protection. The survey should tailor its questions to the unique needs of the premises to be surveyed. Essentially, the survey involves a day and night physical examination of the location requiring a loss prevention program. The list that follows is a beginning point for topics for the survey, which can take several days.

1. Geography and climate (possible natural disaster);
2. Social and political climate surrounding the facility (possible high crime rate and unrest);
3. Past incidents causing loss;
4. Condition of physical security, fire protection, and safety measures;
5. Hazardous substances and protection measures;
6. Policies and procedures and enforcement;
7. Quality of security personnel (e.g., applicant screening, training, and supervision; properly registered and licensed);
8. Protection of people and assets;
9. Protection of information systems and information;
10. Protection of communications systems (e.g., telephones and fax machines);
11. Protection of utilities;
12. Protection of parking lots.[1]

The survey document usually consists of a checklist in the form of questions that remind the loss prevention practitioner or committee of what to examine to isolate vulnerabilities and plan strategies. A list attached to the survey can contain the targets—for example, people, money, equipment—that must be protected by the loss prevention department and the present strategies, if any, used to protect them. Blueprints of the facility and a map of the surrounding area also are helpful.

Identifying Vulnerabilities

Once the survey is completed, vulnerabilities can be isolated. For example, merchandise stacked high in a retail store provides "cover" and aids shoplifters. Poor record keeping and accountability can benefit employee thieves. These vulnerabilities can be minimized through loss prevention measures: an improved store plan and better accountability. Another example might be seen at a petrochemical plant where safety procedures are not being followed. Fire and explosion are serious consequences of such a lax atmosphere. These vulnerabilities can be minimized via loss prevention strategies such as strict adherence to safety policies and procedures and regular inspections.

During a risk analysis "think like a thief." Try to anticipate how not only crimes but also fires, accidents, and other losses can occur.

Determining Probability, Frequency, and Cost

The third step requires an analysis of the probability, frequency, and cost of each loss. Shoplifting and employee theft are common in retail stores, and numerous incidents can add up to serious losses. Fire and explosion are potential risks at a petrochemical facility: Even one incident can be financially devastating. The frequency of shoplifting and employee theft incidents at a retail store will be greater than the frequency of fires and explosions at a petrochemical facility. When the questions of probability, frequency, and cost of losses arise, practitioners must rely on their own experience, records and statistics, special computer programs, communication with fellow practitioners, and information provided by trade publications.

Most loss prevention practitioners maintain statistical records of the number of loss-provoking incidents that occur. These statistics often point out, for example, the number of employee theft incidents reported, direct and indirect losses, the success or failure of prevention strategies, and other information.

It is impossible to pinpoint accurately when, where, and how many times losses will occur. However, the sources of information just mentioned can help in planning protection.

PLANNING

Planning results in a design used to reach objectives. It is better to know where one is going and how to get there than to adhere to a philosophy of "we'll cross that bridge when we get to it," a point of view detrimental to any type of loss prevention effort. One serious consequence of that philosophy is the panic atmosphere that develops when serious losses occur; emotional decisions are made when quickly acquiring needed loss prevention devices and services. This sets up the organization for unscrupulous sales-people who prey on the panic.

An integral purpose of the planning process is to fulfill organizational goals and objectives. Those who plan protection should have a clear under-standing of the organization and its needs. Because of global competitive-ness, downsizing, and restructuring, today's corporations are in a state of constant change and reengineering. To survive, support functions like secu-rity must become part of the team player, adapt quickly to change, meet challenges in a positive and creative manner, and contribute to the corpo-rate mission.[2]

Budgeting is closely related to planning because it pertains to the money required to fulfill plans. Modern practitioners state their protection plans in financial terms that justify the expenditures, save the organization money, and if possible, bring in a return on the investment. The concept of *value added* means that all corporate departments must demonstrate their value to the organization by translating expenditures into bottom-line impact. Corporate financial officers ask, "Is security contributing to our business and profit success and how?" Illustrations of financial leverage for security include calculating total direct and indirect losses for each loss incident (as explained earlier in the text), conducting an undercover investi-gation to pinpoint not only theft but also substance abuse and safety prob-lems, hiring a bad check specialist who recovers several times his or her salary, purchasing an access control system that performs multiple roles such as producing time and attendance data, and installing a CCTV system that not only assists investigations but helps to locate production problems to improve efficiency and cut costs.

> Modern security and loss prevention practitioners state their pro-tection plans in financial terms that justify expenditures, save the organization money, and if possible, bring in a return on the investment.

A risk analysis provides input for planning protection. Security strate-gies generally take the form of personnel, hardware, and policies and proce-dures, as discussed throughout this book. Some of the many factors that go into the planning process follow:

1. Has the problem been carefully and accurately identified?
2. How much will it cost to correct the problem, and what percent of the budget will be allocated to the particular strategy?
3. Is the strategy practical?

4. Is the strategy cost effective? For example, a loss prevention manager debates an increase in the staff of loss prevention officers or the purchase of a closed-circuit television system. The staff increase will cost $20,000 per officer (three officers x $20,000 per year = $60,000 per year). CCTV will cost $75,000. After considering the costs and benefits of each, the manager decides on the CCTV system because by the second year the expense will be much lower than hiring three extra officers.

5. Does the cost of the strategy exceed the potential loss? For example, it would not be cost effective to spend $5000 to prevent the burglary of a $50 petty cash fund.

6. Does the strategy relate to unique needs? Often, strategies good for one location may not be appropriate for another location.

7. How will the strategy relate to the entire loss prevention program? A systems approach is wise. The interrelatedness of each strategy should be considered. For example, CCTV can be used in a retail store to prevent both shoplifting and employee theft. Also, personnel are needed to respond to incidents. Furthermore, a high-quality CCTV system can act as a cost savings by reducing personnel at certain locations.

8. Does the strategy conform to the goals and objectives of the organization or business and the loss prevention program?

9. How does the strategy compare to contract loss prevention programs? Will the strategy interfere with any contract services?

10. How will the insurance carriers react?

11. If a government contract is involved, what Department of Defense regulations must be considered?

12. Does the strategy create the potential for losses greater than what is being prevented? For example, applying a chain and lock to the inside handles of a double door makes it more difficult for a burglar to enter; however, what if a fire takes place and employees must escape quickly?

13. Does the strategy reduce the effectiveness of other loss prevention strategies? For example, a chain-link fence with colorful plastic woven through the links and high hedges will prevent people from seeing into the property and hinder an offender's penetration, but this strategy also will cause observation problems for patrolling police.

14. To what extent will the loss prevention strategy interfere with productivity? For example, in a high-risk environment, how much time will be necessary to search employees who leave and return at lunch time? What if 1000 employees leave for lunch? As another example, if the loss prevention manager requires merchandise loaded into trucks to be counted by three separate individuals, will this strategy slow the shipping process significantly?

15. Will the strategy receive support from management, employees, customers, clients, and visitors? Can any type of adverse reaction be predicted?

16. Does the strategy have to conform to local codes, ordinances, or laws? For example, in certain jurisdictions, perimeter fences must be under a specific height and use of barbed wire is restricted.

17. Will the strategy lower employee morale or lead to a distrust of management?

18. Are there any possible problems with civil liberties violations?

19. How will the union react to the strategy?

20. Was participatory management used to aid in planning the strategy?

21. Can the strategy be effectively implemented with the present number of loss prevention personnel?

22. Will the strategy cause a strain on personnel time?

23. What are the characteristics of the area surrounding the location that will receive the loss prevention strategy? These characteristics must be considered to improve the quality of strategies. For example, if loss prevention strategies are planned for a manufacturing plant, what factors outside the plant must be considered? (Factors of consideration include crime, fire, and accident rates.) Also, certain nearby sites may be subject to disaster: nuclear plants, airports, railroads (transportation of hazardous materials), educational institutions (student unrest), forests (fire), hazardous industries (chemicals), military installations, among others. Weather conditions are important to consider as well. Storms can activate alarms. Excessive rainfall can cause losses due to flooding. Heavy snow can result in a variety of losses. Earthquake and volcanic actions are additional factors to consider.

24. When considering loss prevention strategies such as burglar or fire alarms, what is the response time of public services such as police, fire, and emergency medical service? Where is the nearest facility housing each service?

25. Will loss prevention strategies be able to repel activity from either local criminals, a gang, or organized crime?

26. Is the strategy really needed? Why?

27. Does the strategy attempt to "loss-proof" or eliminate all losses? This often is an impossible objective to reach. Loss prevention practitioners sometimes are surprised by the failure of a strategy that was publicized as a panacea.

28. If the strategy is not implemented, what is the risk of loss?

29. Will a better, less expensive strategy accomplish the same objective? For example, "According to a survey by the U.S. General Services Administration, one 24-hour guard post can cost as much as $100,000 per year, including salaries, maintenance, uniforms, equipment, benefits, and insurance. By injecting an electronic backup such as a CCTV or alarm into the security force, guard manpower can be reduced."[3]

30. Can any other present strategy be eliminated when the new strategy is implemented?

31. What other strategies are more important? Are priorities established?

32. Should a pilot program be implemented (say, at one manufacturing plant instead of all plants) to study the strategy for problems and corrective action?
33. How will the strategy be evaluated?

Incomplete Protection Plans[4]

Andrew Smith, security manager at Tecsonics, Inc., a fast growing electronics firm, was assigned the task of preparing a plan and one-year budget for the protection of proprietary information. Two months later, Andrew was in front of senior executives who were eager to learn how proprietary information would be protected in such a fiercely competitive industry. At the beginning of the presentation, Andrew emphasized that the survival and growth of Tecsonics depended on its information protection program. The three major strategies for protection for the first year included electronic soundproofing, also referred to as shielding, which would involve the use of a copper barrier throughout one conference room to cut off radio waves from a spy's bugging equipment. Cost: $250,000. The second strategy was to spend $85,000 for countermeasure "sweeps" to detect bugs in select locations on the premises. The third strategy was to install a card access control system at a cost of $200,000.

Before Andrew was five minutes into his presentation, the rapid-fire questions began: "What is the return on investment?" "Are the plans cost effective?" "Did you perform a risk analysis?"

"What are other similar businesses doing?" "Why should we spend so much money on shielding and sweeps when we can use cheaper methods, such as holding meetings in unexpected locations, preparing good policies and procedures, promoting employee education, and keeping certain sensitive information out of the computer and locked up in a safe?" One sarcastic, hard-nosed executive quipped: "You would probably spend millions on shielding and sweeps and not realize that one of our male scientists could go out of town to a seminar, get cornered by a foxy broad, and get drunk as she pumps him for information!" Unfortunately for Andrew, everybody was laughing while he wished he had known about these questions beforehand.

Planning from a Systems Perspective

The *systems perspective* looks at interactions among subsystems. When actions take place in one subsystem, other subsystems are affected. For example, the criminal justice system is composed of three major subsystems: police, courts, and corrections. If, during one day, 100 public drunk arrests are made by the police, then the court and corrections subsystems must react by accommodating these arrestees. There are many other examples of systems: a loss prevention department, business, government, school, an automobile, the human body, and so on. All these systems have subsystems that interact and affect the whole system. In each system, subsystems are established to attain overall system objectives and goals.

In a loss prevention system, for instance, the investigation subsystem is dependent on the patrol subsystem for information and assistance. Likewise, the patrol subsystem depends on the investigation subsystem for in-depth follow-up.

Similar to other systems, a loss prevention department can be analyzed in terms of inputs, processes, outputs, and feedback. As an example, look at a loss prevention department's immediate reaction and short-term planning concerning an employee theft (see Figure 3–1). The loss prevention department receives a call from a supervisor who has caught an employee stealing: the input. The process is the analysis of the call; planning; and the action taken, dispatching of loss prevention personnel. The output (activity at the scene) is the arrival of the personnel, questioning, and note taking. Feedback involves communications from the on-site loss prevention personnel to the loss prevention department. This helps to determine if the output was proper or if corrections are necessary. For instance, suppose that an on-the-spot arrest was required. Then additional outputs might be necessary, possibly including assistance from a local public police department.

The systems perspective described in Figure 3–1 is for planning a short-term immediate action. Figure 3–2 illustrates long-term loss prevention planning from a systems perspective.

In Figure 3-2, the inputs of goals and objectives relate to upper management's expectations of the loss prevention function. The resources basically are money, material, and personnel. Information, research, reports,

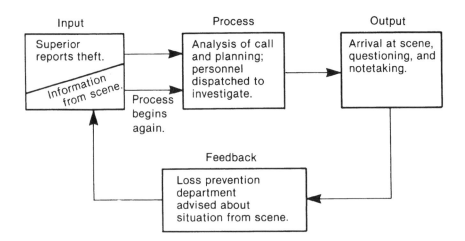

Figure 3–1 A systems perspective of a loss prevention department's immediate reaction and short-term planning relevant to an employee theft incident.

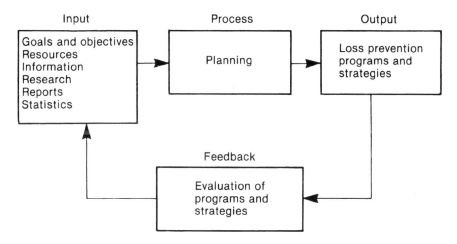

Figure 3–2 Long-term loss prevention planning from a systems perspective.

and statistics all aid in decision making within the planning process. The output is the loss prevention programs and strategies evolving from the planning process that will prevent and reduce losses while increasing profits. Feedback, an often overlooked activity, is essential for effective planning; and evaluation is an integral part of feedback. Ineffective programs and strategies must be eliminated. Other programs and strategies may need modification. Evaluation helps to justify programs and strategies.

Loss prevention practitioners must be prepared when asked by upper management, "How do you know the loss prevention plans and strategies are working?"

Critical Thinking for Security Planning

Maxims of Security

1. Security is never foolproof. The term *foolproof* is a misnomer. Instead of *burglarproof*, *fireproof*, or *bulletproof*, replace *proof* with *resistant*.
2. State-of-the-art security has its vulnerabilities. History is filled with grand security strategies that failed.

continued

3.   Security often is as good as the time it takes to get through it. The longer the time delay facing the offender, the greater the protection and chances that he or she will abort the offense, be apprehended, or seek another victim.
4.   Security must focus on not only what is leaving a facility (e.g., company assets) but also what is entering (e.g., weapons, explosives, illegal drugs, and anger).

Three Models of Security

Each security strategy falls under one of the following models:

1.   It protects people and assets.
2.   It accomplishes nothing.
3.   It helps offenders.

Illustrations of security protecting people and assets are seen when a hospital security officer escorts nurses to their vehicles at night or when a safe proves too formidable for a burglar, who leaves the scene. Security accomplishes nothing when security officers sleep on the job or fail to make their rounds or when alarm systems remain inoperable. Sometimes unknown to security practitioners and those they serve are the security strategies that actually help offenders. This can occur when security officers are poorly screened and they commit crimes. The ordinary padlock is an example of how physical security can assist offenders. An unlocked padlock hanging on an opened gate can invite *padlock substitution* whereby the offender replaces it with his or her padlock, returns at night to gain access, and then secures the gate with the original padlock. Such cases are difficult to investigate because signs of forced entry may be absent. Fences, another example, often are built with a top rail and supports for barbed-wire that are strong enough to assist and support people, rather than the fence and barbed-wire. Also, attractive looking picket fences have been knocked down by offenders and used as ladders.

Security practitioners should identify and classify all security strategies under these models to expose useful, wasteful, and harmful methods. This endeavor should be a perpetual process within risk analysis, careful planning, critical thinking, testing, and research to facilitate cost-effective, results-oriented security. Although these challenging goals require time and effort, the net result is a superior security and loss prevention program.

EVALUATION OF LOSS PREVENTION PROGRAMS

How can a loss prevention program be evaluated? First, a research design can assist in the evaluation. A look at a few simplified research designs demonstrates how loss prevention programs are determined to be successful or unsuccessful.

One design is the *pretest-posttest design*. A robbery prevention program can serve as an example. First, the robbery rate is measured (by compiling statistics) before the robbery prevention program is implemented. The program then is implemented and the rate measured again. Robbery rates before and after program implementation are compared. If the robbery rate has declined, then the robbery prevention program may be the causative factor.

A loss prevention training program can serve as another example. Loss prevention personnel are tested prior to the training program, and their test scores are saved. The training program is implemented. After the program is completed, another similar test is given the personnel. The pretest scores are compared to the posttest scores. Higher posttest scores indicate that the training program probably was effective.

Another evaluation design or research method is called the *experimental control group design*. As an example, a crime prevention program within a corporation is subject to evaluation. Within the corporation, two plants that are characteristically similar are selected. One plant (the experimental plant) receives the crime prevention program, while the other plant (the control plant) does not. Before the program is implemented, the rate of crime at each plant is measured. After the program has been in effect for a predetermined period of time, the rate of crime is again measured at each plant. If the crime rate has declined at the "experimental" plant while remaining the same at the "control" plant, then the crime prevention program may be successful.

A good researcher should be cautious when formulating conclusions. In the crime prevention program at the plant, crime may have declined for reasons unknown to the researcher. For instance, offenders at the experimental plant may have refrained from crime because of the publicity surrounding the crime prevention program. However, after the initial impact of the program and the novelty expired, offenders continued to commit crimes without being detected by the program. In other words, the program may have been successful in the beginning but soon became ineffective. Thus, continued evaluations are vital to strengthen research results.

RESEARCH

To assist planning and research the *scientific method* can be used. *Four steps are involved: statement of the problem, hypothesis, testing, and conclusion.* As an example, employee theft will serve as the problem. The hypothesis is a statement whereby the problem and a possible solution (i.e., loss prevention strategy) are noted. Testing involves an attempt to learn whether the strategy reduces the problem. Several research designs are possible. Here is an example of the presentation of the problem according to the style of scientific methodology:

- *Problem*: Employee theft
- *Hypothesis*: Employee theft can be reduced by using CCTV.

- *Testing*: Control group (plant A—no CCTV); Experimental group (plant B—CCTV)
- *Conclusion*: After several months of testing, plant A maintained previous levels of employee theft, whereas plant B showed a drop in employee theft. Therefore, CCTV appears to be an effective loss prevention strategy in reducing employee theft.

To strengthen research results, continued testing is necessary. In the example, CCTV can be tested at other, similar locations. Further, other strategies can be combined with CCTV to see if the problem can be reduced to a greater extent.

Sources of Research Assistance

Obviously, a need exists for more loss prevention research; at this time it is limited. A unified national effort is needed. Five potential sources of research assistance are in-house, university, public service, private consulting, and insurance companies.

In-house research may be the best because proprietary personnel are familiar with the unique problems at hand. Salary costs could be a problem, but a loss prevention practitioner with a graduate degree can be an asset to loss prevention planning and programming. In-house research, however, can result in increased bias by the researcher because superiors may expect results that conform to their points of view.

University researchers usually have excellent credentials. Many educators are required to serve the community and are eager to do research that can lead to publication. The cost is minimal.

Public service research requires assistance from police, fire, EMS, or other public service agencies. Because these agencies frequently are pressed for personnel while coping with tight budgets, acquiring assistance may be difficult. However, if the loss prevention practitioner demonstrates that public service research assistance can reduce losses in the private sector while reducing public safety problems and costs, then assistance may be possible. The size and budget of the public service agency will reveal the quality and quantity of personnel. Costs and contracts vary.

Private consulting firms often have qualified personnel. This source can be the most expensive because these firms are in business for profit. Careful consideration and a scrutiny of the consulting staff are wise. The buyer should beware.

Insurance companies are active in making inspections of risks and recommending strategies (i.e., risk management) to reduce possible losses. They also participate in varying degrees in research projects relevant to crime, fire, and safety. Other sources of research assistance and information are described in the standards section of this chapter.

Performance Measures

Traditionally, public police performance has been measured by reported crime rates, overall arrests, crimes cleared by arrest, and response time to incidents. These measures have become institutionalized, and substantial investments have been made to develop information systems to capture such data. However, this data may tell little about police effectiveness in reducing crime and the fear of crime.[5] Furthermore, do these measures reflect outmoded policing and do they fail to account for many important contributions police make to the quality of life, such as efforts at community cohesion and crime prevention?

Here is an example of performance measures for police which have implications for security:

- Goal: promoting secure communities.
- Methods and activities: promoting crime prevention and problem-solving initiatives.
- Performance indicators: programs and resources allocated to crime prevention, public trust and confidence in police, and reduced public fear of crime.[6]

What lessons can security practitioners learn from research on performance measures in the public sector? Do security programs contain traditional systems of measuring performance that reflect outmoded security efforts, while failing to account for important contributions to protection? Performance measures are surfacing in security programs.[7] (For performance measures in health care security, see Chapter 17.) To improve security programs, research should be directed at enhancing traditional performance measures and introducing new measures that more accurately reflect security expenditures, efforts, and successes.

STANDARDS

Standards are written and tested guidelines that promote uniformity and quality. Manufacturers can adhere to standards in the production of protection products, and businesses in the same industry can follow standards to ensure an adequate level of protection for people and assets on the premises.

Manufacturers have been producing their products in accordance with safety standards for many years. During the 1920s, for example, *Underwriters Laboratory* (UL), an independent testing organization, worked with insurers to establish a rating system for alarm products and installations. This system assists insurance agents in setting premiums for customers. An alarm company may show customers that its service is of a higher standard than a competitor's. UL has various listings, and it requires that an alarm company advertise its listing specifically. What a company has to do to obtain a listing as a central station burglar alarm company differs widely from what it has to do to be listed as a residential monitoring station; providing fire-resistant construction, backup power, access controls, and optimal response time following an alarm are a few examples (UL, 1285 Walt Whitman Rd., Melville, NY 11747-3081; Tel.: 516-271-6200).

Consumers, in general, are more familiar with UL as an organization promoting the electrical safety of thousands of retail products. Companies pay a fee to have UL test their products for safety according to UL standards. The famous UL label often is seen attached to the product.

Another organization producing standards is the *National Fire Protection Association* (NFPA). This group has established standards for fire protection equipment and construction that have been adopted by government agencies, in addition to companies in the private sector. Beginning in 1898, in cooperation with the insurance industry, the NFPA has produced standards covering sprinklers, fire hoses, and fire doors, among other forms of fire protection (NFPA, 1 Batterymarch Park, Quincy, MA 02269-9101; Tel.: 617-770-3000).

The *American Society for Testing and Materials* (ASTM), organized in 1898, has grown into one of the largest voluntary standards development systems in the world. ASTM is a nonprofit organization providing a forum for producers, consumers, government, and academia to meet to write standards for materials, products, systems, and services. Among its 132 standards-writing committees are committees that focus on security, safety and fire protection (ASTM, 100 Barr Harbor Dr., West Conshohocken, PA 19428; Tel.: 610-832-9500).

The *American National Standards Institute* (ANSI), organized in 1918, is a nonprofit organization that coordinates U.S. voluntary national standards and represents the United States in international standards bodies such as the International Organization for Standardization. ANSI serves both private and public sectors in an effort to develop standards that exist in all industries, such as safety and health, information processing, banking, and petroleum (ANSI, 11 West 42nd St., New York, NY 10036; Tel.: 212-642-4900).

Standards have also been set by the U.S. Congress through the *Occupational Safety and Health Act* (1970), which promotes workplace safety through enforcing standards. This law is discussed in Chapter 13.

Standards promote uniformity and quality.

For the security industry as a whole, we should also remember the *Report of the Task Force on Private Security* (1976). As discussed in the previous chapter, this report was prepared by the National Advisory Committee on

Criminal Justice Standards and Goals, which endeavored to set standards that would make the security industry more professional.

Some security standards focus on uniform standards of protection for specific industries, as seen at banks, through the Bank Protection Act; at airports, through the Federal Aviation Administration (FAA); and at companies with a U.S. Department of Defense (DOD) contract. Specific types of security characterize these different industries. Unfortunately, many types of businesses and institutions have no uniform standards of protection (for example, retail businesses, hotels, restaurants, office buildings, and manufacturing plants).

Security magazine states the following:

> Facility security standards, in some form and coverage, do exist at US colleges, some health care facilities, some convenience stores and at some federal government facilities—all where specific federal, state or local laws or industry regulations come into play.
>
> Most existing United States premises security standards exist as ever-changing *de facto* guidelines determined by common application, case law, insurance or arising from liability concerns.[8]

To make matters worse, in settling lawsuits involving negligent security, courts have ruled inconsistently. Acceptable security in one jurisdiction may be unacceptable in another. Security standards would curb this problem and enable the private sector and the courts to foster uniform security. Those against standards cite costs and argue that it is impossible to standardize security because each location and business is unique.

PROPRIETARY SECURITY

Answers to three key questions reveal the quality of a proprietary (in-house) protection program: Does the program have good support from upper management? Does the program have an adequate budget? Does the program have the appropriate authority to fulfill its responsibilities? Any loss prevention manager would be delighted to have affirmative responses to all of these questions, although this is not the case in many instances. In fact, in many corporations, to save money, proprietary security slowly is being phased out and replaced with contract services or a combination of both. Whatever support and resources are available, proprietary security programs, and those programs served by contract services, are characterized by the organization terms and practical management tools in the following two lists.

Basics of Organization: The Vocabulary

- *Division of work.* Work is divided among employees according to such factors as function, clientele, time, and location.
- *Authority.* The right to act.

- *Responsibility.* An obligation to do an assigned job.
- *Power.* The ability to act.
- *Delegation of authority.* A superior delegates authority to subordinates to spread the workload. A superior can delegate authority, but a person must accept responsibility. Responsibility cannot be delegated. For example, the sergeant delegated to loss prevention officers the authority to check employee lunch boxes when employees left the plant.
- *Chain of command.* Communications go upward and downward within an organized hierarchy for the purpose of efficiency and order.
- *Span of control.* The number of subordinates that one superior can adequately supervise. An example of a broad span of control would be one senior investigator supervising 20 investigators. An example of a narrow span of control would be one senior investigator supervising five investigators. An adequate span of control will depend on factors such as the amount of close supervision necessary and the difficulty of the task.
- *Unity of command.* To prevent confusion during an organized effort, no subordinate should report to more than one superior.
- *Line personnel.* Those in the organized hierarchy who have authority and function within the chain of command. Line personnel can include uniformed loss prevention officers, sergeants, lieutenants, captains, and other superiors.
- *Staff personnel.* Specialists with limited authority who advise line personnel. For example, the loss prevention specialist advised the captain about a more efficient method of reducing losses.
- *Formal organization.* An official organization designed by upper management whereby the "basics of organization" are applied to produce the most efficient organization possible.
- *Informal organization.* An unofficial organization produced by employees with specific interests. For example, several employees spend time together (during "breaks" and lunch) because they are on the company bowling team.
- *Organization chart.* A pictorial chart that visually represents the formal organization. Many of the "basics of organization" actually can be seen on organization charts (see Figure 3–3).

Basics of Organization: The Practical Management Tools

- *Directive system.* A formal directive system is a management tool used to communicate information within an organized group. The communications can be both verbal and written. A verbal directive can be as simple as a superior telling a subordinate what work needs to be done. The formal verbal directive system also can include meetings in which verbal communications are exchanged.
- *Policies.* Policies are management tools that control employee decision making. Policies reflect the goals and objectives of management.

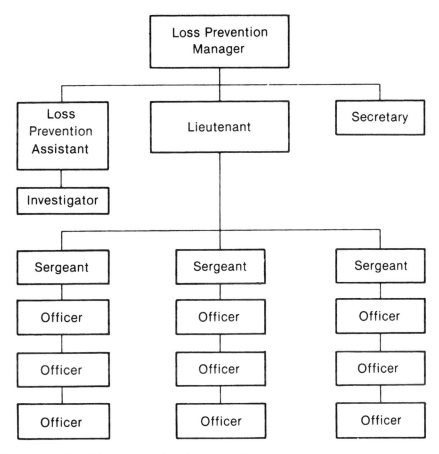

Figure 3–3   Small loss prevention department.

- *Procedures.* Management tools that point out a particular way of doing something: they guide action. Many procedures actually are plans that fulfill the requirements of policies. The loss prevention manager must maintain an open mind when feedback evolves from policies and procedures. For instance, the example in the following Sample Memorandum may cause complications: suppose there are only two fixed posts for searching articles and at 5 P.M. 1000 employees leave the plant. Obviously, the searches will become haphazard while long lines of irritated employees develop. Consequently, changes must be made.
- *The manual.* A manual is like a "rule book" for an organized group; it contains policies and procedures.
- *Participatory management.* Participation by subordinates in management decision making has been shown to increase morale and motivation, and excellent subordinate ideas have evolved from the use of participatory management. As with other management tools, its use varies.

Sample Memorandum

TO: All Loss Prevention Personnel
FROM: Loss Prevention Manager
SUBJECT: Policy and Procedure for Searching Employees
DATE: June 1, 200_

As we all know there has been considerable controversy about loss prevention personnel searching employees at the end of the workday. After negotiations with employees and management, policy and procedure has been revised concerning the searching of employees by loss prevention personnel.

Policy

Our company produces an expensive and easily pilfered product. Unfortunately, several employees have been caught pilfering while leaving the plant. These losses and others are a drain on profits and plans for plant expansion. Therefore, loss prevention personnel will search all articles (e.g., lunch boxes, coats, paper bags, umbrellas) carried by employees only when they leave the plant. A body search is prohibited.

Procedure

1. The fixed posts for searching will be at inner doors located before employee time card racks.
2. Two loss prevention officers must be stationed at each post.
3. Maintain courtesy.
4. If not in uniform, identify yourself by displaying identification.
5. Politely ask the employee to open the article that is being carried.
6. If necessary, use your hands to neatly shift things within the employee's article. Do not touch or search the employee.
7. If a problem develops (e.g., employee refuses article search or pilfered item is found), note the employee's name and number from his or her displayed identification card; radio for assistance; and then hold the employee's time card.
8. In case the problem employee is a decoy or diversion, at least one officer must remain at the fixed post.

What are your suggestions for improving the foundations of security and loss prevention?

CASE PROBLEMS

3A. As a loss prevention manager you have been asked to prepare a speech to a group of security practitioners. The topic is Prerequisites to Planning Security and Loss Prevention Programs and Strategies. Outline the speech or prepare note cards for your presentation.

3B.   Refer to the box in this chapter entitled "Incomplete Protection Plans." If you were an outside security consultant hired by Andrew Smith, what would you suggest to help him prior to his meeting with top executives?

3C.   As a security manager, you believe that the 3 P.M. meeting with the vice president of Finance today will not bring good news. Each business quarter seems to show poor profits and the need for cutbacks in all departments. When you enter her office for the meeting, the VP, Alaine Nell, gets right to the point: "Your security budget to protect the four openings at the plant must be cut by 50 percent." She draws a sketch of the huge square plant and notes that each of the four openings on the sides of the facility is costing $100,000 annually for 24-hour-a-day security officer protection. She states that each post requires four officers (three on and one off during each 24-hour period) at $20,000 apiece. She requests a financial plan for the next five years. Prepare such a plan, providing hypothetical information if needed.

3D.   Design an organization chart for a loss prevention department of 35 people at an industrial plant. Write a one-page justification of your design to satisfy management. Provide hypothetical information about the plant if needed.

NOTES

1. Jay B. Crawford, "Security, Heal Thyself," *Security Management* (May 1995): 85–90.
2. Richard D. Roberts, "Changing of the Guard: Corporate Downsizing's Effect on Security," *Security Technology and Design* (October 1996): 8–12.
3. Wayne Siatt, "Doubled Systems Promise Documented Savings," *Security World* 17 (January 1980): 30.
4. Philip P. Purpura, *Modern Security and Loss Prevention Management* (Boston: Butterworth–Heinemann, 1989), pp. 43–44.
5. U.S. Department of Justice, *A Police Guide to Surveying Citizens and Their Environment* (Washington, DC: U.S. Government Printing Office, October 1993), p. ix.
6. John J. DiIulio, Jr., et al., *Performance Measures for the Criminal Justice System* (Washington, DC: Bureau of Justice Statistics, October 1993), pp. 113–135.
7. Steven Placek, "Smithsonian Displays New Security Model," *Security Management* (August 1996): 62–68.
8. "NFPA Shuts Door, Again, to Security Standards," *Security* (March 1996): 108.

4

Law

OBJECTIVES

After studying this chapter the reader will be able to

1. Explain the origins of law;
2. List and define at least five torts;
3. Discuss premises protection and negligence;
4. Explain contract law;
5. Explain the relationship among administrative law, compliance auditing, and the Federal Sentencing Guidelines;
6. Summarize criminal justice procedure;
7. Explain arrest law, use of force, searches, and questioning.

A good foundation in law is an essential prerequisite to loss prevention programming. Many crucial decisions by practitioners are circumscribed by legal parameters, and the consequences of these decisions can be serious. An arrest without the proper legal authority and evidence can result in civil and criminal action against security personnel. Negligence is a serious concern that results from the failure to exercise due care in the use of force, for example. This is why training is so important; it becomes a major issue in a lawsuit against security. Numerous lawsuits also have been directed at those responsible for security, who are claimed to be negligent for not providing a safe environment, which caused a person to become a crime victim. Consequently, security and loss prevention decisions must take into consideration the legal environment.

ORIGINS OF LAW

Three major sources of law are common law, case law, and legislative law. English common law is the major source of law in the United States. *Common law* generally refers to law founded on principles of justice determined by reasoning according to custom and universal consent. The development of civilization is reflected in common law. Specific acts were, and still are, deemed criminal. These acts, even today, are referred to as common law crimes: treason, murder, robbery, battery, larceny, arson, kidnapping, and rape, among others. Common law is reinforced by decisions of courts of law. After our nation gained independence from England, the common law influence remained. Nineteen states have perpetuated common law through case law (i.e., judicial precedent). Eighteen states have abolished common law and written it into statutes. The remaining states have either adopted common law via ratification or are unclear about exactly how it is reflected in the state system.

Case law, sometimes referred to as *judge-made law*, involves the interpretation of statutes or constitutional concepts by federal and state appellate courts. Previous case decisions or "precedent cases" have a strong influence on court decisions. Precedents clarify both statutes and court views to limit ambiguity. When a new case comes into existence, earlier case decisions are used as a reference for decision making. Because the justice system is adversary in nature, opposing attorneys refer to past cases (i.e., precedents) that support their individual contentions. The court makes a decision between the opposing parties. Societal changes often are reflected in decisions. Because the meaning of legal issues evolves from case law, these court decisions are the law. Of course, later court review of previous decisions can alter legal precedent.

Legislative law from the federal government is passed by Congress under the authority of the U.S. Constitution. Likewise, individual state constitutions empower state legislatures to pass laws. Legislative laws permit both the establishment of criminal laws and a justice system to preside over criminal and civil matters. A court later may decide that a legislative law is unconstitutional; this illustrates the system of "checks and balances" that enables one government body to check on another.

Criminal law deals with crimes against society. Each state and the federal government maintains a criminal code that classifies and defines offenses. *Felonies* are considered more serious crimes, such as burglary and robbery. *Misdemeanors* are less serious crimes such as trespassing and disorderly conduct.

Civil law adjusts conflicts and differences between individuals. Examples of civil law cases are accidental injuries, marital disputes, breach of contract, sales that dissatisfy customers, and disputes with a government agency. When a *plaintiff* (i.e., a person who initiates a lawsuit) wins a case against another party, monetary compensation commonly results.

TORT LAW

Public police officers have greater police powers than private sector officers, who typically possess citizen's arrest powers. In conjunction with greater police powers, public officers are limited in their action by the Bill of Rights of the U.S. Constitution. On the other hand, private officers, possessing fewer powers, for the most part, are not as heavily restricted by constitutional limitations. Authority and limitations on private officers result from *tort law*, the body of state legislative statutes and court decisions that governs citizens' actions toward each other and allows lawsuits to recover damages for injury. Tort law is the foundation for civil actions in which an injured party may litigate to prevent an activity or recover damages from someone who has violated his or her person or property. Most civil actions are not based on a claim of intended harm but a claim that the defendant was negligent. This is especially so in cases involving private security officers. Tort law requires actions that have regard for the safety and rights of others, otherwise negligence results. *The essence of the tort law limitations on private sector officers is fear of a lawsuit and the payment of damages.*

The primary torts relevant to private security are as follows:

1. *False imprisonment.* The intentional and forceful confinement or restriction of the freedom of movement of another person, also called *false arrest.* The elements necessary to create liability are detention and its unlawfulness.
2. *Malicious prosecution.* Groundless initiation of criminal proceedings against another.
3. *Battery.* Intentionally harmful or offensive touching of another.
4. *Assault.* Intentional causing of fear of harmful or offensive touching.
5. *Trespass to land.* Unauthorized entering upon another person's property.
6. *Trespass to personal property.* Taking or damaging another person's possessions.
7. *Infliction of emotional distress.* Intentionally causing emotional or mental distress in another.
8. *Defamation (libel and slander).* Injury to the reputation of another by publicly making untrue statements. *Libel* refers to the written word; *slander*, to the spoken word.
9. *Invasion of privacy.* Intruding on another's physical solitude, the disclosure of private information about another, public misrepresentation of another's actions.
10. *Negligence.* Causing injury to persons or property by failing to use reasonable care or by taking unreasonable risk.

Generally, public police are restrained by the Bill of Rights, whereas private security officers are restrained by tort law.

Civil action is not the only factor that hinders abuses by the private sector. Local and state ordinances, rules, regulations, and laws establish guidelines for the private security industry. This usually pertains to licensing and registration requirements. Improper or illegal action is likely to result in suspension or revocation of a license. Criminal law presents a further deterrent against criminal action by private sector personnel. Examples are laws prohibiting impersonation of a public official, electronic surveillance, breaking and entering, and assault.

Some court cases have applied select constitutional limitations to private sector action. Union contracts also can limit private police. These contracts might stipulate, for instance, that employee lockers cannot be searched and that certain investigative guidelines must be followed.

PREMISES PROTECTION AND NEGLIGENCE

Negligence results when a failure to exercise a reasonable amount of care in a situation causes harm to another (see Figure 4–1). For instance, management should take steps to ensure the safety of individuals on the premises.

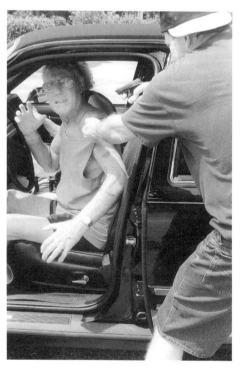

Figure 4–1 Assaults in parking lots have led to lawsuits alleging negligent security. Source: Philip P. Purpura, *Criminal Justice: An Introduction* (Boston: Butterworth–Heinemann, 1997), p. 47.

Numerous lawsuits have been directed at management for failing to provide adequate protection for employees, customers, residents, or students.

Forseeability is a legal test applied in cases involving the question of alleged negligent security; if a plaintiff cannot demonstrate that there had been a prior similar incident on the premises to the crime in question, the court will dismiss the case. This is known as the *prior similar incidents rule*. Courts have become highly critical of this rule. In the case *Sharp v. W. H. Moore, Inc.*, 188 Idaho 297,796 P.2d 506 (1990), the Idaho Supreme Court noted that the prior similar incidents rule had the effect of being a "one free rape rule." During this time, the majority of American jurisdictions abandoned this rule in favor of a *totality of the circumstances* test: prior similar incidents and other factors, such as the nature of the business, its surrounding locale, security training, and whether customary security measures for the particular industry were applied.[1] A third test courts place on security-related cases is *conscious disregard*: whether management or the security program knew of a problem or vulnerability, but did nothing.

Walter A. Stewart v. *Federated Department Stores*, No. 15124, Connecticut Supreme Court, 1995[2]

Marion Javery returned to her car after shopping at a Bloomingdale's department store in Stamford, Connecticut. Her car was located on the ground floor of the store's covered parking garage. As she placed her bags in the trunk of her car, Bernard Williams approached her from behind and made it clear that he intended to rob her. She resisted and was stabbed repeatedly and left on the garage floor where she died.

Walter Stewart, administrator of her estate, sued Bloomingdale's parent company, Federated Department Stores, Inc., for inadequate security. The plaintiff noted that the store employed five security officers inside the building and only one to protect the three-story garage, who, according to the company's own records, was frequently called away to monitor the loading dock. More than 300 fluorescent lights were burnt out or inoperative on the day of the murder. No gates or fences kept undesirables out of the garage. The store was in a high crime area: in the year prior to the murder, 1000 serious crimes were committed within two blocks of the garage. Employees had issued repeated requests for increased security. Even the store's security director requested an additional officer and a perimeter fence for the garage. Management took no steps to increase security.

In a unanimous decision, the Connecticut Supreme Court upheld a $1.5 million liability award to the estate of Marion Javery.

Research results vary on the percent of increase in negligent security cases each year and the average amounts won by plaintiffs. Most cases are settled before the trial stage. Liability Consultants, Inc., found that premises liability tort filings have increased over 260 percent in the last ten years, with an average negotiated settlement of $545,000 and an average jury award of $3.5 million.[3]

Essentially, a lawsuit means that security faces a very big test. Either management pays for adequate protection initially to prevent a serious incident or pays later, following a lawsuit. In addition to providing basic protection for people and assets, a good security and loss prevention program becomes an investment in litigation prevention.

Negligence involves many types of situations pertaining to protection programs. Security personnel have been held liable for negligent use of force and firearms. Managers and supervisors have been found negligent in the areas of applicant screening and the training and supervision of employees. And such negligence is not only restricted to the security industry. Any organization and employee can be subject to negligence. A hospital, for example, may find itself in a lawsuit after a patient is sexually assaulted by an orderly because the personnel department did not check on the orderly's background.

> Do businesses and institutions in your locale provide reasonable protection for people on the premises?

CONTRACT LAW

A *contract* is an agreement between parties to do or to abstain from doing some act. The law may enforce the agreement by requiring that a party perform its obligation or pay money equivalent to the performance. These court requirements are known as *remedies for breach of contract.* Specific circumstances may create defenses for failure to perform contract stipulations. Contracts may be express or implied. In an express contract, written or oral, the terms are stated in words. An implied contract is presumed by law to have been made from the circumstances and relations of the parties involved.

Several areas in the security and loss prevention field are relevant to the law of contracts. The company that provides a service or device to a client company may be liable for breach of contract following a dispute. A contract usually states liabilities for each party. For instance, if a third party is harmed (e.g., a person illegally arrested on the premises by a private officer from a contract service hired by a client company), the contract will commonly establish who is responsible and who is to have insurance for each risk. However, in third-party suits, courts have held a specific party liable even though the contract stipulated that another party was to be responsible in the matter. This principle is known as *nondelegable duty.*

In the common law principle of *respondeat superior* (i.e., let the master respond), an employer (master) is liable for injuries caused by an employee (servant). This is also called *vicarious liability*. Typically, the injured party will look beyond the employee, to the employer, for compensation for damages. Proper supervision and training can prevent litigation.

Another form of contract is the union contract. If a proprietary force is employed on the premises, it may be under a union contract. For regular employees, their union contract may stipulate guidelines for locker searches and investigations.

ADMINISTRATIVE LAW

A discussion of administrative law is important because many U.S. federal and state agencies and executive departments can influence loss prevention policies and programs. On the federal level, these include the Occupational Safety and Health Administration (OSHA), the National Labor Relations Board (NLRB), and the Equal Employment Opportunity Commission (EEOC), among others. (All three are discussed in various sections of this book.) Likewise, on the state level, similar bodies exist to regulate various activities such as the security industry. These agencies were formed because legislative and executive branches of government typically lack the expertise to regulate specialized areas. Therefore, independent agencies are formed that are less susceptible to direct political influence. *Administrative agencies* are government bodies that regulate various activities, make rules, conduct investigations, perform law-enforcement functions, issue penalties, and initiate criminal and civil litigation. Federal agencies document rules in the *Federal Register*, published by the General Services Administration. State agency manuals perform a similar function. Local governments follow generally accepted fire and building codes.

Compliance Auditing

Compliance auditing involves a survey of whether an organization is conforming to government regulations. A business, for example, can prepare its own forms, like a checklist, based on the requirements of regulatory laws such as the posting of laws, licenses, certificates, and policies and plans, and record-keeping functions. OSHA is one of many agencies that requires such compliance, subject to penalties amounting to a $10,000 fine, six months imprisonment, or both.[4]

Environmental compliance is an especially important area of growing concern. During the 1970s and 1980s, federal, state and local governments in the United States passed hundreds of environmental statutes and regulations focusing on discharges to the air, land, and water; the manufacture, transport, storage, and disposal of goods and their by-products; and the location of facilities. The 1990s became the era of enforcement of these laws on the federal, state, and local levels. Consequently, U.S. industry spends tens of billions of dollars to comply with these laws and prevent severe criminal and civil penalties, imprisonment, and liability for personal injuries and property damage. The American Society for Testing and Materials standard practice E1527 on environmental site assessment often is referred to as the foundation for designing an environmental compliance audit. (This type of audit often is used as part of a due diligence investigation when, for example, a company acquires a plant. *Due diligence*, in an investigation, is the attention and care legally expected in checking on the accuracy of information and omissions.) Businesses that audit themselves and put forth efforts to reach compliance may receive a lighter sanction under the Federal Sentencing Guidelines and in certain states.[5]

Federal Sentencing Guidelines

Today, the federal government views incarceration of corporate executives as a strong deterrent to corporate crime. The *Federal Sentencing Guidelines*, which apply to all federal crimes, contain stiff sentencing provisions and strong economic penalties for corporate crimes such as environmental violations, fraud, and safety and health violations. In one case, the Fifth Circuit Court of Appeals affirmed a 33-month term of imprisonment for unlawful industrial waste discharge. The defendant, in the hope of a reduced sentence, pled guilty and later testified at his sentencing to show the offense was not severe. The trial court found this testimony untruthful and imposed an upward adjustment to his sentence of six months for "obstruction of justice."[6] The sentencing guidelines are a judicial strategy to encourage corporations to enforce compliance with legal requirements and avert ignorance of the law throughout a corporation. Communications and training are essential to corporate compliance programs. The guidelines themselves state the importance of corporate programs exercising due diligence (i.e., attention and care) in preventing, detecting, and reporting criminal conduct of employees and other agents—customary duties of security programs. The Ethics Resource Center (see Chapter 2) differs with the federal government strategy and views serious corporate misconduct as not ignorance of the law but the result of unrealistic business objectives. Research by this group reveals that many companies had compliance programs in place when their problems occurred, but the programs failed to penetrate the culture. Consequently, an effective ethics program must embrace the entire corporation.[7]

Do you believe our government is too tough on businesses? Why or why not? Do you agree with the federal government or the Ethics Resource Center as to the cause of corporate misconduct? Explain your answer.

A Comprehensive Environmental Compliance Program[8]

Because environmental compliance is such a serious issue, seven recommendations are presented here that can assist a corporation in proving it has taken steps to comply with environmental laws. These recommendations can apply to other compliance programs as well.

1. Ensure line management is attentive to regulatory compliance.
2. Communicate relevant policies, procedures, and standards to all employees.
3. Audit and monitor all relevant activities.
4. Establish a training program for all employees.
5. Establish an incentive program.
6. Discipline wrongdoers.
7. Evaluate the whole effort through an outside expert.

CRIMINAL JUSTICE PROCEDURE

The following list briefly describes *procedural law*, which covers the formal rules for enforcing substantive law and the steps required to process a criminal case. (*Substantive law* defines criminal offenses and specifies corresponding fines and punishment.) Because jurisdictional procedures vary, a generalization is presented here.

1. The purpose of an arrest is to bring the person into the criminal justice system so that he or she may be held to answer the criminal charges.
2. A citation frequently is used by public police instead of a formal arrest for less serious crimes (e.g., traffic violation). If the conditions set forth in the citation are not followed, a magistrate of the appropriate court will issue a misdemeanor warrant.
3. All arrests must be based on probable cause, which is stated in arrest warrants. *Probable cause* is reasonable grounds to justify legal action, more than mere suspicion. Viewing an assault would be good probable cause.
4. Booking takes place when an arrestee is taken to a police department or jail so that a record can be made of the person's name, the date, time, location of offense, charge, and arresting officer's name. Fingerprinting and a photograph are part of the booking process.
5. Because our system of justice has a high regard for civil liberties as expressed in the Bill of Rights, the accused is informed of the *Miranda* rights, by the public police, prior to questioning.
6. After booking, and without unnecessary delay, the accused is taken before a magistrate for the "initial appearance." At this appearance, the

magistrate has the responsibility of informing the accused of constitutional rights, stating the charge, and fixing bail (if necessary).

7. Also after booking, the arresting officer will meet with the prosecutor, or a representative, to review evidence. A decision is made whether to continue legal action or to drop the case. A case may be dropped by the prosecutor for insufficient evidence or because the defendant is suffering from a problem better handled by a social agency.

8. The prosecutor prepares an "information" when prosecution is initiated. It cites the defendant's name and the charge and is signed by the complainant (e.g., the person who witnessed the crime). Then an arrest warrant is prepared by the proper judicial officer. The defendant already may be in custody at this point.

9. At the initial appearance, the magistrate will inform the defendant about the right to have a preliminary hearing. The defendant and the defense attorney make this decision. This hearing is used to determine if probable cause exists for a trial. The courtroom participants in a preliminary hearing are a judge, defendant, defense attorney, and prosecutor. The prosecutor has the "burden of proof." Witnesses may be called by the prosecutor to testify.

10. Federal law and the laws of more than half the states require that probable cause to hold a person for trial must result from grand jury action. The Fifth Amendment of the Bill of Rights states such a requirement. When probable cause is established in an action ordered by a judge or prosecutor, the grand jury will return an "indictment" or "true bill" against the accused. A "presentment" results from an investigation initiated by a grand jury establishing probable cause. Based on the indictment or presentment, an arrest warrant is issued.

11. At an "arraignment," the accused enters a plea to the charges. The four plea options are guilty, not guilty, nole contendere (no contest), and not guilty by reason of insanity.

12. Few defendants reach the trial stage. Plea bargaining is an indispensable method to clear crowded court dockets. Essentially, it means that the prosecutor and defense attorney have worked out an agreement whereby the prosecutor reduces the charge in exchange for a guilty plea. Charges also may be dropped if the accused becomes a witness in another case.

13. "Pretrial motions" can be entered by the defense attorney prior to entering a plea at arraignment. Some examples would be a "motion to quash" an indictment or information because the grand jury was improperly selected, a "continuance" requested by the defense attorney because more time is needed to prepare the case, or a "change of venue" requested when pretrial publicity is harmful to the defendant's case and the defense hopes to locate the trial in another jurisdiction so that an impartial jury is more likely to be selected.

14. The accused is tried by the court or a jury. The system of justice is basically adversarial, involving opponents. This is apparent in a trial, where the prosecutor and defense attorney make brief opening statements to the jury. The prosecutor then presents evidence. Witnesses are called to the stand to testify; they go through direct examination by the prosecutor, followed by defense cross-examination. The prosecutor attempts to show the defendant's guilt "beyond a reasonable doubt." The defense attorney strives to discredit the evidence. Redirect examination rebuilds evidence discredited by cross-examination. Recross-examination may follow. After the prosecutor presents all the evidence, the defense attorney may move for acquittal. This motion commonly is overruled by the judge. Then, the defense attorney presents evidence. Defense evidence undergoes direct and redirect examination by the defense, and cross- and recross-examination by the prosecutor.

15. Next, the judge will "charge the jury," which means that the jury is briefed by the judge on the charge and how a verdict is to be reached based on the evidence. In certain states, juries have a responsibility for recommending a sentence after a guilty verdict; the judge will brief the jury on this issue. Closing arguments are then presented by opposing attorneys.

16. The jury retires to the deliberation room; a verdict follows. A not guilty verdict signifies release for the defendant. A guilty verdict leads to sentencing. Motions and appeals may be initiated after the sentence.

ARREST LAW

Because our justice system places a high value on the rights of the individual citizen, private and public personnel cannot simply arrest, search, question, and confine a person by whim. A consideration of individual rights is an important factor. The Bill of Rights of the U.S. Constitution affords citizens numerous protections against government. The Fourth and Fifth Amendments of the Bill of Rights demonstrate how individual rights are safeguarded during criminal investigations.

> Amendment IV—The right of the people to be secure in their persons, houses, papers, and effects, against unreasonable searches and seizures, shall not be violated, and no Warrants shall issue, but upon probable cause, supported by Oath or affirmation; and particularly describing the place to be searched, and the person or things to be seized.
>
> Amendment V—. . . nor shall [any person] be compelled in any criminal case to be a witness against himself, nor be deprived of life, liberty, or property, without due process of law.

The Sixth, Eighth, and Fourteenth Amendments are other important amendments frequently associated with our criminal justice process. Briefly, the

Sixth Amendment pertains to the right to trial by jury and assistance of counsel. The Eighth Amendment states that "excessive bail shall not be required, nor excessive fines imposed, nor cruel and unusual punishments inflicted." The Fourteenth Amendment bars states from depriving any person of due process of law or equal protection of the laws.

The Fourth Amendment stipulates guidelines for the issuance of warrants. Public police obtain arrest and search warrants from an impartial judicial officer. Sometimes immediate action (e.g., chasing a bank robber) does not permit time to obtain warrants before arrest and search. In such a case, an arrest warrant is obtained as soon as possible. Private police should contact public police for assistance in securing warrants and in apprehending suspects.

A knowledge of arrest powers is essential for those likely to exercise this authority. These powers differ from state to state and depend on the statutory authority of the type of individual involved. Generally, public police officers have the greatest arrest powers. They also are protected from civil liability for false arrest, as long as they had probable cause that the crime was committed. Those in the private sector usually have arrest powers equal to citizen's arrest powers, which means that they are liable for false arrest if a crime was not, in fact, committed—regardless of the reasonableness of their belief. An exception is apparent if state statutes point out that these personnel have arrest powers equal to public police only on the protected property. If private sector personnel are deputized or given a special constabulary commission, their arrest powers are likely to equal those of public police.

Whoever makes an arrest must have the legal authority to do so. Furthermore, the distinction between felonies and misdemeanors, for those making arrests, is of tremendous importance. *Felonies*, more serious crimes, include burglary, armed robbery, murder, and arson. *Misdemeanors*, less serious crimes, include trespassing, disorderly conduct, and being drunk in public. Generally, public police can arrest someone for a felony or a misdemeanor committed in his or her view. Arrest for a felony not seen by the public police is lawful with probable cause. Arrest for a misdemeanor not seen by the public police generally is unlawful; a warrant is needed based on probable cause. There are exceptions to this misdemeanor rule; for example, public police can arrest in domestic violence cases or cases of driving under the influence, when the offense is fresh although not observed by the police. On the other hand, private police have fewer powers of arrest (equal to citizen's arrest powers). Basically, citizen's arrest powers permit felony arrests based on probable cause but prohibit misdemeanor arrests.

A serious situation exists when, for example, a private officer arrests and charges a person for a felony when in fact the offense was a misdemeanor and the jurisdiction does not grant security officers such misdemeanor arrest power. Many employers in the private sector are so afraid of an illegal arrest and subsequent legal action that they prohibit their officers from making arrests without supervisory approval. It is imperative that private sector personnel know state arrest law; proper training is a necessity.

Force

During the exercise of arrest powers, force may be necessary. The key criterion is *reasonableness*: force should be no more than what is reasonably necessary to carry out legitimate authority. If an arrestee struggles to escape and is subdued to the ground, it would be unreasonable for the arrestor to step on the arrestee's face. *Deadly force* is reserved for life-threatening situations, never to defend property. Unreasonable force can lead to difficulties in prosecuting a case, as well as civil and criminal litigation.

Searches

A legal arrest is a prerequisite to a search. Ordinarily, public police conduct a search of an arrestee right after an arrest. This has been consistently upheld by courts for the protection of the officer who may be harmed by a concealed weapon. However, *evidence obtained through an unreasonable search and seizure is not admissible in court*; this is known as the *exclusionary rule*. In reference to private sector officers, who generally have citizen arrest powers, the law is not clear and varies widely. Generally, a search is valid when consent is given and where, in a retail environment, a shoplifting statute permits the retrieval of merchandise. A search for weapons following an arrest may be justified through common law, which states that citizens have the right of self-defense. The recovery of stolen goods as the basis for a search is typically forbidden, except in some state shoplifting statutes. Whenever possible, private sector personnel should let public police conduct searches in order to transfer potential liability.

Although the law of searches by private police is not as well developed as for public police, court cases are evolving that change this situation. In the California Supreme Court decision *People* v. *Zelinsky*, 24 Cal. 3d. 357, handed down in 1979, the court ruled, in essence, that the exclusionary rule applies to private security officers. This decision involved a shoplifting case in which Virginia Zelinsky placed a blouse in her purse without paying for it. She was stopped outside the store and escorted to the security office. When the officers opened her purse and found the blouse, they also discovered a vial of heroin. She went to trial on a charge of possession of narcotics. Zelinsky requested the judge to suppress the heroin because it had been seized illegally. The judge denied her request, stating that store detectives are not governed by the prohibition against unreasonable searches. On appeal, the California Supreme Court disagreed. What also was significant about this case was that the court had ruled that when private security officers investigate crimes, their acts are "government actions," so the full force of the Constitution governs those acts.

Call It "Inspection," Not "Search and Seizure"[9]

Norman M. Spain, an authority on legal issues in security, states that private security officers generally are not bound by constitutional constraints of search and seizure as public police, unless they are "tainted by the color of law"; that is, jointly working with public police. Spain favors the term *inspection* instead of *search* for private security, because the Fourth Amendment does not apply in most private settings. He cites various targets for inspections in private settings: a locker, a vehicle entering or leaving a facility, or the belongings of an employee.

Spain recommends a formal inspection policy that would be backed by common law—employers have the right to take reasonable measures to protect their property against theft. All parties (e.g., employees, contractors, visitors) should be given notice through, for example, signs and publications. The policy should have four components:

1. A formal statement that the company reserves the right to inspect;
2. Illustrations of types of inspections;
3. A list of items that employees should not have in their possession (e.g., illegal drugs, weapons, company property removed without authorization);
4. A statement of penalties, including those for not cooperating.

Spain cautions that a "pat-down" of a person's body or inspections of pockets may result in a civil action alleging invasion of privacy, unless the site requires intense security.

Questioning

An important clause of the Fifth Amendment states that a person cannot be compelled in any criminal case to be a witness against himself or herself. Therefore, what constitutional protections does a suspect have on being approached by an investigator for questioning? Here again, the law differs with respect to public and private sector investigations.

A person about to be questioned about a crime by public police must be advised of

1. The right to remain silent;
2. The fact that statements can be used against the person in a court of law;
3. The right to an attorney, even if the person has no money;
4. The right to stop answering questions.

These rights, known as the *Miranda warnings*, evolved out of the famous 1966 U.S. Supreme Court case known as *Miranda* v. *Arizona*. If these rights are not read to a person (by public police) before questioning, statements or a confession will not be admissible as evidence in court.

Are private police required to read a person the *"Miranda* warnings" prior to questioning? The U.S. Supreme Court has not yet required the reading. However, any type of coercion or trick during questioning is prohibited for private as well as public police. A voluntary confession by the suspect is in the best interests of public and private investigators. Many private sector investigators read suspects the *"Miranda* warnings" anyway, to strengthen their case.

Employee Privacy

Privacy issues involving employees have become increasingly complex as technology changes. The use of e-mail, voice mail, computers, phone banks, and security cameras illustrates the types of technology that can have an impact on privacy concerns. Courts attempt to balance business justifications against the employee's expectation of privacy. Attorneys recommend that employers require employees to sign a declaration of understanding that they have been advised of policies and that they understand that they have no right to privacy as to activities in the workplace.[10] However, such an approach has resulted in lawsuits by employees. To prevent litigation, attorneys also recommend that employers develop guidelines or rules for acceptable monitoring.[11]

You Be the Judge[*]

Facts of the Case: "I've received letters and phone calls from the wives of employees claiming that their husbands are losing money during card games in our cafeteria at lunchtime," the personnel manager said to Jack Swanson, security manager. "In fact, two mechanics can't make their mortgage payments this month, because they lost money in poker games last week. You know we have a strict policy against gambling on company premises, Jack. I've mentioned this problem to you before."

"I know," Swanson said. "My guards have been keeping an eye on the cafeteria during lunch breaks. There's no gambling when they're on the scene, but they have plenty of other responsibilities to carry out. I don't have the personnel to monitor the lunchroom on a three-shift basis," Swanson said.

"Then you have to come up with a different strategy to catch the gamblers in the act. Either that or I'm going to have some of these angry wives call you directly," the personnel manager warned.

continued

The next day, Swanson called a local firm and had a concealed video camera installed in the cafeteria. Three days later, he was back in the personnel manager's office with a videotape showing employees from all shifts playing poker. From the amount of money on the table, it was obvious that they weren't playing for matches.

The employees featured in the video were shown the playback and given three-day suspensions. Two days later, the company received a certified letter from an attorney claiming that the evidence used against his clients had been gathered illegally by "secret" video cameras in a site where the employees had a right to expect reasonable privacy.

Neither side would budge, and the case went to court. Was the company able to play the videotape in court and thus prove that the employees had committed policy violations?

Make your decision; then turn to the end of the chapter for the court's decision.

* Reprinted with permission from *Security Management Bulletin,* a publication of the Bureau of Business Practice, Inc., 24 Rope Ferry Road, Waterford, CT 06836.

CASE PROBLEMS

4A. You are a loss prevention officer with three years of experience and a newly acquired college degree. The plant manager of loss prevention has selected you for a special assignment: design and conduct an eight-hour training program on law for company loss prevention officers. The grapevine indicates that success on this project could lead to a promotion to training officer, a position vacant at this time. You are required to (1) formulate an outline of topics to be covered and the hours for each topic, (2) justify in one to three sentences why each topic is important, and (3) prepare an examination of 10 (or 20) questions.

4B. Research and prepare a report on the laws of arrest and search and seizure in your state for citizens, private security officers, private detectives, and public police.

4C. Create, in writing, situations where each of the previous types of individuals in problem 4B can make a valid arrest. In each of the situations you create, describe appropriate search and seizure guidelines.

4D. You are a member of a jury on a civil case involving the question of negligent security. In this case, a young man was killed by a stray bullet at a restaurant parking lot at night during the weekend as he approached a group of rowdy people about to fight. The restaurant had a history of three gun incidents prior to the murder: one month earlier a shot was fired into the restaurant, without injury; three months earlier police arrested a subject for assault in the parking lot and confiscated a pistol; and five months earlier police found a revolver in the bushes in the parking lot following an arrest for public intoxication.

Each incident occurred at night during the weekend. Following these three incidents the restaurant maintained the same level of security on the premises, which was good lighting and training for employees to call police when a crime occurred. Does the business owe a duty to provide a safe environment to those who enter the premises? Is the restaurant negligent? Why or why not?

THE DECISION FOR YOU BE THE JUDGE

No. The court ruled that no evidence obtained by the secret cameras could be used, because it had been obtained illegally. Although a company has a right to enforce its policies, it has no right to do so by using illegal methods. Planting hidden cameras in locker rooms, restrooms, cafeterias, or any areas where employees have reasonable expectations of privacy is illegal, the court noted. In these areas (although not necessarily in all workplace situations and areas), employee privacy takes precedence, the court said. Police are not allowed to introduce evidence that has been obtained illegally, and as this court noted, neither are security managers. This case is based on *Hawaii* v. *Bonnel*, HI Sup. Ct., No. 16031 1993. The names in this case have been changed to protect the privacy of those involved.

NOTES

1. Corey L. Gordon and William Brill, *The Expanded Role of Crime Prevention Through Environmental Design in Premises Liability* (Washington, DC: National Institute of Justice, April 1996), pp. 2–3.
2. Teresa Anderson, "Judicial Decisions," *Security Management* (January 1996): 74.
3. William F. Blake, "Putting a Lid on Premises Liability," *Security Management* (January 1996): 64.
4. John D. McCann, "Preparing a Case for Compliance," *Security Management* (February 1994): 72–73.
5. Dan M. Chilcutt, "Making Sense of Environmental Compliance," *Risk Management* (November 1995): 41–43.
6. Janet S. Kole and Hope Lefeber, "The New Environmental Hazard: Prison," *Risk Management* (June 1994): 39.
7. Gary Edwards and Rebecca Goodell, "Three Years Later: A Look at the Effectiveness of Sentencing Guidelines," *Ethics Journal* (Fall–Winter 1994): 1 and 4.
8. Kole and Lefeber, "New Environmental Hazard," pp. 37–40.
9. "Call It 'Inspection' (Not 'Search and Seizure')," *Security Management Bulletin* (May 10, 1996): 4–7.
10. Gillian Flynn, "Balance on the Fine Line of Employee Privacy," *Personnel Journal* (March 1995): 90.
11. Richard A. West, "What's in the Rear View Mirror on the Information Superhighway," *Security Risk* (Summer 1995): 4–5.

5

Internal and External Relations

OBJECTIVES

After studying this chapter the reader will be able to

1. Define internal and external relations;
2. Differentiate between public relations and effective loss prevention relations;
3. Discuss internal relations;
4. Define marketing and explain how marketing strategies can be applied to security planning;
5. Discuss external relations;
6. List the advantages and disadvantages of prosecution.

This chapter explains why it is so important to recruit people and organizations to assist with security and loss prevention efforts. With practitioners being asked to handle increasingly complex problems, often with limited resources, it is vital that all possible sources of assistance be solicited. Strategies are delineated here for improving relations between the loss prevention department and those groups that loss prevention serves and works with in reducing losses. *Internal relations* refers to cooperative efforts with individuals and groups within an organization that a loss prevention department serves. *External relations* refers to cooperative efforts with external individuals and groups that assist in loss prevention objectives.

To elaborate on the internal and external relations charts (Figures 5–1 and 5–2), lines of communications are important for an improved loss prevention program. For instance (clockwise, Figure 5–1, internal relations chart), upper management dictates loss prevention goals. Both the personnel and loss prevention departments should coordinate activities relevant to applicant screening and disciplinary actions. When labor problems (e.g., unrest, strike) are anticipated, losses can be minimized. In addition, labor union contracts may stipulate limitations on loss prevention activities (e.g., the questioning of suspect employees). Loss prevention practitioners are

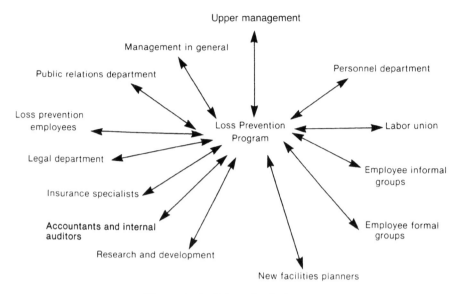

Figure 5–1   Internal relations.

Figure 5–2   External relations.

wise to tune in on feedback and criticism from formal and informal employee groups. By listening to and satisfying employee needs (e.g., clean restrooms, a well-run cafeteria, and recreational programs), losses can be reduced. When new facilities are being planned, architects, engineers, and loss prevention practitioners can jointly design prevention strategies into the plan and thereby save money by not having to install equipment (e.g., alarms) after construction is completed. Trade secrets and other proprietary information must be under strict security, especially in research and development. Accountants and auditors can help create cooperative strategies against losses. Furthermore, the loss prevention manager should be given an opportunity to review their findings. Insurance specialists often assist in planning prevention strategies and reducing premiums. At various times, legal assistance may be required by a loss prevention department. Because loss prevention personnel are the backbone of the program, the manager should do everything possible (e.g., give praise and pay raises, and institute participatory management) to satisfy their needs. Good rapport with the public relations department ensures that appropriate loss prevention information is released to outsiders and that this information is in the best interest of the organization. Communicating with management in general is vital for many reasons. For instance, the objectives of the loss prevention program can be transmitted to all employees via meetings with management. Feedback from management also assists in planning loss prevention strategies that do not hinder productivity or profit.

In reference to the external relations chart (clockwise, Figure 5–2, beginning with law enforcement), public service agencies are an essential ingredient of private sector loss prevention programs. Good communications and cooperation are important in case crimes occur or a disaster strikes. Educational institutions also can provide research assistance as well as potential employees. The loss prevention manager may want to serve on an advisory committee or speak to classes to spread the word about loss prevention. When possible, the news media should be recruited to aid in loss prevention objectives. Other businesses and loss prevention peers with similar problems can be a good source of ideas. Insurance companies, like internal insurance specialists, can provide information to improve prevention strategies while reducing premiums. Independent auditors and certified public accountants can point out weaknesses in the loss prevention program. When people (e.g., customers) visit the organization, they should not be seriously inconvenienced by loss prevention devices (e.g., access control), but at the same time, losses must be prevented. Friendly dialogue and cooperative efforts should be emphasized when OSHA and other government agencies are involved in a loss prevention program.

LOSS PREVENTION RELATIONS VERSUS PUBLIC RELATIONS

What is public relations? *Public relations*, PR for short, is primarily concerned with developing a positive image for the organization being represented.

A loss prevention program can use some of the concepts featured in (public) police-community relations. PR is only a part of police-community relations (PCR). To many police agencies, PR refers to an outward projection to the community to educate residents about police activity and law. Other police PR objectives involve building respect for the police and developing an environment for compliance with the laws. The mass media have helped police agencies reach these PR objectives. However, this PR approach represents one-way communication flowing from the police department to the community. Progressive police agencies have considered PR as only a part of PCR. PCR differs from PR by attempting to develop two-way communication. The basic prerequisite is a free flow of communication between both groups. PCR is interested in mutual understanding of each other's problems and concerns and mutual cooperation and broader based action against crime by not only the police but also by the community. This approach has developed into *community policing*, which aims to control crime through a partnership of police and citizens.

To develop effective loss prevention relations, PR, two-way communication, and partnership are important. These strategies can be used internally and externally. Good internal relations can mean meetings between loss prevention personnel and regular employees to talk over various vulnerabilities, prevention strategies, and associated problems. Likewise, good external relations can involve meetings between loss prevention personnel and public service officials to seek solutions to mutual problems.

Benefits of Good Relations

The following are reasons why good internal and external relations are important to a loss prevention program. Good relations

1. Build respect for the loss prevention department, its objectives, and its personnel;
2. Reinforce compliance with policies and procedures to prevent losses;
3. Foster assistance with loss prevention activities such as programs and investigations;
4. Provide a united front against vulnerabilities, which creates lower losses, extends the impact of strategies, and saves money;
5. Educate employees, community residents, and others;
6. Improve understanding of complex security problems;
7. Reduce rumors and false information;
8. Improve understanding of the loss prevention program;
9. Stimulate consciousness-raising relevant to loss prevention;
10. Make the loss prevention job easier.

> Good internal and external relations enhance the effectiveness of security and loss prevention programs.

INTERNAL RELATIONS

Too often in security and loss prevention texts and in practice attention is given to public relations while internal relations are ignored. A loss prevention program is wise to focus on internal relations; many experts state that the greatest threat to business or an organization is from within and employees throughout an organization can be recruited to aid loss prevention efforts.

Human Relations on the Job

Getting along with others is a major part of almost everyone's job. Many say it is half of the job. The result of such effort is increased cooperation and a smoother working environment.

These suggestions can help a person develop good human relations:

1. Make getting along with all employees as well as possible a conscious goal. Cooperation increases productivity.
2. Say hello to as many employees as possible, even if you do not know them.
3. Smile.
4. Think before you speak.
5. Be aware that nonverbal communication such as body language, facial expression, and tone of voice may reveal messages not included in your oral statements.
6. Listen carefully.
7. Maintain a sense of humor.
8. Try to look at each person as an individual. Avoid stereotyping (applying an image of a group to an individual member of a group).
9. Personalities vary from one person to another.
10. People who are quiet may be shy, and these people should not be interpreted as being aloof.
11. Carefully consider rumors and those who gossip. Such information often is inaccurate.
12. Remember that when you speak about another person your comments often are repeated.

13. If possible, avoid people with negative attitudes. A positive attitude increases the quality of human relations and has an impact on many other activities (e.g., opportunity for advancement).
14. Do not flaunt your background.
15. Everybody makes mistakes. Maintain a positive attitude and learn from mistakes.

Management Support

Management support is indispensable for an effective loss prevention program, and management support can be enhanced through good human relations. Frequent dialogue between loss prevention practitioners and management should be a high priority. One method of gaining the interest of management is to emphasize loss prevention as an investment for increasing profits. A good knowledge of business principles and practices can aid the practitioner who must speak "business management language" for effective communications. A loss prevention practitioner who does not speak "business management language" would be wise to enroll in management and accounting courses at a local college.

In one large corporation, the strategy of the security department to gain management support is to quantify its worth and prove it can provide services more efficiently than an outside contractor. This is the reality of proprietary (in-house) security today as it struggles to survive and escape the outsourcing and downsizing trends. This corporation's security department tracks everything from the number of investigations conducted to the turnover rate of security officers. Such information helps the security function evaluate and improve its services to its in-house customers. Internal customer satisfaction is further measured via written and telephone surveys. Additionally, the department measures losses avoided because of security action. For example, the department takes credit for the annual savings from an investigation that reveals that a workers' compensation claim that the corporation has been paying for several years is fraudulent. Another avenue to gain management support is to show that a $50,000-a-year investigator can recover an average of $500,000 in lost inventory each year.[1]

Orientation and Training Programs

Beginning with a new employee's initial contact with a business, an emphasis should be placed on loss prevention. Through the employment interview, orientation, and training, an atmosphere of loss prevention impressed on the new people sets the stage for consciousness-raising about the importance of reduced losses through prevention strategies.

Specifically, orientation and training sessions should include a description of the loss prevention plan pertaining to crime, fire, and accident. Program objectives, benefits to employees, and how employees can help reduce losses also are topics of concern. Other possible topics include prosecution policies, photo ID cards, emergency exits, and various loss prevention services, devices, policies, and procedures.

Loss Prevention Meetings

Meetings with superiors, with employees on the same level as the prevention manager, and with subordinates all strengthen internal relations because communication is fostered. When the loss prevention manager meets with superiors, goals and objectives often are transmitted to the manager. Essentially, the manager does a lot of listening. However, after listening, the manager usually has an opportunity to explain the needs of the loss prevention program while conforming to upper management's expectations. This two-way communication facilitates mutual understanding.

Meetings with other managers vary, depending on the type of organization. For instance, a meeting between the personnel manager and the loss prevention manager helps to resolve problem areas. One typical conflict pertains to disciplinary decisions. Another problem area between both departments evolves from applicant screening. Both departments should meet, work together, and formulate a cooperative plan.

When a loss prevention manager meets with subordinates, internal relations are enhanced further. Morale and productivity often are heightened when subordinates are given an opportunity to express opinions and ideas. A manager who is willing to listen to subordinates fosters improved internal relations.

Loss Prevention Bulletins

This strategy fosters communications while improving internal relations. Bulletins can be directed at superiors, loss prevention personnel, and the general in-house workforce.

A bulletin for superiors can be prepared at intervals of, say, every three months. It can emphasize vulnerabilities, past losses, prevention strategies, and achievements by the loss prevention department. Vulnerabilities show upper management where future losses are expected. Past losses document the losses that have taken place. A dollar amount of direct and indirect losses increases upper management's interest. A concise explanation of various prevention strategies serves as an educational tool. The achievements of the loss prevention department show that the department is not just sitting idle. "Tooting one's own horn" should not be perceived as bragging but a method to tell others that the past budget allocation was worthwhile. For example, achievements may include lowering of shrinkage and increasing profits, a low accident rate, foiling a criminal conspiracy, quickly extinguishing a fire, and a favorable report from an OSHA inspector. The bulletin for superiors will better prepare them for meetings, budgets, and decisions associated with loss prevention.

A bulletin for loss prevention personnel is worthwhile, too. Two primary objectives are to disseminate information (i.e., educate) and to build morale. Examples of educational topics are policies and procedures, criminal law, discussions of actual incidents, prevention strategies, practical aids, interesting statistics, and other information related to crime, fire, and safety. This information dissemination also reinforces professionalism. Morale can be strengthened by devoting a section of the bulletin to items of an interpersonal nature; for instance, promotions, officer of the month, accomplishments of personnel (on and off the job), birthdays, anniversaries, and birth announcements.

A bulletin for employees in general can serve to reinforce loss prevention as an integral part of the working environment; educate employees about crime, fire, and accident hazards; review emergency procedures; and discuss general protection methods such as locking vehicles.

If bulletins are not feasible, then perhaps a section in the company newspaper will be available. Other methods of disseminating information and improving internal relations are to use bulletin boards and signs.

Involvement Programs

The essence of involvement programs is to motivate employees who are not directly associated with the loss prevention department to participate in loss prevention objectives. How can this be accomplished? The following ideas are suggested. The employee responsible for the lowest shrinkage among several competing departments within a business wins $200 and a day off. The employee with the best loss prevention idea of the month wins $25. The employee with the best loss prevention question of the month wins $10. Those people who become involved should be mentioned in loss prevention bulletins to show others the benefits of interest in loss prevention.

Don't Just Sell Security, Market It!

Marketing consists of researching a target market and the needs of customers and developing products and services to be sold at a profit. Marketing also is considered the study of consumer problems as opportunities.

The concepts of marketing are universally applicable. *Market segmentation* divides a market into distinct groups of consumers. When one or more of the market segments is chosen for a specific product or service, this is known as *target marketing*. To illustrate, for security programs, market segmentation within a corporation can yield the following groups: executives, women, salespeople, production workers, and truck drivers. Once the market is segmented, a protection program can be designed for each target market. Research and risk analyses will produce a foundation from which to satisfy the protection needs of each type of customer. For those security programs that are so general in nature that few customers find them appealing, marketing strategies may be the solution to generate interest. Loss prevention influence over a target group or groups is better than no influence at all.[2]

These seven strategies contain a heavy emphasis on marketing and are designed to produce a high-quality security program:

1. Identify all internal and external customers of security services and determine what the customers want and how security can tell whether they are satisfied with the quality of the services rendered.
2. Focus on the customer and his or her perspective. Security should avoid a "we versus them" viewpoint.
3. Facilitate teamwork by meeting with representatives of all internal departments to discuss security issues and to seek solutions.
4. Listen and be receptive to customer concerns. In one hospital, employees complained about the need to enter their departments outside of regular business hours. In response, the security department used its technology to customize access control for each department.
5. Develop definitions. Ensure that customers and security share each group's definitions of security and loss prevention.
6. Set priorities among customers. One hospital ranked its customers as follows: patients or outside customers, employees, and employees' families.
7. Take action and be prepared to constantly adapt to new circumstances.[3]

What other ideas can you suggest to improve internal relations?

EXTERNAL RELATIONS

In this discussion of external organizations and groups that should be recruited to aid loss prevention objectives, emphasis is placed on law enforcement and other public service agencies, the community, the media, and external loss prevention peers.

Roger Herren, Loss Prevention Manager, Improves Relations with Roy Bounty, Chief of Police

Because of poor crime prevention strategies, the Multistructure Company sustained continued losses from burglaries. After five such incidents and strained relations with local law enforcement, the company finally fired the loss prevention manager. A short time later, Roger Herren was hired as the new manager because of his impressive experience and education. He was instructed to solve quickly the problems of burglary and strained relations.

Herren's first objective was to meet with Chief Roy Bounty to ask for advice on how a cooperative effort could reduce the burglary problem. The chief was pleased at this suggestion. He stated that the previous loss prevention manager was never interested in any of his ideas about crime prevention. The chief also had previously offered to visit the plant to perform a crime prevention survey, but nobody seemed interested. Herren told the chief that a survey would be most welcome and shared his belief that a cooperative effort surely would solve the burglary problem.

During the following week the chief conducted the survey. Over lunch, several ideas were pooled by Bounty and Herren. Thereafter, the strategies were implemented, and burglaries and strained relations no longer were a problem.

Law Enforcement

Without the assistance of public law enforcement agencies, criminal charges initiated by the private sector would not be possible. Public police and prosecutors are the main components of public law enforcement. Police frequently are guided by a prosecutor, who is often referred to as the "chief law enforcement officer." The prosecuting attorney has broad discretion to initiate criminal cases. Community sentiment and powerful groups almost always have an influence on a prosecutor's discretion. Various alternatives are open to a prosecutor. If there is sufficient evidence, the prosecutor can charge an individual. Charges frequently are reduced after a defendant has agreed to plead guilty to a lesser offense. This is called *plea bargaining.* It avoids an expensive trial and the prosecutor obtains a conviction.

Unless private security officers adhere to the basic requirements within local jurisdictions, cases cannot be prosecuted successfully. An example can be seen in shoplifting cases. Depending on state law and local prosecutor requirements, a jurisdiction may require apprehension of a shoplifter after the offender leaves the store with the item, rather than apprehending within the store. Many prosecutors feel that this strengthens the case.

External relations with law enforcement agencies are vital for loss prevention programs. Mutual dependence and cooperation foster improved crime-fighting capabilities. Sharing information is a major factor in enhancing this working relationship. Law enforcement agencies often provide information that aids the private sector. Intelligence information pertaining to the presence in an area of professional criminals, bad-check violators, counterfeiters, and con artists assists the private sector in preventing losses.

Public Service Agencies

In addition to law enforcement, other public service agencies such as fire departments, emergency medical units, and rescue squads are useful in helping a loss prevention program. An analysis of these services is particularly important when a new facility is being planned. Factors relevant to emergency response time and efficiency assist in planning the extent and expense of a loss prevention program.

Very little is accomplished by overtly criticizing local public service agencies for their deficiencies. This action results in negative attitudes and strained relations. Moreover, in the future, the severity of losses very well may depend on action taken by these public service agencies.

Several strategies help create good relations with public service agencies:

1. Do not become too aggressive when striving toward good external relations.
2. Speak on the same vocabulary level as the person with whom you are communicating.
3. Do not brag about your education and experience.
4. Do not criticize public service practitioners, because these comments often are repeated.
5. Try to have a third party, such as a friend, introduce you to public service personnel.
6. Join organizations to which public service personnel belong.
7. Join volunteer public service organizations (e.g., the local public police reserve or volunteer fire department), if possible.
8. Speak to civic groups.
9. Ask to sit in on special training programs and offer to assist in training.
10. Try to join local or regional criminal intelligence meetings, where information is shared and crimes are solved.
11. Create a softball league with private and public sector participation. Have a picnic at the end of the season. Try to obtain company funds for these activities.
12. Obtain a position on an advisory committee at a college that has a criminal justice, security and loss prevention, or fire science program.

13. Form an external loss prevention advisory board and ask local public service heads to volunteer a limited amount of time. Secure company money to sponsor these as dinner meetings.
14. Accept official inspections and surveys by public service practitioners.
15. Begin an organization, such as a local private sector–public sector cooperative association, that has common goals.

The Community

When a new industry is planned for a certain locale, external relations become especially important. Good relations are necessary, particularly when the industry has been known to alter the environment and cause pollution problems. Therefore, residents must be informed about safety plans. Safety is a moral obligation, as well as a necessity, to ensure limited losses and business survival. As shown in the media, over and over again, community resistance to certain industries is strong. Consequently, an industry with a history of adverse environmental impacts must cultivate relations that assure residents that safety has improved to the point of causing minimal problems and an extremely low probability of accidents. A loss prevention manager working alone, representing the industry, would find such a job extremely difficult. Engineers, scientists, upper management, and other support personnel are needed to provide community residents, politicians, and resistance groups with a variety of information and answers.

Another consideration involves reassuring the community that a proposed industry will not adversely drain public service resources while creating additional community problems. Careful planning must ensure that the industry does not compound crime problems while causing an increase in local police expenditures. This same consideration should be applied to fire, medical, and other emergency services.

If an industry becomes directly involved in a special program to aid the community, then external relations are even further enhanced. In Quincy, Massachusetts, the Earn-It Program has helped rehabilitate juvenile delinquents while enabling them to compensate the victims of their crime. Through this restitution program, probation personnel contact victims and ascertain losses. The backbone of the program consists of the over 75 area businesses that have made available work opportunities to the Earn-It Program.[4]

The Media

The media can help or hinder a loss prevention program. Efforts must be made to recruit the media. Difficulties often arise because members of the media usually are interested in information beyond that offered by interviewees. It is worthwhile to maintain positive relations; negative relations may create a vicious cycle leading to mutual harm.

In almost all large organizations, educated and experienced public relations personnel handle the media. Loss prevention practitioners should take advantage of such an organizational structure. This, in effect, insulates the loss prevention department from the media. Policy statements should point out that comments to the media are released through a *designated spokesperson* in the public relations department. When all loss prevention personnel clearly understand the media policy, mistakes and embarrassing situations are minimized. An example of a mistake is the story about a young police officer who was confronted by an aggressive news reporter about a homicide investigation. Investigators had one lead: clear shoe prints under the window of entry to the crime scene. It was hoped that one of the suspects would be discovered with the shoes that matched the prints. Unfortunately, the news reporter obtained this information from the young officer. The local newspaper printed the story and mentioned the shoes. After reading the newspaper, the offender destroyed the shoes, and the case became more difficult to solve. There had never been a clear policy statement concerning the media within this organization. Another blunder may take place if the amount of valuables (e.g., cash) stolen in a burglary or robbery is revealed to the media or that the offenders overlooked high-priced valuables during the crime. Both types of information, broadcast by the media, have been known to cause future crimes at the same location.

An article in *Security Management*, "Stress from the Press—and How to Meet It,"[5] points out many useful ideas concerning relations with the media. The article stresses the importance of preparation, knowing what you want to say, being prepared for tricky questions, and carefully phrasing answers. Numerous firms are training executives in effective communication techniques. These courses vary, but most participants learn how to deal with hostile questioning and receive feedback and coaching with the assistance of videotaping. The courses generally run for one to three days and can cost thousands of dollars per participant.

The article recommends several "don'ts" for interviews with the media:

1. Don't return any hostility from the interviewer.
2. Don't lose the audience. Remember the type of audience you are communicating with at home.
3. Don't say, "no comment." If you can't answer the questions, at least tell the audience why.
4. Don't make up answers. If you do not know an answer, say so.
5. Don't say "off the record." If you don't want it repeated, don't say it.
6. Don't offer personal opinions. You are on the air to represent your company, and everything you say will appear to be company policy.

External Loss Prevention Peers

The practitioner who exists in a vacuum is like a student who doesn't pay attention. No knowledge is obtained. Through formal and informal associations with peers, the practitioner inevitably becomes involved in a learning experience. One of the results of relations with peers is information that can improve loss prevention programming.

No individual is an expert about everything. If a group of experts comes together, a broad spectrum of ideas results. When a loss prevention practitioner does not know the answer to a particular question, a call to a peer can produce an answer. Peers are helpful in the selection of services and devices, budget preparation, and even presentations to management.

Many formal organizations are open to practitioners. The one organization known by almost all practitioners is the American Society for Industrial Security. This organization is at the forefront in upgrading the security and loss prevention field by educating members and increasing professionalism. Local chapters, national meetings, specialized seminars, and other activities bring peers together for mutually beneficial relations.

> What other ideas can you suggest to improve external relations?

SPECIAL PROBLEMS

Certain select areas of concern overshadow both internal and external relations. Two important areas are prosecution decisions and loss prevention attire.

Prosecution Decisions

Prosecution decisions concerning employee-offenders, usually for theft, often are difficult for management. The difficulty arises because a wise manager considers numerous variables. No matter what decision is made, the company may suffer in some way. The situation is tantamount to "damned if we do and damned if we don't." The following are benefits of prosecuting:

1. Prosecuting deters future offenders by setting an example. This reduces the potential for future losses.
2. The company will rid itself of an employee-offender who may have committed previous offenses.

3. The company will appear strong, and this will generate greater respect from employees.
4. Morale is boosted when "rotten apple" employees are purged from the workforce.
5. If a company policy states that all offenders will be prosecuted, then after each prosecution, employees will know that the company lives up to its word and will not tolerate criminal offenses.
6. The company aids the criminal justice system and the community against crime.
7. Local law enforcement will feel that the company is part of the war against crime. This will reinforce cooperation.
8. A strong prosecution policy will become known inside and outside the company. Those seeking employment who also are thinking of committing crimes against the company will be deterred from applying for work.

The following are benefits of not prosecuting:

1. The company shows sympathy for the employee-offender. Therefore, employees say the company has a heart. Morale is boosted.
2. Not prosecuting saves the company time, money, and wages for those employees, such as witnesses and the investigator, who must aid in the prosecution.
3. If the employee-offender agrees to pay back the losses to the company and he or she is not fired, the company will not lose an experienced and trained employee in whom it has invested.
4. The criminal justice system will not be burdened by another case.
5. Sometimes companies initiate prosecution, an arrest is made, and then management changes its mind. This creates friction with law enforcement agencies.
6. Possible labor trouble is avoided.
7. Possible litigation is avoided.
8. Prosecution sometimes creates friction among the public relations, personnel, and loss prevention departments.
9. Giving bad news to financial supporters, stockholders, customers, and the community is avoided.

To complicate the prosecution decision even more, the policy statement concerning prosecution must be carefully worded by management. There is no perfect statement that can apply to all incidents. A look at a strict policy statement illustrates this problem. Suppose a company policy states that all employees committing crimes against the business will be impartially and vigorously prosecuted. Thereafter, what if a 15-year employee, with an excellent work record, and accumulated company-paid training, is caught stealing a box of envelopes? Obviously, such a strong policy statement can be detrimental.

Employees Smoking Marijuana

An undercover investigation at the Southern Manufacturing Plant has revealed that seven experienced and well-trained employees smoke marijuana before work.

The company loss prevention manager met with upper management to decide what to do. One solution was to fire all the employees; however, these offending employees have good work records, considerable work experience, and the company has invested heavily in their training. The loss prevention manager suggested that the employees be confronted and threatened with firing unless they participate in a local alcohol and drug abuse program. The manager stated that another local business had a similar problem and a contract was formulated between the business and the government agency dealing with alcohol and drug abuse problems. Upper management at Southern favored this idea.

Later, the employees were confronted and surprised. They all admitted that they liked their jobs and were willing to participate in a drug abuse program on their own time to avoid being fired. By this time, the local alcohol and drug abuse commission had agreed to conduct a program for these employees. The local police chief and prosecutor favored the program as an innovative diversion from the criminal justice system.

Upper management was satisfied. Internal and external relations were improved. The company did not lose experienced workers nor the money invested in their training.

The *Report of the Task Force on Private Security* adds interesting perspectives to the prosecution issue:

> [I]t would appear that a large percentage of criminal violators known to private security personnel are not referred to the criminal justice system. A logical conclusion would be that there is a "private" criminal justice system wherein employer reprimands, restrictions, suspensions, demotions, job transfers, or employment terminations take the place of censure by the public system. . . . [I]n many instances private action is more expedient, less expensive, and less embarrassing to the company. Fear of lawsuits or protecting the offender from a criminal record may be important. However, violations of due process, right to counsel, and other individual rights are more likely to occur under such a system. The criminal justice system is established for the purpose of resolving criminal offenses and can be a viable resource for the private security sector in this regard.[6]

Another factor affecting a company's prosecution decision is the *prosecution threshold*, which is the monetary level of the alleged crime that must be met before prosecution. Trends indicate a rise in dollar amounts of individual instances of theft that are partly tied to employee perception of changes in company and prosecutor policies concerning prosecution thresholds. "In the 1970s, an employee who stole $10,000 would have been prosecuted. Today, in many places, that amount won't even produce a criminal referral."[7]

Loss Prevention Attire

The appearance of loss prevention personnel has a definite impact on how people perceive a loss prevention program. A vital part of appearance is attire (i.e., uniforms). Wrinkled, messy uniforms send a message to observers that loss prevention objectives are not very important. A variety of people observe loss prevention personnel: employees, customers, visitors, salespeople, truck drivers, law enforcement personnel, and the community in general. What type of message to these people is desired from an effective loss prevention program? Obviously, neat, good-looking attire is an asset.

Attire can project two primary images: subtlety or visibility. Subtle attire consists of blazers or sports jackets (see Figure 5–3). It projects a

Figure 5–3   Security officers at a museum. Courtesy of Wackenhut Corporation. Photo by Ed Burns.

warmer, less threatening, and less authoritarian image. Increased visibility and a stricter image are projected through traditional uniforms. However, it is vital that traditional uniforms do not look similar to those worn by public police; this can cause mistakes by citizens needing aid, and the public police resent private sector officers wearing such uniforms. The type of loss prevention program and particular needs dictate the attire.

All security and loss prevention personnel must realize that they have only one opportunity to create a first, favorable impression.[8]

CASE PROBLEMS

5A. As a security supervisor you have received reports that a security officer assigned to the employee parking lot is having repeated verbal confrontations with employees. One report described the officer's use of profane language and threats. Specifically, what do you say to this officer, and what actions do you take? How do you repair internal relations?

5B. You are a loss prevention supervisor, and two company employees report to you that a loss prevention officer is intoxicated while on duty. You approach the officer, engage in conversation, and smell alcohol on his breath. What do you do? An added complication is that this particular officer has a brother on the local police department who has provided valuable aid during past loss prevention investigations. Furthermore, the officer has had a good work record while employed by the company for five years. After carefully analyzing the advantages and disadvantages of various internal and external ramifications to proposed actions, what do you do?

5C. While a loss prevention officer was routinely patrolling the inner storage rooms of a plant, he accidentally stumbled on two employees engaged in sexual intercourse. All three were shocked and surprised. The man and woman should have been selecting orders for shipment. The woman cried and begged the loss prevention officer to remain silent about this revelation. The man also pleaded for mercy, especially because both were married to other people. When the officer decided that he should report the matter, the man became violent. A fight developed between the officer and the man and woman. The officer was able to radio his location and within 10 minutes other officers arrived. The pair has been brought to the loss prevention office. What do you do as the loss prevention supervisor?

5D. An unfortunate explosion and injuries took place at Smith Industries and a company vice president designates you, a loss prevention supervisor, to speak to the media. It has been only one hour since the explosion, the investigation is far from complete, and you have no time to prepare for the media representatives who have arrived. As you walk to the front gate of the plant, several newspeople are anxiously waiting. The rapid fire questions begin: "What is the extent of injuries and damage?" "Is it true that both high production quotas and poor safety have caused the explosion?" "What dangers will the community face due to this explosion and future ones?" "What are your comments about reports that safety inspectors have been bribed by Smith Industries executives?" As a loss prevention supervisor with the authority and responsibility to respond to media questions, what are your answers to each question?

5E. Because of your experience and college education you are appointed manager of loss prevention at a large manufacturing plant in a small city. It is your understanding that the local police chief is introverted and uncooperative with strangers. The chief has an eighth-grade education and is extremely sensitive about this deficiency. He refuses to hire college graduates. Despite these faults, he is respected and does a good job as a police administrator.

The local fire chief is the police chief's brother. Both have similar backgrounds and character traits. Furthermore, the local prosecutor is a cousin of both chiefs. A "clannish" situation is apparent.

As the loss prevention manager you know that you will have to rely on as much cooperation as possible from these public officials. What do you do to develop good relations with them?

5F. Allen Dart has worked for the AM Radio Manufacturing Plant for 14 years. He has always done above-average work and recently has been promoted to production supervisor. One afternoon when Allen was leaving the plant, he dropped an expensive radio from under his coat in front of a loss prevention officer. Allen was immediately approached by the officer who asked Allen to step inside to the loss prevention office. At this time, Allen broke down and began crying. Before anybody could say a word, Allen stated that he was very sorry and that he would not do it again. Later, the plant, loss prevention, and personnel managers met to discuss the incident. An argument developed because the loss prevention manager wanted to seek prosecution, whereas the personnel manager did not. The plant manager stopped the argument and instructed both managers to list the advantages and disadvantages of prosecuting. As a liaison to both of these managers, what do you suggest in terms of advantages and disadvantages to prosecution?

NOTES

1. Brian R. Hollstein, "Internal Security and the Corporate Customer," *Security Management* (June 1995): 61–63.
2. Philip P. Purpura, *Modern Security & Loss Prevention Management* (Boston: Butterworth–Heinemann, 1989), pp. 141–148.
3. Dennis Wozniak, "Seven Steps to Quality Security," *Security Management* (March 1996): 25–28.
4. International City Management Association, "Businesses Provide Jobs for Juvenile Offenders," *Target* (May 1978): 4–5.
5. "Stress from the Press—and How to Meet It," *Security Management* 24, no. 2 (February 1980): 8–11.
6. U.S. Department of Justice, *Report of the Task Force on Private Security* (Washington, DC: U.S. Government Printing Office, 1976), p. 128. Research in 1980 and 1990 confirmed that much economic crime is disposed of privately. See William C. Cunningham et al., *Private Security: Patterns and Trends* (Washington, DC: National Institute of Justice, August 1991), p. 4.
7. "Finding Where the (Financial) Bodies Are Buried," *Security Management Bulletin* (August 25, 1993): 4–5.
8. Philip P. Purpura, *Security Handbook* (Albany, NY: Delmar, 1991), p. 41.

6

Applicant Screening and Employee Socialization

OBJECTIVES

After studying this chapter the reader will be able to

1. Define applicant screening and employee socialization;
2. Summarize the legal guidelines for applicant screening;
3. Explain each of the following and how it relates to the employment environment—equal employment opportunity, affirmative action, quotas, diversity, and sexual harassment;
4. List and explain at least four applicant screening methods;
5. Describe how to enhance employee socialization.

One of the most important assets of an organization is its personnel. The purpose of *applicant screening* is to find the most appropriate person for a particular job. Several methods are available for screening applicants, such as interviewing and testing.

The culmination of the applicant screening process results in hiring an applicant. At this stage, an organization already has invested considerable personnel, money, and time into making the best possible choice. The next step is to develop a productive employee. This can be accomplished through adequate *socialization*, which is a learning process that, it is hoped, produces an employee who will benefit the organization. Two primary methods of socialization are employee training and example setting by superiors.

Both applicant screening and employee socialization are primary loss prevention strategies. If an organization can select honest and productive people, losses are prevented. If employees can be socialized to act safely and protect company assets, security and loss prevention strategies are enhanced further.

Applicant screening and employee socialization are primary loss prevention strategies.

LEGAL GUIDELINES

Laws and regulations had a major impact on the process of staffing organizations. Here is an overview of major legislation and court decisions that guide the employment relationship.

Federal Legislation

- *The Equal Pay Act of 1963.* This legislation requires that men and women be paid equally if they work at the same location at similar jobs. Exceptions include a seniority or merit system and earnings through quantity or quality of production. The act is enforced by the Equal Employment Opportunity Commission (EEOC).
- *The Civil Rights Act of 1964, Title VII.* This law prohibits employment discrimination based on race, color, religion, sex, or national origin. Title VII prohibits discrimination with regard to any employment condition, including recruiting, screening, hiring, training, compensating, evaluating, promoting, disciplining, and firing. Congress established the Equal Employment Opportunity Commission to enforce Title VII.
- *The Age Discrimination in Employment Act of 1967.* Age discrimination in the workplace against individuals 40 years of age and older is prohibited. The act is enforced by the EEOC.
- *The Equal Employment Opportunity Act of 1972.* The purpose of this federal law (EEO) is to strengthen Title VII by providing the EEOC with additional enforcement powers to file suits and issue cease-and-desist orders. Further, EEO expands coverage to employees of state and local governments, educational institutions, and private employers of more than 15 persons. EEO programs are implemented by employers to prevent discrimination in the workplace and to offset past employment discrimination.
- *The Rehabilitation Act of 1973.* This act requires government agencies and contractors with the federal government to take affirmative action to hire those with physical or mental handicaps. The act is enforced by the Office of Federal Contract Compliance Procedures.
- *The Americans with Disabilities Act of 1990.* This legislation prohibits discrimination against individuals with disabilities and increases their access to services and jobs. The act is enforced by the EEOC.

- *The Civil Rights Act of 1991.* This legislation permits women, persons with disabilities, and persons who are members of religious minorities to have a jury trial and sue if they can prove intentional hiring and workplace discrimination. Also, it requires businesses to prove that the business practice that led to the charge of discrimination was not discriminatory but job related for the position and consistent with business necessity. The act is enforced by the EEOC.
- *The Family and Medical Leave Act of 1993.* This legislation requires employers to provide 12 weeks of unpaid leave for family and medical emergencies without employees suffering job loss. The act is enforced by the Department of Labor.

U.S. Supreme Court Decisions

When laws are passed, the courts play a role in helping to define what the legislation means. Such court cases evolve, for example, when the EEOC develops and enforces guidelines based upon their interpretation of legislation. Confusion over how to interpret the legislation has led to many lawsuits and some conflicting court decisions. The U.S. Supreme Court has provided guidelines by ruling on cases from lower courts.

- *Griggs* v. *Duke Power* (1971). In 1968, several employees of the Duke Power Company in North Carolina were given a pencil-and-paper aptitude test for manual labor. Willie Griggs and 12 other black workers sued their employer with the charge of job discrimination under the Civil Rights Act of 1964. Their contention was that the pencil-and-paper aptitude test had little to do with their ability to perform manual labor. The Supreme Court decided that a test is inherently discriminatory if it is not job related and differentiates on the basis of race, sex, or religion. Furthermore, employers are required to prove that their screening methods are job related.
- *Albermarle Paper Co.* v. *J. Moody* (1975). The Court decided that tests or other screening methods that disqualify a disproportionate number of minorities have to be validated. In other words, employers must prove that a test predicts on-the-job performance.
- *Washington* v. *Davis* (1976). This case involved the Washington, DC, police department, where, between 1968 and 1971, 57 percent of blacks failed the entrance exam compared to 13 percent of whites. The department demonstrated that the exam was related to those given during recruit training. According to the Court, the police department did not discriminate. If a test is job related, it is not necessarily illegal even though a greater percentage of minority group members do not pass it. This case departed from several others while supporting the use of tests as a screening tool.

- *Bakke* v. *University of California* (1978). Reverse discrimination was the main issue of this case. Allan Bakke, a white man, sued the Davis Medical School under the "equal protection" clause of the Fourteenth Amendment because it set aside 16 of 100 openings for minorities, who were evaluated according to different standards. The Court concluded that the racial quota system was unacceptable because it disregarded Bakke's right to equal protection of the law, and that affirmative action programs are permissible as long as applicants are considered on an individual basis and a rigid number of places has not been set aside. Race can be a key factor in the selection process; however, multiple factors must be considered.

- *Weber* v. *Kaiser* (1979). Reverse discrimination again was the issue. Brian Weber sued Kaiser Aluminum under Title VII of the 1964 Civil Rights Act because he had been bypassed for a position under a company-union rule that set aside 50 percent of jobs of a certain category for blacks. The Court ruled that employers can give preference to minority group members in hiring and promoting for "traditionally segregated job categories." Affirmative action programs were strengthened.

- *Fire Fighters Local Union 1784* v. *Stotts* (1984). This case showed that not all affirmative action programs are acceptable. The Court ruled that a seniority system cannot be subservient to an affirmative action program during a layoff. A last-hired, first-fired plan by the union and the city of Memphis survived.

- *Adarand* v. *Pena* (1995). The U.S. Supreme Court questioned the constitutionality of government measures aimed at helping minority group members obtain contracts, jobs, or education. This case resulted from a lawsuit by Adarand because, despite submitting the lowest bid, a contract was lost and given to a minority group member-owned business. The Court decision requires lower courts to apply "strict scrutiny," meaning the government may have to prove that each program assists only those individuals who can prove they were victims of past discrimination, rather than assisting all minority groups.

In addition to federal legislation and court cases, executive orders have been issued by presidents of the United States to deal with problems of discrimination. Furthermore, every state has equal employment laws of one form or another, and state court decisions have interpreted these state laws.

What do all these laws and cases mean for those involved in applicant screening? Basically, all screening methods must be job related, valid, and nondiscriminatory. Included in this mandate are interviews, background investigations, and tests. Simply put, the EEOC regards all screening tools as capable of discriminating against applicants.

According to the EEOC, 87,500 cases were filed during fiscal year 1995 and 50 percent of all cases filed are won by employees. The average jury award in employment cases is about $842,000, with average legal fees and court costs estimated to be $125,000 per case. If the case does not go to court, the cost of defending a case before an administrative agency such as the EEOC is between \$10,000 and \$20,000 per case.[1] To prevent such lawsuits, an audit of human resource management practices should be conducted, with attention to applicable laws and personnel policies and procedures.

You Be the Judge[*]

Facts of the Case: When security guard Bronislav Zaleszny was passed over for promotion to supervisor, he decided that his Eastern European origin was at least one of the reasons (his English was rather thickly accented). So he went to the Equal Employment Opportunity Commission and filed a charge against his employer, Hi-Mark Home Products, alleging discrimination on the basis of national origin.

During the month after the EEOC notified the company of the charge, Zaleszny's troubles multiplied. First, Hi-Mark informed the police that products had been disappearing for months, that the disappearances evidently had occurred during Zaleszny's shift, and that Zaleszny was a reasonable suspect. Second, the company terminated the guard on suspicion of theft. Police arrested Zaleszny, but a preliminary hearing resulted in dismissal of the charges against him.

The ex-guard fumed with anger at his former employer. He sued, alleging that Hi-Mark had prosecuted him maliciously and had fired him in retaliation for his EEOC complaint.

Exactly Who Prosecuted, and Exactly Who Knew About the EEOC Complaint?

In court, the company argued that Zaleszny's allegations really couldn't stand up to logical analysis. *We didn't prosecute him, maliciously or otherwise,* Hi-Mark noted. *We truthfully told the police everything we knew about the disappearance of our products, and we said that on the basis of the facts, Mr. Zaleszny seemed to us to be a logical suspect. Then, completely on their own discretion, the police and the district attorney initiated charges against him. We disagree that the prosecution was malicious, but whether it was or not, we're not the ones who prosecuted.*

In answer to the guard's retaliatory-firing allegation, Hi-Mark's director of corporate security took the stand. "I'm the company official who recommended Mr. Zaleszny's termination," she testified, "and when I made the recommendation, I *didn't know* about his EEOC complaint. Yes, the Commission had notified our company, and yes, our HR department knew, but I didn't! And if I didn't know about the complaint when I fired him, then the firing obviously wasn't a retaliation."

Did the ex-security guard win his suit against Hi-Mark Home Products?

Make your decision; then turn to the end of the chapter for the court decision.

[*] Reprinted with permission from *Security Management Bulletin,* a publication of the Bureau of Business Practice, Inc., 24 Rope Ferry Road, Waterford, CT 06386.

EEO, AA, and Quotas [2]

Equal employment opportunity, affirmative action, and quotas are important terms relevant to staffing organizations. *Equal employment opportunity*
(EEO) refers to practices that are designed so that all applicants and employees are treated similarly without regard to protected characteristics such as
race and sex. For example, suppose a vacant position requires applicants to
undergo a written job knowledge test and an interview to assess applicants.
Anyone is free to apply for the position and all that apply will be given both
the test and the interview. How well each performs on both screening methods determines who is hired. Thus, all applicants have an equal opportunity
and the job will be offered following an unbiased assessment.

Affirmative action (AA) focuses on procedures employers use to correct and abolish past discriminatory employment practices against minority
group members, women, and those in other groups, while setting goals for
hiring and promoting persons from underrepresented groups. AA may be
voluntarily undertaken by an employer or court ordered. In our previous
example, AA could result if there was a failure to recruit women and minority group members or if the job knowledge test was biased. Then, management would make a good faith effort to meet certain hiring goals, for
instance, by improved recruiting.

Quotas are rigid hiring and promotion requirements. In our previous
example, a hiring formula would be set that specifies the number or percent
of women and minorities to be hired.

These concepts, as applied in the workplace, have raised considerable
legal turmoil and controversy over whether in fact they have been successful in correcting discrimination. The issue of "reverse discrimination" has
intensified the debate. Court decisions provide guidelines for employers.

Diversity

Diversity in the workforce encompasses many different dimensions, including sex, race, national origin, religion, age, and disability.[3] The workforce, historically dominated by white men, is being increasingly replaced with
workers from diverse backgrounds. The U.S. Bureau of Labor Statistics estimates that, by the year 2005, the U.S. labor force will consist of only 38 percent white, non-Hispanic men.[4] The reasons for this change go beyond
affirmative action plans that have brought nontraditional employees into
many positions. More than half of the new entrants into the workplace will be
women, the average age of employees will climb, immigrant employees will
have language and cultural differences, and as companies become more global, there will be an increasing need to respond to the unique needs of individual employees, including their languages, values, and customs. Diversity
facilitates tolerance to different behavioral styles and wider views, which can
lead to greater responsiveness to diverse customers. The challenge of learning
to manage a diverse workforce is an investment in the future.[5]

Sexual Harassment

In October of 1991 viewers watched television with intensity during the confirmation hearing for the appointment of ex-EEOC chairman Clarence Thomas as associate justice of the U.S. Supreme Court. Thomas's ex-EEOC assistant, Anita Hill, testified in detail to sexual harassment by Thomas. Although he was confirmed by the Senate, complaints of sexual harassment filed with the EEOC increased by more than 50 percent—from 6,883 complaints in 1991 to 10,532 in 1992. In 1995, the number increased to 15,549, with monetary benefits to victims at $24.3 million. Several surveys have shown that sexual harassment is a serious, widespread problem, although only about 5 percent of incidents are reported.[6]

The EEOC defines *sexual harassment* as unwelcome sexual conduct that has the purpose or effect of unreasonably interfering with an individual's work performance or creating an intimidating, hostile, or offensive work environment. Although the *Civil Rights Act* was passed in 1964, only during the 1970s did courts begin to recognize sexual harassment as a form of gender discrimination under Title VII. Thereafter, the EEOC issued guidelines for determining what activity is sexual harassment, and these guidelines influence courts.

The two theories upon which an action for sexual harassment may be brought are explained here. *Quid pro quo* involves an employee who is required to engage in sexual activity in exchange for a workplace benefit. For example, a male manager tells his female assistant that he will get her a promotion and raise if she engages in sex with him. A second theory of sexual harassment is *hostile working environment*, which occurs when sexually offensive behavior by one party is unwelcome by another and creates workplace difficulties. Examples include unwelcome suggestive remarks or touching or posted jokes or photos of a sexual nature.

The following list offers guidance when taking action against the problem of sexual harassment:

1. Ensure that top management takes the lead to establish a zero tolerance policy.
2. Communicate the policy and reporting procedures to all employees.
3. Provide relevant training.
4. Ensure that reported incidents are taken seriously, thoroughly investigated, and corrective action taken if the allegations are true.
5. Ensure that the personnel department is notified about each complaint.
6. Maintain confidentiality, providing information only on a "need to know" basis.

An employer must take immediate and appropriate corrective action, otherwise civil and criminal legal action can be devastating. Under the *Civil Rights Act of 1991*, an employee suing for sexual harassment can ask for up to \$300,000 in compensatory and punitive damages, unlimited medical damages, and request a jury trial. Furthermore, these tort actions may be initiated: assault, battery, intentional infliction of emotional distress, and false imprisonment. In addition, these criminal charges may be filed: assault, battery, and rape.[7]

SCREENING METHODS

Screening methods vary among organizations and depend on such factors as budget, the number of personnel available to investigate applicants, and the types of positions open. Certain employers expend minimal efforts to properly screen, using the excuse that their hands are tied because of legal barriers. Others follow legal guidelines and screen carefully. The EEOC, the Office of Personnel Management, the Department of Justice, and the Department of Labor have adopted and published the *Uniform Guidelines on Employee Selection Procedures*, which is a guide for determining the proper use of tests and other selection procedures for any employment decision such as hiring, promotion, demotion, retention, training, and transfers. These guidelines also contain technical standards and documentation requirements for the validation of selection procedures as described in the *Standards for Educational and Psychological Tests*, prepared by the American Psychological Association and other groups. Courts rely on such guidelines in deciding cases.

The courts also have established screening standards from negligence cases; awards have been made to victims who have sued, claiming the employer was negligent in not conducting a reasonable inquiry into the background of an employee who, for example, had a history of physical violence. The term *reasonable inquiry* has various definitions; however, an employer can take a number of steps to screen applicants.

First, careful planning is required. Input from a competent attorney can strengthen the legality of the screening process. *No single screening tool should be used to assess an applicant. Multiple measures always are best.*

It is important that the job duties and qualifications be clearly defined. Help-wanted advertisements should be worded carefully to attract only those who meet the requirements of the job. This also prevents expensive turnover and charges of discrimination.

To save money, the most expensive screening methods should be performed last. The time and labor spent reading application forms is less expensive than conducting background investigations.

Resumes and Applications

Applications must be carefully studied. Job seekers are notorious for exaggerating and actually lying. The Port Authority of New York and New Jersey did a study by using a questionnaire to ask applicants if they had ever used certain equipment that really did not exist. More than one-third of the applicants said that they had experience with the nonexistent equipment.[8] The FBI conducted an extensive investigation of diploma mills in 1981 and located 680 "graduates" of phony institutions. Of these "graduates," 171 were federal and state employees. A raid on an Oregon mill netted 32,000 fake diplomas, many marked *Harvard* and *UCLA*.[9] Research in the 1990s shows not only one-third of resumes being fraudulent, but an increase in the problem.[10]

Signs of deception on resumes and applications include inconsistencies in verbal and written statements and among background documents. Periods of "self-employment" may be used to hide institutionalization. Not signing an application may be another indicator of deception. Social security numbers are issued by state, and that can assist in verifying past residence. A thorough background investigation is indispensable to support information presented by the applicant.

Interview

When asking the applicant general questions about work experience and education, open-ended questions should be formulated so the interviewee can talk at length. "What were your duties at that job?" elicits more information than short-answer questions requiring yes or no responses. Answers to questions should be compared to the application and resume.

Some employers ask the applicant to complete an application at home to be mailed in before the interview. Before the interview, while the applicant is waiting in an office, another application is asked to be completed. Both applications are then compared before the interview for consistency.

The following information concerns questions prohibited during the entire screening process. Court rulings under EEO legislation have stressed repeatedly that questions (and tests) must be job related. This legal requirement is known as a *bona fide occupational qualification* (BFOQ).

Questions pertaining to arrest records generally are unlawful. An arrest does not signify guilt. The courts have stated that minority group members have suffered disproportionately more arrests than others. A question that asks about a conviction, however, may be solicited. It is not an absolute bar to employment. Here again, minority group members have disproportionately more convictions. Certain offenses can cause an employer to exclude an applicant, depending on the particular job. Therefore, the question of convictions must be job related (e.g., related to loss prevention) and carefully considered.

Unless a "business necessity" can be shown, questions concerning credit records, charge accounts, and owning one's own home are discriminatory because minority group applicants often are poorer than others. Unless absolutely necessary for a particular job, height, weight, and other physical requirements are discriminatory against certain minority groups (e.g., Latino, Asian, and women applicants often are physically smaller than other applicants).

Other unlawful questions, unless job related, include asking age, sex, color, or race, maiden name of applicant's wife or mother, and membership in organizations that reveal race, religion, or national origin.

The questions that can be asked of an applicant and on an application form, among others, are name, address, telephone number, social security number, past experience and salary, reasons for leaving past jobs, education, convictions, U.S. citizenship, military experience in U.S. forces, and hobbies.

Extensive research on the interview process shows that without proper care it can be unreliable, low in validity, and biased against certain groups. Research has pointed to concrete steps that can be taken to increase the utility of the personnel selection interview. First, the interview should be structured, standardized, and focused on a small number of goals (e.g., interpersonal style or ability to express oneself). Second, ask questions dealing with specific situations (e.g., "As a security officer, what would you do if you saw a robbery in progress?"). Third, use multiple interviewers and ensure that women and minority group members are represented to include their perspectives.[11]

Validity asks how accurately a test predicts job success. *Reliability* asks if a test is consistent in measuring performance.

Tests

The testing of applicants varies considerably. Here is a summary of various types of tests.

- *Aptitude tests* measure a person's ability (e.g., verbal, numerical, reasoning) to learn and perform a job. Because these tests often contain questions that do not relate to the job, and they may have an adverse impact on the hiring of minority group members, many employers have reduced their use of these tests.
- *Job knowledge tests* are written or oral and measure job-related knowledge. *Proficiency tests* measure how well the applicant can do the work; an example is a typing test for a secretarial position. As with other tests, they must be job related.
- *Personality tests* attempt to measure personality characteristics and categorize applicants by what they are like, such as agreeable and conscientious. When such tests ask job applicants to answer intimate

questions, such as their sex practices, class action lawsuits can result. These tests have been criticized for questionable validity and low reliability.

- *Medical examinations* are given to determine whether applicants are physically capable of performing the job. The Americans with Disabilities Act requires employers to make medical inquiries directly related to the applicant's ability to perform job-related duties and requires employers to make reasonable accommodations to help handicapped individuals to perform the job. This act requires that the medical exam cannot be conducted until after the job offer has been provided to the applicant.

Employers and job applicants are becoming increasingly knowledgeable about the validity and reliability of tests, especially because of the need to eliminate or to detect discrimination. The Buros Institute of Mental Measurement (University of Nebraska) evaluates published tests and acts as a consumers' evaluation service.

- *Honesty tests* are paper-and-pencil tests that measure trustworthiness and attitudes toward honesty. Thousands of companies have used this evaluation tool on millions of workers, and its use is increasing as employers deal with the legal restrictions of the polygraph. These tests have helped employers screen job candidates, and validity and reliability studies have been published in scholarly journals.[12]

Preemployment Test Is Security Specific[13]

Builders Square and Oshman's Sporting Goods use a specially designed preemployment test that helps them select the best possible in-store loss prevention agents. The test, designed by a human resources firm, is job specific, rather than for general retail employees. It began with a job profile to determine the most appropriate behaviors for effective, on-the-job performance. The behavior and experiences of the best agents also provided input for the test. It takes one and a half hours to complete and includes basic requirements and conditions of the job, behavior on the job, and critical situations requiring responses. The test is a more effective predictor of job success than an interview and it helps to professionalize the position of loss prevention agent.

- *Drug testing* has grown dramatically in a drug-oriented world. Employers expect workers to perform their jobs free from the influence of intoxicating substances, and accidents must be prevented. Former U.S. Surgeon General C. Everett Koop estimated that between 14 and 25 percent of employees between the ages of 18 and 40 would test positive for illegal substances on any given day. The cost of lost productivity from this problem is estimated at $34 billion annually, and this is a major reason why 22 million employees were tested in 1992 alone.[14] The opposing view favors protection from an invasion of an individual's right to privacy.[15] Drug tests vary in terms of cost, quality, and accuracy. A drug test can result in a "false positive," showing that a person tested has used drugs when that is not so. A "false negative" can show that the individual has not used drugs when, in fact, the opposite is true. Another problem with drug testing is cheating. Simply stated, if an observer is not present when a urine sample is requested, a variety of ploys may be used by an abuser to deceive an employer. For example, "clean" urine may be substituted. Such deception is a huge problem. Another strategy of drug testing is to measure drug usage from a sample of a person's hair. Some experts view this method as more accurate than urine sampling. More on the substance abuse problem in Chapter 18.

An employer can be held liable for negligent hiring if an employee causes harm that could have been prevented if the employer had conducted a reasonable background check.

Background Investigations

With restrictions on the use of the polygraph, employers increasingly are turning to background investigations to verify job applicant information. An applicant's criminal history, if any, is a prime concern of employers, especially when the applicant is applying for a loss prevention position. Asking about an applicant's arrest record is generally unlawful, but conviction records legally are obtainable in most jurisdictions; they usually are public records on file at court offices. If an applicant appears to have no convictions, this does not necessarily mean that he or she has never committed a criminal offense. It is possible that the background investigator did not search court records in other jurisdictions where the applicant has lived.

History and Controversy: Polygraph and PSE

Background information on the polygraph and psychological stress evaluator (PSE) will assist the reader in understanding the controversy and subsequent legal restrictions on these devices. In 1895, Cesare Lombroso used the first scientific instrument to detect deception through changes in pulse and blood pressure. In 1921, Dr. John A. Larson developed the polygraph, which measured blood pressure, respiration, and pulse. By 1949, Leonard Keeler added galvanic skin response (i.e., electrical changes on the surface of the skin).

The PSE was developed for the U.S. Army in 1964 by Robert McQuiston, Allan Bell, and Wilson Ford. After it was rejected by the Army, McQuiston patented a civilian version and marketed it to the private sector.

When questions are asked during a polygraph exam, bodily changes are recorded on graph paper. The examiner interprets these readings vis-à-vis questions asked. Persons have been known to try to "fool" the polygraph by biting their tongue or pressing a toe into a thumbtack previously hidden in their shoe. The PSE has a few variations, but basically it records voice stress as questions are asked. There is no hookup, so it can be used covertly.

A disadvantage of the PSE is that only one factor is being recorded, as opposed to the multiple factors of the polygraph. Training for administering and interpreting the PSE is shorter than for the polygraph. The accuracy of either device is subject to considerable debate, especially concerning the PSE. University of Utah research concluded that the polygraph can be over 90 percent accurate.[16] Much depends on the skill of the examiner behind the device. The polygraph has been responsible for eliminating undesirable job applicants, in addition to assisting with criminal and civil cases, but at the same time, abuses have occurred that resulted in the passage of the Employee Polygraph Protection Act.

Employee Polygraph Protection Act of 1988

The Employee Polygraph Protection Act (EPPA) was passed by Congress and signed into law by then-president Ronald Reagan on June 27, 1988. It became effective on December 27. The act prohibits most private employers from using polygraph or "lie detector" tests to screen job applicants and greatly restricts the use of these instruments to test present employees. The EPPA defines the term *lie detector* to include any device that is used to render a diagnostic opinion regarding the honesty of an individual. The congressional Office of Technology Assessment estimated that 2 million polygraph exams had been conducted each year—90 percent by private employers.

The EPPA states that it is unlawful for an employer to directly or indirectly force an employee to submit to a polygraph test. Discrimination against
continued

those who refuse to be tested or who file a complaint under the EPPA is pro-hibited. Employers who violate the EPPA may be assessed a civil penalty up to $10,000 for each violation. In addition, the Secretary of Labor may seek a restraining order enjoining the employer from violating the act. The law pro-vides individuals with the right to sue employers in federal and state courts for employment reinstatement, promotion, and payment of lost wages and benefits.

A few kinds of employees are exempt from the act and can be tested, including employees of

- national security organizations or defense industries;
- federal, state, and local governments;
- businesses involved with controlled substances;
- certain security service firms, such as armored car or security alarm firms.

In addition, a limited exemption exists for any employer who is conducting an ongoing investigation involving economic loss or injury; the suspect employee must have had access to the subject of the investigation, and reasonable suspicion must be present. Considerable justification and documentation is required. Chapter 10 contains proper testing procedures under the EPPA.

Past employment is a crucial area of inquiry because it reveals past job per-formance. An investigator should check the applicant's employment history by telephone or in person. Personnel offices may be reluctant to supply information due to potential defamation suits.

The personal references supplied by the applicant usually are those of people who will make favorable comments about the applicant. If an inves-tigator can obtain additional references from contacting references, more will be learned about the applicant.

Most colleges will verify an applicant's attendance and degree over the telephone. College transcripts can be checked out by mail as long as a copy of the applicant's authorization is enclosed. This conforms to privacy legis-lation. When educational records are received, the investigator should study characteristics (e.g., name, social security number) and look for inconsisten-cies.

The financial condition of the applicant may reveal the potential for theft. Remember that unless a business necessity can be shown, questions and employment decisions related to credit can be discriminatory, since certain minority groups are often poorer than others.

According to the *Fair Credit Reporting Act of 1971*, credit bureaus are barred from maintaining adverse information more than seven years old, except for certain categories (e.g., bankruptcies and criminal records). The act requires disclosure of the credit or background check to the individual being investigated. Consumers have the right to inspect credit agency records and make corrections.

The private use of public records is on the increase for background investigations. As we know, conviction records are available in most jurisdictions. Records from state motor vehicle departments can reveal a history of careless driving behavior and substance abuse (i.e., driving under the influence). A motor vehicle report (MVR) can serve as a cross-check for name, date of birth, social security number, physical description, and impairments. Federal court records expose violations of federal laws, civil litigation, and bankruptcy. Chapter 10 discusses on-line databases for acquiring information.

Organizations should inform applicants about background investigations. The subject's written authorization for the search, inspection of the results, and confidentiality should be a part of this process. Many employers outsource background investigations to a third party, such as a credit reporting agency, to reduce the risk of a lawsuit.

Inadequate Applicant Screening Results in Serious Problems[*]

Reporter Blasts Security at TMI

HARRISBURG, PA—A reporter who got himself hired as a guard at the Three Mile Island nuclear plant later gained entry through an unlocked door to the sensitive control room, his newspaper reported Tuesday in an article the plant's operators tried to suppress.

The *Guide*, a muckraking Harrisburg area weekly, printed copyright stories about the exploits of cub reporter Robert Kapler following a court battle in which Metropolitan Edison Co. tried to block publication.

"TMI: it's a Paradise Island for the saboteur," said one headline. "I waltz into unlocked control room of Unit 2," said another.

Kapler said he was hired as an unarmed watchman, a lowlevel [sic] guard who is not supposed to have access to the control room. Armed guards, who have a higher security clearance, do have such access.

Unit 2 is the facility severely damaged last March in the worst accident in the history of U.S. commercial nuclear power. Its control room is where vital reactor functions are still maintained.

The *Guide* published photographs by Kapler identified as the interior of the control room and an unlocked control room door, with the knob missing so that a piece of rope was used to pull it open.

The photos were taken, the *Guide* said, with a concealed Minox spy camera—"the kind the CIA uses."

The newspaper also detailed what it claimed was laxity in the plant security operation, which allowed Kapler to get a job as a security guard with bogus identification and apparently without having his background checked.

continued

Sandy Polon, a spokesman for Metropolitan Edison Co., declined comment on the newspaper articles, as did the contractor that supplies the company with guards, Gregg Security Co.

The stories have thrust the *Guide* into international attention. The 26-year-old Kapler, who had never worked for a newspaper before the *Guide* hired him in November, has been interviewed on national television, and the newspaper has received a deluge of phone calls from around the United States and Canada.

"We had to give him a raise," said *Guide* editor Richard Halverson, the paper's only other full-time news staffer. Kapler's weekly pay jumped from $239 to $250.

Metropolitan Edison had sought an injunction Monday from Dauphin County Court Judge John C. Dowling, claiming the stories would hurt national security. Dowling refused, saying publication should be permitted under constitutional guarantees of a free press.

Kapler reported in his articles that the plant goes to great lengths to protect against outside threats, even carefully logging the numbers of airplanes that get too close.

But he said it "is doing little to protect vital areas from potentially hazardous inside forces—like saboteurs."

He told of making his way unchallenged to the door of the control room.

"I pull on a piece of knotted clothesline rope where a doorknob should be and step inside a room covered wall-to-wall, floor-to-ceiling, with panels of instruments," Kapler wrote.

He said he encountered two control room operators and other workers, but was not noticed until one of the operators casually looked at him.

"'Howyadoin,' I say in a friendly voice. He looks away and sighs, 'Not bad,'" said the story.

Kapler said he used another man's birth certificate to get a job with Gregg Security and worked as a guard at the plant from Jan. 2 to Jan. 19.

* Source: Associated Press Release, February 6, 1980.

Why do you think there is so much government legal regulation of staffing organizations?

EMPLOYEE SOCIALIZATION

Socialization, the learning process whereby an employee gains knowledge about the employer and how to become a productive worker, is broader in scope than orientation and training programs. Employers who understand the socialization process are likely to enhance the value of employees to the organization. Furthermore, losses can be reduced as employees adhere to loss prevention strategies. The following emphasizes orientation, training programs, examples set by superiors, and employee needs.

Loss Prevention Orientation for New Employees

When new employees begin to work for an organization, the orientation session plays a significant role in the socialization process. Examples set at the beginning can go a long way in preventing future problems and losses. The orientation program should be designed to acquaint the new employees with the "big picture" of loss prevention. Such discussions can enhance the employee's understanding of the objectives of the loss prevention program, how employees can help, and the benefits to everyone.

Employee Training

In this discussion the focus is on training protection personnel, but the principles that follow can apply to a variety of training programs for a broad spectrum of employees.

Today, increasing numbers of practitioners in the field realize the importance of training. Consequently, training standards and programs constantly are being upgraded for uniformed officers, investigators, and supervisory personnel. This also is important because the traditional security philosophy is expanding to the broader concept of loss prevention, in which fire and safety strategies are being implemented to prevent losses. Unfortunately, many proprietary loss prevention departments and service businesses have instituted improved training programs after a critical incident, when an armed, uniformed officer reacted inappropriately and used a weapon to harm or kill someone, for example. False arrest is another common problem; litigation often results in sizable losses.

Although training costs money, the investment is well worth it. Training helps to prevent problems such as critical incidents and litigation. Training provides personnel with an improved understanding of what is expected of them, heightens morale and motivation, and reduces disciplinary problems. All these benefits are impossible unless there is management support for training.

Planning Training

Step 1. Training Needs

Several questions need to be answered. Who are the recipients of the training (loss prevention personnel or regular employees; new or experienced employees)? What training programs are available? What deficiencies were noted in employee evaluations? What are the suggestions from supervisors? What are the suggestions from employees? Of particular importance is to conduct a *job and task analysis* to pinpoint the skills required for the job.

Training for Security Officers[17]

This curriculum is used in an Ohio training program.

Course	Hours	Course	Hours
Registration and Orientation	1	Handling Juveniles	5
Role of Law Enforcement	4	Mental Illness,	
Note Taking	1	Drug Abuse, and	
Report Writing	3	Alcohol Addiction	6
Criminal Law and Procedures	4	Self Defense	10
Law of Arrest	4	First Aid	12
Search and Seizure	4	Surveillance Techniques	4
Rules of Evidence	4	Sex Offenders	
Techniques and		and Offenses	2
Mechanics of Arrest	4	Patrol of Private Property	2
Crimes and Elements	4	Crowd and Mob Control	4
Interview Techniques	2	Fire Control Techniques	4
Testifying in Court	4	Firearms Training	16
Legal Phrases and Definitions	2	Final Examination	2
Motor Vehicle Crime	2	Total Program Hours	114
Vehicle Traffic			
Law and Control	4		

Step 2. Budget

Before the training program is prepared, an estimate of money available is necessary, since one cannot spend what one does not have.

Step 3. Behavioral Objectives

Each behavioral objective consists of a statement, usually one sentence, that describes the behavioral changes that the student should undergo because of the training. For example, loss prevention officers must explain how the Fifth Amendment to the Bill of Rights relates to the private sector.

Step 4. Training Program Outline

With the use of the behavioral objectives, an outline is prepared. It can be considered a step-by-step sequence for training.

Step 5. Learning Medium

The method of presentation is described. Various strategies are available, such as lecture, discussion, demonstration, case method, and role playing. Audiovisual aids can enhance the program by increasing student interest. Handouts that guide the student also are helpful.

Step 6. Evaluation, Feedback, and Revision

After the training is completed, the students should provide valuable feedback to the instructor. An evaluation questionnaire, completed by students, can guide the instructor in revising the training program. The training is further validated through interviews of participants and supervisors a few months after the training to see if the training helped participants to perform their tasks effectively and to identify topics requiring more or less attention.

Learning Principles

1. Learning results in a behavioral change. Learning objectives are stated in terms of specific behaviors. When a student is able to perform a task that he or she was unable to perform before a training program, then behavior has changed.
2. Tests are used to measure the changed behavior.
3. If the proper conditions for learning are presented to students, learning will take place. The teacher should help the student to learn by facilitating learning through effective instructional methods.
4. An instructional program should begin with basic introductory information to develop a foundation for advanced information.
5. Feedback, an instructor informing the student whether a response was correct or incorrect, is vital to learning.
6. An instructional program must consider the learner's ability to absorb information.
7. A student will be more receptive to learning if information is job related.
8. Conditioning aids the learning process. Conditioning can be perceived as a method of molding or preparing a student for something through constant practice; for example, repetitive drills so that employees know exactly what to do in case of fire.
9. Increased learning will take place if the practice is spread out over time as opposed to a single, lengthy practice session.
10. Information that is learned and understood is remembered longer than that which is learned by rote.

Wasted Training

In an article in *Administrative Management*, "How Not to Waste Your Train-ing Dollars," Donald J. Tosti declares that "American businesses and govern-ment agencies spend about $7 billion a year on training, and by the best estimates half of that amount is wasted."[18] He also states that "the company training instructor who assumes the traditional chalk-in-hand teacher role will have little effect in changing worker behavior."[19] Tosti describes "Seven Deadly Sins of Training," which are paraphrased here:

1. Using training to solve motivational problems;
2. Making training more complicated than is necessary;
3. Training personnel at the wrong time, such as training all of an organi-zation's employees for a program that will be instituted in two years;
4. Overtraining, such as instructing retail clerks on the theoretical aspects of their job before explaining important procedural aspects of retailing.
5. Failing to understand the true costs of training;
6. Failing to calculate training on a cost-effective basis. Evaluations of training programs help to predict benefits. Questions of concern are these: Did employees learn and apply the new information? Are losses reduced? Was the training worth the money?
7. Following fads in training.

Think about a training program or course you attended in the past. In what ways could it have been improved?

Examples Set by Superiors

Poor example setting is pervasive in many organizations. All organizations have informal rules that serve as guides to action. These rules often are transmitted to subordinates from superiors. The length of the 15-minute cof-fee break varies within organizations; the amount of time allowed before being considered late also varies; the number of minor safety violations per-mitted before strict disciplinary action differs from one organization to another as well as from one superior to another. Clearly, superiors serve as teachers and role models. The actions of superiors greatly affect subordinate performance. Poor supervision results in both low subordinate productivity and losses.

A supervisor can be perceived to be what sociologists call an *agent of socialization*, a person who plays a dominant role in the socialization of an individual. In society, parents, teachers, and clergy are agents of socialization. In a business organization, a supervisor becomes an agent of socialization after establishing a working relationship with a new employee. The superior first makes the new employee feel some degree of belonging, in calming the uneasy new worker. The superior may have to skillfully break down the old methods that the new subordinate may have carried over from a previous job.

Because first impressions are lasting, the initial part of the socialization process is important. A good example must be set in the beginning.

Based upon your experience, can you think of any poor examples set by superiors in the workplace?

Employee Needs

The way an organization responds to employee needs has a great impact not only on the socialization process, but also on losses. When employee needs are met, workers also learn about the employment environment. They learn that management and supervisors care; the employee learns to respect and appreciate the employment environment while helping to reduce losses.

What are employee needs? Psychologist *Abraham Maslow* became famous for designing a "hierarchy of needs" in the early 1950s[20] (see Figure 6–1). Maslow's view is that people are always in a state of want, but what they want depends upon their level within the hierarchy of human needs.

Figure 6–1   Maslow's hierarchy of needs.

Poor Example Set by Ralph Marks, Loss Prevention Manager

The Locost retail store chain emphasized the importance of loss prevention procedures as an aid to increased profits. All employees were expected to adhere to these procedures. The loss prevention managers at each store were expected to do their part in reinforcing the program. Each store's employees looked to the loss prevention manager for guidance.

At one particular store, Ralph Marks, the loss prevention manager, made a serious mistake. All retail employees were permitted to make purchases and receive a 15 percent discount. Procedures dictated that items bought were to be recorded and then stored under a designated counter until the end of the day. When Ralph Marks bought a stereo for his car, he did not follow the appropriate procedures. He installed the stereo during working hours, which also compounded the poor example. By the end of the working day, all retail employees had seen or heard of this incident. This poor example caused many employees to lose respect for the manager and the loss prevention program.

Lower level needs must be satisfied before upper level needs. Maslow's hierarchy of needs follows:

- *Basic physiological needs.* Survival needs like food, water, and the elimination of wastes can be satisfied with employer assistance. A well-run company cafeteria and clean lavatories are examples.
- *Safety and security needs.* This need relates to order in one's life. A person needs to feel free from anxiety and fear. Adequate wages, medical insurance, and workplace safety help to satisfy these needs.
- *Societal needs.* The need to be loved and have friends and the need for esteem can be fulfilled by supervisors. A supervisor should praise a subordinate when appropriate. Employees should receive recognition or awards after completing a good job. Employee socials also are helpful.
- *Esteem and status needs.* A person needs to be competent, to achieve, and to gain approval and respect.
- *Self-actualization needs.* This need is at the top of the hierarchy of needs. It signifies that a person has reached his or her full potential, whether as a janitor, homemaker, doctor, or whatever. An organization and its superiors can do a lot (e.g., training, promotion) in assisting an employee to fulfill this need.

Employees learn which needs are satisfied and which are not. Suppose a workplace has a terrible cafeteria, dirty lavatories, poor wages, limited medical insurance, an inadequate safety program, authoritarian supervisors, and poor training and promotional opportunities. What level of losses would be sustained at this workplace in comparison to another that adhered to Maslow's hierarchy of human needs?

How do you think corporate downsizing affects Maslow's hierarchy of human needs and loss prevention?

CASE PROBLEMS

6A. Plan and write a step-by-step screening process for applicants interested in uniformed loss prevention positions. Formulate an application form. Pay particularly close attention to applicable laws.

6B. You are a candidate for the position of security manager for a large shopping mall near a major city. The number of candidates has been narrowed to six and the mall human resources manager has decided to use an in-basket exercise to further narrow the list of candidates. The in-basket exercise consists of a series of memoranda, telephone calls, and radio transmissions that the mall security manager would encounter in the job. Your task is to read all items, set priorities among them, and write what action you would take and the reasoning for your action for each item. The time to complete this case is 60 minutes. It is possible that all candidates will be handed additional memoranda, telephone messages, or radio transmissions during the exercise. A review panel (police captain, firefighter, college educator, and mall security officer) will evaluate each candidate's work without knowing the identity of the writer.*

Item 1

TO: Mall Security Manager
FROM: Mall Manager
SUBJECT: Security Seminar
DATE: September 20
Several merchants would like a seminar on security before the busy holiday season. Please get back to me as soon as possible.

Item 2

TO: Mall Security Manager
FROM: Human Resources Manager, Bigmart Department Store

---

* Source: Philip P. Purpura, *Retail Security and Shrinkage Protection* (Boston: Butterworth–Heinemann, 1993), pp. 327–329.

SUBJECT: Selection of Store Detective
DATE: September 24
Please walk over to review the applications for store detective. I have no idea who would be the best one.

Item 3

TELEPHONE MESSAGE: September 21
Mr. John Poston, a mall customer, called again. He is still irate about the damage to his car window when Security Officer Mallory broke into the vehicle after Mr. Poston left his keys in the ignition. Mr. Poston is threatening to sue.

Item 4

TELEPHONE MESSAGE: September 20
Mrs. Johnson, owner of the Befit Health Store, thinks someone is entering her store at night. She is very upset and worried, and wants you to meet her at her store.

Item 5

TO: Mall Security Manager
FROM: Mall Manager
SUBJECT: Application Verification
DATE: September 22
The Westwood Mall office called to verify your application for their job opening in security. Are you planning to begin another job? Please let me know immediately. Let's talk.

Item 6

RADIO TRANSMISSION: September 24, 11:15 A.M.
"Four year old boy lost at south end of mall. We have not been able to locate for one hour."

Item 7

TELEPHONE MESSAGE: September 23
Attorney for the plaintiff who was assaulted in the parking lot last month wants you to call him right away.

Item 8

TO: Mall Security Manager
FROM: Mall Manager
SUBJECT: Security/Safety Plan
DATE: September 16
In speaking with other mall managers at a recent seminar, they mentioned their security/safety plans. We probably need to have one, too. Please respond.

Item 9

RADIO TRANSMISSION: September 24, 11:20 A.M.
"Small fire in stock room of Smith's Department Store. We can put it out."

Item 10

TO: Mall Security Manager
FROM: Paula Reed, Security Officer
SUBJECT: Pay Raise
DATE: September 23

I am not pleased about my raise of only $0.15 per hour. I have been doing a good job and I really work hard when we get busy. The male security officers are making much more than my rate per hour. I believe that this difference is because I am a black woman. We have talked about this already, but you haven't done anything about it. I want something done right away or I will take legal action.

Item 11

TELEPHONE MESSAGE: September 22
The manager of Hall Stuart Clothes wants to know why it took so long for security to respond to a shoplifting incident yesterday.

THE DECISION FOR YOU BE THE JUDGE

Ultimately, no, but the company had to run a gauntlet before breaking out into the clear. There were conflicting judgments at two lower court levels, but finally a higher court ruled in favor of Hi-Mark. In the end, Zaleszny did not win anything. This case is based on *Griffiths* v. *CIGN,* 988 F 2nd 457 3rd Circuit Court (1993). The names in this case have been changed to protect the privacy of those involved.

Comment

The fact that this company had to go through appeals can give you pause. You might suppose that simple logic should have upheld Hi-Mark from the outset. If the company didn't prosecute, how could it be guilty of malicious prosecution? If the manager who fired Zaleszny didn't know about the guard's EEOC complaint, how could the firing have been a retaliation for the complaint? And why didn't these lines of reasoning prevail right away? Because logic doesn't always prevail in court. Often, other variables are in play, including the effectiveness with which a case is presented, a jury's understanding of a judge's instructions, the extent to which all parties understand the relevant law, and even the personalities in the courtroom.

The two questions that confronted this company can be minefields. What to do about prosecution of a crime suspect? Can you safely fire an employee who has engaged in a protected activity, such as complaining to a federal watchdog agency? Be sure to get a qualified attorney's advice whenever you face these questions.

NOTES

1. Donald Caruth and Gail Handlogten, "Effective Human Resource Management: An Antidote for Costly Lawsuits," *Security Dealer* (August 1996): 32–34.
2. Herbert G. Heneman et al., *Staffing Organizations*, 2nd ed. (Middleton, WI: Irwin Pub., 1997), pp. 62–64.
3. Lloyd Byars and Leslie Rue, *Human Resource Management*, 5th ed. (Chicago: Irwin Pub., 1997), p. 8.
4. Howard N. Fullerton, Jr., "The American Work Force, 1992–2005: Another Look at the Labor Force," *Monthly Labor Review* (November 1993): 31–40.
5. Byars and Rue, *Human Resource Management*, p. 10.
6. Dawn D. Bennett-Alexander and Laura B. Pincus, *Employment Law for Business* (Chicago: Irwin Pub., 1995), pp. 193–194.
7. Ibid., p. 219.
8. "Lying on Job Applications May Be Widespread," *Security* (February 1988): 13.
9. "Bogus Diplomas Present Hiring Danger," *Creative Management* (August 1987): 7.
10. Christopher J. Bachler, "Resume Fraud: Lies, Omissions, and Exaggerations," *Personnel Journal* (June 1995): 51–60.
11. Raymond A. Noe et al., *Human Resource Management: Gaining a Competitive Advantage* (Chicago: Irwin Pub., 1997), pp. 320–321.
12. Ibid., p. 326.
13. "Pre-Employment Test Is Security Specific," *Chain Store Age Executive* (April 1995): 104.
14. Bennett-Alexander and Pincus, *Employment Law*, p. 386.
15. See Erich Goode, *Drugs in American Society*, 3rd ed. (New York: Alfred A. Knopf, 1989).
16. U.S. Department of Justice, *Validity and Reliability of Detection of Deception* (Washington, DC: U.S. Government Printing Office, 1978), p. 8.
17. Wayne Siatt, "Curing the Ills of Hospital Security," *Security World* 17, no. 7 (July 1980), p. 31, copyright 1980. Cahners Publishing Co., Division of Reed Holdings, Inc. Reproduced with permission.
18. Donald J. Tosti, "How Not to Waste Your Training Dollars," *Administrative Management* 41, no. 2 (February 1980): 44.
19. Ibid., p. 45.
20. Abraham H. Maslow, *Motivation and Personality* (New York: Harper and Row, 1954).

7

Internal Threats and Countermeasures

OBJECTIVES

After studying this chapter the reader will be able to

1. Describe the seriousness of the internal theft problem;
2. Explain why and how employees steal;
3. Outline at least five management countermeasures to prevent internal theft;
4. List and explain the steps involved in confronting an employee suspected of internal theft;
5. Outline access control methods and systems, including the types of cards used for access;
6. List and describe at least three types of locks;
7. List and describe at least five types of intrusion alarm sensors;
8. Describe CCTV technology;
9. Explain the characteristics of safes.

Internal loss prevention focuses on threats from inside an organization. Theft, fires, and accidents are major internal loss problems, but there are others. Productivity losses can result from poor plant layout or substance abuse by employees. Other productivity losses result from employees who loaf, arrive at work late, leave early, abuse coffee breaks, socialize excessively, and prolong work to create overtime; these abuses can be referred to as *thefts of time.* Faulty measuring devices, which may or may not be known to employees, are another cause of losses. Scales or dispensing devices that measure things ranging from truck weight to copper wire length are examples.

The spectrum of internal threats is broad. Although this chapter focuses on internal theft (that is, employee theft) and associated countermeasures, the strategies covered also apply to external threats such as burglary, vandalism, arson, sabotage, and espionage.

To personalize the information presented, three businesses are described: a retail lumber business (see Figure 7–1), a clothing manufacturing

123

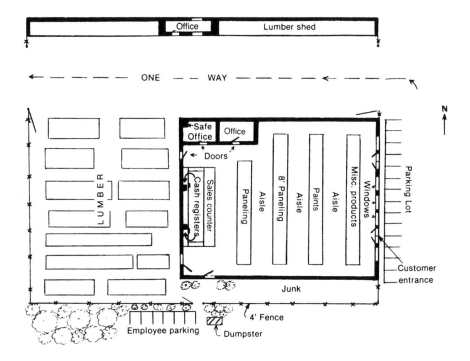

Figure 7–1   Woody's Lumber Company. Woody's lumber company has suffered declining profits in recent years. A new manager recently was hired who quickly hired six people to replace the previous crew, which was fired for internal theft. Four additional people were quickly hired for part-time work. The process for conducting business is to have customers park their cars in the front of the store, walk to the sales counter to pay for the desired lumber, receive a pink receipt, drive to the rear of the store, pick up the lumber with the assistance of the yard crew, and then depart through the rear auto exit. At the lumber company, loss prevention is of minimal concern. An inoperable burglar alarm and two fire extinguishers are on the premises.

plant (see Figure 7–2), and a research facility (see Figure 7–3). Suppose you are a loss prevention specialist working for a corporation that has just purchased these three businesses. Your supervisor informs you that you are responsible for recommending modifications at these facilities to improve internal loss prevention. First read this chapter then proceed to the case problem pertaining to these businesses at the end of the chapter.

INTERNAL THEFT

How Serious Is the Problem?

Internal theft also is referred to as employee theft, pilferage, embezzlement, stealing, peculation, and defalcation. *Employee theft* is stealing by employ-

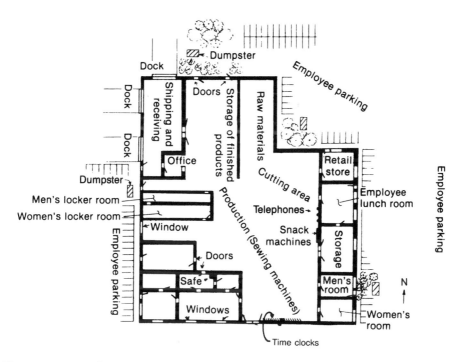

Figure 7–2 Smith Shirt manufacturing plant. In the last two years, the Smith plant has shown declining profits. During this time, managers believed that employee theft might be the cause, but they were unsure of what to do and were worried about additional costs. Employees work one shift from 8 A.M. to 5 P.M. five days per week and are permitted to go to their cars to eat lunch from noon to 1 P.M. A total of 425 employees are divided as follows: 350 sewing machine operators, 15 maintenance personnel, 20 material handlers, 20 miscellaneous workers, 2 retail salespeople, 5 managers, and 13 clerical support staff members. A contract cleanup crew works from 6 to 8 A.M. and from 5 to 7 P.M. on Monday, Wednesday, and Friday; Sunday cleanup is from 1 to 4 P.M. The crew members have their own keys. Garbage dumpster pickup is 7 A.M. and 7 P.M. Monday, Wednesday, and Friday. The plant contains a fire alarm system and four fire extinguishers. One physical inventory is conducted each year.

ees from their employers. *Pilferage* is stealing in small quantities. *Embezzlement* occurs when a person takes money or property that has been entrusted to his or her care; a breach of trust occurs. *Peculation* and *defalcation* are synonyms for embezzlement. Whatever term is used, this problem is an insidious menace to the survival of businesses, institutions, and organizations. This threat is so severe in many workplaces that employees steal anything that is not "nailed down."

The total estimated cost of employee theft varies from one source to another, mainly because theft is defined and data is collected in so many different ways. The Hallcrest report estimated the amount at $100 billion.[1] The Association of Certified Fraud Examiners found that 6 percent of an

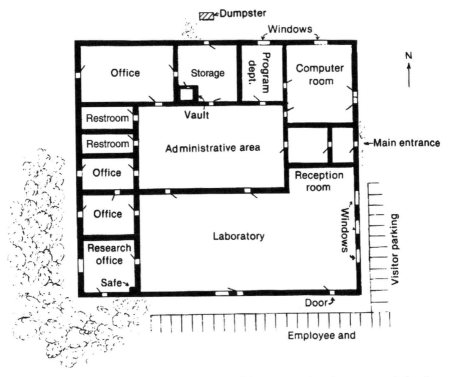

Figure 7–3   Compulab Corporation. Compulab Corporation is a research business with tremendous potential. However, it seems that when it produces innovative research results, a competitor claims similar results soon afterward. Compulab employs 33 people, including a research director, 2 assistants, 10 scientist-researchers, 8 computer specialists, and an assortment of office staff. The facility is open 24 hours a day, 7 days per week, and employees work a mixture of shifts each month. Almost every employee has his or her own key for entrance into the building.

organization's revenues are lost to employee fraud and abuse, totaling nearly $400 billion annually.[2] Shepard and Duston analyzed several studies of total annual economic losses to U.S. businesses from employee theft and concluded that a realistic figure ranges from $15 billion to $25 billion per year.[3] However, these figures may be only the tip of the iceberg when direct and indirect costs are totaled. Indirect costs can include a slowing of production or an insurance premium hike after a claim. Research by Baker and Westin mention employee morale and damage to public image as expensive indirect costs following major internal crimes.[4]

Why Do Employees Steal?

There is no one reason why employees steal from their employers. However, two major causes of employee theft are employee personal problems and the environment.

"Let's Not Fire Him for Stealing, He's a Good Employee"

An undercover investigation at Smith's lumber yard #7 revealed that the yard boss, Joe Crate, was stealing. The undercover investigator, Jimmy Wilson, worked at yard #7 and found that Joe was stealing about $80 worth of building products per week. Each evening Joe would hide merchandise near the back gate, and when it was time to close up and lock the gate, he would quickly load his auto, which was conveniently parked nearby.

Before Jimmy was assigned to another yard, he met with a vice president and the manager of yard #7 at company headquarters. During the meeting, Jimmy asked, "Are you going to fire Joe Crate?" The VP stated, "Let's not fire him for stealing, he's a good employee." Then the VP explained: "Joe's salary is $10 per hour, which is equal to $400 per week. If Joe steals about $80 per week, then Joe's salary is about equal to $480 per week. If we hired a carpenter to build the lumber sheds that Joe is building at yard #7, it would cost us almost twice as much." Jimmy could not believe what he was hearing, especially from the VP. He did not say a word and listened to instructions for his next assignment.

What are your views of the way in which internal theft was handled at Smith's lumber yard #7 in the preceding box?

Employee personal problems often affect behavior on the job. Financial troubles, domestic discord, drug abuse, and excessive gambling can contribute to theft. It is inappropriate to state that every employee who has such problems will steal, but during trying times, the pressure to steal may be greater. A wise employer should be alert to troubled employees and even suggest referral to a community helping agency.

The environment is perhaps the strongest factor behind internal theft. Politicians, corporate executives, and other "pillars of society" are constantly being found guilty of some form of crime. Inadequate socialization results. In other words, poor examples are set: employees may observe managerial illegalities and then act similarly. In many businesses, so many people are stealing that those who do not steal are the deviants and outcasts; theft becomes normal and honesty becomes abnormal. Some managers believe that employee theft improves morale and makes boring jobs exciting. In many workplaces employees are actually instructed to be dishonest. This can be seen when receiving department workers are told by their supervisor to accept overages during truck deliveries without notifying the vendor.

When employees steal, a hodgepodge of rationalizations (excuses) are mentally reviewed to relieve guilt feelings. Some of these rationalizations are "everybody does it," "it's a fringe benefit," and "they aren't paying me enough."

Dr. Donald R. Cressey analyzed thousands of offenders to ascertain common factors associated with inside thievery.[5] He found three characteristics that must be present in a person before theft will be committed. Cressey's *employee theft formula* is

$$\text{Motivation} + \text{Opportunity} + \text{Rationalization} = \text{Theft}$$

Motivation develops from a need for money to finance a debt or a drug problem or to win approval from others. Opportunity occurs at many unprotected locations (such as a cash register or a loading dock). Rationalizations relieve guilt, as stated already. This formula illustrates the need for security and an honest environment.

How Do Employees Steal?

The methods used to steal money or items from employers are limited by employee imagination. Typically, employees pilfer items by hiding them under their clothing before leaving the workplace. More sophisticated methods involve the careful manipulation of accounting records. Collusion among several employees (and outsiders) is common. The kinds of item to be taken (e.g., pocket radio, piano, cash) and the obstacles (e.g., loss prevention strategies) dictate the method of theft. A pocket radio can be hidden in a person's pocket or underwear, and a piano might be pilfered piece by piece over a year and then assembled in a home garage. Some employee theft methods follow:

1. Wearing manufactured items while leaving the workplace, for example, wearing pilfered underwear or wearing scrap lead that has been molded to one's body contours;
2. Smuggling out pilfered items by placing the item in a lunchbox, pocketbook, bundle of work clothes, radio, umbrella, newspaper, hat, or even one's hair;
3. Hiding merchandise in garbage pails, dumpsters, or trash heaps to be retrieved at a later time;
4. Returning to the workplace after hours, with a pass key, and helping oneself to goods;
5. Truck drivers turning in fictitious bills to employers for fuel and repairs and then splitting the money with truck stops;
6. Collusion between truck drivers and receiving personnel;
7. Executives padding expense accounts;
8. Purchasing agents receiving kickbacks from vendors for buying high-priced goods;

9.   Retail employees pocketing money from cash sales and not recording the transaction;
10. Padding payrolls as to hours and rate of pay;
11. Maintaining nonexistent or fired employees on a payroll and then cashing the paychecks;
12. Accounts payable employees paying fictitious bills to a bogus account and then cashing the checks for their own use.

Possible Indicators of Theft

Certain factors may indicate that theft has occurred:

1.   Inventory records and physical counts that differ;
2.   Inaccurate accounting records;
3.   Mistakes in the shipping and receiving of goods;
4.   Increasing amounts of raw materials needed to produce a specific quantity of goods;
5.   Merchandise missing from boxes (e.g., every pallet of 20 boxes of finished goods has at least 2 boxes short a few items);
6.   Merchandise at inappropriate locations (e.g., finished goods hidden near exits);
7.   Security devices found to be damaged or inoperable;
8.   Windows or doors unlocked when they should be locked;
9.   Workers (e.g., employees, truck drivers, repair personnel) in unauthorized areas;
10. Employees who come in early and leave late;
11. Employees who eat lunch at their desks and refuse to take vacations;
12. Complaints by customers about not having their previous payments credited to their accounts;
13. Customers who absolutely have to be served by a particular employee;
14. An unsupervised, after-hours cleaning crew with their own keys;
15. Employees who are sensitive about routine questions concerning their jobs;
16. An employee who is living beyond his or her income level;
17. Expense accounts that are outside of the norm.

MANAGEMENT COUNTERMEASURES

The problem of internal theft is reduced by successful preventive strategies, such as

- Management support;
- Effective planning and budgeting system;
- Good internal and external relations;
- Job applicant screening and employee socialization;

- Accountability, accounting, and auditing;
- Policy and procedural controls;
- Signs;
- Toll-free number and reward;
- Investigation;
- Property losses and theft detection;
- Insurance, bonding;
- Confrontation with employee suspect;
- Prosecution;
- Research.

Strategies

Management Support

Without management support, efforts to reduce losses are doomed. *A good management team sets both a foundation for strategies and an atmosphere in which theft is not tolerated.* Support for budget requests and appropriate policies and procedures is vital.

Effective Planning and Budgeting

Before implementing measures against internal theft, a thorough analysis of the problem is necessary. Questions to consider include the following. How serious is the problem? What are the shrinkage statistics? Is the last inventory accurate? Should another inventory be taken? What strategies are cost effective?

Internal and External Relations

Good internal and external relations can play a role in preventing employee theft. Loss prevention practitioners who show appropriate courtesy, demeanor, and appearance are respected by employees. Prompt investigations of incidents indicate that losses are a major concern.

With a heightened prevention atmosphere within a workplace, an external reputation is sure to follow. Outside people with ulterior motives will think twice before applying for a job.

Job Applicant Screening and Employee Socialization

The screening of job applicants from full-time to part-time and temporary workers is a major theft-prevention technique. Whatever steps are taken, an atmosphere of loss prevention should exist from every applicant's initial contact.

Accountability, Accounting, and Auditing

Accountability defines a responsibility for and a description of something. For example, John Smith is responsible (i.e., is held accountable) for all finished products in a plant, and he maintains accurate records (i.e., a description) of what is in stock. *Accounting* is concerned with recording, sorting, summarizing, reporting, and interpreting business data. For example, business records may show that shrinkage has increased in the last year. *Auditing* is an examination or check of a system to uncover deviations. Personnel audit physical security by checking alarms, CCTV, and so on. An auditor audits the accounting records of a company to see if the records are reliable and to make sure embezzlement has not occurred.

Policy and Procedural Controls

These controls coincide with accountability, accounting, and auditing. In each of these three functions, policies and procedures are dictated to employees through manuals and memos. *Policies* are management tools that control employee decision making and reflect the goals and objectives of management. *Procedures* guide action to fulfill the requirements of policies.

As an example, a company policy states that, before trash is taken to outside dumpsters, a loss prevention officer must be present to check for stolen items. Procedures point out that to conform to this policy the head of the cleaning crew must call the loss prevention office and wait for an officer to arrive before transporting the trash outside.

Signs

Placing messages about loss prevention on the premises is another method. The message must be brief, to the point, and in languages for diverse readers. An example of a message is "let's all work together to reduce losses and save jobs."

Toll-Free Number and Reward System

Numerous organizations have established a toll-free number to facilitate ease of loss reporting. A reward system is another strategy to reinforce reporting. One method employed is to provide the caller with a secret number that is required to pick up reward money at a bank at a time convenient to the caller, who is encouraged to send a substitute to strengthen anonymity.

Investigation

Employee thieves often are familiar with the ins and outs of an organization's operation and can easily conceal theft. In addition, a thorough knowledge of the loss prevention program is common to employee thieves. Consequently, an undercover investigation is an effective method to outwit and expose crafty employee thieves and their conspirators.

Property Losses and Theft Detection

To remedy property or tool losses within a firm, three recommendations are (1) set up an inventory system, (2) mark property, and (3) use metal detectors.

An *inventory system* maintains accountability for property and tools. When employees borrow or use equipment or tools a record is kept of the item, its serial number, the employee's name, and the date. On return of the item, a notation is made, including the date, by both the clerk and the user.

Marking property (e.g., tools, computers, furniture) serves several useful purposes. When property is marked with a serial number, or a firm's name is etched with an engraving tool, thieves are deterred because the property can be identified if the thief is caught. Publicizing the marking of property reinforces the deterrent effect. Many public police agencies are active in a similar program called *operation identification* and are willing to loan etching tools and supply standard inventory forms.

Fluorescent substances can be used to mark property. An ultraviolet light is necessary to view these invisible marks, which emerge as a surprise to the offender.

Organizations sometimes experience the theft of petty cash. To expose such theft, fluorescent substances, in the form of powder, crayon, or liquid, are used to mark money. The typical scenario involves a few suspects who are the only people with access to petty cash after hours. Before these after-hour employees arrive, the investigator handling the case places bills previously dusted with invisible fluorescent powder in envelopes at petty cash locations. The bills even can be written on with the invisible fluorescent crayon. Statements such as "marked money" can be used to identify the bills under ultraviolet light. Serial numbers from the bills are recorded and retained by the investigator. Before the employees are scheduled to leave, the "planted" bills are checked. If the bills are missing, then the employees' hands are checked under an ultraviolet light. Glowing hands expose the thief, and identification of the marked money carried by the individual strengthens the case. The marked money must be placed in an envelope because the fluorescent powder may transfer to other objects and onto an honest person's hands. A wrongful arrest can lead to a false-arrest suit. A check of a suspect's bills, for the marked money, helps avoid this problem. Many cleaning fluids appear orange under an ultraviolet light. The investigator should analyze all cleaning fluids on the premises and select a fluorescent color that is different from the cleaning substances. The use of a pinhole lens camera for covert surveillance is another investigative technique covered later in this chapter.

Walk-through *metal detectors*, similar to those at airports, are useful at employee exits to deter thefts of metal objects and to identify employee thieves. Such detectors also uncover weapons being brought into an area. Handheld metal detectors are also helpful.

Insurance, Bonding

If insurance is the prime bulwark against losses, premiums are likely to sky-rocket and become too expensive. For this reason, *insurance is best utilized as a supplement to other methods of loss prevention that may fail.* Fidelity bonding is a type of employee honesty insurance for employees who handle cash and perform other financial activities. Bonding deters job applicants and employees with evil motives. Some companies have employees complete bonding applications but do not actually obtain the bond.

Confrontation with the Employee Suspect

Care must be exercised when confronting an employee suspect. The following recommendations, in conjunction with good legal assistance, can produce a strong case. The list of steps presents a cautious approach. Many locations require approval of management before an arrest.

1. Never accuse anyone unless absolutely certain of the theft.
2. Theft should be observed by a reliable person. Do not rely on hearsay.
3. Make sure you can show intent: the item stolen is yours, and it was removed from the premises by the person confronted.

In steps 4 through 14 an arrest has not been made.

4. *Ask* the suspect to come to the office for an interview. Employees do not have a right to an attorney to be present during one of these employment meetings. If the person is a union employee and requests a union representative, comply with the request.[6]
5. Without accusing the employee, he or she can be told: "Some disturbing information has surfaced and we want you to provide an explanation."
6. Maintain accurate records of everything. These records may become an essential part of criminal or civil action.
7. Never threaten a suspect.
8. Never detain the suspect if the person wants to leave. Interview for less than one hour.
9. Never touch the suspect or reach into the suspect's pockets.
10. *Request permission* to search the suspect's belongings. If left alone in a room under surveillance, the suspect may take the item concealed on his or her person and hide it in the room. This approach avoids a search.
11. Have a witness present at all times. If the suspect is female, and you are male, have another woman present.
12. If permissible under the Employee Polygraph Protection Act of 1988, ask the suspect to volunteer for a polygraph test and have the suspect sign a statement of voluntariness. Follow EPPA guidelines.
13. If verbal admission or confession is made by suspect, have him or her write it out, and have everyone present sign it.
14. *Ask* the suspect to sign a statement stipulating that no force or threats were applied.

15. For the uncooperative suspect, or if prosecution is favored, call the public police, but first be sure you have sound evidence as in step 3.
16. Do not accept payment for stolen property, because it can be construed as a bribe and it may interfere with a bond. Let the court determine restitution.
17. Handle juveniles differently from adults; consult the public police.
18. When in doubt, consult an attorney.

Prosecution

Many feel strongly that prosecution is a deterrent, whereas others maintain that it hurts morale and public relations and is not cost effective. Whatever management decides, it is imperative that an incident of theft be given considerable attention so that employees realize that a serious act has taken place. Establish a written policy that is fair and applied uniformly.

Research

Although employee theft is a significant national problem, limited research is available. One such research project was conducted by the University of Minnesota and the American Management Association with funds from the U.S. Department of Justice.[7] Thirty-five corporations including 4985 employee respondents anonymously provided data. Conclusions from this research report that deserve further study are the following:

1. In the three industries studied (retail stores, electronic manufacturers, and hospitals), employees most likely to be involved in theft constitute a significant portion of the work force: salespersons, engineers, and nurses.
2. The dissatisfied employee was found more frequently to be involved in theft.
3. The most consistent predictor of theft involvement was the employee's perceived chance of being caught.
4. Theft decreased when a negative reaction by management and coworkers increased.
5. Informal coworker sanctions are twice as influential in changing behavior as formal management responses.
6. Prevention measures have an effect on theft.
7. Those companies with a clearly defined antitheft policy had a lower incidence of theft.
8. Theft can be lowered by communicating antitheft policies to employees (e.g., through signs, memos).
9. A lesser degree of theft was found in businesses that had theft-prevention strategies within the inventory system.
10. Preemployment screening deters theft.
11. Lower levels of theft can be achieved by instituting several strategies at once.

PHYSICAL SECURITY COUNTERMEASURES

When used properly the effectiveness of the following items is well worth the cost: access controls, locks and keys, key control, alarms, CCTV, patrols, and safes, vaults, and files.

Access Controls

Access controls regulate people, vehicles, and items during movement into, out of, and within a building or facility. With regulation, assets are easier to protect. If a truck can enter a business facility easily, back up to the shipping dock so that the truck driver can load valuable cargo illegally, and then drive away, that business cannot last long. But if the truck has to stop at the facility's front gate, where a uniformed officer issues a pass and records the license and other information, and appropriate paperwork is exchanged at the shipping dock under the watchful eyes of another officer who restricts the driver's access into the facility, then these controls can prevent losses.

Access controls are vital for the everyday movement of employees, customers, vendors, service people, contractors, and government inspectors. Any of these people can be someone who would steal.

In addition to merchandise, confidential information, such as classified industrial documents, and employee and customer information must be protected.

> At one corporation a security officer permitted two salespeople from another company to enter a restricted area involved in new product development. The officer was fired.

Access control varies from simple to complex. A simple setup includes locks and keys, officers checking identification badges, and written logs of entries and exits. More complex systems use access cards that activate electronic locking devices while a CCTV system observes the entry. A prime factor influencing the kind of system employed is need. A research laboratory developing a new product requires strict access controls, whereas a retail business would require minimal controls.

Controlling Employee Traffic

The fewest entrances and exits is best. This permits officers to observe people entering and departing. If possible, employees should be routed to the exit closest to the workplace away from valuable assets.

Unauthorized exits locked from within create a hazard in case of fire or other emergency. To ensure safety yet fewer losses, emergency exit alarms on each locked door are a worthwhile investment. These devices enable quick exit, or a short delay, when pressure is placed against a horizontal bar that is secured across the door. An alarm is sounded when these doors are activated, which discourages unauthorized use.

Searching Employees

Careful planning and legal assistance are important prerequisites to employee searches. Because of the sensitivity involved, management should communicate the issues to employee representatives prior to the formulation of policy and procedure. To strengthen the searching policy, job applicants can be requested to sign a written statement stipulating that employees will be searched when they leave the workplace. In many businesses, body searches are prohibited, but all things carried (e.g., lunch boxes) are subject to searches. To avoid a charge of discrimination, searches should be applied uniformly.

Searches also should be extended to employee locker areas, which are a frequent hiding place for pilfered items and drugs. When employees are informed that locker use is a privilege and employees are notified as a condition of employment (in writing with signature required) that lockers may be subject to unannounced searches, then the constitutionality of these searches is reinforced. Some stipulations point out that employees must be present. U.S. labor law supports this contention. Agreements with unions may play a role in locker searches.

Visitors

Visitors include customers, salespeople, vendors, service people, contractors, and government employees. A variety of techniques are applicable to visitor access control. An appointment system enables preparation for visitors. When visitors arrive without an appointment, the person at reception should lead them to a waiting room. Whatever the reason for the visit, the shortest route to specific destinations, away from valuable assets and dangerous conditions, can avert theft and injuries. Lending special equipment, such as a helmet, may be necessary. A record or log of visits is wise. Relevant information would be name of the visitor, date of visit, time entering and leaving, purpose, specific location visited, name of employee escorting visitor, and temporary badge number. These records aid investigators. The temporary badge, which must be collected and accounted for, can state the visitor's name, date, time, specific location of visit, and badge number.

Whenever possible, procedures should minimize employee-visitor contact. This is especially important in the shipping and receiving department, where truck drivers may become friendly with employees and conspiracies may evolve. When telephones, restrooms, and vending machines are scattered throughout a plant, truck drivers and other visitors who are permitted easy access may actually steal the place blind. These services should be located at the shipping and receiving dock and access to outsiders should be limited.

Controlling the Movement of Packages and Property

The movement of packages and property also must be subject to access controls. Some locations require precautions against packaged bombs, letter bombs, and other hazards. Clear policies and procedures are needed for incoming and outgoing items. To counter employee theft, outgoing items require both scrutiny and accountability. Uniformed officers can check outgoing items while a property pass system serves the accountability function.

Employee Identification System

The use of an employee identification (card or badge) system will depend on the number of employees that must be accounted for and recognized by other employees. An ID system not only prevents unauthorized people from entering a facility but also deters unauthorized employees from entering restricted areas. For the system to operate efficiently, clear policies should state the use of ID cards, where and when the cards are to be displayed on the person, who should collect cards from employees who quit or are fired, and the penalties for noncompliance. A lost or stolen card should be reported so that the proper information reaches all interested personnel. Sometimes ID systems become a joke, and employees refuse to wear them, or they decorate them or wear them in odd locations on their person. To sustain an ID system, proper socialization is essential.

Simple ID cards contain employer and employee names. A more complex system would include an array of information: name, signature, address, social security number, employee number, physical characteristics (e.g., height, weight, hair and eye colors), date of birth, validation date, authorized signature, location of work assignment, thumbprint, and color photo.

Lamination discourages card tampering: if an attempt is made to alter the card, it will be disfigured. To laminate a card, a paper ID card is inserted into a plastic case and then placed in a laminating machine that bonds a clear plastic coating over the card.

Automatic Access Control

Keys are difficult to control and easy to duplicate, so there are limitations to the lock-and-key method of access control. Because of these problems, the need for improved access control, and technological innovations, a huge market has been created for electronic card access control systems. These systems are flexible. Unauthorized duplication of cards can be difficult, and personnel (i.e., an officer at each entrance) costs are saved. The card contains coded information "read" by the system. The so-called cardkey is inserted into a "reader" next to a secured door, and if the card is valid, a locking mechanism is released.

Before an automatic access control system is implemented, several considerations are necessary. Safety must be a prime factor to ensure quick exit in case of emergency. Another consideration deals with the adaptability of the system to the type of door presently in use. Can the system accommodate all traffic requirements? How many entrances and exits must be controlled? Will there be an annoying waiting period for those who want to gain access? Are additions to the system possible? What if the system breaks down? Is a backup source of power available (e.g., generators)?

A summary of major types of cards used in card access systems follows:

- *Magnetic stripe cards* are plastic, laminated cards (like credit cards) that have a magnetic stripe along one edge onto which a code is printed. When the card is inserted, the magnetically encoded data is compared to data stored in a computer and access is granted on verification.
- *Magnetic dot cards* contain magnetic material, often barium ferrite, laminated between plastic layers. The dots create a magnetic pattern that activates internal sensors in a card reader.
- *Weigand cards* employ a coded pattern on a magnetized wire within the card to generate a code number. To gain access, the card is passed through a sensing reader.
- *Bar-coded cards* contain an array of tiny vertical lines that can be visible and vulnerable to photocopying or invisible and read by an infrared reader.
- *Proximity cards* need not be inserted into a reader but placed in its "proximity." A code is sent via radio frequency, magnetic field, or microchip-tuned circuit.
- *Smart cards* contain an integrated circuit chip within the plastic that serves as a miniature computer as it records and stores information and personal identification codes in its memory. These cards permit a host of activities from access control to making purchases, while almost eliminating the need for keys or cash.

Access card systems vary in terms of advantages, disadvantages, and costs. Each card can be duplicated with a sufficient amount of knowledge, time, and equipment. A magnetic stripe is easy to duplicate. A piece of cardboard with a properly encoded magnetic stripe functions with equal efficiency. Magnetic dot cards are vulnerable to deciphering. Although bar-coded cards also are easy to duplicate, they can be made more secure by covering the code with an opaque patch, which prevents photocopying. Many software programs are available that can generate bar codes, so fully concealing the code adds more security. Weigand and proximity cards are more difficult to duplicate but higher in cost. The Weigand card has the disadvantage of wear and tear on the card that passes through a slot for access. Proximity cards have the advantage of the sensing element being concealed in a wall and the card typically can be read without removing it from a pocket. Smart cards are expensive, but they can be combined with other card systems.[8]

Biometric security systems have been praised as a major advance in access control. These systems verify an individual's identity through fingerprints, hand geometry, retinal blood vessel patterns of the eye, voice patterns, physical action of writing, and keystroke dynamics (i.e., typing patterns and rhythms), among other methods. Research continues to improve those systems subject to errors, especially voice and handwriting recognition. Basically, these systems operate by storing identifying information in a computer to be compared with information presented by a subject requesting access. The applications are endless: doors, computers, vehicles, and so on. Although biometric systems have been touted as being invincible, no security is foolproof, as illustrated by terrorists who cut off the thumb of a bank manager to gain entry through a fingerprint-based access control system.

Video identification is another strategy to facilitate positive identification. Two forms are photo ID badges and image storage and retrieval systems. A security officer verifies the image with a host computer on a monitor or display terminal that also contains personal data.

Access controls often use multiple technologies. For example, magnetic stripe and smart card technologies can complement each other on a single card. One location may require a card and a personal identification number, or PIN (see Figure 7–4), whereas another requires scanning a finger and a PIN. Many systems feature a distress code that can be entered if someone is being victimized. Another feature is an alarm that sounds during unauthorized attempted entry. Access systems can be programmed to allow select access according to time, day, and location. The logging capabilities are another feature to ascertain personnel location by time, date, and the resources expended (e.g., computer time, parking space, cafeteria).

In the future, we will see an increasing merger of card access systems and biometric technology. Missing or stolen cards will be less of a concern. It will not be long before people will be recognized through biometrics as they approach an access point. In addition, digital imaging technology, in combination with CCTV systems, eventually will recognize individuals through an archived digital image. We will see more point-of-sale readers that accept biometric samples for check cashing, credit cards, and other transactions. The use of biometric systems will become universal—banking, correctional facilities, welfare control programs, and so forth.

Figure 7–4   Card reader and key pad. Courtesy: Diebold, Inc.

Locks and Keys

The basic purpose of a lock-and-key system is to hinder unauthorized entry. Attempts to enter a secure location usually are made at a window or door to a building or at a door somewhere within a building. Consequently, locks deter unauthorized access from outsiders and insiders. *Many see a lock as only a delaying device that is valued by the amount of time needed to defeat it.*

Locks are often categorized as *mechanical* (e.g., key-in-the-knob lock) or *electromechanical* (e.g., card entry). Almost all locking devices are operated by a key, numerical combination, card, or electricity.

Most key-operated locks (except padlocks) use a bolt or latch. The *bolt (or deadbolt)* extends from a door lock into a bolt receptacle within the door frame (see Figure 7–5). Authorized entry is made by using an appropriate key to manually move the bolt into the door lock. *Latches* are spring loaded and less secure than a bolt. They are cut on an angle to permit them to slide right into the strike when the door is closed (see Figure 7–6). Unless the latch is equipped with a locking bar (deadlatch), a credit card or knife can be used to push the latch back to open the door.

Figure 7–5   Deadbolt lock.

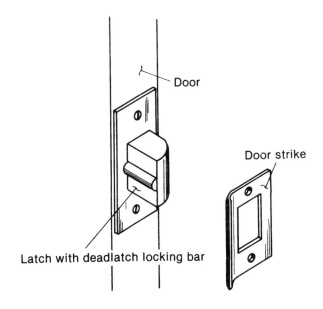

Figure 7–6   Latch and door strike.

The *cylinder* part of a lock contains the keyway, pins, and other mechanisms that permit the bolt or latch to be moved by a key for access (see Figure 7–7). Double-cylinder locks, in which a cylinder is located on each side of a door, are a popular form of added security as compared to single-cylinder

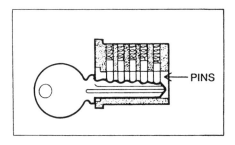

Figure 7–7　Cylinder.

locks. *Double-cylinder locks require a key for both sides* (see Figure 7–5). With a single-cylinder lock, a thief may be able to break glass or remove a wood panel and then reach inside to turn the knob to release the lock. For safety's sake, locations that use double-cylinder locks must prepare for emergency escape by having a key readily available.

Key-in-knob locks are used universally. As the name implies, the keyway is in the knob. Most contain a keyway on the outside and a button on the inside for locking from within (see Figure 7–8). This design is similar in limitations to the single-cylinder lock. Therefore, a double key-in-the-knob lock provides increased security. A double-cylinder lock with a 1-inch bolt is better than a double key-in-the-knob lock, especially because the latter is subject to greater damage by hammering or ripping out the knob.

Entrances for Handicapped

The Internal Revenue Service offers a tax credit to eligible businesses that comply with provisions of the Americans with Disabilities Act to remove barriers and promote access for individuals with disabilities. The door hardware industry offers several products and solutions to aid the disabled (see Figure 7–9). Electrified door hardware such as magnetic locks and electromechanical locks retract the latch when energized. Proximity card readers

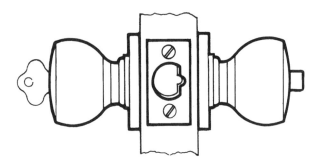

Figure 7–8　Key-in-the-knob lock.

Lever trim reduces force required to unlatch a door.

Push/Pull Latch

Push/Pull latches are popular on institutional doors because of ease of operation.

Proximity Card

Proximity card reader requires only close presence of the user's card to activate door's automatic opener.

Presence detectors are popular with automatic exit doors and require no physical action.

Figure 7–9   Entrances for handicapped. Courtesy: Von Duprin Division of Ingersoll-Rand Company.

and presence (motion) detectors at access points are especially helpful to those with disabilities (as seen in the drawings).

Attacks and Hardware

There are several ways to attack locks. Probably one of the simplest techniques, as stated earlier, is to force a credit card or knife between the door frame (jamb) and the door near the lock to release the latch, which is easily defeated. But, when a deadlatch or bolt is part of the locking mechanism, more forceful methods are needed. In one method, called *springing the door*, a screwdriver or crowbar is placed between the door and the door frame so that the bolt extending from the door lock into the bolt receptacle can be pried out, enabling the door to swing open. This type of attack can be difficult to detect (see Figure 7–10). A 1-inch bolt will hinder this attack.

In *jamb peeling*, another method of attack, a crowbar is used to peel at the door frame near the bolt receptacle so that the door is not stopped from swinging open. Strong hardware for the door frame is helpful. In *sawing the bolt*, a hacksaw is applied between the door and the door frame, similar to the placement of the screwdriver in Figure 7–10. Here again, strong hardware, such as a metal bolt composed of an alloy capable of withstanding a saw blade, will impede attacks. Some offenders use the *cylinder-pulling technique*: the cylinder on the door is actually ripped out with a set of durable pliers or tongs. A circular steel guard surrounding the cylinder (see Figure 7–10) will frustrate the attacker. Offenders also are known to use automobile jacks to pressure door frames away from a door.

Both high-quality hardware and construction will impede attacks, but the door itself must not be forgotten. If a wood door is only $1/4$-inch thick, even though a strong lock is attached, the offender may simply break through the door. A solid wood door $1^3/4$-inches thick or a metal door are worthwhile investments. Wood door frames at least 2-inches thick provide durable protection. When a hollow steel frame is used, the hollow area can be filled with cement to resist crushing near the bolt receptacle. An L-shaped piece of iron secured with one-way screws will deter attacks near the bolt receptacle for doors swinging in (see Figure 7–11). When a padlock

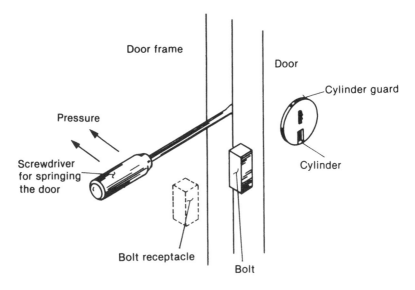

Figure 7–10   Deadbolt lock and door frame.

is used in conjunction with a safety hasp, the hasp must be installed correctly so that the screws are not exposed (see Figure 7–12).

Many attacks are by forced entry, which is easier to detect than when the use of force is minimal. Lock picking is one technique needing a minimum amount of force. It is used infrequently because of the expertise required. *Lock picking* is accomplished by inserting a tension wrench (an L-shaped piece of metal) into the cylinder and applying tension while using metal picks to align the pins in the cylinder as a key would to release the lock (see Figure 7–7). The greater the number of pins the more difficult it is to align them. A cylinder should have at least six pins.

A more difficult attack utilizes a blank key, matches, and a file. The blank key is placed over a lighted match until carbon is produced on the key. Then the key is inserted into the cylinder. The locations where the pins have scraped away the carbon signifies where to file. Needless to say, this method is time consuming and calls for repeated trials.

After gaining access, a professional burglar will employ some tricks to make sure nobody enters while he or she is busy. This is accomplished, for instance, by inserting a pin or obstacle in the keyway and locking the door from the inside.

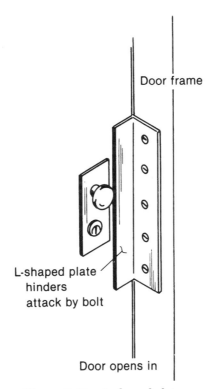

Door frame

L-shaped plate
hinders
attack by bolt

Door opens in

Figure 7–11   L-shaped plate.

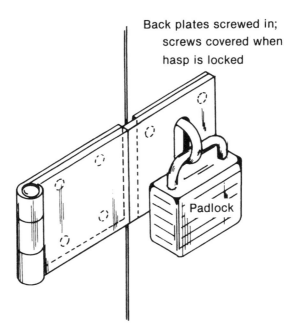

Back plates screwed in;
screws covered when
hasp is locked

Padlock

Figure 7–12   Safety hasp.

Whatever hardware is used, the longer it takes to attack a lock, the greater is the danger for the offender. Six or more pins and pick-resistant, impression-resistant cylinders inhibit unauthorized access. One further point, most burglary insurance policies state that there must be visible signs of forced entry to support a claim.

Other methods of entry may be used by offenders. A thief may simply use a stolen key or a key borrowed from another person. Unfortunately, intruders often enter restricted areas because somebody forgot to use a locking device. This mistake renders the most complex locks useless. *Padlock substitution* is a technique whereby an unlocked padlock is replaced with the thief's similar padlock. When the opportunity is ripe, the thief opens his or her lock, enters, and then replaces the original lock. Therefore, all padlocks should be locked even when not in use. The methods of defeating lock-and-key systems do not stop here. Innovative thieves and various kinds of locks and keys create a hodgepodge of methods that loss prevention practitioners should understand.

Kinds of Locks

Volumes have been written about locks. The following briefly summarizes the common kinds of locks:

- *Warded (or skeleton key tumbler) lock.* This older kind of lock is disengaged when a skeleton key makes direct contact with a bolt and slides it back into the door. It is an easy lock to pick. A strong piece of L-shaped wire can be inserted into the keyway to move the bolt. Furthermore, stores selling sets of skeleton keys add to this lock's limited security characteristics. Warded locks are still in use in many older buildings and are recognized by a keyway that permits seeing through. Locks on handcuffs are of the warded kind and can be defeated by a knowledge-able offender.

- *Disc tumbler (or wafer tumbler) lock*. Originally designed for the auto-mobile industry, its use has expanded to desks, cabinets, files, and padlocks. The operation of this lock entails spring-loaded flat metal discs, instead of pins, that align when the proper key is used. These locks are mass produced, inexpensive, and have a short life expect-ancy. More security is offered than a warded lock can provide, but disc tumbler locks are subject to defeat by improper keys or being jimmied.
- *Pin tumbler lock*. Invented by Linus Yale in 1844, the pin tumbler lock is used widely in industry and residences (see Figure 7–7). Its security surpasses that of the warded and disc tumbler kinds.
- *Lever lock*. Lever locks vary widely. Basically, these locks disengage when tumblers are aligned by the proper key. Those found in cabinets, chests, and desks often provide minimal security, whereas those found in bank safe deposit boxes are more complex and provide greater secu-rity. The better quality lever lock offers more security than the best pin tumbler lock.
- *Combination lock*. This lock requires manipulating a numbered dial(s) to gain access. Combination locks usually have three or four dials that must be aligned in the correct order for entrance. These locks provide greater security than key locks because a limited num-ber of people probably will know the lock combination, keys are unnecessary, and lock picking is obviated. They are used for safes, bank vaults, and high-security filing cabinets. With older combination locks, skillful burglars are able actually to listen to the locking mecha-nism to open the lock; more advanced mechanisms have reduced this weakness. A serious vulnerability results when an offender watches the opening of a combination lock either with binoculars or a tele-scope. Retailers sometimes place combination safes near the front door for viewing by patrolling police; however, unless the retailer uses his or her body to block the dial from viewing, losses may result. This same weakness exists where access is permitted by typing a secret code into a keyboard for access to a parking lot, doorway, or secure area.
- *Combination padlock*. This lock is similar in operation to a combina-tion lock. It is used on employee or student lockers and in conjunction with safety hasps or chains. Some of these locks have a keyway so they can be opened with a key. A security hazard is created when a serial number, on the back of the lock, also is listed in certain factory refer-ence books. It may be wise to obliterate the serial numbers in case a reference book is misused.

- *Padlock.* Requiring a key, this lock is used on lockers or in conjunction with hasps or chains. Numerous kinds of construction are possible, each affording differing levels of protection. Low-security padlocks contain warded locks, whereas more secure ones have disc tumbler, pin tumbler, or lever characteristics. Serial numbers on padlocks are a security hazard similar to combination padlocks.

Other kinds of locks include devices that have a bolt that locks vertically instead of horizontally. Emergency exit locks with alarms or "panic alarms" enable quick exit in emergencies while deterring unauthorized door use. Recording devices on locks print out door usage as to date, time, and key number. Sequence locking devices require locking the doors in a predetermined order; this ensures that all doors are locked because the outer doors will not lock until the inner doors are locked.

The use of *interchangeable core locks* is a quick method to deal with the theft, duplication, or loss of keys. Using a special control key, one core (that part containing the keyway) is simply replaced by another. A different key then is needed to operate the lock. This system, although more expensive initially, minimizes the need for a locksmith or the complete changing of locks.

Automatic locking and unlocking devices also are a part of the broad spectrum of methods to control access. Digital locking systems open doors when a particular numbered combination is typed. If the wrong number is typed, an alarm is sounded. Combinations can be changed when necessary. *Electromagnetic locks* use magnetism, electricity, and a metal plate around doors to hold doors closed. When the electricity is turned off, the door can be opened. Remote locks enable opening a door electronically from a remote location. Before releasing the door lock, an officer seated in front of a console identifies an individual at a door by use of CCTV and a two-way intercom.

Master Key Systems

In most instances, a lock accepts only one key that has been cut to fit it. A lock that has been altered to permit access by two or more keys has been *master keyed.* The master key system allows a number of locks to be opened by the master key. This system should be confined to high-quality hardware utilizing pin tumbler locks. A disadvantage of the master key system is that if the master key is lost or stolen, security is compromised.

A *change key* fits one lock. A *submaster key* will open all locks in, for instance, a wing of a building. The *master key* opens locks covered by two or more submaster systems. The *grand master key* opens all locks within two or more master key systems (a rare occurrence). The *great grand master key* is obsolete and should be avoided. To impede losses, master and submaster keys often are made thin to limit usage; excessive use will destroy the key.

Key Control

Without adequate key control, locks are useless and theft is likely to climb. Accountability and proper records are necessary. Keys should be marked with a code to identify the corresponding lock; the code is interpreted via a record stored in a safe place. A key should never be marked, *Key for room XYZ*. When not in use, keys should be positioned on hooks in a locked key cabinet or vault. The name of the employee, date, and key code are vital records to maintain when a key is issued. These records require continuous updating. Employee turnover is one reason why precise records are vital. Departing employees will return keys (and other valuables) if their final paycheck is withheld. Policies should state that reporting a lost key will not result in punitive action; an investigation and a report will strengthen key control. If key audits check periodically on who has what key, control is further reinforced. To hinder duplication of keys, "do not duplicate" may be stamped on keys, and company policy can clearly state that key duplication will result in dismissal. Lock changes are wise every eight months and sometimes at shorter intervals on an irregular basis. Key control also is important for vehicles such as autos, trucks, and forklifts.

Even the most thorough system of key control is not foolproof. An offender may quickly press a borrowed key into a bar of soap to use as a guide for duplication. A very intelligent offender may even memorize the cuts on a key for subsequent duplication.

Intrusion Alarm Systems

An *intrusion alarm system* detects and reports an event or stimulus within its detection area. A response to rectify the reported problem is essential. The emphasis here is on sensors to thwart employee theft. Sensors appropriate for perimeter protection are stressed in Chapter 8.

What are the basic components of an intrusion alarm system? Three fundamental components are sensor, control unit, and annunciator. *Sensors* detect intrusion by feeling (e.g., pressure mats, contact switches), sound (e.g., vibration detector), or sight (e.g., light beams). The *control unit* receives the alarm notification from the sensor and then activates the *annunciator* (e.g., a bell or siren), which usually produces a human response.

Interior Sensors

A *balanced magnetic switch* consists of a switch mounted to a door (or window) frame and a magnet mounted to a moveable door or window. When the door is closed, the magnet holds the switch closed to complete a circuit. An alarm is triggered when the door is opened and the circuit is interrupted. An ordinary magnetic switch is similar to the balanced type, except simpler, less expensive, and providing a lower level of security. Switches provide good protection against opening a door; however, an offender may cut through a door or glass. (Chapter 8 provides illustrations of switch sensors.)

Mechanical contact switches contain a push-button actuated switch that is recessed into a surface. An item is placed on it that depresses the switch, completing the alarm circuit. Lifting the item interrupts the circuit and signals an alarm.

Pressure-sensitive mats contain two layers of metal strips or screen wire separated by sections of foam rubber or other flexible material. When pressure is applied, as by a person walking on the mat, both layers meet and complete an electrical contact to signal an alarm. These mats are applied as internal traps at doors, windows, main traffic points, and near valuable assets. The cost is low and these mats are difficult to detect. If detected by the offender, he or she can walk around it.

Grid wire sensors are made of fine insulated wire attached to protected surfaces in a grid pattern consisting of two circuits, one running vertical, the other horizontal, and each overlapping the other. An interruption in either circuit signals an alarm. This type of sensor is applied to grill work, screens, walls, floors, ceilings, doors, and other locations. Although these sensors are difficult for an offender to spot, they are expensive to install and an offender can jump the circuit.

Trip wire sensors use a spring-loaded switch attached to a wire stretched across a protected area. An intruder "trips" the alarm (i.e., opens the circuit) when the wire is pulled loose from the switch. These sensors are often applied to ducts, but can be applied to other locations. If spotted by an offender, he or she may be able to circumvent it.

Vibration sensors detect low frequency energy resulting from the force applied in an attack of a structure (see Figure 7–13). These sensors are

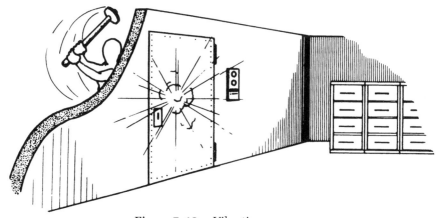

Figure 7–13   Vibration sensor.

applied to walls, floors, and ceilings. Various sensor models require proper selection.

Capacitance sensors create an electrical field around metallic objects that, when disturbed, signal an alarm (see Figure 7–14). These sensors are applied to safes, file cabinets, grills at openings (e.g., windows), and other metal objects. One sensor can protect many objects; however, it is subject to defeat by using insulation (e.g., heavy gloves).

Infrared photoelectric beam sensors activate an alarm when an invisible infrared beam of light is interrupted (see Figure 7–15). If the system is detected, an offender may jump over or crawl under the beam to defeat it.

Ultrasonic motion detectors create a pattern of inaudible sound waves that are transmitted into an area and monitored by a receiver. These detectors operate on the *Doppler effect*, which is the change in frequency that results from the motion of an intruder. These detectors are installed on walls or ceilings or used covertly (i.e., disguised within another object). They are subject to nuisance alarms from high-pitched noises or air currents and can be defeated by objects blocking the sensor or by fast or slow movement.

Microwave motion detectors operate on the Doppler frequency shift principle. An energy field is transmitted into an area and monitored for a change in the pattern and frequency, which results in an alarm. Because microwave energy penetrates a variety of construction materials, care is required for placement and aiming. However, this can be an advantage in protecting multiple rooms and large areas with one sensor. These sensors can be defeated (like ultrasonic ones) by objects blocking the sensor or by fast or slow movement.

Passive infrared intrusion sensors (PIR) are passive in that they do not transmit a signal for an intruder to disturb. Rather, moving infrared radiation (from a person) is detected against the radiation environment of a room (see Figure 7–16). When an intruder enters the room, the level of infrared

Figure 7–14   Capacitance sensor.

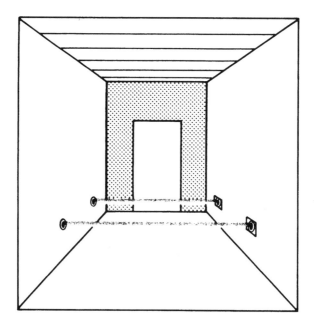

Figure 7–15   Infrared photoelectric beam system.

Figure 7–16   Passive infrared intrusion sensor.

energy changes and an alarm is activated. Although the PIR is not subject to the many nuisance alarms as ultrasonic and microwave detectors, it should not be aimed at sources of heat or surfaces that can reflect energy. The PIR can be defeated by blocking the sensor so it cannot pick up heat.

Passive audio detectors listen for noise created by intruders. Various models filter out naturally occurring noises not indicating forced entry. These detectors can use public address system speakers in buildings, which can act as microphones to listen to intruders. The actual conversation of intruders can be picked up and recorded by these systems. To enhance this system, CCTV can provide visual verification of an alarm condition, video in real-time and still images digitally to security or police, and evidence. The audio also can be two-way, enabling security to warn the intruders. *Such audiovisual systems must be applied with extreme care to protect privacy, confidentiality, and sensitive information.*

Fiber optics is growing in popularity for intrusion detection and for transmission of alarm signals. It involves the transportation of information via guided light waves in an optical fiber. This sensor can be attached to or inserted in many things requiring protection. When stress is applied to the fiber optic cable, an infrared light pulsing through the cable reacts to the stress and signals an alarm.

Intrusion alarm systems only detect and report an alarm condition. These systems do not stop or apprehend an intruder.

Dual Technologies

Two types of sensor technologies often are applied to a location to reduce false alarms, prevent defeat techniques, or fulfill unique needs. The combination of ultrasonic and passive infrared sensors is a popular example of applying dual technologies. Each technology should be considered independently for its advantages and disadvantages in the protected environment. Reporting can be designed so an alarm is signaled when both sensors detect an intrusion (to reduce false alarms) or when either sensor detects an intrusion.[9]

Operational Zoning

Operational zoning means that the building being protected has a segmented alarm system, whereby the alarm can be turned on and off within particular zones depending on usage (see Figure 7–17). For example, if an early morning cleaning crew is in the north end of a plant, then that alarm is turned off while other zones still have the alarm on. Furthermore, zoning helps to pinpoint where an intrusion has occurred.

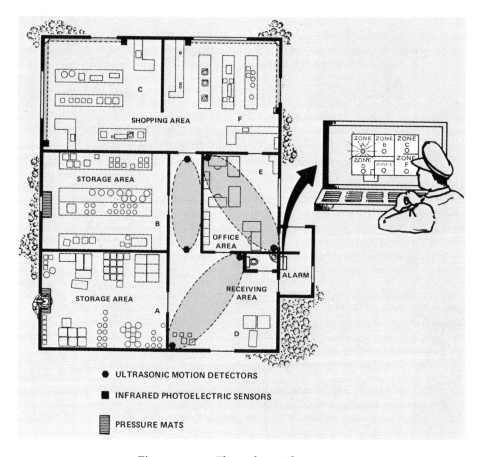

SHOPPING AREA

STORAGE AREA

STORAGE AREA

OFFICE AREA

RECEIVING AREA

ALARM

ZONE A   ZONE B   ZONE C
ZONE D   ZONE E   ZONE F

● ULTRASONIC MOTION DETECTORS

■ INFRARED PHOTOELECTRIC SENSORS

▤ PRESSURE MATS

Figure 7–17   Floor plan with sensors.

Alarm Monitoring

Today, many entities have an alarm system that is monitored by an in-house station (e.g., a console at a secure location) or from a central station (contract service) located off the premises. These services easily can supply reports of unusual openings and closings, as well as those of the regular routine. Chapter 8 covers alarm signaling systems.

Closed-Circuit Television

Closed-circuit television, or CCTV (see Figure 7–18) assists in deterrence, surveillance, apprehension, and prosecution. Although it may be costly initially, CCTV reduces personnel costs because it allows the viewing of multiple locations by one person. A simple *CCTV system* consists of a television camera, monitor (TV), and coaxial cable. The camera and monitor are plugged in, and

Figure 7–18   CCTV and monitor. Courtesy: Diebold, Inc.

the cable is connected between them before both are turned on. An extensive system would have numerous cameras strategically located. For instance, throughout a manufacturing plant, personnel seated in front of a console of monitors could view the targets of many cameras. Accessories include zoom lenses, remote pan (i.e., side-to-side movement), and tilt (i.e., up-and-down movement) mechanisms that enable viewing mobility and opportunities to obtain a close look at any suspicious activity. Low-light-level equipment permits viewing when limited light is present.

Changing technology has brought about the *charged coupled device* (CCD) or *"chip" camera*, a small, photosensitive, solid-state unit designed to replace the tube in the closed-circuit camera. CCD technology is found in camcorders. CCD cameras have certain advantages over tube cameras: CCD cameras are more adaptable to a variety of circumstances, they have a longer life expectancy, "ghosting" (i.e., people appearing transparent) is less of a problem, there is less intolerance to light, less power is required, and less heat is produced, thereby requiring less ventilation and permitting installation in more locations.

Cameras commonly are placed at access points, passageways, shipping and receiving docks, merchandise storage areas, cashier locations, parts departments, computer rooms, and overlooking files, safes, vaults, and production lines. Wherever cameras are located, careful planning is essential to avoid harming employee morale. Employees may find it distasteful being viewed on a production line and might view the workplace as having a "Big Brother" atmosphere, in which management "spying" is more important than employee privacy. An opposing view is that management wants to maintain productivity without losses. Labor arbitrators have ruled that this kind of surveillance is legal; however, labor unions and management are likely to be involved in future controversy concerning this issue.

Constant monitoring of a CCTV system ensures its loss prevention capabilities. Personnel that are not rotated periodically become fatigued from watching too much TV. This is a serious problem that is often overlooked. Regular employees may "test" the monitoring of the system by placing a bag or rag over a camera or even spraying the lens with paint. If employees see that there is no response, CCTV becomes a hoax. The use of dummy cameras is not recommended because, when employees discover the dummy, loss prevention appears to be a deceitful farce.

A *video cassette recorder* (VCR) combined with a CCTV system permits recording visual evidence. This is helpful in the prosecution of offenders and may be used in court. Further, if an employee violates policies and procedures and is fired, a recording is helpful for arbitration hearings or litigation. The time and date of the recording, shown on the cassette, strengthens the case.

The widespread use of video cassette recorders has surpassed the use of the older reel-to-reel video tape recorders (VTR). VCRs generally record for two, four, or six hours. *Time-lapse recorders* (i.e., single frames of video are stored at intervals over an extended period of time) have total recording time of up to several hundred hours, plus an alarm mode in which the recorder reverts to real time when an alarm condition exists. Real-time setting records 30 frames a second; time-lapse video may record between 1 frame a second and 1 frame every eight seconds. Time-lapse recorder features include a quick search for alarm conditions during playback, the playing of recorded video frames according to the input of time by the user, and the interface with other security systems such as access controls to ensure a video record of all people entering and departing.

CCTV capabilities can be enhanced by using a video motion detector. A *video motion detector* operates by sending, from a camera, a static (i.e., having no motion) picture to a memory evaluator. Any change in the picture, such as movement, activates an alarm. These systems assist security officers in reacting to threats. A VCR is applicable.

Increasing "intelligence" is being built into CCTV-computer-based systems. *Multiplex* means sending many signals over one communications channel. *Video multiplex systems* minimize the number of monitors security personnel must watch by allowing up to 16 cameras to be viewed at the same time on one video screen. The pictures are compressed, but a full view is seen of each picture. If an alarm occurs, a full screen can be brought up. The *digital multiplex recorder* enables users to record events without a time-lapse recorder, directly to a hard drive. The images are collected digitally, which improves video quality and permits fast storage and retrieval of information, while avoiding tape degradation. This technology facilitates the move from video monitors to computer monitors, and we will see increasing use of security video at the desktop computer and remote monitoring (e.g., watching a business from many miles away).

CCTV technology, called *intelligent surveillance*, has further reduced the problem of real-time monitoring of dozens of cameras, which is beyond human capacity. Based on machine vision technology, these computerized systems digitize video images and, through specially designed software, automatically identify targets and track people or vehicles. The system alerts security through voice annunciation, the live video is called to the screen, and the video images are filed to a disc.[10]

The extent of the use of hidden surveillance cameras is difficult to measure, especially because many individuals are unaware of the existence of these cameras in workplaces. Pinhole lenses are a popular component of hidden surveillance cameras. They get their name from the outer opening of the lens, which is $1/8$ to $1/4$ inch in diameter and difficult to spot. Cameras are hidden in almost any location, such as clocks, file cabinets, computers, sprinkler heads, and mannequins.

Integrated Systems

"An *integrated system* is the control and operation by a single operator of multiple systems whose perception is that only a single system is performing all functions."[11] These computer-based systems include access controls, alarm monitoring, CCTV, electronic article surveillance, fire protection and safety systems, HVAC, environmental monitoring, radio and video media, intercom, point-of-sale transactions, and inventory control. Such systems are installed within facilities worldwide, controlled and monitored by operators and management at a centralized workstation or from remote locations.

The benefits of integrated systems include lower costs, a reduction in staff, improved efficiency, centralization, and reduced travel and time costs. For example, a manufacturing executive at corporate headquarters can monitor a branch plant's operations, production, inventory, sales, and loss prevention. Likewise, a retail executive at headquarters can watch the sales floor, special displays, point-of-sale transactions, customer behavior, inventory, shrinkage, and loss prevention. *These "visits" to worldwide locations are conducted without leaving the office!*

Integration requires careful planning and clear answers to many questions, such as the following:

- Will the integrated system truly cost less and be easier to operate and maintain than separate systems? Obtain separate quotations on integrated and interconnected systems.
- Does the supplier truly have expertise across all of the applications?
- Is the integration software listed or approved by a third party testing agency such as Underwriters Laboratories?
- Do authorities prohibit integration of certain systems? Some fire departments prohibit integrating fire alarm systems with other systems.[12]

Security Officers

When supervised, uniformed officers patrol on foot inside a facility—through production, storage, shipping, receiving, office, and sales floor areas—an enhanced loss prevention atmosphere prevails. Unpredictable and irregular patrols can play an important role in deterring employee theft (among other losses). A properly trained officer looks for deviations, such as merchandise stored or hidden in unusual places, and tampered devices (e.g., locks, alarms, and CCTV). By thoroughly searching trash containers, employees are deterred from hiding items in that popular spot. Losses also are hindered when officers identify and check people, items, and vehicles at access points.

Safes, Vaults, and File Cabinets

Protective containers secure valuable items (e.g., cash, confidential information). These devices generally are designed to withstand losses from fire or burglary. Specifications vary and an assessment of need should be carefully planned. Management frequently is shocked when a fire-resistive safe in which valuable items are "secured" enables a burglar to gain entry because the safe was designed only for fire. The classic *fire-resistive (or record) safe* has a square (or rectangular) door and thin steel walls that contain insulation. During assembly, wet insulation is poured between the steel walls; when the mixture dries, moisture remains. During a fire, the insulation creates steam that cools the safe below 350° F (the flash point of paper) for a specified time. Record safes for computer tapes and discs require better protection because damage occurs at 150° F and these records are more vulnerable to humidity. Fire safes are able to withstand one fire; thereafter, the insulation is useless.

The classic *burglary-resistive (or money) safe* has a thick, round door and thick walls. Round doors were thought to enhance resistance, but today many newer burglary-resistive safes have square or rectangular doors. The burglary-resistive safe is more costly than the fire-resistive safe.

Ratings

Better quality safes have the UL (Underwriters Laboratory, a nonprofit testing organization) rating. This means that manufacturers have submitted safes for testing by UL. These tests determine the fire- or burglary-resistive properties of safes. For example, a fire-resistive container with a UL rating of 350-4 (formerly designated *A*) can withstand external temperatures to 2000° F for four hours while the internal temperature will not exceed 350° F (see Table 7–1). The UL test actually involves placing a safe in an increasingly hot furnace to simulate a fire. An explosion impact test requires another safe of the same model to be placed in a preheated (2000° F) furnace for half an hour. Then the heat is lowered slightly for another half hour

Table 7–1   Fire-resistant containers

| | UL Record Safe Classifications | | | |
Classification	Temperature	Time	Impact	Old Label
350-4	2000° F	4 hrs	yes	A
350-2	1850° F	2 hrs	yes	B
350-1	1700° F	1 hr	yes	C
350-1	1700° F	1 hr	yes	A
(Insulated record container)				
350-1	1700° F	1 hr	no	D
(Insulated filing device)				
UL computer media storage classification				
150-4	2000° F	4 hrs	yes	
150-2	1850° F	2 hrs	yes	
150-1	1700° F	1 hr	yes	
UL insulated vault door classification				
350-6	2150° F	6 hrs	no	
350-4	2000° F	4 hrs	no	
350-2	1850° F	2 hrs	no	
350-1	1700° F	1 hr	no	

Source: Correspondence (June 3, 1996) with UL, 1285 Walt Whitman Rd., Melville, NY 11747.

before the safe is dropped 30 feet onto rubble. If the safe is still intact, it is returned to the furnace for an hour at 1700° F before it is allowed to cool so that the papers inside can be checked for damage. In reference to burglary-resistive containers, a UL rating of TL-15, for example, signifies weight of at least 750 pounds and resistance to an attack on its door by common tools for a minimum of 15 minutes (see Table 7–2). UL-rated burglary-resistive safes also contain UL-listed combination locks and other UL-listed components. UL is constantly toughening its standards. In the last few years UL has expanded the testing of safes to six sides instead of only the door. When selecting a safe, consider recommendations from insurance companies and peers, whether or not safe company employees are bonded, and how long the company has been in business.

Attacks

Before a skilled burglar attacks a safe, he or she studies the methods used to protect it. Inside information (e.g., a safe's combination) is valuable, and scores of employees and former employees of attacked firms have been implicated in burglaries. Listed next are major attack techniques of two types: with force and without force.

Table 7–2   UL money safe classification

Classification	Description		Construction
TL-15	Tool resistant	Weight	At least 750 lbs. or anchored.
		Body:	At least 1-inch thick steel or equal.
		Attack:	Door and front face must resist attack with common hand and electric tools for 15 minutes.
TL-30	Tool resistant	Weight:	At least 750 lbs. or anchored.
		Body:	At least 1-inch thick steel or equal.
		Attack:	Door and front face must resist attack with common hand and electric tools plus abrasive cutting wheels and power saws for 30 minutes.
TRTL-30[a]	Tool and torch resistant	Weight:	At least 750 lbs.
		Attack:	Door and front face must resist attack with tools listed above, and oxy-fuel gas cutting or welding torches for 30 minutes.
TRTL-30X6	Tool and torch resistant	Weight:	At least 750 lbs.
		Attack:	Door and entire body must resist attack with tools and torches listed above, plus electric impact hammers and oxy-fuel gas cutting or welding torches for 30 minutes.
TXTL-60	Tool, torch, and explosive resistant	Weight:	At least 1000 lbs.
		Attack:	Door and entire body must resist attack with tools and torches listed above, plus 8 oz. of nitroglycerine or its equal for 60 minutes.

[a] As of January 31, 1980, UL stopped issuing the TRTL-30 label, replacing it with the TRTL-30X6 label, which requires equal protection on all six sides of the safe. Some manufacturers, however, continue to produce safes meeting TRTL-30 standards in order to supply lower priced containers, which provide moderate protection against tool and torch attack.
Source: Correspondence (June 3, 1996) with UL, 1285 Walt Whitman Rd., Melville, NY 11747.

Attack methods using force include

- *Rip or peel.* Most common, the method is used on fire-resistive safes that have lightweight metal. Like opening a can of sardines, the metal is ripped from a corner. The peel technique requires an offender to pry along the edge of the door to reach the lock.
- *Punch.* The combination dial is broken off with a hammer. A punch is placed on the exposed spindle, which is hammered back to enable

breakage of the lock box. The handle then is used to open the door. The method is effective against older safes.

- *Chop.* This is the attack of a fire-resistive safe from underneath. The safe is tipped over and hit with an ax or hammer to create a hole.
- *Drill.* A skillful burglar drills into the door to expose the lock mechanism; the lock tumblers are aligned manually to open the door.
- *Torch.* The method is used against burglar-resistive safes. An oxygen-acetylene cutting torch melts the steel. The equipment is brought to the safe, or the offender uses equipment from the scene.
- *Carry away.* The offender removes the safe from the premises and attacks it in a convenient place.

Attack methods using no force include

- *Office search.* Simply, the offender finds the safe combination in a hiding place (e.g., taped under a desk drawer).
- *Manipulation.* The offender opens a safe without knowing the combination by using sight, sound, and touch—a rare skill. Sometimes the thief is lucky and opens a safe by using numbers similar to an owner's birth date, home address, or telephone number.
- *Observation.* An offender views the opening of a safe from across the street with the assistance of binoculars or a telescope. To thwart this, the numbers should be on the top edge of the dial, rather than on the face of the dial.
- *Day combination.* For convenience, during the day, the dial is not completely turned each time an employee finishes using the safe. This facilitates an opportunity for quick access. An offender often manipulates the dial in case the day combination is still in effect.
- *X-ray equipment.* Metallurgical X-ray equipment is used to photograph the combination of the safe. White spots appear on the picture that help to identify the numerical combination. The equipment is cumbersome, and the technique is rare.

The following measures are recommended to fortify the security of safes and other containers:

1. Utilize alarms (e.g., capacitance and vibration), CCTV, and adequate lighting.
2. Locate the safe in a well-lighted spot near a window where police or pedestrians can see it. Hiding the safe gives the burglar better working conditions.
3. Secure the safe to the building so it is not stolen. (This also applies to cash registers that may be stolen in broad daylight.) Bolt the safe to the foundation or secure it in a cement floor. Remove any wheels or casters.

4. Do not give the burglar an opportunity to use any tools on the premises; hide or secure all potential tools. A ladder or torch on the premises can be used.
5. A time lock permits the safe to be opened only at select times. This hinders access even if the combination is known. A delayed-action lock provides an automatic waiting period (e.g., 15 minutes) from combination use to the time the lock mechanism activates. A silent signal lock triggers an alarm when a special combination is used to open a safe.
6. At the end of the day, turn the dial several times in the same direction.
7. A written combination is risky. Change the factory combination as soon as possible. When an employee leaves who knows the combination, change it.
8. Maintain limited valuables in the safe through frequent banking.
9. Select a safe with its UL rating marked on the inside. If a burglar identifies the rating on the outside, an attack is made easier.

Vaults

A walk-in vault is actually a large safe; it is subject to similar vulnerabilities from fire and attack. Because a walk-in vault is so large and expensive, typically only the door is made of steel, and the rest of the vault is composed of reinforced concrete. Vaults are heavy enough to require special support within a building. They commonly are constructed at ground level to avoid stress on a building.

File Cabinets

According to Richard Healy, "There is a correlation between fire damage and business failure. Statistics seem to indicate that almost half of the companies that lose their records are forced out of business."[13] Records help to support losses during insurance claims. Some vital records are accounts receivable, inventory lists, legal documents, contracts, research and development, and personnel data.

File cabinets that are insulated and lockable can provide fair protection against fire and burglary. The cost is substantially lower than a safe or vault, but valuable records demanding increased safety should be placed in a safe or vault. Special computer safes are designed to protect against forced entry, fire, and moisture that destroys computer media.

Which strategies do you view as affording the best protection against internal theft? Support your answer.

CASE PROBLEMS

7A. Consult the floor plans for Woody's Lumber Company, the Smith Shirt manufacturing plant, and Compulab Corporation (Figures 7–1, 7–2, and 7–3). Draw up a priority list of 10 loss prevention strategies for each company, which you think would best solve the internal loss problems. Why did you select as top priorities your first three strategies on each list?

7B. As a security officer at a manufacturing plant, an employee informs you about observing another employee hide company property near a backdoor. You check the area near the door and find company property under boxes. What action do you take?

7C. As a security officer you learn that officers on your shift, and your immediate supervisor, have secretly installed, without authorization, a pinhole lens camera in the women's restroom. You refuse to be involved in peeping. The officers have been your friends since high school and you socialize with them when off duty. One day the corporate security manager summons you to her office and questions you concerning the whereabouts of the pinhole lens camera. What do you say?

NOTES

1. William C. Cunningham and Todd H. Taylor, *Private Security and Police in America: The Hallcrest Report* (Portland, OR: Chancellor Press, 1985), p. 243.
2. Robert King, "Employee Screening—Key for Today's Businesses," *Security Concepts* (October 1996): 15.
3. Ira M. Shepard and Robert Duston, *Thieves at Work: An Employer's Guide to Combating Workplace Dishonesty* (Washington, DC: Bureau of National Affairs, 1988), p. 19.
4. Michael A Baker, Alan F. Westin, and U.S. Department of Justice, *Employer Perceptions of Workplace Crime* (Washington, DC: U.S. Government Printing Office, 1987), p. 12.
5. Banning K. Lary, "Thievery on the Inside," *Security Management* (May 1988): 81.
6. Gillian Flynn, "Legal Insight," *Personnel Journal* (April 1995): 158–166.
7. John P. Clark and Richard C. Hollinger, "Theft by Employees," *Security Management* 24 (September 1980): 106.
8. Joseph A. Barry, "Don't Always Play the Cards You Are Dealt," *Security Technology and Design* (July–August 1993): 75. Bud Toye, "Bar-Coded Security ID Cards Efficient and Easy," *Access Control* (March 1996): 23.
9. Douglas R. Kunze, "Selecting the Right Bells and Whistles," *Security Management* (May 1996): 63–67.
10. Robin Thompson, "Intelligent Surveillance Provides Security Uplift," *National Defense* (May–June 1997): 52.
11. James Keener, "Integrated Systems: What They Are and Where They Are Heading," *Security Technology and Design* (May 1994): 6–9.
12. "Hard Questions to Ask in Integration Projects," *Security* (August 1996): 54.
13. Richard J. Healy, *Design for Security* (New York: John Wiley & Sons, 1968), p. 174.

8

External Threats and Countermeasures

OBJECTIVES

After studying this chapter the reader will be able to

1. Describe methods of unauthorized entry;
2. Explain how environmental design can enhance security;
3. Discuss perimeter security and list and define five types of barriers;
4. Explain window and door protection;
5. Discuss the application of intrusion alarm systems to perimeter protection;
6. List and explain at least four types of alarm signaling systems;
7. Explain lighting, illumination, and at least five types of lamps;
8. Discuss parking lot and vehicle controls;
9. Explain the deployment and monitoring of security officers;
10. Discuss the use of protective dogs;
11. Explain the aura of loss prevention.

External loss prevention focuses on threats from outside an organization. This chapter concentrates on countermeasures to impede intrusions from outsiders. If unauthorized access can be accomplished, numerous losses are possible from crimes such as burglary, robbery, vandalism, arson, and espionage. Naturally, these offenses may be committed by employees as well as outsiders or a conspiracy of both. Outsiders can gain legitimate access if they are customers, repair personnel, and so on. Internal and external countermeasures play an interdependent role in minimizing losses; a clear-cut division between internal and external countermeasures is not possible because of this intertwined relationship.

Many organizations have developed formidable perimeter security to prevent unauthorized entry, while not realizing that the greatest threat is from within.

165

METHODS OF UNAUTHORIZED ENTRY

A good way to begin thinking about how to deter unauthorized entry is to study the methods used by offenders. The characteristics of patrols, fences, alarms, locks, windows, doors, and the like are studied by both management (to hinder penetration) and offenders (to succeed in gaining access). By placing yourself in the position of an offender (i.e., *think like a thief*) and then that of a loss prevention manager, you can see, while studying Woody's Lumber Company, the Smith Shirt manufacturing plant, and Compulab Corporation (discussed in Chapter 7), that a combination of both perspectives aids in the designing of defenses. (Such planning is requested in a case problem at the end of this chapter.)

Forced entry is a common method used to gain unauthorized access. Windows and doors are especially vulnerable to forced entry. Offenders repeatedly break or cut glass (with a glass cutter) on a window or door and then reach inside to release a lock or latch. To stop the glass from falling and making noise, a suction cup or tape is used to remove or hold the broken glass together. Retail stores may be subject to *smash and grab attacks:* a store display window is smashed, merchandise is quickly grabbed, and the thief immediately flees. A complex lock may be rendered useless if the offender is able to go through a thin door by using a hammer, chisel, and saw. Forced entry also may be attempted through walls, floors, ceilings, skylights, utility tunnels, sewer or storm drains, and ventilation vents or ducts.

Even though an attempted intrusion may be unsuccessful, losses inevitably result from damaged construction and locks. But, if offenders can be convinced that security is a discouraging obstacle, attempts will decline. This is accomplished through signs informing people about the extent of the security features such as patrols and alarms.

Unauthorized access also can be accomplished *without force*. Wherever a lock is supposed to be used, if it is not locked properly, access is possible. Windows or doors left unlocked are a surprisingly common occurrence. Lock picking or possession of a stolen key or computerized access card renders force unnecessary. Dishonest employees are known to assist criminals by unlocking locks, windows, or doors and by providing keys and technical information. Offenders sometimes hide inside a building until closing and then break out after stealing something. Tailgating is a method whereby an intruder blends into a group of entering employees. These sly methods of gaining entry are often referred to as *surreptitious entry*.

COUNTERMEASURES

With so many possible techniques of unauthorized entry, prevention methods must be formidable. Strategies for preventing unauthorized access by using the following aspects of the premises are discussed in the remainder of this chapter: construction and environmental security design, perimeter security, barriers, windows, doors, intrusion alarm systems, CCTV, lighting, parking lot and vehicle controls, security officers, communications and the control center, protective dogs, and the aura of loss prevention.

Construction and Environmental Security Design

When planning a new facility, the need for a coordinated effort by architects, loss prevention practitioners, and local police and fire officials cannot be overstated. Pooling ideas and viewpoints surely can produce a facility worthy of reduced loss expectations. Further, money is saved when defenses are planned before actual construction rather than accomplished by modifying the building later.

Years ago, when buildings were designed, loss prevention features were an even smaller part of the planning process than today. Older buildings often have the original warded-type locks that are easy to defeat. Before air conditioning came into widespread use, numerous windows were required for proper ventilation, providing thieves with many entry points. Today's buildings also present problems. For example, ceilings are constructed of suspended ceiling tile with spaces above the tile that enable access by simply pushing up the tile. Once above the tiles, a person can crawl to other rooms on the same floor. Roof access from neighboring buildings is a common problem for both old and new buildings. Many of these weak points are corrected by adequate hardware, locks on roof doors, for example, and alarms.

In the last 30 years, architects have played an increasing role in designing crime prevention into building plans. *Environmental security design* includes natural and electronic surveillance of walkways and parking lots, windows and landscaping that enhance visibility, improved lighting, and other architectural designs that promote crime prevention. Additionally, dense shrubbery can be cut to reduce hiding places and grid streets can be turned into cul-de-sacs by using barricades to reduce ease of escape.

During the late 1960s and early 1970s, *Oscar Newman* conducted innovative research into the relationship between architectural design and crime prevention that developed into the concept of *defensible space*.[1] He studied over 100 housing projects and identified design elements that inhibit crime. For instance, Newman favored the creation of surveillance opportunities through windows for residents and the recognition that the neighborhood surrounding the residential setting influences safety. An essential part of defensible space is to create designs that change residents' use of public places while reducing the fear of crime; this is hoped to have a snowballing effect. Oscar Newman found that physical design features of public housing affect both the rates of victimization of residents and their perception of security. Crime prevention through environmental design (CPTED) is applicable not only to public housing but also businesses, industries, public buildings, transportation systems, and schools, among others. In the past, the U.S. Department of Justice has funded CPTED programs in several cities.

Today, research continues on how the physical environment influences behavior. Offenders may decide whether or not to commit a crime at a location after they determine the following:

1. How easy will it be to enter?
2. How visible, attractive, or vulnerable do targets appear?
3. What are the chances of being seen?
4. If seen, will the people in the area do something about it?
5. Is there a quick, direct route from the location?[2]

The planning of a new building must not overlook fire and safety features as integral components of loss prevention. These topics are described in later chapters.

Perimeter Security

Perimeter means outer boundary, and it is often the property line and the first line of defense against unauthorized access (see Figure 8–1). Building access points such as doors and windows also are considered part of perim-

Figure 8–1   Perimeter security. Courtesy of Wackenhut Corporation. Photo by Ed Burns.

eter defenses at many locations. Typical perimeter security begins with a fence and may include locks, alarms, lighting, CCTV, and patrols. The following variables assist in the design of perimeter security:

1. Whatever perimeter security methods are planned, they should interrelate with the total loss prevention program.
2. Perimeter security needs to be cost effective. When plans are presented, management is sure to ask: "What type of return will we have on such an investment?"
3. Although the least number of entrances strengthens perimeter security, the plan must not interfere with normal business and emergency situations.
4. Perimeter security has a psychological impact on potential intruders. It signals a warning to outsiders that steps have been taken to block intrusions. Offenders actually "shop" for vulnerable businesses.
5. Even though a property line may be well protected, the possibility of unauthorized entry cannot be totally eliminated. For example, a fence can be breached by going over, under, or through it.
6. If intruders are apprehended within a property line, weak perimeter security may be evident. Perimeter security must strive to deter attempts at intrusion, no matter how unsuccessful those attempts are destined to be.
7. Perimeter security often serves as the first line of a series of defenses.
8. Penetration of a perimeter is possible from within. Merchandise may be thrown over a fence or out of a window. A variety of things are subject to smuggling by persons walking or using a vehicle while exiting through a perimeter.
9. The perimeter of a building, especially in urban areas, often is the building's walls. A thief may enter through a wall from an adjoining building.
10. To permit an unobstructed view, both sides of a perimeter should be kept clear of vehicles, equipment, and vegetation. This allows for what is known as *clear zones*.
11. Perimeter security methods are exposed to a hostile outdoor environment not found indoors. Adequate clothing and shelter are necessary for personnel. The selection of proper security devices prevents false alarms from animals, vehicle vibrations, and adverse weather.
12. Perimeter security should be inspected periodically.

Barriers

Post and Kingsbury state that "the physical security process utilizes a number of barrier systems, all of which serve specific needs. These systems include natural, structural, human, animal, and energy barriers."[3] *Natural barriers* are

rivers, hills, cliffs, mountains, foliage, and other features difficult to overcome. Fences, walls, doors, and the architectural arrangement of buildings are
structural barriers. *Human barriers* include security officers who scrutinize
people, vehicles, and things entering and leaving a facility. The typical *animal barrier* is a dog. *Energy barriers* include protective lighting and alarms.

The most common type of barrier is a *chain-link fence* topped with
barbed wire. One advantage of chain-link fencing is that it allows observation
from both sides: a private security officer looking out and a public police officer
looking in. Foliage and decorative plastic woven through the fence can reduce
visibility and aid offenders. Opposition to chain-link fencing sometimes develops because management wants to avoid an institutional-looking environment.
Decorative masonry walls are an alternative, although expensive.

It is advisable that the chain-link fence be made of at least 9-gauge or
heavier wire with 2" x 2" diamond-shaped mesh. It should be at least 7 feet
high. Its posts should be set in concrete and spaced no more than 10 feet
apart. The bottom should be within 2 inches of hard ground; if the ground is
soft, the fence can become more secure if extended a few inches below the
ground. Recommended at the top is a *top guard*: supporting arms about 1 or
2 feet long containing three or four strands of taut barbed wire 6 inches
apart and facing outward at 45 degrees.

Barbed wire fences are less effective and used less frequently than
chain-link fences. Each strand of barbed wire is constructed of two 12-gauge
wires twisted and barbed every 4 inches. For adequate protection, vertical
support posts are placed 6 feet apart, and the parallel strands of barbed wire
are from 2 to 6 inches apart. A good height is 8 feet.

Concertina fences consist of coils of steel razor wire clipped together
to form cylinders weighing about 55 pounds. Each cylinder is stretched to
form a coil-type barrier 3 feet high and 50 feet long. The ends of each 50-foot
coil need to be clipped to the next coil to obviate movement. Stakes also sta-
bilize these fences. This fence was developed by the military to act as a
quickly constructed barrier. When one coil is placed on another, they create
a 6-foot-high barrier. One coil placed on two as a base provides a pyramid-
like barrier difficult to penetrate. Concertina fences are especially helpful
for quick temporary repairs to damaged fences.

Razor ribbon or *coiled barbed tape* are increasing in popularity. They
are similar to concertina fencing in many ways. Every few inches along the
coil are sharp spikes, looking something like a sharpened bow tie.

Gates are necessary for traffic through fences. The fewer gates, the better because, like windows and doors, they are weak points along a perimeter. Gates usually are secured with a chain and padlock. Uniformed officers
stationed at each gate and fence opening increase security while enabling
the observation of people and vehicles.

Vehicle barriers control traffic and stop vehicles from penetrating a
perimeter. The problems of drive-by shootings and vehicle bombs have
resulted in greater use of vehicle barriers. These barriers are assigned gov-

ernment-certified ratings based on the level of protection; however, rating systems vary among government agencies. One agency, for example, tests barriers against 15,000-pound trucks traveling up to 50 miles per hour, while another agency tests 10,000-pound trucks traveling the same speed. *Passive vehicle barriers* are fixed and include decorative bollards, large concrete planters, specially engineered and anchored park benches, hardened fencing, fence cabling, and trees. *Active vehicle barriers* are used at entrances and include gates, barrier arms, and pop-up type systems that are set underground and, when activated, spring up to block a vehicle.[4] As we know, no security method is foolproof, and careful security planning is vital. In 1997, to protest government policy, the environmental group Greenpeace penetrated government security in Washington, DC, and dumped four tons of coal outside the Capitol building. The driver of the truck drove the wrong way up a one-way drive leading to the building.

Walls are a good substitute for fences when management is against the use of a wire fence. Attractive walls can be designed to produce security equal to fences while blending into surrounding architecture. Walls are made from a variety of materials: bricks, concrete blocks, stones, cement. Depending on design, the top of walls 6 or 7 feet high may contain barbed wire, spikes, or broken glass set in cement. Offenders often avoid injury by throwing a blanket or jacket over the top of the wall (or fence) before scaling it. Many jurisdictions prohibit ominous features at the top of barriers. Check local ordinances. An advantage of a wall is that outsiders are hindered from observing inside. However, observation by public police during patrols also is hindered; this can benefit an intruder.

Hedges or shrubbery are useful as barriers. Thorny shrubs have a deterrent value. These include holly, barberry, and multiflora rose bushes, all of which require a lot of watering. The privet hedge grows almost anywhere and requires minimal care. A combination of hedge and fence is useful. Hedges should be less than 3 feet high and placed on the inside to avoid injury to those passing by and to create an added obstacle for someone attempting to scale the fence. Any plants that are large and placed too close to buildings and other locations provide a climbing tool, cover for thieves, and a hiding place for stolen goods.

Municipal codes restrict the heights of fences, walls, and hedges to maintain an attractive environment devoid of threatening-looking barriers. Certain kinds of barriers may be prohibited to ensure conformity. Planning should encompass research of local standards.

The following list can help a security manager eliminate weak points along a perimeter or barrier.

1. Utility poles, trees, boxes, pallets, forklifts, tools, and other objects outside of a building can be used to scale a barrier.
2. Ladders left outside are a burglar's delight. Stationary ladders are made less accessible via a steel cage with a locked door.

3. A *common wall* is shared by two separate entities. Thieves may lease and occupy or just enter the adjoining building or room and then hammer through the common wall.

4. A roof is easy to penetrate. A few tools, like a drill and saw, enable offenders to actually cut through the roof. Because lighting, alarms, and patrols rarely involve the roof, this weakness is attractive to thieves. A rope ladder often is employed to descend from the roof, or a forklift might be used to lift items to the roof. Vehicle keys should be hidden and other precautions taken. Alarms, lights, patrols, and a roof fence to hinder access from an adjoining building's roof deter burglars.

5. Roof hatches, skylights, basement windows, air-conditioning and other vent and duct systems, crawl spaces between floors and under buildings, fire escapes, and utility covers may need a combination of locks, alarms, steel bars, heavy mesh, fences, and inspections. A widely favored standard is that any opening greater than 96 square inches requires increased protection.

Windows

Glazing

Two basic kinds of protective windows are bullet-resistant and burglar-resistant windows. Underwriters Laboratories classifies *bullet-resistant windows* into eight protection levels, with levels 1 to 3 rated against handguns and 4 to 8 rated against rifles. Level 4 or higher windows usually are applied by government agencies and the military. Protective windows are made of either glass or plastic or mixtures of each. *Laminated glass* absorbs a bullet as it passes through various glass layers. The advantage of glass is in its maintenance: easy to clean and less likely to scratch than plastic. It is less expensive per square foot than plastic, but heavier, which requires more workers and stronger frames. Glass has a tendency to spall (i.e., chip) when hit by a bullet. UL752-listed glass holds up to three shots, then it begins to shatter from subsequent shots. Two types of plastic used in windows are acrylic and polycarbonate. Both vary in thickness and are lighter and more easily scratched than glass. *Acrylic windows* are clear and monolithic, whereas glass and polycarbonate windows are laminates consisting of layers of material bonded one on top of the other. Acrylic, sometimes referred to by the brand name Plexiglas, will deflect bullets and hold together under sustained hits. Some spalling may occur. *Polycarbonate windows* are stronger than acrylics against high-powered weapons. In addition to protective windows, wall armor is important because employees often duck below a window during a shooting. These steel or fiberglass plates also are rated.[5]

Burglar-resistant windows are UL rated, available in acrylic and polycarbonate materials, and protect against hammers, flame, "smash and grab," and other attacks. Combined bullet- and burglar-resistant windows are available. Although window protection is an expense that may be difficult to justify, insurers offer discounts on insurance premiums for such installations.

Shatter-Resistant Film

Following the Oklahoma City bombing, considerable interest focused on the vulnerability of flying glass due not only to explosions but also accidents or natural disasters. Conversely, a report on the World Trade Center bombing in New York City claimed that the destroyed windows permitted deadly gases to escape from the building, enabling occupants to survive. Because of this controversy, and the limited objective performance data on various window films on the market, the U.S. Army Corps of Engineers is studying how different types of materials perform during bomb blasts.[6]

If you were a security director in charge of protecting a high-rise office building, would you apply shatter-resistant film to the building?

Window Protection

By covering windows with grating or security screens, additional steps have been taken to impede entrance by an intruder or items being thrown out by a dishonest employee. Window grating consists of metal bars constructed across windows. These bars run horizontally and vertically to produce an effective form of protection. Although these bars are not aesthetically pleasing, they can be purchased with attractive ornamental designs. Security screens are composed of steel or stainless steel wire (mesh) welded to a frame. Screens have some distinct advantages over window grating. Employees can pass pilfered items through window bars more easily than through a screen. Security screens look like ordinary screens, but they are much heavier in construction and can stop rocks and other objects.

When planning window protection, one must consider the need for emergency escape and ventilation. To ensure safety, certain windows can be targeted for the dismantling of window protection during business hours.

Window Locks

Businesses and institutions often contain windows that do not open. For windows that do open, a latch or lock on the inside provides some protection. The double-hung window, often applied at residences, is explained here as a foundation for window protection. It consists of top and bottom windows that are raised and lowered for user convenience. When the top window is pushed up and the bottom window pushed down, a sash lock containing a curved turnknob locks both parts of the whole window in place (see Figure 8–2). By inserting a knife under the sash lock where both window sections meet, a burglar can jimmy the latch out of its catch. If an offender breaks the glass, the sash lock can be unlocked by reaching inside. With such simple techniques known to burglars, more complicated defenses are necessary. Nails can be used to facilitate a quick escape while maintaining good window security: one drills a downward-sloping hole into the right and left sides of the window frame where the top and bottom window halves overlap and inserts nails that are thinner and longer than the holes. This enables the nails to be quickly removed during an emergency escape. If a burglar attacks the window, he or she cannot find or remove the nails (see Figure 8–2). Another method is to attach a window lock requiring a key (see Figure 8–2). These locks are capable of securing a window in a closed or slightly opened position. This can be done with the nail (and several holes) as well. The key should be hidden near the window.

Electronic Protection for Windows

Four categories of electronic protection for windows are foil, vibration, glass-breakage, and contact-switch sensors. *Window foil,* which has lost much of its popularity, consists of lead foil tape less than 1 inch wide and paper thin that is applied right on the glass near the edges of a window. In the nonalarm state, electricity passes through the foil to form a closed circuit. When the foil is broken, an alarm is sounded. Window foil is inexpensive and easy to maintain. One disadvantage is that a burglar may cut the glass without disturbing

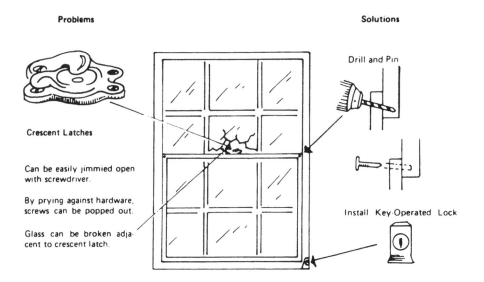

Figure 8–2 Double-hung window (view from inside).

the foil. *Vibration sensors* respond to vibration or shock. They are attached right on the glass or window frame. These sensors are noted for their low false alarm rate and are applicable to fences, walls, and valuable artwork, among other things. *Glass-breakage sensors* react to glass breaking. A sensor the size of a large coin is placed directly on the glass and can detect glass breakage several feet away. Some types operate via a tuning fork, which is tuned to the frequency produced by glass breaking. Others employ a microphone and electric amplifier. *Contact switches* activate an alarm when the contact is interrupted by opening the window. (In Figure 8–3, this sensor protects a door.)

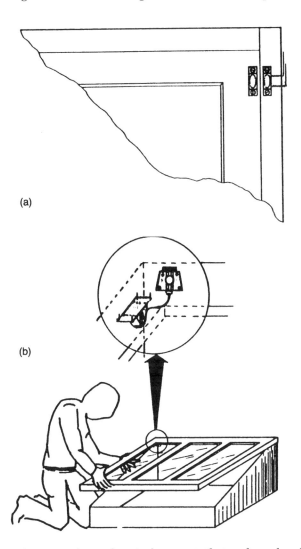

(a)

(b)

Figure 8-3   Switch sensors have electrical contacts that make or break an electrical circuit in response to a physical movement.

Additional ideas for window protection follow:

1. A strong window frame fastened to a building prevents prying and removal of the entire window.
2. First floor windows are especially vulnerable to penetration and require increased protection.
3. Consider tinting windows to hinder observation by offenders.
4. Windows (and other openings) no longer used can be bricked.
5. Expensive items left near windows invite trouble.
6. Cleaning windows and windowsills periodically increases the chances of obtaining clear fingerprints in the event of an attack.

Doors

Hollow-core doors render complex locks useless because an offender can punch right through the door. Thin wood panels or glass on the door are additional weak points. More expensive, *solid-core doors* are stronger; they are made of solid wood (over an inch thick) without the use of weak fillers. To reinforce hollow-core or solid-core doors, one can attach 16-gauge steel sheets, via one-way screws. An alternative is to install an all-metal door.

Intruding Neighbors

The Finch Brothers Supermarket Company maintained a busy warehouse stocked with hundreds of different items for local Finch supermarkets. The company leased the large warehouse to accommodate the increasing number of supermarkets. After 18 months at this location, managers were stumped as to why shrinkage was over 4 percent. Several precautions were taken to avert losses: perimeter security consisted of alarms, lighting, and a security officer. A perpetual inventory was maintained.

Eventually, Finch's loss prevention manager's job was on the line, so he began a secret, painstaking, and continuous surveillance of the warehouse at night. After an agonizing week went by, he made an astonishing discovery. A printing company building next door was only 7 feet away from the warehouse and printing company employees on the late shift were able to slide a 12′ x 16″ x 2″ board from a third-story window to a window of the same height at the warehouse. Within 30 minutes, the group of thieves hauled and threw many burlap sacks of items from one building to another. With a sophisticated camera, the manager snapped several pictures. Police were later notified and arrests made.

The thieves confessed that, when they worked the 11 P.M. to 8 A.M. shift, they stole merchandise from the warehouse. They stated that a maintenance man, who visited the warehouse each day, left the window open so the board could be slipped in. They added that dim lighting and the fact that alarms existed on the first floor only were factors that aided their crimes.

Aluminum doors generally are used by businesses and institutions. Composed of an aluminum frame, most of the door is covered by glass. Without adequate protection, the glass is vulnerable, and prying the weak aluminum is not difficult.

Whenever possible, door hinges should be placed on the inside. Door hinges that face outside enable easy entry. By using a screwdriver and hammer, one can raise the pins out of the hinges to enable the door to be lifted away. To protect the hinge pins, it is a good idea to weld them so they cannot be removed in this manner. Another form of protection is to remove two screws on opposite sides of the hinge, insert a pin or screw on the jamb side of the hinge so that it protrudes about half an inch, and then drill a hole in the opposite hole to fit the pin when the door is closed. With this method on both top and bottom hinges, even if the hinge pins are removed, the door will not fall off the hinges (see Figure 8–4).

Contact switches applied to doors offer electronic protection. Figure 8–3 illustrates their use. Greater protection is provided when contact switches are recessed in the edges of the door and frame. Other kinds of electronic sensors applied at doors include vibration sensors, pressure mats, and various types of motion detectors aimed in the area of the door.

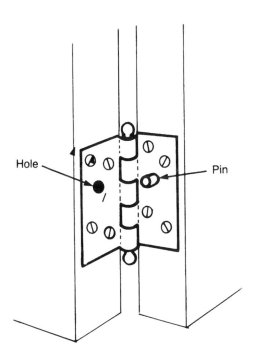

Figure 8–4   Pin to prevent removal of door.

More hints for door security follow:

1. Doors (and windows) are afforded extra protection at night by chain closures. These frequently are seen covering storefronts in malls and in high-crime neighborhoods.
2. To block "hide-in" burglars (those who hide in a building until after closing) from easy exit, require that openings such as doors and windows have a key-operated lock on the inside as well as on the outside.
3. Almost all fire departments are equipped with power saws that cut through door locks and bolts in case of fire. Many firefighters are capable of easy access to local buildings because building owners have provided keys that are located in fire trucks. Although this creates a security hazard, losses can be reduced in case of fire.
4. All doors need protection, including garage, sliding, overhead, chain-operated, and electric doors.

Intrusion Alarm Systems

Table 8–1 describes widely used intrusion alarm systems. This table will help you cut through the jungle of systems on the market. A comparison of Table 8–1 with a comprehensive 1997 article on sensors in *Security Management*, by two noted experts, showed the information in the table to be applicable today. Exceptions were that balanced capacitance was not mentioned in the article, while magnetic field was covered. A *magnetic field* consists of a series of buried wire loops or coils. Metal objects moving over the sensor induce a current and signal an alarm. According to research by Ronald W. Clifton and Martin L. Vitch, the vulnerability to defeat (VD) for magnetic field, infrared photo beam, and taut wire systems is high. Microwave, electric field, fence disturbance, seismic sensor cable, and video motion systems all have a medium VD. The VD for ported coaxial cable systems is low. Visible sensors are relatively easy to defeat but cost effective for low-security applications. Multiple sensors, and especially covert sensors, provide a higher level of protection.[7]

Fiber optics is a growing choice for intrusion detection and transmission. *Fiber optics* refers to the transportation of data by way of guided light waves in an optical fiber. This differs from the conventional transmission of electrical energy in copper wires. Fiber optic applications include video, voice, and data communications. It is more secure and less subject to interference than older methods of transmitting data.

Fiber optic perimeter protection can take the form of a fiber optic net installed on a fence. When an intruder applies stress on the cable, an infrared light source pulsing through the system notes the stress or break and activates an alarm. Optical fibers can be attached to or inserted within numerous items to signal an alarm, including razor ribbon, security grilles, windows, and doors, and it can protect valuable assets such as computers.

No one technology is perfect; many protection programs rely on dual technology to strengthen intrusion detection. When selecting a system, it is wise to remember that manufacturers' claims often are based on perfect weather. Security decision makers must clearly understand the advantages and disadvantages of each type of system under a variety of conditions.

Applications

Intrusion alarm systems can be classified according to the kind of protection provided. There are three basic kinds of protection: point, area, and perimeter. *Point protection* (see Figure 8–5) signals an alarm when an intrusion is made at a special location. It is also referred to as *spot* or *object protection*. Files, safes, vaults, jewelry counters, and artworks are targets for point protection. Capacitance and vibration systems provide point protection and are installed right on the object. These systems often are used as a backup after a burglar has succeeded in gaining access. *Area protection* (see Figure 8–6) detects an intruder in a selected area such as a main aisle in a building or at a strategic passageway. Ultrasonic, microwave, and infrared systems are applicable to area protection. *Perimeter protection* (see Figure 8–7) focuses on the outer boundary of the premises. If doors and windows are part of the perimeter, then contact switches, vibration detectors, and other devices are applicable.

Control Unit

As described in Chapter 7, intrusion alarm systems contain three major components: once a *sensor* detects an intruder, a *control unit* receives this information and activates an *annunciator* (e.g., noise or light) to summon security or police. Figure 8–8 shows a control unit with user instructions.

Alarm Signaling Systems

Alarm signaling systems transmit data from a protected area to an annunciation system. Local ordinances and codes may restrict certain systems, designate to whom the alarm may be transmitted, or limit the length of time the alarm is permitted to sound.

Local alarm systems notify, by sound or lights, people in the hearing or seeing range of the signal. This includes the intruder, who may flee. Typically, a bell rings outside of a building. Often, local alarms produce no response—in urban areas responsible action may not be taken, and in rural areas nobody may hear the alarm. These alarms are less expensive than other signaling systems but are easily defeated. If a local alarm is used during a robbery, people may be harmed.

A *central station* alarm system receives intrusion or fire signals or both at a computer console located and monitored a distance away from the protected

Table 8–1 Types of Intrusion Alarm Systems

System	Graphic Idea	Concept	Advantages	Disadvantages
Motion detection				
Fence-mounted sensor	Wire on Fence	Detection depends on movement of fence	Ease of installation; early detection on interior fence; relatively inexpensive; requires little space; follows terrain easily	Frequent false alarms (weather and birds); conduit breakage; dependent on quality, rigidity of fence, and type of installation
Seismic sensor cable (buried)	Buried cable	Detection depends on ground movement (intruder walking over buried movement sensors, or other seismic disturbances)	Good for any site shape, uneven terrain; early warning; good in warm climate with little rain	False alarms from ground vibrations (vehicles, thunderstorms, heavy snow); not recommended for heavy snow regions; difficult installation and maintenance
Balanced capacitance		Detection depends on touching of cable, interfering with balance of cable	Few false alarms; good for selected areas of fence, rooftops, curves, corners, any terrain	Not to be used independently; for selected areas only
Taut wire		Detection depends on deflecting, stretching, or releasing the tension of wire that triggers alarming mechanism	Good for any terrain or shape; can be used as interior fence; extremely low false alarm rates	Relatively expensive; possible false alarms from snow, ice, birds, etc.; temperature changes require adjustments

Energy field

		Detection	Advantages	Disadvantages
Microwave sensor		Based on line of sight; detection depends on intrusion into volumetric area above ground between transmitter and receiver	Does not require a great deal of maintenance	Not good on hilly or heavily contoured terrain; costly installation; potential false alarms caused by weather (snow, ice, wind, and rain); vegetation must be removed
Infrared photo beam sensor		Based on line of sight; detection depends on intrusion into beam(s) stacked vertically above ground	Good for short distances, building walls, and sallyports	Distances between transmitter and receiver must be short, requiring more intervals; potential false alarms by animals and weather conditions (fog, dust, snow); voltage surges
Ported coaxial cable		Detection depends on interruption of field in terms of mass, velocity, and length of time	Adaptable to most terrains	False alarms caused by heavy rain (pooling of water), high winds, tree roots; relatively expensive installation and maintenance
Video motion detection		Detection depends on change in video-monitor signal	Good for enhancing another system; good for covering weak spots	Lighting is a problem
Electric field sensor		Detection depends on penetration of volumetric field created by field wires and sensor wires	Good on hilly or heavily contoured terrain; can be freestanding or fence-mounted	Requires more maintenance; sensor wires must be replaced every 3 years; vegetation must be controlled

Sources: Information from New York State Department of Corrections, Pennsylvania Department of Corrections, and Federal Bureau of Prisons. Reproduced from U.S. Dept. of Justice, National Institute of Justice, *Stopping Escapes: Perimeter Security* (U.S. Government Printing Office, August 1987). p. 6.

Figure 8–5   Point protection.

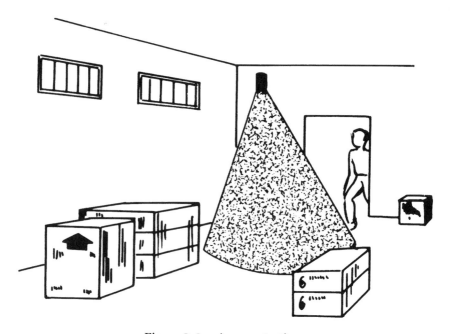

Figure 8–6   Area protection.

Figure 8–7   Perimeter protection.

location. When an alarm signal is received, central station personnel contact police, firefighters, or other responders. Central station services employ sales, installation, service, monitoring, and response personnel. Proprietary monitoring systems are similar to central station systems, except that the former does the monitoring and the system is operated by the proprietary organization.

A variety of data transmission systems are utilized to signal an alarm.[8] Telephone lines have been used for many years. Here, the earlier technology is covered first before the more modern technology.

Automatic telephone dialer systems are of two kinds: tape dialer and digital dialer. Tape dialer systems seldom are used today. They deliver a prerecorded or coded message to an interested party (e.g., central station, police department) after that party answers the telephone. Digital dialers do not use a recorded tape message; coded electronic pulses are transmitted, and an electronic terminal decodes the message onto a panel or teletype.

With *direct connect* systems the intrusion device is connected by wire directly to an alarm receiver located on the premises, at a police station, or some other location. Local ordinances may not permit direct reporting to

Figure 8–8 Alarm control unit with user instructions.

police stations. A variation of this method is the "buddy" alarm system, in which the alarm signal is transmitted via direct wire to a neighbor, who calls the police. These systems usually are silent alarms.

Radio frequency (RF) and *microwave* data transmission systems often are applied where telephone lines are not available or where hardwire lines are not practical. The components include transmitter, receiver, repeaters to extend range, battery backup, and solar power.

Fiber optic data transmission systems, as discussed earlier, transport data by way of light waves within a thin glass fiber. These cables are either underground or above ground. The components include transmitter, receiver, repeaters, battery backup, and solar power. Fiber optic systems often support computer-based multiplex data communications systems and are more secure than direct wire.

Among the advances in alarm monitoring is remote programming. By this method, a central station can perform a variety of functions without ever visiting the site. Capabilities include system arming and disarming, unlocking doors, diagnostics and corrections, and with access systems, adding or deleting cards.[9]

Alarm systems also may be multiplexed or integrated. *Multiplexing* is a method of transmitting multiple information signals over a single communications channel. This single communications channel reduces line requirements by allowing signal transmission from many protected facilities. Two other advantages are that more detailed information can be transmitted, such as telling which detector is in an alarm state, and transmission line security is enhanced through the use of encoding. *Integrated systems*, as covered in Chapter 7, combine multiple systems (e.g., alarm monitoring, access controls, and CCTV).

CCTV

Closed-circuit television allows one person to view several locations. This is a distinct advantage when protecting the boundaries of a facility, because it reduces personnel costs. An entire facility, both outside and inside, can be put under CCTV surveillance, with recording capabilities for future reference.

Television programs and movies sometimes portray an intruder penetrating a perimeter barrier by breaking through when a CCTV camera had momentarily rotated to another location. Usually the camera just misses the intruder by returning to the entry point right after the intruder gains access. Such a possibility can be averted via overlapping camera coverage. If cameras are capable of viewing other cameras, personnel can check on viewing obstructions, sabotage, vandalism, or other problems. Tamperproof housings will impede those interested in disabling cameras. Different models are resistant to bullets, explosion, dust, and severe weather. Housings are manufactured with heaters, defrosters, windshield wipers, washers, and sun shields. Low-light-level cameras provide the means to view outside when very little light is available.

An essential aspect of CCTV is proper monitoring. To reduce fatigue and ensure good quality viewing, it is a good idea to rotate personnel every two hours if possible, limit TV monitors to fewer than 10, arrange the monitors in a curved configuration in front of the viewer, control the lighting over the console to avoid glare on the monitor screens or tilt the monitors if necessary, place the monitors in an order that permits easy recognition of camera locations, provide a swivel chair that hampers the opportunity for sleeping, and assign tasks to the viewer (e.g., communications, logging). The previous chapter covers technology that has enhanced CCTV systems.

Lighting

From a business perspective, lighting can be justified because it improves sales by making a business and merchandise more attractive, promotes safety and prevents lawsuits, improves employee morale and productivity, and enhances the value of real estate. From a security perspective, two major purposes of lighting are *to create a psychological deterrent to intrusion* and *to enable detection*. Good lighting is considered such an effective crime control method that the law, in many locales, requires buildings to maintain adequate lighting.

One way to analyze lighting deficiencies is to go to the building at night and study the possible methods of entry and areas where inadequate lighting will aid a burglar. Before the visit, one should contact local police as a precaution against mistaken identity and to recruit their assistance in spotting weak points in lighting.

Negligence Caused by Lighting Deficiency

Entities have an obligation to create a safe environment through lighting. In addition to moral and societal obligations, legal responsibilities are illustrated in the Illinois case of *Fancil v.Q.S.E. Foods, Inc.* In this case, a police officer's widow won a wrongful death suit because a store owner had disconnected his backdoor light even though the location had been burglarized several times and the owner was aware that local police checked the business during the evenings. The officer was shot by a burglar hidden in a dark area. The court found the store owner guilty of negligence through his failure to provide adequate lighting.[10]

What lighting level will aid an intruder? Most people believe that under conditions of darkness a criminal can safely commit a crime. But this view may be faulty, in that one generally cannot work in the dark. Three possible levels of light are *bright light, darkness*, and *dim light*. Bright light affords an offender plenty of light to work but enables easy observation by others; it will deter crime. Without light—in darkness—a burglar finds that he or she cannot see to jimmy a door lock, release a latch, or whatever work is necessary to gain access. However, dim light provides just enough light to break and enter while hindering observation by authorities. Support for this view was shown in a study of crimes during full-moon phases, when dim light was produced. This study examined the records of 972 police shifts at three police agencies, for a two-year period, to compare nine different crimes during full-moon and non-full-moon phases. The crime showing the greatest difference between full moon and non-full-moon phases was breaking and entering.

> [T]he principle that light is a form of crime prevention could be criticized. . . . [A] threshold effect may be apparent with light. . . . [B]right light may be a deterrent to crime, but dim light (similar to moonlight) may increase the likelihood for crimes. . . . [D]imly lit houses, businesses, and streets may be an asset for offenders. . . [p]ersonnel may want to consider the dangers of dimly lit areas as a greater crime-provoking condition than darkness or bright light.[11]

Although much case law supports lighting as an indicator of efforts to provide a safe environment, security specialists are questioning conventional wisdom about lighting.[12] Because so much nighttime lighting goes unused, should it be reduced or turned off? Does an offender look more suspicious under a light or in the dark with a flashlight? Should greater use be made of motion-activated lighting? How would these approaches affect safety and cost-effectiveness? These questions are ripe for research.

What are your views on nighttime lighting?

Illumination[13]

Lumens (of light output) per watt (of power input) is a measure of lamp efficiency. Initial lumens-per-watt data are based on the light output of lamps when new; however, light output declines with use. *Illuminance* is the intensity of light falling on a surface, measured in foot-candles (English units) or lux (metric units). The *foot-candle* (FC) is the measure of how bright the light is when it reaches one foot from the source. One lux equals 0.0929 FC. The light provided by direct sunlight on a clear day is about 10,000 FC, an overcast day would yield about 100 FC, and a full moon about 0.01 FC. A sample of outdoor lighting illuminances recommended by the Illuminating Engineering Society of North America are self-parking area, 1 FC; attendant parking area, 2 FC; covered parking area, 5 FC; active pedestrian entrance, 5 FC; building surroundings, 1 FC. It generally is recommended that gates and doors, where identification of persons and things takes place, should have at least 2 FC. An office should have a light level of about 50 FC.

Care should be exercised when studying FC. Are they horizontal or vertical? Horizontal illuminance may not aid in the visibility of vertical objects such as signs and keyholes. (The preceding FC are horizontal.) FC vary depending on the distance from the lamp and the angle. If you hold a light meter horizontally, it often gives a different reading than if you hold it vertically. Are the FC initial or maintained? Maintenance and bulb replacement ensure high-quality lighting.

Although instruments can measure light levels, a reasonable rule of thumb is that, at night, outside of a building or at a parking lot, one should be able to read a driver's license or newspaper with some eyestrain.

Lamps[14]

The following lamps are applied outdoors:

- *Incandescent* lamps are commonly found at residences. Light is produced by passing electrical current through a tungsten wire that becomes white hot. These lamps produce 10 to 20 lumens per watt, are the least efficient and most expensive to operate, and have a short lifetime of from 1000 to 2000 hours.
- *Halogen* and *quartz halogen* lamps are incandescent bulbs filled with halogen gas (like sealed-beam auto headlights) and provide about 25 percent better efficiency and life than ordinary incandescent bulbs.
- *Fluorescent* lamps pass electricity through a gas enclosed in a glass tube to produce light, producing 40 to 80 lumens per watt. They create twice the light and less than half the heat of an incandescent bulb of equal wattage and cost 5 to 10 times as much. Fluorescent lamps do not provide high levels of light output. The lifetime is 10,000 to 15,000 hours. They are not used extensively outdoors, except for signage.
- *Mercury vapor* lamps also pass electricity through a gas. The yield is 30 to 60 lumens per watt and the life is about 20,000 hours.
- *Metal halide* lamps are also of the gaseous type. The yield is 80 to 100 lumens per watt, and the life is about 10,000 hours. They often are used at sports stadiums because they imitate daylight conditions and colors appear natural. Consequently, these lamps complement CCTV systems, but they are the most expensive light to install and maintain.
- *High pressure sodium* lamps are gaseous, yield about 100 lumens per watt, have a life of about 20,000 hours, and are energy efficient. These lamps are often applied on streets and parking lots, cut through fog, and are designed to allow the eyes to see more detail at greater distances.

- *Low pressure sodium* are gaseous, produce 150 lumens per watt, have a life of about 15,000 hours, and are even more efficient than high pressure sodium. These lamps are expensive to maintain.

Each type of lamp has a different *color rendition*, which is the way a lamp's output affects human perceptions of color. Incandescent, fluorescent, and certain types of metal halide lamps provide excellent color rendition. Mercury vapor lamps provide good color rendition but are heavy on the blue. High pressure sodium lamps, which are used extensively outdoors, provide poor color rendition, making things look yellow. Low pressure sodium lamps make color unrecognizable and produce a yellow-gray color on objects. People find sodium vapor lamps, sometimes called *anticrime lights*, to be harsh because they produce a strange yellow haze. Claims are made that this lighting conflicts with aesthetic values and that it affects sleeping habits. In many instances, when people park their vehicles in a parking lot during the day and return to find their vehicle at night, they are often unable to locate it due to poor color rendition from sodium lamps; some report their vehicle as being stolen. Another problem is the inability of witnesses to describe offenders accurately.

Mercury vapor, metal halide, and high pressure sodium take several minutes to produce full light output. If they are turned off, even more time is required to reach full output because they first have to cool down. This may not be acceptable for certain security applications. Incandescent, halogen, and quartz halogen have the advantage of instant light once electricity is turned on. Manufacturers can provide information on a host of lamp characteristics including the "strike" and "restrike" time.

The following three sources provide additional information on lighting:

- *National Lighting Bureau*
  1300 N. 17th Street, Suite 1847
  Rosslyn, VA 22209
  301-587-9572
  Publications.
- *Illuminating Engineering Society of North America*
  120 Wall Street, Floor 17
  New York, NY 10005
  212-248-5000
  Technical materials and services; many members are engineers.
- *International Association of Lighting Management Companies*
  214 Oakwood Avenue
  Newark, OH 43055
  515-243-2360
  Seminars, training, and certification programs.

Lighting Equipment

A variety of lighting equipment is on the market. For instance, streetlights are stationary and part of a continuous lighting system. Incandescent or gaseous discharge lamps are used in streetlights. Fresnel lights have a wide flat beam that is directed outward to protect a perimeter, glaring in the faces of those approaching. A floodlight "floods" an area with a beam of light, resulting in considerable glare. Floodlights are stationary, although the light beams can be aimed to select positions. Manufacturers provide catalogues on the numerous components of lighting systems.

The following strategies reinforce good lighting:

1. Locate perimeter lighting to allow illumination of both sides of the barrier.
2. Direct lights down and away from a facility to create glare for an intruder. Make sure the directed lighting does not hinder observation by patrolling officers.
3. Do not leave dark spaces between lighted areas for burglars to move within. Design lighting to permit overlapping illumination.
4. Protect the lighting system: locate lighting inside the barrier, install protective covers over lamps, mount lamps on high poles, bury power lines, and protect switch boxes.
5. Photoelectric cells will enable lights to go on and off automatically in response to natural light. Manual operation is helpful as a backup.
6. Consider motion-activated lighting for external and internal areas.
7. If lighting is required in the vicinity of navigable waters, contact the U.S. Coast Guard.
8. Try not to disturb neighbors by intense lighting.
9. Maintain a supply of portable, emergency lights and auxiliary power in the event of a power failure.
10. Good interior lighting also deters burglars. Having lights over safes, expensive merchandise, and other valuables, and large clear windows (especially in retail establishments), lets passing patrol officers see in.
11. If necessary, join other business owners to petition local government to install improved streetlighting.

Parking Lot and Vehicle Controls

In the previous chapter, considerable attention focused on access controls. This chapter stresses parking lot and vehicle controls as integral components of access controls.

A well-designed parking lot is a chief prerequisite to construction. Space usually is limited, and the layout of parking spaces and traffic lanes demands care. Employee access control to a building is easier when a parking lot is on one side of a building rather than surrounding the building. If possible, a parking lot should be located a reasonable distance from buildings and have a complete perimeter fence so that the lot is separated from buildings. These characteristics dissuade employees and others from parking vehicles near shipping and receiving docks, garbage dumpsters, and other locations near buildings. Furthermore, while employees and visitors walk to their vehicles, they are funneled through gates for observation.

Executives and other employees should have permanent parking stickers, whereas visitors, delivery people, and service groups should be given a temporary pass to be displayed on the windshield. Stickers and passes allow uniformed officers to locate unauthorized vehicles. Tight accountability of the stickers and passes frustrates abuses. By communicating relevant policies and procedures, via memos and signs, people will know what is expected of them.

Parking lots are more secure when these specific strategies are applied: security patrols, panic buttons and emergency phones, lighting, and CCTV. At certain times, patrols and stationary posts are in greater need. For example, shift changes, breaks, and meal times produce heavy traffic and opportunities for theft. But employee theft is not the only danger. Management has an obligation to protect employees from street crimes. Assault, rape, robbery, and larceny committed in parking areas can harm morale and create lawsuits, unless employees (and customers) are protected. Hospitals, for example, supply an escort for nurses who walk to their vehicles after late shifts. Employee vehicles also require protection, or else stereos, batteries, and other property will disappear. Employee education about personal safety, locking vehicles, and additional precautions will cut losses. Furthermore, the threat of drive-by shootings and vehicle bombs may necessitate vehicle barriers as discussed earlier in the chapter.

Certain types of equipment can aid a parking lot safety program. Cushman patrol vehicles, capable of traveling through narrow passageways, increase patrol mobility, provide shelter during adverse weather, contain lights for night viewing, and are inexpensive to operate. Bicycles are another option. Loss prevention booths or guardhouses (unfortunately called *guard shacks* at times) are useful as command posts in parking lots. They may include a telephone, portable radios, weapons, records, parking stickers and passes, heating and cooling units, and restrooms. Raising the floor at least 2 feet above the ground for increased visibility and locating the booth near a main entrance or gate will enhance its effectiveness.

Security Officers

Officers normally are assigned to stationary (fixed) posts or to patrol. A *stationary post* is at a door or gate where people, vehicles, and objects are observed and inspected. Stationary posts also involve directing traffic or duty at a command post where communications, CCTV, and alarms are monitored. *Foot or vehicle patrols* conducted throughout the premises and along perimeters identify irregularities while deterring offenders. Examples of unusual or harmful conditions that should be reported are damaged security devices, holes in perimeter fences or other evidence of intrusion, hidden merchandise, unattended vehicles parked inappropriately, keys left in vehicles, employees sleeping in vehicles or using drugs, blocked fire exits, cigarette butts in no-smoking areas, accumulations of trash, and odors from fuels or other combustibles.

Officers assigned to either stationary posts or patrols are obligated by the nature of their position to strive to provide a safe and secure environment for people and assets. In contrast to public police officers, private security officers act in primarily a preventive role and *observe and report.*

Before security officers are employed, farsighted planning ensures optimum effectiveness of this service. What are the unique characteristics of the location? What assets need protection? How many hours per day is the facility open? How many employees? How many visitors and vehicles are admitted daily? What are the particular vulnerabilities? How will security officers interact with other loss prevention measures?

Security officers are expensive. Wages, insurance, uniforms, equipment, and training add up to a hefty sum per officer per year. If each officer costs $25,000 per year for a proprietary force and 5 officers are required for the premises at all times, to maintain all shifts seven days per week requires approximately 20 officers. The cost would be about $500,000 per year.

Several specific steps can be taken to improve the effectiveness of officers. Three of the most critical are *careful applicant screening, sound training,* and *proper supervision.* Management should ensure that officers know what is expected of them. Policies, procedures, and day-to-day duties are communicated via verbal orders, memos, and training programs. Policies should ensure that supervisors check on officers every hour. Irregular, unpredictable patrols hinder offenders. Rotating officers reduces fatigue while familiarizing them with a variety of duties. Providing inspection lists for adverse conditions will keep them mentally alert. The formal list should be returned with a daily report. Courtesy and a sharp appearance command respect from employees and visitors.

Monitoring Officers

Historically, *watchclocks* have been used to monitor officer patrols along preplanned routes. This older technology is carried by the officer while on patrol. It is a timepiece that contains a paper tape or disc divided into time segments. The watchclock is operated by an officer via keys mounted in walls at specific locations along the patrol route. These keys are often within metal boxes and chained to walls. When inserted into the watchclock, the key makes an impression in the form of a number on the tape or disc (see Figure 8–9). Supervisor examination of this will show whether the officer visited each key location and completed the scheduled route. It is

Figure 8–9   Watchclock.

best to locate the keys at vulnerable locations (e.g., entry points, flammable storage areas).

Lower burglary and fire insurance premiums are possible through the use of monitored patrols. Records may be subjected to inspection by insurance personnel. Good supervision thwarts officers from disconnecting all the keys, bringing them to one location for use in the watchclock, and thus avoiding patrols.

Automatic monitoring systems are another way to monitor patrols. With this system, key stations are visited according to a preplanned time schedule and route. If an officer does not visit a key station within a specific time period, a central monitoring station receives a transmitted signal. At the central station, a receiver prints a record of the time and location of the key stations visited and those not visited. After a signal indicates that a key station was not visited, an attempt is made to communicate with the patrol officer. If contact cannot be made, personnel are dispatched.

Bar-code technology provides another avenue for monitoring patrols (see Figure 8–10). Officers are assigned a scanner the size of a pen or credit card and a keypad for use when a bar-coded label will not read. While on patrol, an officer scans bar codes located at critical points, such as at doorways. Officers also carry a pocket-size book of bar codes representing various conditions; these bar codes are scanned when appropriate. One great advantage of this technology is that bar-coded labels can be removed and placed at critical locations as conditions change without the installation expense of traditional key stations.[15]

Armed versus Unarmed Officers

The question of whether to arm officers is controversial. Probably the best way to answer this question is to study the nature of the particular officer's assignment. If valuable assets are being protected and robbery or

Figure 8–10   Security officer using a Data Scanner to record security activities from a bar code. Courtesy: TISCOR, San Diego, CA.

some other type of violent crime is probable, then officers should be armed. Officers assigned to locations where violent crimes are unlikely do not need weapons. Industrial plants producing inexpensive merchandise and select institutions that are rarely confronted with violent criminal acts are examples of sites at which weapons become unnecessary and even offensive.

If weapons are issued to officers, proper selection of officers and training are of the utmost importance. Instructions on the use of force and firearms safety, as well as practice on the firing range every four months, will reduce the chances of accidents, mistakes, and costly lawsuits.

The question of whether more or fewer security officers are being armed is difficult to answer. Only 12 states track armed versus unarmed officers; and of these, only 6 maintain statistics for consecutive years. In the 12 states, the percentage of armed officers averaged 10 to 20 percent.[16] The viewpoint that the number of armed security officers is declining and will be at 5 percent by the year 2000, especially because of the liability issue, as stated by the second Hallcrest report, may be faulty and awaits further research.

Communications and the Control Center

As emergency personnel know, the ability to communicate over distance is indispensable. Every officer should be equipped with a portable two-way radio; this communication aid permits officers to summon assistance and notify superiors about hazards and impending disasters. Usually, officers on assignment communicate with a control center that is the hub of the loss prevention program. The control center is the appropriate site for a console containing alarm indicators, CCTV monitors, door controls, the public address system, and an assortment of other components for communication and loss prevention (see Figure 8–11). Because personnel will seek guidance from the control center in the event of an emergency, that center must be secure and operational at all times. The control center is under increased protection against forced entry, tampering, or disasters when it contains a locked door, is located in a basement or underground, and is constructed of fire-resistant materials. An automatic, remotely operated lock, released by the console operator after identifying the caller, also enhances security. Retail stores and other locations, where customers and visitors are common, often allow observation of the control center through a large glass window. This approach, although debatable, has merit as a deterrent. Bullet-resistant glass is wise for high-crime locations. Whoever designs the control center should be well versed in human engineering, which deals with the efficient partnership between people and machines. Human engineering results in an improved working environment and reduced fatigue and mistakes. For instance, rotating chairs and wraparound consoles permit easy reach by the operator. An acoustically treated control room absorbs excess noise (a cause

Figure 8–11   Security officer at console managing access control, CCTV, alarm monitoring, and video imaging. Courtesy: Diebold, Inc.

of fatigue) from alarms, printers, and other devices. A raised floor of the kind often built for a computer room facilitates wiring changes and expansion.

Protective Dogs

Classified as an animal barrier, a dog can strengthen security around a protected location. An *alarm dog* patrols inside a fenced area or building and barks at the approach of a stranger but makes no attempt to attack. These dogs retreat when threatened but continue to bark. Such barking may become so alarming to an intruder that he or she will flee. A *guard or attack dog* is similar to an alarm dog with an added feature of attacking the intruder. Serious problems develop if a dog escapes and attacks someone. To minimize the possibility of a lawsuit, these dogs should be selectively applied, adequately fenced in, and warning signs posted. An experienced person on call at all times is needed to respond to emergencies. Another type of attack dog is the *sentry dog*. This dog is kept on a leash and responds to commands while patrolling with a uniformed officer. The advantages are numerous. These animals protect officers. Their keen sense of hearing and smell is a tremendous asset when trying to locate a hidden burglar (or explosives or drugs). Dogs can discern the slightest perspiration from people under stress, enabling the dog to sense those individuals who are afraid of them. An ingredient in stress perspiration irritates dogs, which makes frightened persons more susceptible to attack. When an "attack" command is given, a German shepherd has the strength in its jaws to break a person's arm.

In addition to the possibility of a lawsuit if a dog attacks someone, there are other disadvantages to the use of dogs. If a proprietary dog is part of the protective team, personnel and kennel facilities are needed to care for the dogs. These costs and others include the purchase of dogs and their training, medical care, and food. Using a contract service would eliminate some of these costs and would probably be more feasible. Another disadvantage is the possibility that dogs may be poisoned, anesthetized, or killed. A burglar also may befriend a dog. Dogs should be taught to accept food only from the handler. Neighbors near the protected premises often find dogs noisy or may perceive them as offensive for other reasons.

Which strategies do you view as affording the best protection against unauthorized entry? Support your answer.

The Aura of Loss Prevention

An *aura* is a distinctive atmosphere surrounding something. When something is *mystifying* it perplexes the mind and becomes mysterious. If an aura of mystification is projected from loss prevention devices and personnel, an added dimension enhances the effectiveness of loss prevention programming. How is this accomplished? The primary requirements are supportive management and professional personnel. Both management and personnel must maintain secrecy concerning what security devices are present and how they operate, what patrol and investigative procedures exist, system weaknesses, and other topics not requiring disclosure. The more a criminal knows, the better he or she can predict the defenses and plan an attack. Discretion is advised when releasing information. Safety and fire protection information is important for everyone. But signs can help project an aura of mystification by stating that the premises are protected by a sophisticated system of hidden alarms, surveillance devices, and patrols. These signs also can state that trespassers will be prosecuted. Signs should be placed along perimeter lines, at openings, and inside buildings. Such an aura is capable of producing a strong *psychological deterrent*. The offender (insider or outsider) would perceive danger and risk from an attempted attack and thereby become discouraged, considering success to be unlikely.

Is an "aura of loss prevention" really possible? Why or why not?

Additional Strategies

Loss prevention programming is never static. Offenders repeatedly test defenses for weaknesses. Losses are averted when strategies are superior to the arsenal of the offender. Effective loss prevention programming constantly changes to reduce never-ending threats from innovative criminals or technological breakthroughs. Practitioners who stay abreast of the state of the art are better prepared to hold down losses.

People are the backbone of any loss prevention program. If they can be motivated, productivity surely will result. Managers should pay personnel bonuses when major weaknesses in defenses are detected or when intruders are apprehended. Some type of monetary or symbolic reward boosts morale and creates an incentive.

Neighbors in the vicinity of the premises may add considerable surveillance capabilities to defenses. Careful selection is advised; the loss prevention manager should make a personal visit. One or two residents on each side of the facility can provide added protection. Retired people, who often are home, may be eager for this opportunity. Debris along a common fence should be removed to allow a clearer view. The company might pay neighbors a small reward for reporting an alarm, a truly suspicious activity, a fire, or other problems.

International Perspective: UN Efforts at Global Crime Prevention

In 1951, the United Nations established the Ad Hoc Advisory Committee of Experts to advise the UN on crime matters. In 1971, the group's name changed to the Committee on Crime Prevention and Control.

Several strategies are employed by the UN to prevent crime and improve justice. The UN fosters UN norms in national legislation, conducts research, and provides technical expertise to countries. Every five years since 1955, the UN holds a congress on crime issues, where successful policies and strategies are shared.[17]

According to the UN, the global crime picture is not an encouraging one and the crime rate at the turn of the century may be four times higher than it was in 1975. In light of the crime problem, the UN asked its member states to prepare an inventory of crime prevention measures so the information can be published and shared worldwide. The inventory focuses on four sections:

- *Crime Prevention through Social Measures.* This approach tackles the root causes of crime and works to improve the family, schools, activities for youth, employment, and health.

- *Situational Crime Prevention.* These measures involve the management, design, or manipulation of the environment to reduce opportunities for criminal behavior and increase the risk for the offender. Specific strategies include hardening the target through security surveys, building and design codes, publicity and awareness campaigns, and insurance incentives to install physical security. Additional measures are marking property, natural surveillance (i.e., designing the inside and outside of buildings so people can more easily observe others), neighborhood watch, and citizen patrols.
- *Community Crime Prevention.* This approach recognizes that physical security should be part of a broader, community-based response to crime. Crime can be prevented through housing policies that decentralize housing management, provide maintenance and caretaking services, speed up renting and transfers to reduce the number of vacant properties, and encourage a sense of cohesion among residents. Community policing and multiagency cooperation are also a part of this approach.
- *Planning, Implementation, and Evaluation of Crime Prevention.* The first step in this approach is an analysis of crime and victimization. By compiling and analyzing the location and nature of offenses and many other characteristics of crime, crime prevention planning and implementation are enhanced. Evaluation assesses whether preventive measures were successful.[18]

In essence, crime is a global problem and many of the crime prevention methods employed in the United States also are employed overseas. The UN is asking member nations to compile and share their ideas on how best to reduce crime.

CASE PROBLEMS

8A. Study the characteristics of Woody's Lumber Company, the Smith Shirt manufacturing plant, and Compulab Corporation (Figures 7–1, 7–2, and 7–3). Establish a priority list of what you think are the 10 most important countermeasures for each location to prevent unauthorized entry. Why did you select as top priorities your first three strategies from each list?

8B. As a security manager for a corporation, you made several written recommendations to management to improve perimeter security at corporate headquarters located in a suburban environment. Management rejected your plans because "headquarters will look like a prison." What measures can you include in your new plan that provide security and are aesthetically pleasing?

8C. As a newly hired security manager for an office building, a site for research and development, you are faced with three immediate challenges:

(1) some employees are not wearing required ID badges from when they first enter the building to when they depart; (2) during off-hours there are too many security system false alarms; and (3) public police are responding to about half of these alarms. What do you do?

NOTES

1. Oscar Newman, *Defensible Space* (New York: Macmillan, 1972).
2. Ralph B. Taylor and Adele V. Harrell, *Physical Environment and Crime* (Washington, DC: National Institute of Justice, May 1996), pp. 1–32.
3. Richard S. Post and Arthur A. Kingsbury, *Security Administration: An Introduction*, 3rd ed. (Springfield, IL: Charles C Thomas Publishing Co., 1977), pp. 502–503.
4. Tim True, "Raising the Ramparts," *Security Management* (October 1996): 49–53.
5. Sharon Durst, "Dodging the Bullet," *Security Management* (October 1996): 55–58.
6. "Framing the Debate on Window Safety," *Security Management* (August 1996): 13.
7. Ronald W. Clifton and Martin L. Vitch, "Getting a Sense for Danger," *Security Management* (February 1997): 57–61.
8. See Robert L. Barnard, *Intrusion Detection Systems*, 2nd ed. (Boston: Butterworth–Heinemann, 1988).
9. Kerry Lydon, "Alarm Monitoring: What's New, What's Next," *Security* (August 1988): 52–55.
10. U.S. Department of Justice, *Report of the Task Force on Private Security* (Washington, DC: U.S. Government Printing Office, 1976), p. 183.
11. Philip P. Purpura, "Police Activity and the Full Moon," *Journal of Police Science and Administration* 7, no. 3 (September 1979): 350.
12. Henri Berube, "New Notions of Night Light," *Security Management* (December 1994): 29–33.
13. National Lighting Bureau, *Lighting for Safety and Security* (Washington, DC: National Lighting Bureau, n.d.), pp. 1–36; Mary S. Smith, *Crime Prevention Through Environmental Design in Parking Facilities* (Washington, DC: National Institute of Justice, April 1996), pp. 1–4; Dan M. Bowers, "Let There Be Light," *Security Management* (September 1995): 103–111; Douglas R. Kunze and John Schiefer, "An Illuminating Look at Light," *Security Management* (September 1995): 113–116.
14. Ibid.
15. "Bar-Code Technology for Security Patrol," *Security Management: Protecting Property, People and Assets* (April 10, 1989): 1–7.
16. Sherry Harowitz, "A Shot in the Dark" *Security Management* (October 1995): 47.
17. United Nations, "Work of the United Nations in Crime Prevention and Criminal Justice," *Crime Prevention and Criminal Justice* (June 1993): 1–19.
18. Eighth United Nations Congress on the Prevention of Crime and the Treatment of Offenders, *Inventory of Comprehensive Crime Prevention Measures* (Havana, Cuba, September 1990).

9

Services and Devices: Methods Toward Wise Purchasing Decisions

OBJECTIVES

After studying this chapter the reader will be able to

1. Discuss the dangers when purchasing security/loss prevention services and devices;
2. List five specific purchasing rules;
3. List guidelines and inquisitive questions that improve purchasing decisions when obtaining security services;
4. List guidelines and inquisitive questions that improve purchasing decisions when obtaining security devices.

One topic often neglected in the security literature focuses on how to make wise purchasing decisions when obtaining security services and devices. Are security specialists wise consumers? The best security plans are useless when poor purchasing decisions are made to implement those plans. *Services* refers to activities performed by personnel to further the goals of security and loss prevention. Uniformed officers, commonly referred to as *contract guards*, represent a large part of available services. *Devices* refers to manufactured items and systems that increase security and prevent losses. This chapter emphasizes security services and devices, keeping in mind the understanding that fire protection and safety are integral components of an effective loss prevention program.

Most business executives and institutional administrators do not know how to select security services or devices or even what questions to ask vendors. Frequently, money is wasted and the results after the purchases are made are disappointing. A specialist in the field who is not a salesperson can improve decision making.

During their careers loss prevention practitioners are most likely to purchase all kinds of services and devices. Purchasing decisions have a definite impact on career opportunities and on the success of loss prevention programs. Care is required during decision making to obtain the best services and devices for the money at hand. This task is difficult when one is confronted with a multitude of salespeople and a varied market that is taking in billions of dollars per year.

THE DANGERS OF PURCHASING

Suppliers of services and devices are not immune to the temptation to be involved in unethical and illegal activities. Vendors (sellers) have been known to misrepresent information, exaggerate, lie, and fail to deliver what was promised. The rotten-apple syndrome is prevalent in this industry just as it is in other facets of life—there are unscrupulous vendors as well as honest ones. Even honest vendors occasionally may act in an unethical manner when attractive sums of money are at stake. Thus, the profit motive produces a minefield of dangers for the purchaser.

A U.S. Department of Justice publication, *Private Police in the United States: Findings and Recommendations*, states:

> On the basis of regulatory-agency reports of the number of complaints filed and the reasons for licenses being suspended and revoked, and on the basis of impressions gleaned from security executives, we conclude that substantial dishonesty and poor business practices exist. The former entails common crimes by some security employees and employers, including burglary, robbery, theft, and extortion. The latter include franchising licenses, operating without a license, failure to perform services paid for, misrepresenting price or service to be performed, and negligence in performing security duties.[1]

Purchasers of security officer services may be billed for hours not worked. Because this service industry is so competitive, some companies bid very low, knowing that they will have to bill the client for phantom services (services not rendered) to make a profit. Other companies lie to clients about training and experience. Promised supervision may not take place. Liability insurance coverage may be exaggerated or nonexistent.

Investigative companies that conduct overt and undercover investigations are known to deceive clients about excessive losses through scary weekly reports in order to lengthen investigations and thereby reap greater profits. Various types of investigative services abuse clients and have an adverse impact on other reputable services. George O'Toole, in *The Private Sector*, writes about dishonest reporting by credit investigators:

> Given such brief and sometimes imaginary interviewing, it might well be wondered how the Retail Credit investigators can report anything of sub-

stance about the people on their lists. Nevertheless they manage to, and four former field men testified to a Senate investigating committee that they were given quotas requiring them to turn up derogatory information on from 6 to 10 percent of all insurance applicants. Obviously the harried gossip brokers of Retail Credit are under considerable pressure to come up with some dirt; when none can be found, there must be strong temptation to invent it.[2]

Techniques employed by people selling devices include selling unneeded devices and equipment. Alarm systems composed of outdated technology, which are overstocked at warehouses, are pushed on buyers who do not realize that burglars can easily defeat these systems. Salespeople conveniently delete information concerning extra personnel needed, additional hardware required, software problems, and expensive maintenance. *One specific tactic involves reinforcing the purchaser's fear.* Crime, fire, and accident dangers are intertwined within high-pressure sales pitches. Newspapers aid salespeople by providing locations where crimes, fires, and accidents occur.

The Consumer Federation of America, in a study for the U.S. Department of Housing and Urban Development, found that burglar alarm systems worth less than $750 were being sold for over $5000, plus finance charges. Contractors then sold the loan contracts to finance companies or savings and loan companies at a discount. When customers called about system malfunctions, it was discovered that the contractor was no longer owed any money, thus reducing the ability to rectify the problem.[3]

Most salespeople are not dishonest. Many vendors adhere to ethical conduct. The point of the industry criticism is that the buyer should be aware of these practices when confronted with a purchasing decision.

The *Report of the Task Force on Private Security* and the first Hallcrest report stated several recommendations for improving the services and devices industry with the consumer in mind. For example, both reports favor certified training for alarm service personnel.[4]

The following five cardinal rules, designed with the consumer in mind, can put the buyer on the road toward making wise purchasing decisions:

1.   Buyer beware.
2.   Properly evaluate the needs of the organization to be protected.
3.   Acquire information and know the state of the art.
4.   Analyze the advantages and disadvantages of each service or device.
5.   Avoid panic buying.

A survey of the premises will assist the buyer in pinpointing weaknesses and evaluating needs. If the buyer has a list of weaknesses and needs, the salesperson will be hindered from influencing the buyer into purchasing something unnecessary. To acquire information about services and devices, five beneficial sources are *trade publications, peers, salespeople, consultants,* and *college and training courses.* When the advantages and disadvantages of whatever is to be bought are analyzed, decision-making capabilities are improved and mistakes are less probable. Panic buying and an emotional reaction to a loss can render these efforts useless. Executives are particularly susceptible to panic buying after a loss, and salespeople know this. To avoid panic buying, the buyer should wait at least 24 hours before making purchases, calm down, and concentrate on the other four cardinal rules.

Is the security industry the only industry where the buyer should beware? Support your answer.

PURCHASING SERVICES

Contract Security Officers

When it is decided to engage a contract company, how can one know when a company is a competent one? Answers to the following questions will improve decision making:

1. Does the company conform to state and local regulatory law, such as registration, licensing, training, and bonding?
2. What is the contract company's liability and other insurance coverage? Request copies of policies. Are there any lawsuits pending against the company?
3. Have there been any EEO complaints against the company?
4. What is the company's Dun and Bradstreet financial rating?
5. Is the company willing to customize service for client company needs?
6. Does the company have the ability to provide extra officers?
7. Can the company perform expanded services, such as investigations?
8. Have you been invited to visit the company's offices?
9. Have you read the employment application form and company publications (e.g., orders, regulations, training literature)?
10. What type of background screening is employed for applicants? Can you set up an agreement whereby your company interviews officers before assignment? Do you require personnel folders to help you select the best candidates?
11. How often during a shift does a supervisor visit?
12. How does the company ensure the honesty of its officers?
13. How are disciplinary problems handled?

14. In general, how is morale? What is the turnover rate?
15. What is the extent of training? Topics in training programs should include laws of arrest, search and seizure guidelines, use of force, weapons, patrol procedures, fire protection, safety, report writing, and other subjects required by state or local law.
16. What equipment is supplied to officers?
17. What are the pay scales and benefits?
18. What is the wage-to-rate ratio? This shows the portion of the total rate received by each officer. The norm is the low to middle 60 percentile.
19. Don't expect honesty to all answers. Some vendors have standard lies!

Many security firms draft their contracts so that much of the risk is on the customer. An attorney should review contracts and negotiate changes. It is important that both parties know the amount of duty the security company is agreeing to. The contract should specify number of officers and hours, location of officers and equipment (e.g., foot or motorized, radio). If, for example, an assault takes place on the tenth floor of a building, the security company may go back to the contract and read that an officer was assigned only to the lobby and that more services were available, but the client refused.[5]

When dealing with contract companies, it is good to know the views of these business people: many of the managers in contract guard companies refer to their vocation as a "nickel-and-dime-business" with a "never-ending turnover of bodies." The former comment refers to the awarding of contracts by clients based on slim differences in bids. The latter comment refers to the high turnover of officers because of low wages. These views have considerable validity. However, when a manager allows such "facts of life" to demoralize him or her and interfere with the ability to strive for contracts, then alternative employment is best.

International Perspective: Are China's Private Security Services Superior to Those of the United States?[6]

Security service companies (SSC) are crime control organizations set up in post-Mao China. They perform security services similar to those in the United States.

As foreign investments increased in China, several questions evolved concerning the security of businesses. Foreign companies refused to have a police-controlled security force inside their companies. At the same time, Chinese police will not allow private security forces controlled by foreign owners. This dilemma lead to the SSC, a buffer in which foreign managers feel comfortable and the police retain a certain amount of control.

continued

The SSC is characterized by the following:

- The SSC concept has spread throughout China. The services offered depend on the contract with the client and include gate keeping, patrol, fire protection, escort for valuables, and selling security equipment.
- SSC security officers are equipped with uniforms, a badge and ID, "nonoffensive tools," and cars. They search, detain, and arrest.
- It is an independent organization whose managers assume responsibility for profit and loss.
- It works on a fee-for-service design by contracting with clients.
- Each SSC must be approved by the government and police, issued a license, and its service fees are controlled by a government agency.
- The police play a heavy role in SSC organization, management, screening of security officers, and training. The SSC leaders are civilians, often retired police or police demobilized for SSC service. The police also control the profits of the SSC.
- Proponents of the SSC claim that crime is a growing problem that community crime control and police are not able to curb and SSC profits can be diverted to public crime control programs.
- Detractors claim that pay for service in public security is an illicit levy.
- One problem is that many nonprofit security forces have changed their names to SSC to make a profit and this leads to disorganization of community crime prevention. Some SSCs sell nonsecurity merchandise and use their license to run other businesses.
- Security services in Western societies are characterized by low pay, high turnover, and difficulty in justifying high-quality training. The SSC pays a stable income, has lower turnover, and requires from one to three months of training.

Do you view China's private security services as superior to those of the United States? Support your answer.

Contract Undercover Investigators

A common scenario in businesses is the panic atmosphere after the discovery of a high inventory-shrinkage statistic following an inventory. When this happens, management wants immediate action even when it is predisposed to avoid panic buying. An outside firm specializing in undercover investigations often is recruited by management. The undercover investigator secretly infiltrates employee informal groups, as a regular employee, to gather information about losses.

With an understanding of how contract undercover investigation services operate, the client will obtain better results. When speaking to a service representative, the client needs to find out the cost and probable length of the investigation. These investigations last from six to eight weeks but may require months to yield success. The cost varies from $500 to $1000 per week depending on the expertise needed and the number of investigators. The client should ask the representative about the backgrounds of investigators, selection methods (for employment and assignment), training, and supervision. Are investigators bonded? Proof should be provided. Are they prepared to testify in court, if necessary? How many reports will the client receive each week? Undercover investigators send reports to their immediate supervisor, who edits them before sending a report to the home of the client. The reporting phase of the investigation is when unscrupulous activity by the service company may take place. Supervisors are known to withhold from clients good information to submit later during "dry weeks," when no substantial information is uncovered. Reports may be repeatedly exaggerated. Frightening reports about losses can scare clients into paying for unnecessarily lengthy investigations. When clients become impatient and ask why the investigation is taking so long, sometimes the service company response is that "a break in the case is right around the corner and we just need a few more weeks." If put under excessive pressure by supervisors, investigators may succumb to exaggerated reports and may even invent information. Although these practices produce a negative image of undercover investigative services, not all of these companies are unethical. Undercover investigations are a widely used and effective method to combat losses.

Consultants

Why would an executive require the services of a loss prevention consultant? Two major reasons are that (1) the executive lacks knowledge about loss prevention and the absence of a proprietary loss prevention practitioner or (2) the executive is a loss prevention practitioner but lacks expertise in a specialized field.

A consultant is commonly called in when a loss problem needs to be corrected; for instance, a baffling shrinkage problem, the loss of trade secrets, or numerous workplace accidents. Consultants also can be a tremendous asset when an organization is contemplating a loss prevention program for the first time or when an established program suffers from morale or training problems. New ideas can stimulate greater efficiency and effectiveness. Consultants can act as a company's representative in negotiating contract services and purchasing devices.

Executives sometimes refrain from hiring a consultant because they feel that it will reflect adversely on their ability. A consultant can be a cost-effective investment, but the buyer must beware.

The client interested in a successful consulting experience will be involved in three specific phases: (1) selection, (2) direction, and (3) evaluation. The objective of the selection phase is to contact the most appropriate person for the job. To do this the executive must first *clearly define the problem* and then search for the individual with the required background.

Executives often find that the private consultant is the most convenient and readily available. It is best to obtain one who is independent, that is, not affiliated with any particular service or device.

Before the final selection is made, the client should answer three questions. Does the consultant's background fit the problem? How much money and time are required to complete the work? Did the initial contact with the consultant suggest that he or she will stimulate me and my subordinates in solving the problem?

In the second phase, the client directs the chosen consultant. This means that the client assists the consultant in becoming familiar with the business and the problem. The consultant is introduced to select personnel. A tour of the premises is another part of what is known as the startup time, which can easily consume a day. The consultant will be preoccupied with collecting information via interviews, observation, and records. Many questions will be asked by the consultant. A previously prepared survey or checklist form is brought by the consultant as a reminder of what specific questions to ask or areas to check. Clients may request a one-day survey followed by verbal advice, whereas other assignments may last for weeks, months, or years.

When sufficient information has been collected, and the consultant has a good grasp of the problem and possible solutions, he or she presents a report of findings and recommendations to the client. Naturally, the consultant is in an advisory capacity and the executives in charge have the authority and must accept the responsibility of instituting the recommendations.

The third and final phase for the client pertains to evaluating the consultant. A standard personnel evaluation form provides several relevant questions (e.g., works well with others, is flexible, communicates clearly). But the primary question is this: was the problem uncovered and satisfactorily remedied?

Certified Protection Professional

Most states have no regulation for the security and loss prevention consultant. When registration or licensing is required, it often is accomplished via the laws regulating security officers and private investigators. With such minimal controls, almost anybody can call himself or herself a consultant.

Hence, charlatans appear who tarnish the field and create a bad image that reflects on competent professionals.

In light of the scarcity of regulations or standards for loss prevention consultants and managers and to reinforce professionalism in this field, the American Society for Industrial Security (ASIS) created the Certified Protection Professional program in 1972. To qualify for CPP certification, the applicant must meet certain education and experience requirements, affirm adherence to the CPP Code of Professional Responsibility, receive endorsement by a person certified as a CPP, and achieve a passing grade on the written examination.

The education and years of security experience and responsible charge of a security function (within the years of experience) that applicants need to qualify for the CPP examination are as follows:

Degree	Years of Experience	Responsible Charge
None	9	2
Associate	7	2
Bachelor's	5	2
Master's	3	2
Doctoral	2	2

The CPP examination is approximately four and one-half hours long and consists of 225 multiple-choice questions covering knowledge application in the field of security and loss prevention. Many of the topics on the examination are covered in this book. Non-U.S. and Non-Canadian candidates take a 200 question examination containing no legal aspects questions. About 75 percent of candidates taking the examination obtain a passing score.[7] Recertification occurs every three years and is accomplished by attending educational programs, among other professional activities. Of the almost 30,000 ASIS members, over 3,000 are CPPs. For information call ASIS Customer Services at 703-522-5800.

In addition to ASIS CPPs as a source of consultants, another source, although small, is the *International Association of Professional Security Consultants* (IAPSC), founded in 1984. Members of this professional association are required to have education and experience, and the CPP is accepted as a component of the qualifications for membership. Like ASIS, the IAPSC requires its members to adhere to a code of ethics. The newsletter published by the IAPSC is an excellent, specialized source for security consultants. There are only about 70 IAPSC members. (Address: IAPSC, 808 17th Street NW, Suite 200, Washington, DC, 20006; Tel.: 202-466-7212.)

What are the benefits of obtaining the Certified Protection Professional designation?

PURCHASING OR LEASING SECURITY DEVICES

Acquiring an Alarm System[8]

When considering the acquisition of alarm system protection, the consumer should become as familiar as possible with available systems. This can be accomplished by (1) consulting security periodicals, (2) reviewing books on the physical security and alarm systems industry, (3) attending trade shows, (4) obtaining brochures from alarm sales companies, (5) contacting organizations such as the National Burglar and Fire Alarm Association (NB&FAA, 1701 Wisconsin Ave., Suite 901, Bethesda, MD 20814; Tel.: 301-907-3202), (6) contacting security consultants, and (7) speaking with customers who use the system of interest.

The NB&FAA has published a consumer guide, *Considerations When Looking for a Burglar Alarm System.* This pamphlet outlines procedures for the consumer:

1. Locate reputable alarm companies by contacting
   a. Local law enforcement agency,
   b. Underwriters' Laboratories, Inc.,
   c. NB&FAA;
2. Conduct a security survey to determine alarm needs;
3. Consider all available systems to determine
   a. Type of alarm devices required,
   b. Type of total alarm system required;
4. Check local laws for
   a. Type of alarm systems permissible,
   b. Length of time an alarm can sound,
   c. Penalties for false alarms;
5. Study any contract or sales agreement prior to purchase for
   a. List of points of protection,
   b. Itemization of equipment to be installed,
   c. Service arrangements and fees;
6. The consumer's role in the use of an alarm system is to
   a. Provide a thorough working knowledge of the system for all persons in contact with it,
   b. Take responsibility for ensuring that public law enforcement officers are not endangered by improper use.

Leasing

With needs and budget limitations in mind, the buyer may want to consider leasing the chosen device or system (e.g., CCTV, alarm, access control). Leasing is an alternative to purchasing through which the vendor retains ownership of the equipment even though it is on the customer's premises for use. A leasing contract ordinarily lasts from one to five years. There are several types of leasing agreements. In addition to an agreement between the manufacturer and buyer, a manufacturer can offer leasing through a third party: the manufacturer sells the product to a leasing agent, who holds title to the product and leases the product to a customer. The customer usually has an option to purchase the device. Certain restrictions are placed on the purchaser to protect the vendor. For instance, the customer is barred from modifying the leased device. Insurance must be obtained for the leased product by the customer. Costs include an installation charge as well as a monthly leasing fee, and a down payment and maintenance fees also may be required.

Leasing holds several advantages. Because of the never-ending ability of offenders to circumvent new devices and constant technological innovations that result in system improvements, the customer can change to new devices when a lease expires. If the customer had purchased the device, changing would not be so easy. Leasing enables temporary use when only short-term protection is needed; for example, a one-year lease of an intrusion detection system for a building construction site. Leasing facilitates acquiring a system immediately when a capital expenditure is difficult to justify and receive acceptance from upper management. Purchasing may be too expensive for the entity, especially when cash is not available and interest rates to borrow funds are too high. When depreciation (for tax purposes) is considered, the long-term benefits are in purchasing over leasing. Planners should consult with a financial advisor to see which alternative is beneficial.

Installation

The manufacturer of the product is the best source for installation and service. However, the manufacturer may contract this work to others. Without proper guidance and supervision, subcontractors are likely to take shortcuts. To reduce this problem, a buyer should check with the manufacturer and subcontractor to ensure compliance with manufacturer's standards and establish controls by requesting frequent inspections by the manufacturer. These requirements should be negotiated into the contract. Furthermore, purchaser needs or specifications relevant to installation should be included in the contract—the more specific the better—for instance, type of wiring, concealment of wiring, and type of screws (e.g., "one-way" screws to hinder removal). At the end of installation, the owner requests copies of drawings of wiring and the design of the system for review and future problems.

You Be the Judge[*]

Carl Simpson, the security director at Southeast Tool Company, was fighting mad. The plant had been burglarized again, but that was nothing new. What had him fighting mad was that the alarm system the company had leased recently had failed to detect the intrusion.

continued

"Get Security Systems International on the phone," snapped Simpson at his secretary.

Once SSI came on the line, Simpson began his attack: "We had $135,000 worth of precision machine tools stolen last night, and your people are responsible. According to our contract, you're supposed to make sure this alarm system works. It doesn't, so your company had better come up with $135,000."

The manager of SSI just laughed. "Calm down and reread your contract," he said. "It has what's called an exculpatory clause, which says that SSI is not responsible for any loss caused by burglary."

"But this was your fault!" Simpson cried.

"It doesn't matter," replied the manager. "The clause covers us even if we're negligent." He chuckled, "I can tell you've never dealt with a burglar alarm company before. Almost all alarm contracts have an exculpatory clause in them."

But Simpson refused to give up without a fight. He had Southeast sue SSI for breach of contract, breach of warranty, and negligence, despite the exculpatory clause in the contract. "It's not fair," Simpson argued. "When we contracted with SSI we put the safety of our company in their hands. They took on the responsibility, and they shouldn't be able to use a catch-all clause to escape liability for their negligence."

Did the court agree?

Make your decision; then turn to the end of the chapter for the court's decision.

* Reprinted with permission from *Security Management—Plant and Property Protection,* a publication of Bureau of Business Practice, Inc., 24 Rope Ferry Road, Waterford, CT 06386.

Maintenance

The importance of maintenance cannot be overstated. *Any device or system is useless when it fails and is not repaired.* Two major forms of maintenance are preventive and emergency. *Preventive maintenance* consists of periodic inspections and the replacement of parts before failure. Specially trained technicians are needed for replacing or fixing components, checking standby batteries, and so on. Loss prevention personnel can inspect systems for reliability. These inspections are as simple as having personnel open an alarmed door or window and then call an alarm monitoring station to verify that the alarm was received. Quick *emergency maintenance* is indispensable after a breakdown. Can the manufacturer or contractor respond to an emergency within a reasonable time? Will the manufacturer or contractor pay for extra loss prevention officers if a lengthy period is needed to repair the system? As a customer, negotiate these stipulations into maintenance contracts.

Proprietary maintenance is possible if qualified employees are available. This reduces the potential of the system being compromised by outsiders. The maintenance supervisor on the premises can render assistance during and after system planning. These supervisors are familiar with building construction characteristics such as new plumbing and electrical work that may cause problems. Also, the maintenance supervisor will know the skills of subordinates and whether they are capable of learning how to maintain the system. The manager should assign this supervisor to check on the system during installation and maintenance.

The *Report of the Task Force on Private Security* suggested the following standard to strengthen buyer satisfaction and the reliability of systems:

> There should be a certified training program for alarm sales personnel and alarm service technicians. . . . A major cause of problems involving alarm systems can be traced back to inadequacies of the person selling, installing, or servicing the system. . . . Many salesmen tend to be more sales oriented rather than technically oriented, but the consumer depends on the salesman's advice regarding which system to buy. Concerning installers: Many are not knowledgeable of installation methods required for the more sophisticated systems on the market.[9]

PURCHASER'S CHECKLIST

Before a buyer purchases an expensive protection device, he or she should answer the questions on the following checklist.

Questions to Ask Before Purchasing a Security Device

1. What can the product do?
2. What is the *total cost* of the product, including installation, additional personnel, training, maintenance, finance charges, and so on? When the purchaser buys in large volume, the greater profit for the vendor may result in lower prices.
3. Is the total price competitive with other vendors?
4. Can the product adapt to new technological developments? What modifications are possible? Costs?
5. How long will it take for the product to be installed and become operational? Can the deadline be met?
6. Does the vendor allow the product to be examined under trial use on our premises, so we can evaluate it before purchase and compare the product specifications from the manufacturer with actual performance? Does the system perform properly? Can our personnel work with it?
7. Before, during, and after installation, who from the manufacturer or contractor is responsible for the product?
8. What is the product life?
9. How often will malfunctions take place?

10. What does the warranty cover?
11. What maintenance is required?
12. Does the manufacturer or contractor provide preventive maintenance and emergency service? What are the costs of each before and after the warranty expires?
13. How quickly can repair personnel respond to an emergency? Where are they based? Are they available at all times?
14. What are the costs of replacement parts? Are they readily available?
15. How frequently is preventive maintenance conducted?
16. Does the installer provide field inspections and testing to assure that the product is functioning properly? What are the testing guidelines? Costs?
17. Are reports concerning maintenance and inspections presented to the user?
18. What is the background and training of maintenance personnel?
19. What is the background of each vendor and product?
20. Have we contacted local police and the Better Business Bureau for information about vendors?
21. Have we checked the company's Dun and Bradstreet rating?
22. Does the vendor have appropriate business licenses? Does the vendor conform to applicable state laws requiring training or registration?
23. Is the vendor a member of trade associations that help members stay current on new technology and product developments?
24. How does the vendor react to questioning by a potential buyer? Are the vendor's answers adequate?
25. What is the background of personnel involved with the product? Are professional engineers employed? Is electrical work done by licensed contractors?
26. Have we requested references from the vendor from current users of the same product? Have we followed up on those references?
27. Does the manufacturer freely release information about its product to outsiders? (Burglars are known to pose as writers, reporters, or buyers to acquire system information.)
28. Has the product and its components been evaluated by an independent testing organization (e.g., UL, Factory Mutual)? If applicable, does it meet National Fire Protection Association (NFPA) standards?
29. Have we checked out these important product characteristics: trouble indicator, auxiliary energy source, battery trouble indicator, control cabinet lock, tamper alarm, and good product mounting characteristics (e.g., wiring, screws, supports)?
30. How will the system be evaluated?

When utilizing a checklist it is helpful to assign a value to each item depending on its importance. For instance, 30 for a very important item (e.g., cost) and 5 for an item of moderate importance (e.g., vendor membership in a trade association). To rate each vendor on each item of the list, a simple rating method such as 1 through 5 (5 being the best rating) is sufficient; multiply the value of the item times the vendor rating and record the amount next to the question. Then add the points for all questions to obtain a grand total. The vendor with the most points may very well be the best choice. A self-designed checklist and rating method will facilitate easier comparisons and selection.

CASE PROBLEM

9A. Select a specific service or device. Study the state of the art. Then, list in order of priority, ten questions you would ask vendors. Explain why the first three questions are placed at the top of the list.

THE DECISION FOR YOU BE THE JUDGE

The court did not agree with Simpson's reasoning and dismissed Southeast's lawsuit against SSI. The court held that the clause was valid and clear in totally absolving SSI from liability for the burglary. If your company has leased a burglar alarm system, check the contract to see if it has an exculpatory clause. If it does, take heart. Not all courts have upheld the validity of such clauses in all circumstances. Check with your company's lawyer to find out where your state courts stand on this issue.

This case is based on *L. Luria & Son* v. *Alarmtech International*, 384 So2d 947. The names in this case have been changed to protect the privacy of those involved.

NOTES

1. U.S. Department of Justice, *Private Police in the United States: Findings and Recommendations*, vol. 1 (Washington, DC: U.S. Government Printing Office, 1972), p. 59.
2. George O'Toole, *The Private Sector* (New York: W.W. Norton Co., 1978), p. 157.
3. "Home-Improvement Frauds: The Costliest Rip-Off," *Changing Times* 34 (November 1980): 8.
4. U.S. Department of Justice, *Report of the Task Force on Private Security* (Washington, DC: U.S. Government Printing Office, 1976), pp. 146–147; and U.S. Department of Justice, National Institute of Justice, *Crime and Protection in America (Executive Summary of the Hallcrest Report)* (Washington, DC: U.S. Government Printing Office, 1985), p. 71.
5. John P. Finnerty, "Who's Liable, The Security Firm or You?"*Risk Management Advisor* (May 1996): 4–7.

6. Hualing Fu, "The Security Service Company in China," *Journal of Security Administration* 16, no. 2 (1993): 35–43.

7. Bill Cornelius, "Reflections on the CPP Designation," *Dynamics* (January–February 1990): 13.

8. U.S. Department of Justice, *Report of the Task Force on Private Security*, p. 244.

9. Ibid., p. 147.

10

Investigations

OBJECTIVES

After studying this chapter the reader will be able to

1. List and discuss the six basic investigative questions;
2. Describe at least five types of investigations in the private sector;
3. Differentiate among proprietary and contract investigations, private and public investigations, and overt and undercover private investigations;
4. Explain the relationship between an investigator and an auditor;
5. List and explain at least five aids to the investigative process.

An investigation is a search for information. Information usually is obtained from people, such as victims, witnesses, suspects, and informants, and from physical evidence, such as fingerprints, bloodstains, shoe prints, and toolmarks.

There are six basic questions to ask in an investigation:

1. *Who?* Who are the individuals involved in the particular incident being investigated? Names, addresses, and telephone numbers are important.
2. *What happened?* What is the story of the incident? For instance, what happened before, during, and after a theft incident at a manufacturing plant?
3. *Where?* The location of the incident and the movement of people and objects are important. For example, where exactly were witnesses and the suspect when the theft occurred?
4. *When?* A notation of the times of particular activities during an incident is necessary for a thorough investigation. If a particular theft occurred between 7 and 8 P.M. on April 9, and Joe Doe is suspect, he later can be exonerated because he really was at another location at that time.
5. *How?* The focus of this question is on how the incident was able to take place in the face of (or absence of) loss prevention measures. After

217

a theft, investigators often attempt to find out how the thief was able to circumvent alarms. In the case of an industrial accident, investigators attempt to find out how the accident occurred while safety equipment was supposedly in use.

6.   *Why?* This question can be difficult to answer. However, the answer can lead to the discovery of a pressing problem that may not be obvious. An example is seen with numerous loss-provoking activities in a manufacturing plant brought about by low employee morale. In this case, theft and destruction of company property can be reduced by, for example, increasing management's concern for employees through praise, a sports program, contests, and high-quality meals in the cafeteria.

The answer to the why question helps to establish the motive for the loss activity. Once the motive is established, suspects can be eliminated. A recently fired employee would have a motive of retribution for setting fire to his or her former place of employment.

Investigations are not always criminal in nature, and not every investigation requires answering all six investigative questions. Once an investigator gathers sufficient information, a report is written and submitted to a supervisor. After that, the information in the report causes action or inaction by supervisors and management. Typically, investigative reports lead to either punitive or nonpunitive action. Punitive action can include firing or prosecution or both. Nonpunitive action can include exonerating a suspect, hiring an applicant, promoting an employee, or insurance reimbursement. Investigations can also result in corrective action such as the creation of a better loss prevention program. Investigations can result in numerous possible consequences.

Investigations are unique to each type of business, institution, or organization served. The varieties and depths of investigations vary; they reflect management's needs, objectives, and budget. The personnel involved also vary and may include company investigators, auditors, managers, contract investigators, public police, and attorneys.

TYPES OF INVESTIGATIONS

There are several types of investigations in the private sector. The following list illustrates some of the more common ones, categorized according to the target of the investigation: applicant background, criminal, accident, fire and arson, civil or negligence and liability, insurance, labor, and due diligence.

The ground rules or laws for each type of investigation vary. An *applicant background* investigation requires adherence to the laws discussed in Chapter 6. A private investigation of a *criminal* offense requires knowledge of criminal law and evidence. In a private-sector criminal investigation, the notification of public police will depend on such factors as whether the suspect was arrested by company investigators and whether management wants to prosecute. In an *accident* investigation, the investigator usually is knowledgeable about safety, the Occupational Safety and Health Act, workers' compensation insurance, and applicable laws. One major objective of a *fire and arson* investigator is to determine the probable cause of a fire. Sophisticated equipment may be used to identify what substance was employed to accelerate a fire. A *civil or negligence and liability* investigation involves, among other things, gathering evidence to show that failure to exercise reasonable care in a situation caused harm to someone or something. For example, a retail store has poor housekeeping, which caused customer injury. Both the plaintiff initiating the suit (the customer) and the defendant (the retail store) may conduct investigations and present evidence in court. A civil court decides on both liability (who is responsible) for a negligent act and any obligation (money award to the plaintiff) enforceable by the court. *Insurance* investigations, which at times result in litigation, are conducted to determine losses, their causes, and to assist in deciding on indemnification. Both an insurance company and the insured may conduct separate investigations before an insurance claim is settled. Investigations of *labor* matters (e.g., workers' activities during a strike) are often sensitive. Legal counsel is necessary to guide the investigator because of associated federal and state laws. *Due diligence*, as defined in Chapter 4, is the attention and care legally expected in checking the accuracy of information and omissions. It can range from determining a customer's financial status to desirability of acquisition targets. Investigators frequently specialize in one or two types of investigations.

Proprietary and Contract Investigations

Proprietary investigations are undertaken by in-house company employees, who perform investigative work. A *contract investigation* requires the contracting of an outside company (agency) to supply investigative services for a fee. Which is better?

There are inadequate and varied laws regulating contract investigative employees and firms. But several jurisdictions have effective regulation (e.g., license requirements, residency, training, experience, no felony convictions, examination, and insurance) that protects clients.

For the most part, proprietary investigators are not subject to government regulation. Many businesses, institutions, and organizations maintain their own investigators. Large corporations, utilities, insurance companies, and banks are some of the many concerns that rely on a large staff of proprietary investigators.

Numerous firms utilize both contract and proprietary investigators. If a large corporation has a particular season when the investigative workload is heavy, some of the extra workload can be assigned to a contract investigation company. This approach frees proprietary investigators for more pressing and specialized problems.

Managers often prefer proprietary investigations for two reasons. First, an extended contract investigation becomes more expensive than a proprietary investigation. Second, a proprietary investigator knows the surroundings. Beginning an investigation with knowledge of the environment can be a tremendous asset.

Citizens frequently obtain a distorted picture of private investigations via television, which produces misconceptions that falsify the various kinds of investigative work, work that is interesting, exciting, and also often boring. Another misconception is that many investigators in the private sector are armed. Few are armed, and those who are rarely use their weapons.

Private and Public Investigations

Private investigations serve the private sector (e.g., businesses). Public investigations feature public police agencies, for the most part serving the public. Both investigative efforts often are entwined. This can be seen, for example, when an office building is burglarized and company investigators call local police in a joint effort to solve the crime. But how much time and effort can the public police devote to the office building burglary in comparison to the company investigators? Public police can devote only limited resources to such a crime. Typically, a uniformed public police officer will arrive for a preliminary investigation, and an incident report will be completed. Next, the incident report is transferred to a detective unit. Within a day or two, a detective arrives at the scene of the crime and conducts a follow-up investigation that involves gathering additional information and perhaps some placation, a public relations effort that assures the citizens that the police are doing everything possible to solve the crime.

The inability of the criminal justice system to assist adequately in private loss prevention efforts can also be illustrated by clearance rates. "[L]aw enforcement agencies clear or solve an offense when at least one person is arrested, charged with the commission of the offense, and turned over to the court for prosecution."[1] The method of compiling clearance rates varies among police agencies. Also, many researchers point out that clearance rates are not suitable for measuring the investigative process.[2]

The figures in Table 10–1 reveal that many property crimes, such as burglaries and larceny-thefts, are not solved. The major reason for this inadequacy is limited resources, namely, personnel. The success of private-sector investigations is difficult to gauge since many firms do not prosecute and the outcome of investigations is usually confidential and unpublished.

Table 10–1 Offenses Cleared by
Arrest, 1995, *FBI Uniform Crime Reports*

Offense	Percentage Cleared by Arrest
Murder	65
Forcible rape	51
Aggravated assault	56
Robbery	25
Burglary	13
Larceny/theft	20
Motor vehicle theft	14
Arson	16

Source: U.S. Department of Justice, *Crime in the United States,
1995, Uniform Crime Reports* (Washington, DC: U.S. Government Printing Office, 1996), pp. 198–199.

Overt and Undercover Private Investigations

An *overt investigation* is an obvious investigation. People coming into contact with the overt investigator know that an investigation is taking place. A
common scenario would be a company investigator, dressed in a conservative suit, arriving at the scene of a loss to interview employees and collect
evidence. An *undercover investigation*, on the other hand, is a secret investigation. A typical approach is when an undercover investigator is hired as a
regular employee, a truck driver, for example, and collects information by
associating with employees who are not knowledgeable about the undercover investigation.

Each type of investigation serves many useful purposes. An overt investigation that begins immediately after a loss shows that the loss prevention
staff is on the job. This in itself acts as a deterrent. An overt investigation
does not have to be in response to a loss; for example, preemployment investigations prevent losses.

Accident at Hardy Furniture Plant

The Hardy Furniture Plant provided over 700 jobs to Clarkston residents as
sales boomed. Most workers at the plant were satisfied with their jobs.
Unfortunately, a group of young forklift drivers were becoming increasingly
bored while transporting furniture throughout the plant. One day two forklifts collided and both drivers were hospitalized with broken arms and legs.
The forklifts were slightly damaged; furniture on the forks was a total loss.

continued

Immediately, the company loss prevention staff began an investigation. The forklift drivers and witnesses were interviewed. All interviewees reported that neither forklift operator saw the other because excessive furniture on the forks obstructed the views. Investigators and a forklift mechanic inspected the forklifts and found no irregularities.

The investigators became suspicious when all of the interviewees produced identical stories during questioning. Later, another round of questioning included nonwitnesses. Finally, after two weeks of persistent interviewing, the case broke when an older employee, loyal to the company, informed investigators that several bored employees bet on forklift drivers who were "playing chicken" while racing toward each other. It was learned that five previous contests had taken place involving hundreds of dollars of cash. Also, one minor accident had occurred that resulted in damaged furniture. Two supervisors were involved in covering up the loss of the damaged furniture.

When the investigation was complete, loss prevention investigators filled out appropriate reports and presented their findings to management. The two forklift drivers and the two supervisors were fired.

Undercover investigations (UI) are sometimes referred to as *secret* or *covert* investigations. The participating investigator is often referred to as the *operative* or *undercover operator*. Whereas public police undercover investigations usually infiltrate organized crime, radical, or spy groups, private sector undercover investigations usually infiltrate employee informal groups.

An example can illustrate the usefulness of a UI. The XYZ warehouse is losing hundreds of dollars of merchandise every week. Management believes that employees are stealing the merchandise. In an effort to reduce the losses, management decides to hire a private investigator. The investigator interviews numerous employees over a two-week period, but the case remains unsolved. An executive of the company argues to management that the private investigator idea is a waste. The executive points out that the private investigator is unfamiliar with the warehouse operations, cannot penetrate the employee informal organization, has no informers, is wasting time during surveillance from another building, and has no substantial leads. After three weeks, the private investigator is terminated. The vocal executive argues for a UI. A loss prevention service company is contacted, and an undercover investigator is placed in the warehouse. After three weeks, the new investigator penetrates the informal employee organization. Four key employees are implicated and fired. Losses are reduced. The company decides to conduct a yearly UI as a loss prevention strategy.

Undercover Investigation of Missing Shirts

The Chester Garment Company, headquartered in New York City, experienced a loss of hundreds of men's shirts at its plant in North Carolina. Company executives were concerned and worried because they had no experience with losses and no loss prevention program.

The plant manager in North Carolina had notified the New York office that 900 shirts were missing. Because of their limited knowledge of loss prevention strategies, company executives decided to contact Harmon Lorman Associates, a company specializing in loss prevention and investigation. A meeting between managers of the investigative company and the garment company decided that an undercover investigator, assigned to the North Carolina plant, would be a wise strategy. The UI would cost $700 per week for an unspecified time period.

One week later, the investigator, Gary Stewart, arrived at the Chester Garment Plant in North Carolina to seek employment. The plant manager, who was the only plant employee who knew about the UI, hired Gary and assigned him to shipping and receiving.

Gary was from New York and educated at a college in North Carolina. The investigative company felt that his experience, a college degree in criminal justice, and his living experience in the South, would add up to a good background for this assignment. Anyway, he was the only company investigator who had lived in the South.

Harmon Lorman executives told Chester executives that Gary had been working with them for a year and a half. Also, they told them that Gary had extensive experience and loss prevention training. The truth was that Gary had been recently hired with six months previous investigative experience. Gary had no previous loss prevention training; he had a criminal justice degree with no loss prevention or business courses.

After two weeks in the plant, Gary had established numerous contacts. His fictitious background ("cover") pointed out that he grew up in Maryland. He arrived at the Chester Garment plant because a friend said that he could get a job there while taking a semester off from college. Gary obtained North Carolina license plates as soon as he entered North Carolina from New York.

Gary mailed three to five reports per week to his supervisor at Harmon Lorman Associates. The first few reports contained background information on the plant like the plant layout and the names, addresses, telephone numbers, description of autos, and plate numbers of select employees. Thereafter, the reports contained information pertaining to loss prevention features and loss vulnerabilities. Janitorial service, employee overtime, Saturday activities, and any unusual events were also reported.

Within three months of undercover investigation, Gary had made close contacts with employees and had worked in numerous assignments throughout the plant. His findings showed numerous instances of pilferage by many

continued

employees. Women sewing machine operators were hiding several manufac-tured shirts under their outer clothes immediately before the work day ended.

Gary's reports were "edited" by his superiors and then sent to the home of one of Chester Garment's executives. After three months and expenditures over $8400, Chester Garment executives became impatient. They wanted bet-ter quality results and threatened to terminate the investigation.

Harmon Lorman executives assured Chester Garment executives that "a break in the case was imminent." Increased pressure was put on investigator Gary Stewart, who realized that the investigation was being prolonged for profit. He responded by withholding information from reports for dry spells when good information was unavailable. As the investigation went on, the report quality went down.

Finally, after two more weeks, Chester Garment executives ordered an inventory at the plant. Surprisingly, half of the missing shirts were accounted for, and a previous inventory was criticized as inaccurate. The undercover investigation was terminated. Gary returned to New York.

Investigator and Auditor

An auditor examines accounting records to check on irregularities. These irregularities usually include (1) deviations from the particular firm's accounting methods, (2) mistakes, and (3) criminal activity. Auditors also are referred to as *internal auditors* or *investigative auditors.*

An ideal background for an auditor would include not only accounting education and experience but also criminal investigation education and experience. Obviously, accounting irregularities are discovered by those knowledgeable about accounting principles and procedures. But, once pos-sible criminal activity is discovered, the auditor needs to know about crimi-nal law and evidence to develop a successful case.

Often, experienced and educated criminal investigators apply for investigative positions at private firms and are asked, "What kind of an accounting background do you have?" The applicant's response usually reveals limited knowledge of accounting.

There is a shortage of people with backgrounds in both accounting and criminal investigation. Therefore, many firms rely on people with an exper-tise in either area and expect cooperation. In the past few years, public (e.g., federal, state, municipal) and private investigation practitioners have expanded their competency in accounting. A major reason for this is a response to increased investigations into the white-collar crime arena.

If needed, cross-training can be used to reduce the knowledge gap between auditor and criminal investigator. Cross-training involves the audi-tor being trained in criminal investigation and the criminal investigator being trained in auditing. An auditor's training could include criminal law, evidence, interviewing, and interrogation. A criminal investigator's training could include accounting principles and procedures and auditing.

Many businesses and other concerns that rely heavily on computers need competent investigative personnel with knowledge of data processing. It is a rare occurrence when one investigator has a good knowledge of the techniques of investigation, auditing, and computer operations. For a solid case against a computer offender, physical evidence in the form of computer data or equipment often is required. Consequently, if the investigator or auditor lacks expertise in computer crimes, then a third member of the investigator–auditor team is necessary. The next chapter contains information on auditing, fraud, legislation, and professional organizations for investigators and auditors.

What type of investigative work do you think you would prefer as a career?

Important Considerations

The following considerations relate to investigations in general:

1. The supervision of investigators must be adequate enough to produce tangible results. Rarely will a supervisor–investigator ratio of 1:20 prove adequate. Investigators may require close supervision by attorneys and other specialists. Poor supervision and excessive pressure on investigators can be adverse to investigations because investigators may save an abundance of information for "dry" weeks or even fabricate information.
2. Sensitive and confidential information must be safeguarded.
3. Information resulting from investigations can be used to improve loss prevention efforts and reduce vulnerabilities. For example, if machine shop workers constantly are stealing company tools, then it may be a good idea to have all workers provide their own tools.
4. Investigations can support the loss prevention budget by documenting vulnerabilities and losses.
5. Investigations should be cost effective. If an investigation costs more than the loss, the expense of the investigation may not be worthwhile. Therefore, priorities need to be established. For example, the loss of a box of pencils is not worth an investigator's time when more serious losses are occurring.
6. The investigator's job is to collect information and facts. Supervisors and managers decide what to do with the investigative results.

7.   Sometimes investigators are assigned to tasks outside of their normal duties. For example, a company executive requests that a company investigator investigate the possibility that the executive's wife is unfaithful.

LAW

A knowledge of law is indispensable to the investigative process. As previously stated, there are various types of investigations, and each requires a knowledge of the laws surrounding the particular investigation. To illustrate, if an employee is suspected of stealing tools in a machine shop, an investigator should know about criminal law before the suspect is questioned.

What other legal concerns are important to the private-sector investigator involved in criminal cases? One important area pertains to electronic surveillance (electronic devices used to listen to conversations) and wiretapping (listening to telephone communications). The U.S. Supreme Court has called these techniques a *dirty business*. Generally, both are prohibited unless under court authority. However, because of the difficulty of detection and the advantages in information gathering, some private (and public) sector investigators violate the law. Federal law imposes a $10,000 fine and up to five years in prison for these offenses.

Another area of law that concerns the investigator in the private sector is conflict of interest. An example of conflict of interest can be seen when a full-time public police officer works part-time for a private firm. The *Report of the Task Force on Private Security* states that "a citizen might file a defamation-of-character suit against a city, law enforcement agency, or officer by claiming that surveillance conducted by an off-duty law enforcement officer working as a private investigator gave others the impression he was the target of a law enforcement criminal investigation."[3] Other problems can evolve, such as a suspect's rights during private-sector questioning by a public police officer working part-time for private police. States have prohibited public police from obtaining a private investigator license. The task force recommended that public police officers should be "strictly forbidden" from performing private-sector investigatory work.

International Perspective: Overseas Investigations[4]

Global business has resulted in increasing demand for overseas investigations. Such investigations are conducted for a variety of reasons, including potential locations for investment. The following information provides tips and guidelines for overseas investigations.

Carefully plan and check with the following U.S. agencies: (Chapter 18, in the section on terrorism, also covers U.S. agencies and their telephone numbers.)

- *U.S. Department of State* ensures that passports are current and valid for all countries not off limits to U.S. citizens. Some countries require a special visa. Fact sheets are provided on 197 countries and include information on such topics as political stability and crime. U.S. embassies are located in capital cities and consulates are located in large urban areas.
- *U.S. Department of Health and Human Services* determines whether travel to particular countries requires immunization. HHS's Centers for Disease Control and Prevention in Atlanta provides current information on immunizations (Tel.: 404-332-4555) and publishes *Health Information for International Travel* (single copies are free).
- *U.S. Department of Commerce* publishes information to alert U.S. citizens to countries that may be dangerous to U.S. travelers.
- Because legal systems vary among countries, a major rule in conducting a foreign investigation is to study the legal and policing system of the respective country.
- Investigations are fundamentally about personal interaction, so another major rule is to study and understand the host culture and try to speak some of the language.
- The international investigator who travels to many countries and freely investigates is actually Hollywood fantasy. Foreign countries do not permit such activities and neither does the U.S. State Department. Without careful research, an investigator can find himself or herself in jail in a foreign country.
- An option is to work with an official of the foreign country, such as a police official or attorney, or contract the investigation to an investigator in that country. The key is to select someone who has experience in the country, has reliable contacts, and speaks the language.
- Avoid bringing a firearm to a foreign country. Possession of a firearm aboard any U.S. airline is a felony.
- If documents are sought in a foreign country, obtain certified copies. This will prevent the need for foreign officials to testify in the United States.

INTERVIEWING AND INTERROGATION

Interviewing and interrogation are methods of gathering information from people. During an *interview*, the investigator obtains information willingly; but during an *interrogation*, the suspect is often unwilling to supply information. The investigator needs to know the techniques associated with each type of situation. There is no one correct method of conducting an interview or interrogation. The circumstances of each particular situation dictate the characteristics of these investigative functions. Members of private security are more likely to interview, whereas public police are more likely to interview and interrogate.

Why are interviews or interrogations conducted? A primary reason is to learn the truth. Other possible reasons are to obtain evidence or a confession to aid in prosecution, eliminate suspects, recover property, and obtain information that results in corrective action. This chapter emphasizes investigations in the private sector, although many of the ideas presented are used in public-sector investigations.

The preliminaries include

1. Maintaining records;
2. Planning the questioning;
3. Making an appointment, if necessary;
4. If a procedure or law question arises, consulting with a superior or an attorney;
5. Questioning in privacy, if possible;
6. Making sure someone of the same sex as the interviewee is present;
7. Identifying yourself to the interviewee;
8. Openly recording the questioning, if possible, on audio or videotape.

Regarding the interviewee,

1. Consider the interviewee's background, intelligence, education, biases, and emotional state;
2. Communicate on the same level;
3. Watch for nervousness, perspiration, and fidgeting;
4. Reluctance to talk can indicate that the interviewee feels the need to protect himself or herself or others;
5. Responding freely can indicate that the interviewee may need to relieve guilt or may want to cause problems for an enemy not involved in the loss.

The objectives of the investigator include

1. Establishing good rapport (e.g., asking, "How are you?");
2. Maintaining good public relations;
3. Maintaining eye contact;
4. Not jumping to conclusions;
5. Maintaining an open mind;
6. Listening attentively;
7. Being perceptive to every comment and any slips of the tongue;

8. Maintaining perseverance;
9. Controlling the interview;
10. Carefully analyzing hearsay (what one person says another person told him or her, unverified information).

Strategies by the investigator include

1. Asking *open-ended questions,* those questions that require lengthy answers; for example, "What happened at the plant before the accident?" *Close-ended questions* require short yes or no answers that limit responses; for example, "Were you close to the accident?"
2. Maintaining *silence* makes many interviewees feel uncomfortable. Silence by an investigator, after an interviewee answers an open-ended question, may cause the interviewee to begin talking again.
3. Building up interviewee memory by having the interviewee relate the story of an incident from its very beginning.
4. To test honesty, asking questions to which you know the answers.

The reader probably is familiar with movies and television programs that portray the interrogation process as a "third degree," in which one bright light hangs over the seated suspect in a dark room and investigators stand around constantly asking questions and using violence when they try to "break" the suspect. Court action against public and private police has curbed this abuse. However, because of the unpleasant connotations associated with interrogations, for the private sector, to prevent litigation, a less threatening term such as "intensive interview" is more appropriate.

During interrogation or "intensive interview" (an extension of the interview),

1. Discuss the seriousness of the incident.
2. Request the story several times. Some investigators request the story backward to catch inconsistencies.
3. Appeal to emotions; for example, "Everybody makes mistakes. You are not the first person who has been in trouble. Don't you want to clear your conscience?"
4. Point out inconsistencies in statements.
5. Confront the interviewee with some of the evidence.

Why would a private security investigator choose to "interview" rather than "interrogate"?

Polygraph: Proper Testing Procedures Under the EPPA*

In the course of a workplace investigation, an employer cannot suggest to employees the possible use of a polygraph instrument until satisfying these ten conditions:

1. *Economic loss or injury.* The employer must administer the test as part of an investigation of a *specific incident* involving economic loss or injury to the business, such as theft or sabotage.
2. *Access.* The employee who is to be tested must have had access to the property that is the subject of the investigation.
3. *Reasonable suspicion.* The employer must have a reasonable suspicion of the worker's involvement in the incident under investigation.
4. *Before the test*, an employer's failure to adhere to guidelines can void a test, and subject the employer to fines and liability. The employee who is to be tested must be notified in writing at least 48 hours, not counting weekends and holidays, prior to the test:
    *   Where and when the examination will take place;
    *   The specific matter under investigation;
    *   The basis for concluding that the employee had access to the property being investigated;
    *   The reason the employer suspects the employee of involvement;
    *   The employee's right to consult with legal counsel or an employee representative before each phase of the test.

    Also before the test, the employee must be provided
    *   Oral and written notice explaining the nature of the polygraph, its physical operation, and the test procedure;
    *   Copies of all questions that will be asked during the test;
    *   Oral and written notice, in language understood by the employee and bearing the employee's signature, advising the worker of his or her rights under the EPPA.
5. *Procedural requirements for polygraph examinations* include
    *   The test must last at least 90 minutes unless the examinee terminates the test.
    *   Either party, employer or employee, can record the test with the other's knowledge.
    *   Questions cannot pertain to religious, political, or racial matters; sexual behavior; or beliefs, affiliations, or lawful activities related to unions or labor organizations; and cannot be asked in a degrading or needlessly intrusive manner.
    *   A worker can be excused from a test with a physician's written advisement that the subject suffers from a medical or psychological condition or is undergoing treatment that might cause abnormal responses during the examination.
    *   An employee has the right to consult with counsel before, during, and after the examination but not to have counsel present during the actual examination.

- An employee must be advised that his or her confessions may be grounds for firing or demotion and that the employer may share admissions of criminal conduct with law enforcement officials.
- A worker can terminate or refuse to take a test and cannot be demoted or fired for doing so. But, the employer can demote or fire the worker if he or she has enough separate supporting evidence to justify taking that action.

6. *After the test*, the employee has a right to a written copy of the tester's opinion, copies of the questions and corresponding replies, and an opportunity to discuss the results with the employer before an employer can take action against a worker based on the test results. An employee may be disciplined, fired, or demoted on the basis of the test results if the employer has supporting evidence, which can include the evidence gathered to support the decision to administer the test, to justify such action. Test results cannot be released to the public, only to the employee or his or her designate; the employer; a court, government agency, arbitrator, or mediator (by court order); or appropriate government agency if disclosure is admission of criminal conduct (without court order). The examiner may show test results, without identifying information, to other examiners in order to obtain second opinions.

7. *Qualifications of examiners.* An employer can be liable for an examiner's failure to meet requirements, which cover licensing, bonding, or professional liability coverage; testing guidelines; and formation of opinions.

8. *Waiving employee rights.* A worker cannot be tested—even at his or her insistence—if the employer cannot meet procedural requirements and prove reasonable suspicion and access. Employees may not waive their rights under the EPPA except in connection with written settlement of a lawsuit or pending legal action.

9. *State law and collective bargaining agreements.* The EPPA does not pre-empt any state or local law or collective bargaining agreement that is more restrictive than the act.

10. Recordkeeping requirements: Records of polygraph exams should be kept for at least three years by the employer and the examiner, who must make them available—within 72 hours upon request—to the Department of Labor.

* Source: U.S. Chamber of Commerce. See Chapter 6 for the Employee Polygraph Protection Act of 1988.

INFORMATION SOURCES

An investigator can become handicapped and frustrated unless he or she knows where and how to obtain information from the billions of records on file. George O'Toole, in *The Private Sector*, describes a CIA employee who investigated prospective employees and was extremely skilled in his job.

Before retirement, this employee was given a fellowship to write a book, *Where's What*. O'Toole states that the guidebook lists "6,723 different record systems maintained by the federal government, which contain a total of 3.9 billion files." Also included was a listing of "countless dossiers compiled by state, county, and municipal governments."[5] O'Toole points out that there are more records maintained by the private sector than by the federal government. *Where's What* also contains information sources in the private sector.

In *Confidential Information Sources: Public and Private*,[6] John M. Carroll lists four questions that describe what is important to know before information is sought:

1. What information is on record?
2. Who has custody of those records?
3. How can I or my surrogate [substitute] get it?
4. How much faith can I place in what I get?

The reality of information acquisition must be explained. No information is totally secure from unauthorized acquisition. Although difficult to measure, information often is obtained in an unethical or illegal manner; that is the reality of information acquisition. An example can be seen when a private-sector investigator pays money to an employee of a bank to secure nonpublic information about an individual. This activity should be condemned because it violates individual rights and laws.

The following list presents some sources of information for the investigator. A case-by-case approach to each source of information is advised because availability varies and laws can be restrictive.

Less Restrictive	*More Restrictive*
Libraries	Hospitals
Newspapers and periodicals	Insurance companies
Professional and trade associations	Educational institutions
Government agencies containing public records (e.g., court records)	Credit bureaus
	Financial Institutions

Databases and Electronic Mail

Security people increasingly are making use of on-line databases to acquire information. A personal computer and a modem that connects a computer to telephone lines are required to communicate with information brokers. A subscriber uses electronic mail (e-mail): a message sent from one computer to another. A subscriber brings up a simple menu on his or her personal computer. The menu provides directions to an electronic request form. Questions asking what information is needed are answered, and e-mail sends the request to the information broker. Examples of information in databases include names and addresses nationwide, all the listed telephone numbers in the United States, real property records in most states, national civil court records, and a national movers index. One airport security director uses such databases to locate owners of vehicles abandoned in the airport's parking lots. Another security practitioner conducts asset searches of employees suspected of fraud; a database may show that an employee earning $45,000 per year has purchased a $600,000 house.

One problem with these databases is selecting the most appropriate information broker. Another problem is that data may not be verified. Also, the scope of the search must be considered. What geographic area and what months or years were searched? Information brokers must adhere to legal restrictions and should provide such guidelines to clients.

Legal Restrictions when Collecting Information

Investigator ability to obtain usable information in today's privacy-protected environment has been greatly reduced. In earlier years, the "old boy" network was in greater use. It consists of employees in both the public and private sectors who informally assist each other with information. An example is when a retired police officer joins an investigative firm and contacts friends from the police agency where previously employed to obtain criminal history information on individuals subject to a private-sector investigation. Because of indictments against people involved in acquiring nonpublic information, the effectiveness of the "old boy" network has decreased.

Another problem for the investigator results when he or she mistakenly collects information that is not usable in court. In litigation, information improperly obtained and not authenticated or certified by the respective agency could subject a litigation team to civil or criminal action, unless the records are subpoenaed or part of a court action (civil or criminal). What makes matters worse is waiting for a Freedom of Information Law request to obtain documents, which can take as long as a year. The *Freedom of Information Law* (FOIL) grants access to public documents, because an informed electorate is essential to safeguard democracy and because publicity is a protection against official misconduct. This law requires all federal agency documents to be publicly disclosed, unless exempted. This law also recognizes the need to restrict intrusions into a private individual's affairs.

Because of the difficulty of obtaining information today, the on-line databases (also referred to as *information resellers*) and Internet sources become especially valuable. But again, caution is advised because certain resellers illegally obtain information, which can result in criminal and civil action against all users. Many government agencies have published a listing of available records and a point of contact is the agency FOIL officer. Relevant directories are available at libraries and large bookstores.[7]

INVESTIGATIVE LEADS

Investigative work requires patience and perseverance, and difficult cases often tax the abilities of investigators as they search for answers. Investigative leads are aids to the investigator.

Scene of the Loss

A search of the scene of the loss can provide answers to investigative questions. *Offenders at a crime scene often leave something (e.g., fingerprints) or take something with them (e.g., stolen item), either of which ties them to the crime.*

The loss scene needs to be protected from unauthorized people. Photographs, video, and sketches should be made without disturbing the characteristics of the scene and before evidence is removed.

Evidence

Evidence is used to prove a fact. It usually consists of testimony by a victim or witness and physical evidence. Good evidence answers questions. In addition to interviewing, physical evidence at the loss scene can aid investigators. Physical evidence is varied and can include fingerprints, documents, clothing, fibers, chemicals, explosives, weapons, or almost anything visible or even invisible. When a person was at the scene of a loss, it is possible that he or she left something that is unique to that individual.

If physical evidence is removed from the scene of the loss, careful documentation and preservation are necessary. Documentation includes statements about the evidence such as the investigator's name, date, and exact location where found.

Victim

Good leads are possible by checking the background of the victim. The victim can be a business or organization or a person. A failing business person may have perpetrated an accident, arson, or other crime to collect on an insurance policy. A male employee may falsely claim that he was attacked at work by his wife's lover. Sometimes employees are hurt off the job but are able to go to work, claim injury on the job, and hope for improved compensation. In most instances, the victim has not perpetrated the loss; however, the investigator must maintain an open mind.

Motive

The motive behind the loss is an important consideration. Questions of concern include these. Who will gain from the loss? Are there any ulterior motives? What types of persons would create such a loss? Why? The investigator also must recognize that the human factor may not be involved in the loss. Equipment malfunction or weather may be the cause.

Witnesses

Investigative leads frequently are acquired from witnesses. Good interviewing is important and can turn up valuable leads.

Informants

Why do informants divulge information? Sometimes, it is to seek favors or money or because they see it as their duty or because they want to get someone in trouble (e.g., competitor, unfaithful lover). Informants often supply misinformation to investigators. An investigator can test the informant by asking questions to which he or she knows the answers. The investigator must never become too involved with informants or perform any unethical or criminal activity to acquire information. Obviously, the informant's identity must be protected, unless a court requires otherwise. Many investigators (private and public) have money in their budgets specifically designed to pay informants for information. A common practice of investigators is to catch an individual in violation of a rule or law but not seek punishment (e.g., prosecute) if that individual supplies the investigator with useful information.

Modus Operandi

MO stands for modus operandi, or method of operation. An investigator may ask, "What method was used by the burglar?" Because people differ, they commit crimes in different ways. Many police departments have MO files on offenders. When a crime takes place, investigators may check the MO files for suspects who are known to commit crimes in a certain way. A particular offender may use a specific tool during a burglary. A robber may wear a unique style of clothing during robberies. A saboteur at a manufacturing plant may be using a particular type of wire cutter. Sometimes, an uncommon MO is discovered: a burglar who defecates at the crime scene.

> Offenders at a crime scene often leave something or take something with them, either of which ties them to the crime.

SURVEILLANCE

Surveillance, watching or observing, is an investigative aid used widely to acquire information. Among the kinds of cases in which surveillance is helpful are these examples: assembly line workers are suspected of stealing merchandise, an employee is suspected by company investigators of passing trade secrets to another company, truck drivers while on their routes experience unexplainable losses between company facilities, an employee claiming to be unable to work because of an accident at the plant is observed building an extension on his home.

Two major kinds of surveillance are stationary and moving. *Stationary surveillance* requires the investigator to remain in one spot while observing; for example, an investigator sitting in an auto watching a suspect's house. This type can be tedious and frustrating. In *moving surveillance*, investigators follow a suspect; for example, tailing a truck driver whose cargo was "lost."

During surveillance, an investigator must be careful not to attract attention. The person being watched usually has the advantage and can attempt to lose the investigator by a variety of quick moves (e.g., going out a backdoor, jumping on a bus, driving through a red light). Therefore, the investigator must blend into the environment to prevent detection.

Another type of surveillance is audio surveillance. This includes wiretapping and eavesdropping, which are restricted by law. The sophistication of audio surveillance devices is impressive. "Radio transmitters called microcircuits can now be made so small that hundreds can be hidden in an ordinary postage stamp. The life span of these 'bugs' is indefinite since they siphon all the energy they need from a local radio broadcast."[8]

Equipment used during surveillance can include binoculars, a telescope, communication equipment, cameras, CCTV, listening devices, video and audio recorders, and auto tracking devices. The loss prevention investigator must keep informed about the devices and the laws that restrict some of them during investigations.

INFORMATION ACCURACY

An investigation is essentially an information-gathering process. The accuracy of the information not only reflects on the investigator but also has a direct bearing on the consequences of the investigation. The following guidelines are helpful in obtaining accurate information:

1. Double-check information whenever possible.
2. Ask the same questions of several people. Compare the results.
3. To check on the reliability of a source, ask questions for which you know the answers.
4. Cross-check information; for example, if you have a copy of a person's employment application and college transcript, cross-check name, date of birth, social security number, and so on.
5. Read information back to a source to check for accuracy.

6. If possible, check the background of a person providing information or check the accuracy of a records system.
7. Maintain accurate notes, records, photographs, and sketches; do not depend on memory for details.
8. If you are unable to write notes or a report, for instance while driving an auto, record the information on a tape recorder.
9. Provide adequate security for information and records to prevent tampering or loss.
10. Reread reports after they are typed.

REPORT WRITING

Report writing is another aid to the investigator. Report writing usually begins after the investigator has invested time and energy in collecting sufficient information on the basic investigative questions: who? what happened? where? when? how? why? How well these reports are prepared will have a definite impact on the investigator's career. Many supervisors get to know their subordinates more through reports than from any other means of communication. Furthermore, many supervisors consider report writing a major skill when promoting investigators.

Reports have a variety of uses aside from punitive results. They are used by management to analyze critical problems (e.g., excessive thefts or accidents). Summations of many reports can assist planning and budgetary efforts. Reports also may be used in litigation.

Investigators usually record information in a small notebook before formulating a report. An investigator has many thoughts in mind during an investigation that prevent the report from being written as the investigation proceeds. Also, after appropriate information is collected, the investigator has a bird's-eye view of the incident; this assists in the development of an outline that will improve the structure of the report.

Standard reports are used by many investigators. These reports are formulated by management to guide investigators in answering important questions. A typical standard report begins with a heading that includes the type of incident, date, time, and location. Next is a list of persons involved in the incident along with their addresses, telephone numbers, ages, and occupations. Another section can include a list of evidence. The narrative, sometimes called the *story*, follows, usually written in chronological order. The end of the report contains a variety of information such as the investigator's name and the status of the investigation. Diagrams and photographs may be attached. Report characteristics vary depending on need.

During report writing, the investigator should get to the point in easily understood language. An impressive vocabulary is not an asset to a report. Neatness and good grammar are important. Supervisors often complain about poor narratives by subordinates. Let's look at some blunders that have reflected on the investigator.

- "When the employee was approached by loss prevention staff he had a switchblade he had bought in his lunch box."
- "A telephone pole of manufacturing plants within our corporation showed that 15 percent of employees were ignoring loss prevention rules."
- "The woman caused the loss because her newborn son was branded as illiterate."
- "The sick employee was honestly in bed with the doctor for two weeks even though he did not give her any relief."

COURTROOM TESTIMONY

Most private-sector investigations do not result in judicial activity. But when a private-sector investigator appears in court, well-prepared court-room testimony is important.

The investigator (or loss prevention practitioner) may become involved in two kinds of court cases: criminal or civil. A judge presides over both kinds, which are adversary in nature. (One individual or group opposes another.) A jury may be present, depending on the characteristics of the case. In criminal cases, the prosecutor represents the state against the defendant; the defendant is represented by a defense attorney. In civil cases, the plaintiff initiates a lawsuit (sues) and is represented by an attorney. The defendant also is represented by an attorney. Each side in either kind of case is permitted to present evidence while the judge presides over the court-room activity and interprets the law for the jury.

Well-prepared courtroom testimony by an investigator in both criminal and civil courts can be assured most readily by the following suggestions. (See Table 10–2 for additional advice.)

1. Prepare for court. Review notes and reports. Coordinate witnesses. Recheck physical evidence that has been properly labeled and identified. Confer with an attorney.
2. Dress in a conservative manner, if not in uniform. Appear well groomed.
3. Maintain good courtroom demeanor (conduct, behavior). Do not slouch or fidget. Do not argue with anyone. Remain calm (take some deep breaths without being obvious).
4. Pause and think before speaking. Do not volunteer information beyond what is requested. Never guess. If you do not know an answer, say so.

Table 10–2 Brief Review of Common Tactics of Cross-Examination

Counsel's Tactic	Example	Purpose	Officer's Response
Rapid-fire questions	One question after another with little time to answer.	To confuse you; attempt to force inconsistent answers.	Take time to consider the question; be deliberate in answering, ask to have the question repeated, remain calm.
Condescending counsel	Benevolent in approach, over-sympathetic in questions to the point of ridicule.	To give the impression that you are inept, lack confidence, or may not be a reliable witness.	Firm, decisive answers, asking for the questions to be repeated if improperly phrased.
Friendly counsel	Very courteous, polite; questions tend to take you into his confidence.	To lull you into a false sense of security, where you will give answers in favor of the defense.	Stay alert; bear in mind that the purpose of defense is to discredit or diminish the effect of your testimony.
Badgering, belligerent	Counsel staring you right in the face, shouts "That is so, isn't it, officer?"	To make you angry so that you lose the sense of logic and calmness. Generally, rapid questions will also be included in this approach.	Stay calm, speak in a deliberate voice, giving prosecutor time to make appropriate objections.
Mispronouncing officer's name; using wrong rank	Your name is Jansen, counsel calls you Johnson.	To draw your attention to the error in pronunciation rather than enabling you to concentrate on the question asked, so that you will make inadvertent errors in testimony.	Ignore the mispronunciation and concentrate on the question counsel is asking.

239

Table 10–2 *(continued)*

Counsel's Tactic	Example	Purpose	Officer's Response
Suggestive question (tends to be a leading question allowable on cross-examination)	"Was the color of the car blue?"	To suggest an answer to his or her question in an attempt to confuse or to lead you.	Concentrate carefully on the facts, disregard the suggestion. Answer the question.
Demanding a yes or no answer to a question that needs explanation	"Did you strike the defendant with your club?"	To prevent all pertinent and mitigating details from being considered by the jury.	Explain the answer to the question; if stopped by counsel demanding a yes or no answer, pause until the court instructs you to answer in your own words.
Reversing witness's words	You answer, "The accident occurred 27 feet from the intersection." Counsel says, "You say the accident occurred 72 feet from the intersection?"	To confuse you and demonstrate a lack of confidence in you.	Listen intently whenever counsel repeats back something you have said. If counsel makes an error, correct him or her.
Repetitious questions	The same question asked several times slightly rephrased.	To obtain inconsistent or conflicting answers from you.	Listen carefully to the question and state, "I have just answered that question."

Conflicting answers	"But, Officer Smith, Detective Brown just said . . ."	To show inconsistency in the investigation. This tactic is normally used on measurements, times, and so forth.	Remain calm. Conflicting statements have a tendency to make a witness extremely nervous. Be guarded in your answers on measurements, times, and so forth. Unless you have exact knowledge, use the term "approximately." Refer to your notes.
Staring	After you have answered, counsel stares as though there were more to come.	To have a long pause that one normally feels must be filled, thus saying more than necessary. To provoke you into offering more than the question called for.	Wait for the next question.

5. If you take notes to court, remember that the opposing attorney can request that the notes become part of the evidence. Recheck notes prior to court to prevent any unwanted information from entering the case.
6. Request feedback from associates to improve future performance.

CASE PROBLEMS

10A. The Loreton Company, a California manufacturer of radios, continuously increased profits due to high output at six company-owned plants. A recent inventory at the largest plant located outside of Los Angeles showed that over 4000 radios were missing. The management of the Loreton Company became desperate about the losses. You are a partner at Klein and Smith Loss Prevention Associates, a small consulting firm specializing in loss problems. Loreton Company executives contact you for assistance. A meeting is arranged. After competition with two other security and loss prevention firms, Loreton executives decide on a two-month contract for your firm's services. You are in charge. What are your specific plans and actions?

10B. You are a senior investigator for the Bolt Corporation, which is a top 100 corporation with large holdings in electrical supplies, oil and gas exploration, and drugs. Because you have an excellent record and 11 years of varied investigative experience with Bolt, you are selected by the Director of Loss Prevention to train five newly hired college-educated investigators. The director stresses that you will design a 105-hour training program to span three weeks. Practical investigative aids will be the essence of the program. After three weeks, the investigators will be assigned to various divisions within Bolt, where they will receive specialized training while working with experienced investigators. The director states that your typed curriculum design is due tomorrow for a 4 P.M. loss prevention meeting. He requires that you list the topics, hours for each topic, and why the particular topics and hours were chosen.

NOTES

1. U.S. Department of Justice, *Crime in the United States, 1995, Uniform Crime Reports* (Washington, DC: U.S. Government Printing Office, 1996), p. 197.
2. U.S. Department of Justice, *The Criminal Investigation Process: A Dialogue on Research Findings* (Washington, DC: U.S. Government Printing Office, 1977), part IV, p. 5.
3. U.S. Department of Justice, *Report of the Task Force on Private Security* (Washington, DC: U.S. Government Printing Office, 1976), p. 238.
4. George Van Nostrand and Anthony J. Luizzo, "Investigating in a New Environ-

ment," *Security Management* (June 1995): 33–35.

5. George O'Toole, *The Private Sector* (New York: W.W. Norton Co., 1978), p. 152.
6. John M. Carroll, *Confidential Information Sources: Public and Private* (Stoneham, MA: Butterworths Publishers, 1976), p. 27.
7. Gary Trobe, "Be on Guard when Collecting Information," *Security Risk* (Summer 1995): 1–5.
8. J. Shane Creamer, *The Law of Arrest, Search and Seizure*, 3rd ed. (New York: Holt, Rinehart and Winston, 1980), p. 49.

11

Accounting, Accountability, and Auditing: Keys to Survival

OBJECTIVES

After studying this chapter the reader will be able to

1. Define and explain the importance of accounting, accountability, and auditing;
2. Explain why the loss prevention function should work closely with accounting operations;
3. Describe how accountability is applied to the areas of evidence collection, cashier operations, purchasing, and shipping;
4. Explain why loss prevention professionals should work with auditors to uncover fraud and the misappropriation of assets.

The purpose of this chapter is to explain and illustrate how accounting, accountability, and auditing are loss prevention strategies and keys to survival for businesses, institutions, and organizations. Before they are discussed, definition of the three terms is helpful.

Accounting, often referred to as the language of business, is concerned with recording, sorting, summarizing, reporting, and interpreting data related to business transactions. Accounting information aids managers in decision making. Virtually every type of concern requires accounting records. For the most part, the day-to-day recording of business data is performed by bookkeepers; accountants design the accounting systems and prepare and interpret reports. For example, a bookkeeper in a business, after counting cash and checking cash sales receipts, records the amount in the cash receipts journal. Or, based on accounting data—specifically, inventory reports—an accountant decides that shrinkage is too high in a particular business; the loss prevention department is notified.

Accounting is the language of business.

Accountability defines a responsibility for and a description of something. For example, John Smith is responsible (i.e., is held accountable) for all finished products in a plant, and he maintains accurate records (i.e., a description) of what is in stock. Another example would be a loss prevention officer keeping a log of people entering and leaving a restricted area. Or, while a truck is being loaded for shipment, a clerk records on a tally the number of items being shipped. In both examples, employees sign their names to the documents (log, tally, or inventory); they are responsible, and accountability is maintained.

Auditing is the examination or check of something; the major purpose of an audit is to uncover deviations. An audit can be simple or intricate. For example, a loss prevention officer audits (checks) a CCTV system to ensure that it is working properly. Or, an auditor audits the financial records of a company and reports that they are fair, reliable, and conform to company policies and procedures.

ACCOUNTING

Within a business, for example, the accounting department has control over financial matters that are vital to business operations. Common components of an accounting department are cashiering operations, accounts receivable, accounts payable, payroll, and company bank accounts. Each component of an accounting department has the responsibility for maintaining accounting records that are scrutinized by management to ascertain the financial position of the business. Without adequate loss prevention strategies or controls in these important areas, businesses, institutions, or organizations could not survive.

Potential losses are possible throughout the accounting department. A cashiering operation must be protected not only from burglary and robbery but also from employee theft. Accounts receivable must be protected from opportunities that allow employees to destroy bills and pocket cash. Accounts payable also needs protection; employees in collusion with supply company employees have been known to alter invoices to embezzle money. A frequent scheme by some payroll clerks is to maintain fictitious employees on the payroll and cash their paychecks. Company bank accounts also are subject to manipulation and embezzlement.

Accounting also is a system of principles and procedures that enable clerks and bookkeepers to record financial data in a logical manner. A record of an individual transaction does not have as much impact as the summation of transactions in a financial statement or business report (see Table 11–1). The accounting statements assist management in decision making. Loss prevention practitioners may be contacted if these statements signify losses.

Accounting statements assist management in answering many questions, a few of which are

What is the financial condition of the concern?

What is the financial value?

Was there a profit or loss?

Which part of a firm is doing well (or poorly)?

How serious are losses attributed to crime, fire, or poor safety?

The concern of this book concentrates on the last question, although the losses affect all the questions that preceded it. Those who plan a career in loss prevention and may have to investigate a crime associated with accounting records are well advised to study accounting at the college level to prepare for investigative tasks that involve interpretation of accounting procedures and records.

ACCOUNTABILITY

The definition of formal accountability points to the documentation or description of something. Informal accountability usually is verbal and results in no documentation; for example, a loss prevention manager asks a subordinate if a fire extinguisher was checked (audited). The subordinate states that it was audited. Thus, a basic audit of a loss prevention device is accomplished. What if two weeks pass, a fire takes place near the particular fire extinguisher, and it is found to be inoperable? An employee who tries to extinguish the fire with the inoperable extinguisher complains to management. The loss prevention manager is asked, by superiors, if the extinguisher was checked. The manager states that it was audited. The superiors ask for documentation to support the statements. Because of the verbal accountability no record exists. From that point on, the loss prevention manager realizes the value of formal accountability and develops an excellent system of records and files.

Obviously, it is impractical to document every activity. Also, it sometimes is difficult to decide when to effectuate formal rather than verbal accountability. When in doubt, a loss prevention practitioner should lean toward formal accountability and fill out the paperwork, make a copy of the document if intending to send it out, and file the original.

Table 11–1   Financial Statements of Two Separate Companies

Trico Corporation
*Balance Sheet June 30, 20_*

Assets		Liabilities		
Cash	4,000	Accounts payable	44,000	
Accounts receivable	100,300	Notes payable	100,000	
Inventory	100,000			144,000
Equipment	34,000			
Land	80,000	Capital		
Buildings	300,400			
	618,700	Preferred stock	74,700	
		Common stock	400,000	
				474,700
		Total liabilities		
Total assets	618,700	and capital		618,700

Simple examples of an income statement and a capital statement are presented below. Note that "expenses" and "net income" are two additional major categories of accounting besides assets, liabilities, and capital.

Quality Loss Prevention Service
Income Statement
*for month ended October 31, 20_*

Sales and service		5,800
Operating expenses:		
Salary expenses:	3,000	
Supplies expense	100	
Rent expense	400	
Miscellaneous expense	300	
		−3,800
Net income		2,000

Quality Loss Prevention Service
Capital Statement
*for month ended October 31, 20_*

Capital, October 2, 20_		10,000
Net income for the month	2,000	
Less withdrawals	−1,000	
Increase in capital		1,000
Capital, October 31, 20_		11,000

The importance of accountability must not be underestimated. It is a key survival strategy. The documentation that is filed can be the result of many types of loss prevention activities (see the box for a list of common documents). As well as aiding a loss prevention practitioner when supporting a contention, documentation can assist in planning, budgeting, preparing major reports, and general reference. The information listed is limited to only a sample of common activities requiring accountability.

Accountability is a key survival strategy.

Common Documents (Records) in a Loss Prevention File Cabinet or Computer

Accident reports

Alarms (locations, incidents)

Applicant investigation notes

Audit and shrinkage reports

Bad checks (copies)

Budget

Building construction plans

Burglary reports

Computer loss prevention strategies

Correspondence, in

Correspondence, out

Emergency and disaster plans

External loss prevention plans

Fire plans

Incident reports

Insurance contracts

Internal loss prevention plans

Investigation reports

Litigation reports

Locks and keys

Loss prevention devices

Loss prevention organizations, notes

Loss prevention program (crime, fire, safety strategies)

Loss prevention services

Meetings with subordinates, notes

Meetings with superiors, notes

Memoranda, in

Memoranda, out

OSHA reports

Periodicals

Personnel lists

Planning and risk management

Policies and procedures

Polygraph examinations, reports

Public police reports

Public relations, notes

Purchase reports

Research notes

Robbery reports

Safes

Safety strategies

Shipping and receiving loss reports

Surveys

Traffic notes

Training and education reports

Uniforms and equipment

Visitors lists and log

Evidence Collection and Presentation

The accountability for physical evidence, especially before it reaches a court of law, can have a definite impact on a case. The "chain of possession" of evidence must be controlled. A loss scene should be protected, photographed, videotaped, and sketched before evidence is touched.

The proper labeling, packaging, and storage of evidence is equally important. The accountability for evidence often is brought forth in court. Attorneys are sure to scrutinize the paperwork and procedures associated with the evidence. The following questions are among the many frequently asked in court. Who saw the evidence first? Who touched it first? Where was it taken? By whom? How was it stored? Was the storage area locked? Who had the keys? How many keys were there?

Cashier Operations

A detailed procedure for accountability in retailing is illustrated by this description from an article in *Security World:*

> The key to front end control is accountability. Each cashier must have his or her own cash register drawer. Relief cashiers should bring their own drawer, and the cashier going on relief should lock up her cash or remove her drawer during relief periods. The relief person should also sign the register tape when taking over, and the regular cashier should sign when leaving the register.
>
> The head cashier should periodically review register detail tapes, watching for continuity of transaction numbers. If the last transaction on the register Monday night was number 112334, then the first transaction on Tuesday morning must be 112335. If it is not, the missing chronological numbers may indicate theft of several sales by the cashier and destruction of the tape containing the missing transaction numbers.[1]

Purchasing

Because procedures vary and various types of computer software are available to enhance purchasing systems, a generalized approach to purchasing is presented here. Four forms are discussed in the subsequent purchasing system: purchase requisition, purchase order, invoice, and receiving report.

When a company orders merchandise, equipment, or supplies, for example, the order should be in writing to avoid any misunderstanding. Suppose a maintenance department head at a plant is ordering something. Generally, the documentation process begins when the order is written on a standard form known as a *purchase requisition*. This form lists, among other things, the originator (who placed the order), the date, the item, a description, justification for need, and cost. Once the originator completes the purchase requisition and makes a copy for filing, superiors approve or disapprove the purchase and sign the original order. If approved, the purchasing department reviews the purchase requisition and selects the best vendor. A prenumbered *purchase order* is completed by the purchasing staff. Copies of the purchase order are sent to the originator, the receiving department, and the accounts payable department; the original purchase order is retained by the purchasing department. The purchase order contains, among other things, the originator, the item, quantity, possibly an item code number from a vendor catalogue, and the cost. The purchase order is mailed to the vendor. On fulfillment of the order, the vendor mails an *invoice* to the buyer's accounts payable department. An invoice contains the names and addresses of both the buyer and the vendor, cost, item, quantity, date, and method of shipment.

When the accounts payable department receives the invoice it checks it for accuracy by comparing it with a copy of the purchase order. Cost, type of item, proper quantity, and address of buyer are checked.

The receiving and purchasing departments of the buyer receive copies of the invoice to be able to check them for accuracy. To decrease the possibility of mistakes (or collusion), the purchase order and invoice sent to the receiving department may have the number of items deleted. When the merchandise arrives, the receiving person records the number of items, type, and also checks for irregularities (e.g., damage). This form often becomes a *receiving report*. Copies are made and then sent to the purchasing and accounts payable departments. The purchasing department compares the receiving report with the invoice. The accounts payable department makes payment after examining the purchase order, invoice, and the receiving report. These three documents and a copy of the check constitute the inactive file for this purchase (see Figure 11–1).

The system may appear complicated; however, without such accountability, losses can increase. Consider the following example of losses within a poor accountability system. The purchaser in a company and a receiving clerk are in collusion with an outside supply company employee. Their scheme is that several items on the purchase order are paid for but never delivered. All three split the money made from selling the undelivered items. Taking advantage of an inadequate accountability system, the purchaser completes a purchase order and mails it to the supplier. The supplier mails the invoice to the purchaser. The purchaser alters the invoice by inserting additional numbers to increase quantity and costs. Then, the accounts payable department receives a copy of the altered invoice from the purchaser. When the receiving clerk verbally "verifies" receiving the merchandise from the supplier, accounts payable mails a check to the supplier. Thus, more items are paid for than are received.

The preceding example is only one variation of numerous types of schemes that result in losses. Only the imagination of the offender limits the variations.

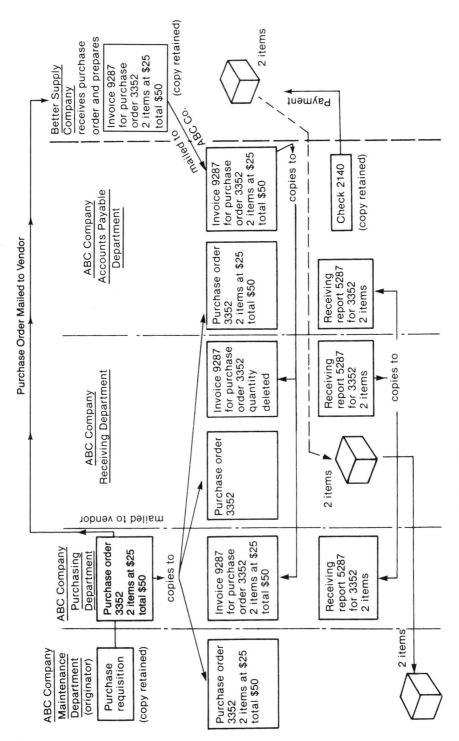

Figure 11-1 Accountability and paper trail for purchase of two items by ABC Company.

252

Another widespread loss-provoking activity in purchasing results from *kickbacks*, when the purchaser receives favors or cash from the seller for buying the seller's product or service. Losses occur, especially if the product or service is inferior and overpriced in comparison to the competition. For example, in a secret deal, John Doe Forklift Company agrees to pay Richard Ring, purchaser for Fence Manufacturing, $1000 cash for each forklift purchased. After the forklifts are delivered, it is discovered that the forklift tires are too smooth for the outside gravel and dirt grounds of the manufacturing company. With limited traction, the forklifts frequently get stuck and employees are unable to work until delivery trucks return and pull the forklifts free. The losses include both cash and lost time.

Loss prevention strategies in purchasing include the following suggestions:

1. Institute an effective accountability system that is customized to particular needs.
2. Establish adequate training relevant to the system.
3. Centralize all purchasing through a purchasing department.
4. Maintain accountability through documents (standard forms), signatures, and carefully designed computer software.
5. Separate duties and responsibilities so that each person and department can check on the others' work.
6. Test by deliberate error.
7. Use unalterable paper to prevent alterations or erasures.
8. Prenumber purchase order forms (and other forms when needed).
9. Make purchases accounted for when received.
10. Conduct loss prevention checks without notice.
11. Conduct periodic audits.
12. Reinforce quality by requiring competitive bids.
13. Scrutinize the purchasing department to prevent favoritism and kickbacks.
14. Prohibit gifts or favors from vendors (sellers).
15. Report irregularities to the loss prevention department.
16. Utilize competent undercover investigators.
17. Screen applicants for employment.
18. Utilize devices when needed (e.g., CCTV).
19. Develop clear policies and procedures.

Shipping

Shipping is another activity requiring accountability. A simplified system is described by Gion Green and Raymond C. Farber as follows:

> This accountability must start from the moment an order is received by the shipper. . . . We might refer to a firm that supplies its salesmen with

sales slips or invoices that are numbered in order. . . . Without numbering, sales slips could be destroyed and the cash . . . pocketed; or they
could be lost so that the customer might never be billed.

Merchandise should only be authorized for shipment to a customer
on the basis of the regular invoice form. This form is filled out by the
salesman receiving the order and sent to the warehouse or shipping
department. The shipping clerk signs one copy, signifying that the order
has been complied with, and sends it to accounts receivable for billing
purposes. The customer signs a copy of the invoice indicating receipt of
the merchandise, and this copy is returned to accounts receivable. It is
further advisable to have the driver sign the shipping clerk's copy as a
receipt for his load.[2]

Many of the loss prevention strategies for shipping are similar to those for
purchasing. In both, there are numerous points of accountability. Each system enables a narrowing of responsibility (and suspects).

Inventory

In a wholesale or retail business, merchandise is continuously purchased
and sold. This sale of merchandise is the primary source of revenue. A substantial amount of a business's resources is invested in salable merchandise,
and this merchandise is the largest asset. Therefore, this asset must be protected. The term *inventory* includes merchandise for sale, raw materials,
and unfinished goods. Inventory is reported on the balance sheet as an asset.

Shrinkage is the amount of merchandise that has disappeared through
theft, or has become useless due to breakage or spoilage, or is unaccounted
for due to sloppy recording. This often is expressed as a percentage. In many
businesses, shrinkage of 3 percent or more is a serious loss problem. Loss
prevention managers frequently express the objective of their job as lowering shrinkage. An accurate measurement of shrinkage depends on the quality of the inventory system; both have a definite impact on the loss
prevention program and its manager.

Two primary inventory systems are the periodic and the perpetual systems. The *periodic inventory system* results in a physical count of merchandise only at specific intervals, usually once per year. When this system is
used, daily revenue from sales is recorded in accounting records but no
transaction is recorded to adjust the inventory account to reflect the fact that
a sale was made. The periodic system makes it difficult to measure shrinkage accurately. To make matters worse, when a monthly or quarterly financial statement is necessary for a particular business using the periodic
inventory system, managers sometimes estimate the inventory without taking a physical count.

The *perpetual inventory system* uses accounting records that maintain
an up-to-date inventory count. These systems typically are computerized.
Handheld microcomputer technology and point-of-sale (POS) computers

capture data through bar-code scanning. In addition to recording daily revenue from sales, an individual inventory record is maintained for each type of merchandise sold, which enables a continuous count. Thus, the accounting records reflect cost of goods sold and the inventory quantity. This information provides a better opportunity to measure shrinkage than that available with the periodic system.

To increase the accuracy of an inventory and the shrinkage statistic, these strategies are recommended:

1. Maintain a careful inventory system.
2. Establish accountability.
3. Standardize forms and procedures for the count.
4. Make sure employees can count accurately.
5. If possible, do not subject employees to extensive inventory counts at any one time.
6. Automate the process by using handheld microcomputer technology that captures data through bar codes on merchandise.
7. Conduct surprise counts of a sample of the merchandise at erratic time intervals. Compare manual counts with computer data.
8. If possible, require prenumbered requisition forms for merchandise taken out of inventory.
9. Prohibit unnecessary people (e.g., truck drivers, service people, other employees) from entering merchandise storage areas.
10. Use an undercover investigator to participate in the inventory count.
11. The loss prevention manager should have an opportunity to examine the methods used to formulate the shrinkage statistic, especially because it will reflect on him or her and on the loss prevention program.

Another type of inventory focuses on assets such as equipment, tools, and supplies. Knowing what a company or institution owns and where assets are at all times is an important aspect of protection programs. This task is made easier by applying innovations such as bar-code technology. With this method, a number is assigned to each asset to be tracked. Software generates a bar-code tag (to be attached to each item) encoded with the respective item's asset identification number. The number links each item to its electronic file which may contain information on the person assigned to the item, its location, restrictions on movement, monetary value, vendor, and warranty. Such a system can generate reports on assets and assist with investigations.[3]

AUDITING

A popular and convenient way to conduct an audit is through an audit questionnaire. A typical audit questionnaire has a list of questions to remind the person conducting the audit to focus attention on specific areas of concern.

Questionnaire results provide feedback that helps to pinpoint and correct deviations and deficiencies.

In the box that follows, an example of an audit questionnaire from *The Journal of Accountancy* is presented.[4] This internal control questionnaire is designed for small businesses, but many of the questions are relevant to other concerns.

Certified Public Accountants

A person does not have to be a *certified public accountant* (CPA) to perform an audit. Obviously, there is a difference between an audit of a fire extinguisher by a loss prevention officer and an audit of a company's accounting records by a CPA. Both types of audits serve useful purposes.

What is involved when an independent CPA audits the accounting records of a business? First, the qualifications for a CPA certificate generally require a college degree with an accounting emphasis plus a passing grade on an examination prepared by the *American Institute of Certified Public Accountants* (AICPA). Most states require a few years of experience before successful candidates can practice as independent CPAs. The Board of Accountancy in each state can supply specific information about qualifications.

During an audit by an independent auditor, the CPA is guided by professional standards and "generally accepted accounting principles." Because it is impossible to check every financial record and transaction, the CPA narrows the audit to certain records like financial reports and areas where problems are common to the particular concern. How accounting data are recorded and summarized is frequently studied.

Internal Control Questionnaire

1.   General
    a.   Are accounting records kept up to date and balanced monthly?
    b.   Is a chart of accounts used?
    c.   Does the owner use a budget system for watching income and expenses?
    d.   Are cash projections made?
    e.   Are monthly or quarterly financial reports available to the owner?
    f.   Does the owner take a direct and active interest in the financial affairs and reports that are available?
    g.   Are the personal funds of the owner and his or her personal income and expenses completely segregated from the business?
    h.   Is the owner satisfied that all employees are honest?
    i.   Is the bookkeeper required to take annual vacations?

2.   Cash receipts
   a.   Does the owner open all mail?
   b.   Does the owner list mail receipts before turning them over to the bookkeeper?
   c.   Is the listing subsequently traced to the cash receipts journal?
   d.   Are over-the-counter receipts controlled by cash register tapes, counter receipts, and so on?
   e.   Are receipts deposited intact daily?
   f.   Are employees who handle funds bonded?
   g.   Do two different people reconcile the bank records and make out the deposit slip?
3.   Cash disbursements
   a.   Are all disbursements made by check?
   b.   Are prenumbered checks used?
   c.   Is a controlled, mechanical check protector used?
   d.   Is the owner's signature required on checks?
   e.   Does the owner sign checks only after they are properly completed?
   f.   Does the owner approve and cancel the documentation in support of all disbursements?
   g.   Are all voided checks retained and accounted for?
   h.   Does the owner review the bank reconciliation?
   i.   Is an imprest petty cash fund used?
   j.   Does the owner never sign blank checks?
   k.   Do different people reconcile the bank records and write the checks?
4.   Accounts receivable and sales
   a.   Are work order or sales invoices prenumbered and controlled?
   b.   Are customer's ledgers balanced regularly?
   c.   Are monthly statements sent to all customers?
   d.   Does the owner review statements before mailing them himself or herself?
   e.   Are account write-offs and discounts approved only by the owner?
   f.   Is credit granted only by the owner?
5.   Notes receivable and investments
6.   Inventories
   a.   Is the person responsible for inventory someone other than the bookkeeper?
   b.   Are periodic physical inventories taken?
   c.   Is there physical control over inventory stock?
   d.   Are perpetual inventory records maintained?
7.   Property assets
   a.   Are there detailed records available of property assets and allowances for depreciation?
   b.   Is the owner acquainted with property assets owned by the company?
   c.   Are retirements approved by the owner?

continued

8. Accounts payable and purchases
   a. Are purchase orders used?
   b. Does someone other than the bookkeeper always do the purchasing?
   c. Are suppliers' monthly statements compared with recorded liabilities regularly?
   d. Are suppliers' monthly statements checked by the owner periodically if disbursements are made from invoice only?
9. Payroll
   a. Are the employees hired by the owner?
   b. Would the owner be aware of the absence of any employee?
   c. Does the owner approve, sign, and distribute payroll checks?

At times, the CPA may encounter misleading financial information that attempts to make a business look better than its true financial position. The misleading information often is an attempt by management to attract investors. To reduce this problem, cautious investors are more likely to favor a business that has had an audit by an outside independent CPA, as opposed to no audit or one performed by an internal auditor.

When the independent CPA has completed the audit, a report is prepared. If the business's financial records are dependable and credible, then the CPA expresses this favorable opinion in the audit report. This is known as the *attest function*.

Many firms maintain internal auditors. These internal auditors audit various internal activities that independent auditors may or may not audit. For instance, in addition to studying specific accounting records, internal auditors may examine whether management's policies and procedures are being followed. An internal auditor also can conduct surprise audits.

Fraud

Fraud is a broad term that includes a variety of offenses that share the elements of deceit or intentional misrepresentation of fact, with the intent of unlawfully depriving a person of property or legal rights. Until 1995, pressure on auditors to uncover fraud was only moderately strong. However, in 1995 Congress passed the *Private Securities Litigation Reform Act*, which requires CPAs who audit publicly held companies to take steps to detect fraud. Following this legislation, the AICPA, the national body that sets standards for the accounting profession, revised its auditing standard and specifically replaced the word *irregularity* with the word *fraud* and formally holds accounting professionals responsible for detecting fraud. The standard, entitled Consideration of Fraud in a Financial Statement Audit, identifies two areas that auditors should diligently work to detect: *financial reporting fraud* and *misappropriation (theft) of assets.* The second area, especially, is likely to bring auditors to rely on the expertise of loss prevention professionals who can provide documentation that the company has controls in place to prevent losses.[5] As well as offering assistance to auditors, this also is *a ripe opportunity for loss prevention professionals to show the value of security and to strengthen the protection budget.*

For accounting and loss prevention professionals interested in developing their expertise against fraud, the *Association of Certified Fraud Examiners* (ACFE), established in 1988, is a professional organization dedicated to reduce the incidence of fraud and white-collar crime. The ACFE assists its membership in the deterrence and detection of fraud through publications, training, and the professional designation, *certified fraud examiner* (CFE). (ACFE, 716 West Avenue, Austin, TX 78701; Tel.: 1-800-245-3321).

In light of compliance auditing and federal sentencing guidelines (both covered in Chapter 4) and our discussion here, we can see a trend where our government is focusing increased attention on corporate crime. This new perspective views environmental violations, health and safety violations, and fraud as more harmful to society than before. Whereas in earlier years, business people who violated the law were punished, more by bad publicity, humiliation, and fines, today, the federal government views incarceration of executives as a stronger deterrent.[6] *Here again, the loss prevention professional should seize this opportunity to show his or her value to the business community by communicating the seriousness of the law to executives, while illustrating the value of protection programs in assisting corporations to survive and prosper.*

How does the Private Securities Litigation Reform Act provide opportunities for loss prevention professionals?

Loss Prevention Auditing

A loss prevention audit can focus on only loss prevention services, devices, policies, and procedures; or instead, the focus can extend to all aspects of a business. This could include all policies and procedures and operating activities (e.g., cash handling, shipping and receiving, warehousing, production, purchasing).

Management can prepare an audit form to remind loss prevention employees what to audit. Questions can emphasize the conditions of locks, alarms, doors, windows, fire extinguishers, and the like and ask for reports of unusual incidents. When audit forms are returned, supervisors can review and provide feedback to subordinates, which is helpful as a training technique. These forms should be filed.

Loss prevention officers commonly are assigned to fixed posts or they are mobile. Many "fall asleep mentally" while on the job. By performing an audit, these officers can obtain increased satisfaction from their jobs while performing a useful activity.

Computerization

Management has become increasingly dependent on computers because of cost savings, efficiency, and speed. Computers can perform an array of activities such as monitor inventories, issue purchase orders, and bill customers. As with manual accounting systems, computerized accounting systems need controls and audits.

Computerized accounting systems are not totally exempt from manual activities. Raw data (e.g., cash receipts and receiving reports) must be entered into the computer. Consequently, the human factor is involved in computer accounting systems; and error, manipulation, and losses are possible. For instance, instructions can be entered into a computer to overpay an invoice or to favor a high-priced vendor.

Controls and auditing are necessary for computerized accounting systems, especially because many systems are designed for efficiency and not with loss prevention in mind. Controls are numerous and can include permitting no changes in the system without authorization, requiring that accountability be maintained when changes are allowed, making sure no one person is responsible for the complete processing of any transaction, and periodic rotation of personnel. Many of the controls used in manual accounting systems are applicable to computerized accounting systems.

Auditing for computerized accounting systems is varied. One technique to audit a computerized inventory system, for example, is to have employees count the physical inventory and compare this count to the computer count. A variety of software programs are available that perform controls and auditing of computerized accounting systems.

CASE PROBLEM

11A. With reference to the purchasing accountability section of this chapter and Figure 11–1, design an accountability system to strengthen control and prevent losses when merchandise travels from the receiving department to the originator. Look for any other weaknesses and suggest controls.

NOTES

1. Bob Curtis, "Executive Insights," *Security World* 17, no. 2 (February 1980): 14.
2. Gion Green and Raymond C. Farber, *Introduction to Security* (Boston: Butterworth–Heinemann, 1978), p. 263.
3. Frederick C. Herdeen et al., "Get a Lock on Inventory," *Security Management* (October 1996): 71–76.
4. "A Small Business Internal Control Questionnaire," *The Journal of Accountancy* (July 1978), p. 54. Copyright © 1978 by the American Institute of Certified Public Accountants.
5. "Soon, Auditors Will Demand More from Security Managers," *Security Management Bulletin* (January 25, 1997): 1–3.
6. Philip Purpura, *Criminal Justice: An Introduction* (Boston: Butterworth–Heinemann, 1997), pp. 37–38.

12

Fires and Other Disasters

OBJECTIVES

After studying this chapter the reader will be able to

1. Discuss the problem posed by fire;
2. Explain the role of public fire departments;
3. List and explain five fire prevention strategies;
4. List and explain five fire suppression strategies;
5. List five suggestions for improving planning and decisions for integrated fire and security systems;
6. List three human-made disasters and three natural disasters;
7. List ten strategies for emergency planning and disaster recovery.

THE PROBLEM POSED BY FIRE

The National Fire Protection Association reported that, in 1995, in the United States, public fire departments responded to 1,965,550 fires, of which 573,500 were fires in structures. The remaining fires were at outside locations such as wildlands and highways. During 1995, civilian deaths due to fire totaled 4,585, and property damage was estimated at $8.9 billion. Of all structure fires in 1995, 16 percent, or 90,500 fires, were deliberately set or are suspected of having been deliberately set.[1]

Private Organizations Involved in Fire Safety

A number of private organizations assist the federal government, state governments, and local fire departments in searching for ways to minimize this costly problem. The *National Fire Protection Association* (NFPA), established in 1896, is a potent voice in fire prevention and suppression (NFPA's address and telephone number are in Chapter 3). The NFPA publishes fire standards and codes that often are incorporated into state and local fire laws. Two popular codes are the National Electric Code and the Life Safety

Code. Among other groups, property owners, insurance companies, and associations have input into the formulation and revision of NFPA standards. The *Fire Protection Handbook*, first published in 1896 by the NFPA, is "presented in the tradition of fulfilling the needs of the fire protection community for a single-source reference book on good contemporary fire protection practices."[2] Topics within this lengthy publication include the characteristics and behavior of fire, fire hazards, building design and construction, water supplies, alarm systems, extinguishing agents, and fire protection systems.

Underwriters Laboratories, Inc., is a nonprofit corporation interested in public safety through the investigation and testing of materials and products (again, the address and telephone number are in Chapter 3). It is supported by fees from manufacturers who request that their products be tested. Each year UL publishes lists of manufacturers whose products have met UL standards for safety. Some specific departments of UL show its relationship to loss prevention: burglary protection and signaling department, casualty and chemical hazards department, and fire protection department. UL representatives make periodic examinations of products at factory sites. From time to time, factory product samples are selected to determine compliance with UL requirements. Manufacturers of products that are not in compliance must correct the deviation or remove the UL label (see Figure 12–1) from the product.

Another private organization involved in fire safety is the *Factory Mutual System* (1151 Boston-Providence Turnpike, Norwood, MA 02062; Tel.: 617-255-4681). This group works on improving the effectiveness of fire protection systems, new fire suppression chemicals, and cost evaluation of fire protection systems. The Approval Group tests materials and equipment, submitted by manufacturers, to see if they can withstand fire tests. An approval guide is published each year. Like UL, it issues labels to indicate that specific products have passed its tests.

Figure 12–1   One of UL's registered marks, which can be found on products that meet safety standards of Underwriters Laboratories, Inc.

The *American Insurance Association*, or AIA (1130 Connecticut Ave., Suite 1000, Washington, DC 20036; Tel.: 1-800-242-2302) studied contributing causes of major fires in the United States during the late 1800s and early 1900s. With this information as a foundation and with NFPA standards, AIA developed codes for fire prevention in urban areas. The National Building Code evolved, which has been adopted by many local governments. A Fire Prevention Code for cities also was published by the AIA. The AIA continues to serve the insurance industry by providing safety services, publications, and database services covering hundreds of topics.

Fire Department Prevention Efforts

Because this book is primarily prevention oriented, it stresses public fire prevention tasks that often involve private-sector loss prevention practitioners. These tasks include facility planning, prefire planning, public education, codes, inspections, and legal implications.

Facility Planning

In many locales, it is legally mandatory that public fire personnel review construction plans for new facilities. This may entail consultation with architects, engineers, and loss prevention practitioners on a number of subjects ranging from fire codes to water supplies for sprinkler systems. On-site inspections by fire personnel ensure compliance with plans. Fire and water department officials often prepare recommendations to local government bodies concerning improvements in water supply systems for new industrial plants to ensure an adequate water supply in the event of a fire. Cooperation and planning with interested parties can create an improved atmosphere for preventing and suppressing fires.

Prefire Planning

Preparatory plans assist fire personnel in case of fire. An on-site survey is made of a particular building with the aid of a checklist. Then the actual prefire plans are formulated for that structure. Drawings are used to identify the location of exits, stairs, fire fighting equipment, hazards, and anything else of importance. Additional information is helpful: construction characteristics and that of adjacent buildings, type of roofs, number of employees, and the best response route to the building. Prefire plans also serve as an aid to training. Naturally, fire fighting personnel do not have the time to prepare prefire plans for all structures in their jurisdiction. One- and two-family residential structures are omitted in favor of more complex structures where greater losses can occur, such as schools, hospitals, theaters, hotels, and manufacturing plants.

Public Education

This fire prevention strategy involves educating the public about the fire problem and how to prevent it. The public can become a great aid in reducing fires if people are properly recruited through education campaigns. Public education programs utilize mass media, contests, lectures, and tours of firehouses. Building inspections also educate the public by pointing out fire hazards.

Codes

Years ago, as the United States was evolving into an industrial giant, buildings were constructed without proper concern for fire prevention. Building codes in urban areas were either nonexistent or inadequate to ensure construction designed to prevent fire-related losses. In fact, a year before the great Chicago fire in 1871, Lloyd's Insurance Company of London halted the writing of policies in that city because of fire-prone construction practices.

Prompted by the difficulty in selling insurance due to higher rates for hazardous buildings and the losses incurred by some spectacular fires, insurance companies became increasingly interested in fire prevention strategies. Improvements in building construction and fire departments slowly followed.

Although insurance associations played an important role in establishing fire standards, government support was necessary to enforce fire codes. Today, local governments enforce state regulations and local ordinances that support fire codes. Fire department personnel inspect structures to ensure conformance to standards and codes that are specified in regulations and ordinances. To strengthen compliance by owners of buildings, penalties are meted out for violations so that fire hazards are reduced. Penalties usually are in the form of fines.

Codes can be in the form of fire codes and building codes. Frequently, there is disagreement about what should be contained in each and what responsibility and authority should be given to fire inspectors as opposed to building inspectors. Generally, construction requirements go into building codes, and these codes are enforced by building inspectors. *Building codes* usually contain construction requirements pertaining to materials, roofs, electrical installations, sprinkler systems, exits, vents, and the like. *Fire codes*, enforced by fire fighting personnel, deal with the maintenance and condition of various fire prevention and suppression features of buildings (e.g., sprinkler systems). Also, fire codes cover hazardous substances, hazardous occupancies, and general precautions against fire.

A code that has been adopted in whole by many federal, state, and local jurisdictions is the *Life Safety Code* from the NFPA. Its objective is to establish minimum requirements for safety from fire in buildings and other structures. Examples of requirements include an ample number of exits for evacuation and the avoidance of locks that prevent escape during an emergency. Codes often are used in litigation when there is a claim of negligence.

Local fire codes have afforded buildings greater fire protection, especially when compared to earlier days. But there are numerous localities where these codes are of poor quality. A prime factor is construction costs. Interest-group (e.g., the construction industry) pressure on government officials who stipulate codes has been known to weaken fire codes. A typical sad case is when a high-rise building catches fire and people perish because no sprinklers were installed on upper floors, and the fire department was ill-equipped to suppress a fire so high up. Later, the media broadcasts the tragedy and government officials meet to satisfy the public outcry. Stronger fire codes often emerge.

Inspections

The primary purpose of building inspections by fire fighting personnel is to uncover deviations from the fire code. The frequency and intensity of these inspections vary. Because of budget constraints and a shortage of personnel, many fire departments are not able to conduct enough inspections to equal national standards of several inspections per year for hazardous buildings. The *NFPA Inspection Manual* outlines methods for conducting inspections.

Legal Implications

Fire marshals are provided with broad powers to ensure public safety. This is especially evident in fire inspections and investigations, rights to subpoena records, and in fire marshal's hearings. Most courts have upheld these powers.

In almost all local jurisdictions, the state has delegated police powers so that local officials regulate safety conditions through ordinances. Fire ordinances stipulate inspection procedures, number of inspections, violations, and penalties. When differences of opinion develop over individual rights (e.g., of a building owner) versus fire department police powers (e.g., building inspection), the issue is often resolved by the courts. Courts have stated that administrative searches are significant intrusions on individual liberties protected by the Fourth Amendment. *Probable cause* is required for a warrant as stipulated in the Fourth Amendment. To establish probable cause, the courts have pointed to the time span since the last inspection, the type of building, and associated hazards.

FIRE PREVENTION AND FIRE SUPPRESSION STRATEGIES

Fire prevention focuses on strategies that help to avoid the inception of fires. *Fire suppression* applies personnel, equipment, and other resources to suppress fires.

The following practical strategies are emphasized for loss prevention programs:

Fire Prevention	Fire Suppression
Inspections	Technology and computers
Planning	Detection of smoke and fire
Safety	Contact the fire department
Good housekeeping	Extinguishers
Storage and transportation of hazardous substances and materials	Sprinklers
	Standpipes and hose systems
Prevention of injuries and deaths	Fire walls and doors
Training	Fire-resistive buildings
	Training and fire brigades

The fire triangle (see Figure 12–2) symbolizes the elements necessary for a fire. Fire requires heat, fuel, oxygen, and then a chemical chain reaction. When all three characteristics, plus a chemical chain reaction, are present, there will be fire. If any one is missing, either through prevention strategies (e.g., good housekeeping, safety) or suppression (i.e., extinguishment), fire will not exist. Heat often is considered the ignition source. A smoldering cigarette, sparks from a welder's torch, or friction from a machine can produce enough heat to begin a fire.

Almost every working environment has fuels, heat, and oxygen. Loss prevention practitioners, and all employees in general, must take steps to reduce the chances for fire by isolating fuels and controlling heat. Not much can be done about pervasive oxygen, but fuels such as gasoline and kerosene should be stored properly away from sources of heat.

Fire Prevention Strategies

Inspections

Inspections or audits to check on fire hazards are the mainstay of any organization's strategy against fires.[3] Checklist questions include the following. Are new facility designs and manufacturing processes being submitted to appropriate personnel for fire protection review? Do employees receive periodic training on fire prevention and suppression policies and procedures? What is the condition of fire suppression equipment? Are plant wastes, oily rags, and other combustibles properly disposed of? What is the condition of electrical wiring? Are machines properly lubricated to reduce friction? The basic purpose of inspections is to uncover deficiencies. Then, corrective action becomes the heart of the inspection prevention strategy.

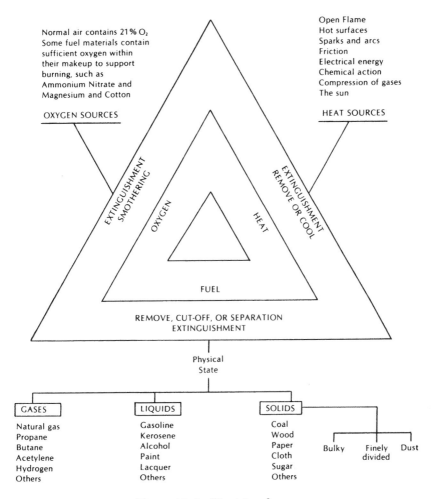

Normal air contains 21% O_2
Some fuel materials contain
sufficient oxygen within
their makeup to support
burning, such as
Ammonium Nitrate and
Magnesium and Cotton

OXYGEN SOURCES

Open Flame
Hot surfaces
Sparks and arcs
Friction
Electrical energy
Chemical action
Compression of gases
The sun

HEAT SOURCES

EXTINGUISHMENT
SMOTHERING

EXTINGUISHMENT
REMOVE OR COOL

OXYGEN

HEAT

FUEL

REMOVE, CUT-OFF, OR SEPARATION
EXTINGUISHMENT

Physical
State

GASES	LIQUIDS	SOLIDS		
Natural gas	Gasoline	Coal		
Propane	Kerosene	Wood		
Butane	Alcohol	Paper	Bulky	Finely Dust
Acetylene	Paint	Cloth		divided
Hydrogen	Lacquer	Sugar		
Others	Others	Others		

Figure 12–2   Fire triangle.

Planning

Feedback from inspections helps in planning for strategies against fire losses. An interdisciplinary planning group often is an excellent source for plans. Fire department personnel, architects, engineers, insurance specialists, loss prevention practitioners, and others can provide a multitude of ideas. Management support is an important ingredient in the planning process. By supplying adequate personnel, money, and policies and procedures, management can strengthen the fire protection program.

Many changes that occur in organizations have fire protection implications. To illustrate, a new manufacturing process may create the need for additional fire prevention training and fire suppression devices. A new computer room will require fire protection. Expanded operations often will result in increased fire insurance premiums.

Careful planning can prevent fires and losses. The following questions can serve as important reminders to reinforce planning:

1. Is a competent employee assigned to coordinate fire protection?
2. Are plans carefully analyzed, detailed in writing, adequately implemented, and revised to conform to changes?
3. Have local codes been adhered to in terms of strategies like sprinkler systems, alarms, fire extinguishers, hoses, and exit signs?
4. Do employees know what to do in case of fire?
5. Is there adequate training for fire prevention and suppression?
6. Are high-quality fire prevention and suppression devices and equipment present?
7. Is there a continuing liaison with public service agencies and public utilities?
8. Are first aid and emergency medical services available?
9. Does the entity have adequate insurance coverage?
10. In the event of fire-related losses, are contingency plans available? Can production be maintained or restored quickly through establishing alternative sources of equipment and resources?
11. Are high-value items separated to avoid large losses?

In reference to local public fire departments, the following questions are helpful to the planning process:

1. Have public fire personnel visited the facility and examined fire prevention and suppression capabilities?
2. Have the water supplies been analyzed?
3. Have prefire plans been formulated?
4. What type of public fire protection is available?
5. How long will it take for public fire equipment to reach the facility?
6. Are outside fire fighters paid or volunteer?
7. How often are joint private-public sector training and drills conducted?

Safety

Some safety strategies for a fire prevention program follow:

1. Set up smoking and no smoking areas that are supervised, safe, and clearly marked with signs.
2. In smoking areas, provide cigarette butt and match receptacles or sand urns.

3. When equipment or devices are selected, select those that have been approved by a reputable testing organization (e.g., Underwriters Laboratories, Inc.)
4. In the use of heating systems, like boilers, maintain safety when lighting up, during usage, and when shutting down.
5. Examine motors frequently to ensure safe operation and to prevent overheating.
6. Never overload electrical circuits.
7. Maintain lightning protective devices (e.g., lightning rods).
8. Employ an electrician who is safety conscious.
9. Prohibit the use of welding equipment near flammable substances or hazardous materials.
10. Watch sparks during and after welding.
11. Train employees to create an atmosphere of safety.
12. Conduct inspections and correct deficiencies.
13. Ensure fire protection standby for hazardous operations.

Good Housekeeping

Good housekeeping is another fire prevention strategy. It consists of building care, maintenance, cleanliness, the proper placement of materials, careful waste and garbage disposal, and other general housekeeping activities.

Storage and Transportation of Hazardous Substances and Materials

The prevention of disasters from hazardous substances and materials is extremely important. Such materials are used in every community and transported by trucks, railcars, ships, barges, and planes. All communities are subject to possible losses. Examples of hazardous substances and materials are plastics, fuels, corrosive chemicals (e.g., acids), and radioactive materials. A tremendous amount of information exists concerning their physical and chemical properties, methods for storage and transportation, and the most appropriate strategies in the event of fire.

Prevention of Injuries and Deaths

Whatever fire prevention strategies are planned, a key factor must be to prevent injuries and deaths. Two vital considerations are *evacuation* and *medical services.* Evacuation plans and drills help people prepare for a possible fire. Smoke and fire alarms often provide warning for escape. Emergency exit maps and properly identified emergency doors also prevent injuries and deaths. Employees should turn off all equipment, utilize designated escape routes and fire escapes, avoid elevators, and report to a predetermined point on the outside to be counted. While employees are evacuating, firefighters may be entering the premises. Here is where a coordinated traffic flow is crucial. Fire fighting equipment and personnel need to be directed to the fire location. Personnel should also be assigned to crowd control.

If injuries do take place, the quickness and quality of emergency medical services can save lives and unnecessary suffering. Preplanning will improve services. Within a plant, for example, specific employees should be trained to administer first aid.

Training

Without training, fire prevention becomes a narrowly conceived strategy. *Through training, fire prevention becomes everybody's responsibility.* Employees must first understand the disastrous effects of serious fire losses. This includes not only harm to humans but also lost productivity and jobs. Topics within training can include safety, good housekeeping, hazardous substances and materials, evacuation, and first aid. Knowledge is transmitted via lectures, videos, demonstrations, drills, visits by public fire prevention personnel, pamphlets, and posted fire prevention signs. By actually starting a small outside fire in a controlled area with the assistance of the local fire department, employees can practice using fire suppression equipment. Incentive programs, whereby employees compete for prizes (e.g., the best fire prevention poster), also can increase fire prevention awareness.

What do you think can improve fire prevention in the United States?

Fire Suppression Strategies

The success of fire suppression strategies depends primarily on preplanning, preparation, equipment quality, and the readiness of personnel.

Technology and Computers

Detectors can measure smoke and the rate of temperature rise. If danger is evident, an alarm is sounded at the earliest stages of a fire. The fire can be extinguished automatically by water from sprinklers. A computer system can be programmed to perform a variety of functions; for example, displaying written text and CCTV pictures on a computer screen to pinpoint the fire, notifying the fire department, activating a public address (PA) system to provide life and safety messages to occupants, starting up emergency generators for emergency lights and other equipment, detecting changes in sprinkler system water pressure, turning off certain electrical devices and equipment (e.g., shutting down fans that spread fire and smoke), venting specific areas, closing doors, creating safe zones for occupants, and returning elevators to ground level to encourage the use of emergency stairways. If a human being were to analyze the fire threat and make these decisions, the time factor would obviously be greater than the split second needed by a computer.

Haphazard Fire Protection at Bestbuy Service Company

The Bestbuy Service Company was a unique and rapidly growing business that sold numerous consumer items similar to those in department stores. Bestbuy's success was due to a no-frills store design and customer self-service. Each store essentially was a warehouse located away from main roads. Loss prevention was of minimal concern to management. Strategies against crime, fire, and accidents were haphazard.

One store, which also served as a distribution center, had an unfortunate experience. Late one afternoon, before closing, a salesperson threw a lighted cigarette butt into a trash container. The trash and then some boxes nearby caught fire. When store personnel were surprised by the spreading fire, they panicked. The first thing they all did was to run out of the warehouse with the customers. While the employees watched the burning warehouse in amazement, the manager asked if anybody had called the fire department. Nobody responded, so he told a young salesperson to run to a nearby gas station to call the fire department. The manager continued to watch the fire and remembered that the automatic sprinklers were turned off because of freezing temperatures. Also in his thoughts were the thousands of dollars worth of merchandise burning up.

For the Bestbuy Company, the store and its contents were a tremendous loss. Insurance covered only a small part of the losses, especially because many insurance company recommendations went unheeded: the local fire department was never contacted for prefire plans, and employees were never trained for simple fire procedures. Senior management was clearly at fault.

Detection of Smoke and Fire

Many businesses utilize a combination of the following detectors for increased protection:

- *Smoke detectors* are widely used, especially since most human casualties in fires result from smoke and the toxic fumes or gases within smoke. These detectors operate with photoelectric light beams and react when smoke either blocks the beam of light or enters a refraction chamber where the smoke reflects the light into the photo cell.
- *Ionization detectors* are sensitive to invisible products of combustion created during the early stages of a fire. These detectors are noted for their early warning capabilities.
- *Thermal detectors* respond to heat either when the temperature reaches a certain degree or when the temperature rises too quickly. The

latter is known as a *rate-of-rise detector*. Thermal detectors are made with either feature or a combination of both.

- *Flame detectors* detect flame and glowing embers. These detectors are sensitive to flames not visible to the human eye. The infrared kind is responsive to radiant energy that human beings cannot see.
- *Sprinkler water flow detectors* contain a seal that melts when heat rises to a specific temperature. Then, water flows from the sprinkler system. An alarm is activated when the water flow closes pressure switches.
- *Carbon monoxide detectors* protect against what is often called the *silent killer*, because carbon monoxide is difficult to detect. In fact victims, in their drowsy state, may be wrongly diagnosed as being substance abusers.
- *Gas detectors* monitor flammable gases or vapors. These devices are especially valuable in petroleum, chemical, and other industries where dangerous gases or vapors are generated.
- *Combination detectors* respond to more than one fire-producing cause or employ multiple operating principles. Examples include smoke/heat detector or rate-of-rise/fixed temperature heat detector.

Contact the fire department. Sometimes simple things can be overlooked. When a serious fire begins, the local fire department must be contacted as soon as possible to reduce losses. The best strategy to prevent a situation in which everybody thought somebody else had contacted the fire department is to ask: "Who called the fire department?" Another problem develops when *people think that they can extinguish a fire without outside assistance.* It is not until precious time has elapsed and serious danger exists that the fire department is contacted.

Alarm signaling systems are automatic or manual. With *automatic systems*, the attachment of a siren or a bell to a smoke or fire detection device or sprinkler system will notify people in the immediate area about a smoke or fire problem. This kind of alarm is called a *local alarm*. Unless incorporated into this system, the local alarm will not notify the fire department. Automatic systems also consist of a local alarm and an alarm that notifies a central station or the fire department. Many large industries have a central, proprietary monitoring station that monitors smoke, fire, burglar, and other alarms. *Manual fire alarm signaling systems* use a pull station fixed to a wall. This is a local alarm unless an alarm signal is transmitted to a central station or fire department.

Extinguishers

Because fire extinguishers are of various kinds, each used for a specific type of fire, it is helpful first to be able to classify fires:

- *Class A* fires consist of ordinary combustible materials such as trash, paper, fibers, wood, drapes, and furniture.
- *Class B* fires are fueled by a flammable liquid, such as gasoline, oil, alcohol, or cleaning solvents.

- *Class C* fires occur in live electrical circuits or equipment such as generators, motors, fuse boxes, computers, or copying machines.
- *Class D* fires, the rarest of the four types of fires, are fueled by combustible metals such as sodium, magnesium, and potassium.

Figure 12–3 illustrates the proper use of fire extinguishers according to the National Institute for Occupational Safety and Health. Class D fires are omitted from the chart; they are extinguished with dry powder extinguishers.

Employees and loss prevention practitioners must be knowledgeable about the proper use of extinguishers. If the wrong extinguisher is used, a fire may become more serious. Water must not be used on a flammable liquid like gasoline (Class B fire) because the gasoline may float on the water and spread the fire. Neither should one spray water on electrical fires (Class C fires) because water conducts electricity, and electrocution may result. Many locations use multipurpose dry chemical extinguishers that can be applied to either A, B, or C fires. This approach reduces confusion during a fire. Employee training can provide the appropriate response to fires.

Fire extinguishers should be checked at least every week during a loss prevention officer's patrol. Service companies recharge extinguishers when necessary. A seal is attached to the extinguisher that certifies its readiness.

Sprinklers

A sprinkler system consists of pipes along a ceiling that contain water under pressure, with an additional source of water for a constant flow. Attached to the pipes, automatic sprinklers are placed at select locations. When a fire occurs, a seal in the sprinkler head ruptures at a preestablished temperature and a steady stream of water flows.

An Angry Ex-Employee's Revenge

Albert Drucker had been warned numerous times about pilfering small tools from the maintenance department at Bearing Industries. When he was caught for the third time, via a strict inventory system, management decided to fire him. When Drucker was informed, he went into a rage and stormed out of the plant. While leaving, he vowed, "I'm gonna get you back for this." Management maintained that it made the right decision and forgot about the matter.

Two weeks later, Drucker was ready with his vindictive plan. At 2:00 one morning, he entered the Bearing plant by using a previously stolen master key. No loss prevention devices or services hindered his entrance. It took him 15 minutes to collect three strategically located fire extinguishers. When Drucker arrived home, he quickly emptied the contents of the extinguishers and then filled each one with gasoline. By 5:30 A.M., the three extinguishers were replaced and Drucker was home sleeping.

continued

At 2:00 P.M., two days later, when the Bearing plant was in full production, Drucker sneaked into the plant unnoticed and placed, on a pile of old rags, a book of matches with a lighted cigarette underneath the matchheads. By the time Drucker was a few miles away, the old rags and some cardboard boxes were on fire. When employees discovered the fire, they were confident that they could extinguish it. They reached for the nearest extinguishers and approached the fire. To their surprise, the fire grew as they supplied it with gasoline. Their first reaction was to drop the extinguishers and run; one extinguisher exploded while the fire intensified. The fire caused extensive damage but no injuries or deaths. The police and management suspected arson. When police investigators asked management if there was anybody who held a grudge against the company, Albert Drucker was mentioned. He was arrested a week later and charged with arson.

Sprinklers are an effective fire suppression strategy. Statistics from the National Fire Data Center reveal that "the average loss is significantly less where automatic sprinklers are installed and operating properly than where there are no sprinklers."[4] The NFPA has kept records of automatic sprinkler performance for more than 80 years; that organization reports: "These remarkably comprehensive records show that in 95 percent of the some 117,770 fires in sprinklered buildings (where the Association has reliable data), the sprinklers have performed satisfactorily."[5] The failure of a sprinkler system most often is due to human error—the water supply was turned off at the time of the fire.

A sprinkler system is a worthwhile investment for reducing fire losses. Lower insurance premiums actually can pay for the system over time.

There are several kinds of automatic sprinkler systems. Two popular ones are the wet-pipe and dry-pipe systems. With the *wet-pipe system*, water is in the pipes at all times and is released when heat ruptures the seal in the sprinkler head. This is the most common system and is applicable where freezing is no threat to its operation (see Figure 12–4). Where freezing temperatures and broken pipes are a problem, the *dry-pipe system* is useful. Air pressure is maintained in the pipes until a sprinkler head ruptures. Then, the air escapes, and water enters the pipes and exits through the opened sprinklers.

Older buildings may have pipes that apply fire-suppressant chemicals such as *carbon-dioxide* or *Halon*. Fire codes now prohibit these chemicals. The former absorbs oxygen, creating a danger to humans, whereas the latter depletes the earth's ozone layer.

Standpipes and Hose Systems

Standpipes and hose systems enable people to manually apply water to fires in buildings. *Standpipes* are vertical pipes that let a water supply reach an

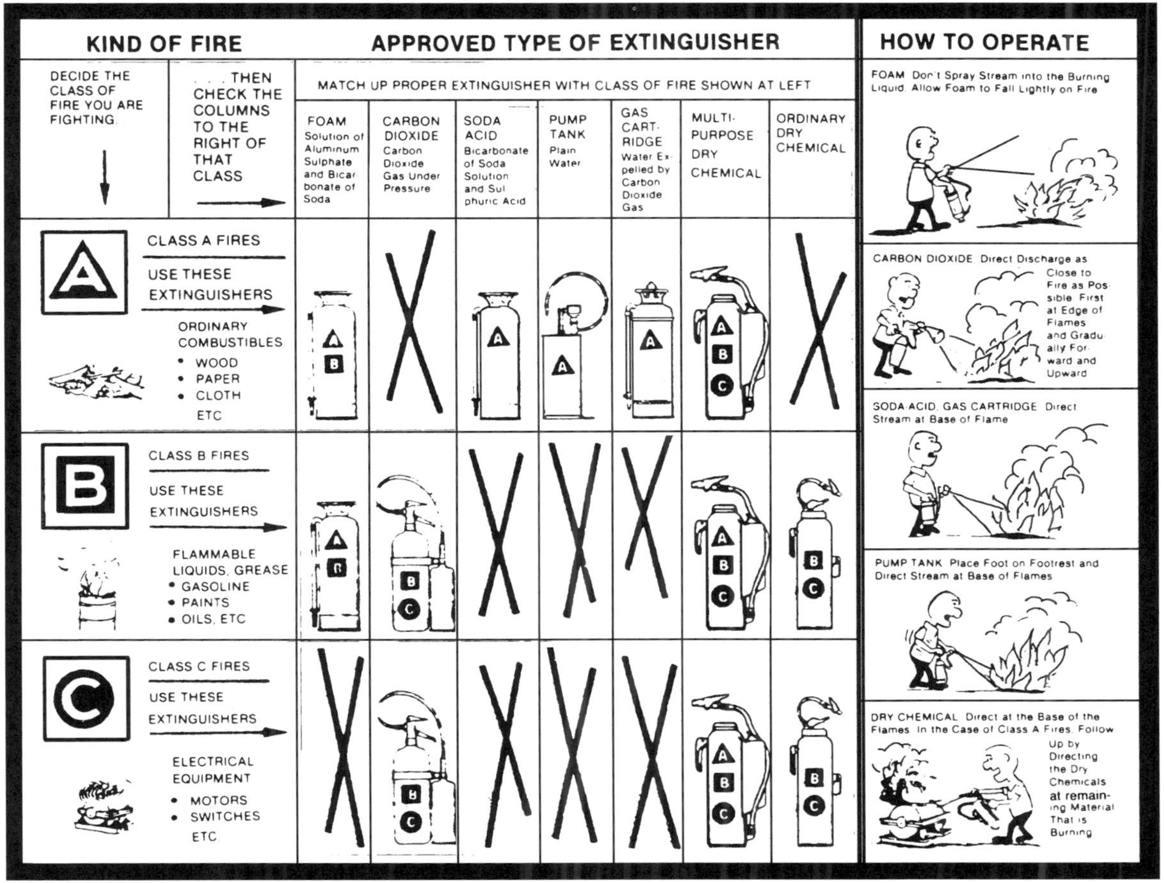

KIND OF FIRE

DECIDE THE CLASS OF FIRE YOU ARE FIGHTING →

THEN CHECK THE COLUMNS TO THE RIGHT OF THAT CLASS ↑

APPROVED TYPE OF EXTINGUISHER

MATCH UP PROPER EXTINGUISHER WITH CLASS OF FIRE SHOWN AT LEFT

	FOAM Solution of Aluminum Sulphate and Bicarbonate of Soda	CARBON DIOXIDE Carbon Dioxide Gas Under Pressure	SODA ACID Bicarbonate of Soda Solution and Sulphuric Acid	PUMP TANK Plain Water	GAS CART-RIDGE Water Expelled by Carbon Dioxide Gas	MULTI-PURPOSE DRY CHEMICAL	ORDINARY DRY CHEMICAL
CLASS A FIRES — USE THESE EXTINGUISHERS ↑ — ORDINARY COMBUSTIBLES • WOOD • PAPER • CLOTH ETC	A–B	X	A	A	A	A–B–C	X
CLASS B FIRES — USE THESE EXTINGUISHERS ↑ — FLAMMABLE LIQUIDS GREASE • GASOLINE • PAINTS • OILS, ETC	A–B	B–C	X	X	X	A–B–C	B–C
CLASS C FIRES — USE THESE EXTINGUISHERS ↑ — ELECTRICAL EQUIPMENT • MOTORS • SWITCHES ETC	X	B–C	X	X	X	A–B–C	B–C

HOW TO OPERATE

FOAM Don't Spray Stream into the Burning Liquid Allow Foam to Fall Lightly on Fire

CARBON DIOXIDE Direct Discharge as Close to Fire as Possible First at Edge of Flames and Gradually Forward and Upward

SODA ACID, GAS CARTRIDGE Direct Stream at Base of Flame

PUMP TANK Place Foot on Footrest and Direct Stream at Base of Flames

DRY CHEMICAL Direct at the Base of the Flames In the Case of Class A Fires Follow up by Directing the Dry Chemicals at remaining Material That is Burning

Figure 12–3 Use of fire extinguishers.

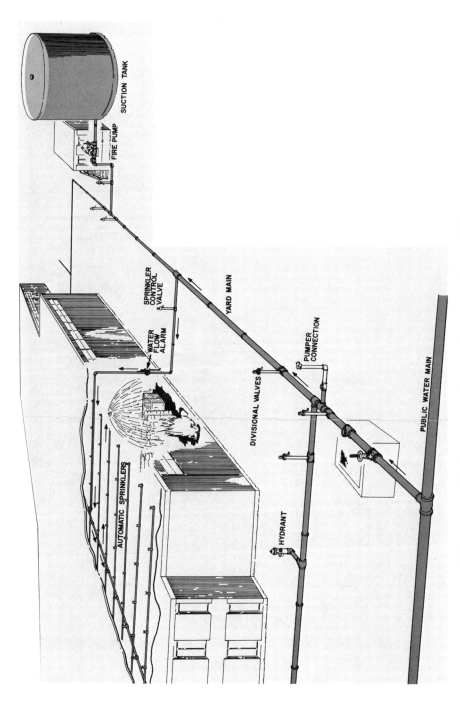

Figure 12–4 Total concept of the wet-pipe automatic sprinkler system.

SUCTION TANK

FIRE PUMP

SPRINKLER CONTROL VALVE

YARD MAIN

WATER FLOW ALARM

PUMPER CONNECTION

DIVISIONAL VALVES

PUBLIC WATER MAIN

AUTOMATIC SPRINKLERS

HYDRANT

278

outlet on each floor of a building. In multiple-story structures, standpipes often are constructed within fire-resistant fire stairs as an added defense for the standpipe, hoses, and fire fighting personnel. The typical setup is a folded or rolled $2^1/_2$-inch hose enclosed in a wall cabinet and identified with fire emergency information. A control valve, which looks like a small spoked wheel, enables water to flow. Automatic extinguishing systems (e.g., sprinklers) often are the preferred system; however, the standpipes and hose systems are advantageous when the automatic system fails or is not present, when sections of a building are not accessible to outside hose lines and hydrants, and when properly trained employees are capable of fire suppression.

Training is needed for employees if they are to have the responsibility for fighting a fire. With hoses, two people are needed; one to stretch the hose to its full length, the other to turn the water flow valve. Without training, employees may be injured if they do not understand the danger of turning the valve before the hose is stretched. This could cause the coiled section of the hose to react to the water pressure by acting like a whip and possibly striking someone.

Fire Walls and Doors

Fire walls are constructed in buildings to prevent the spread of fire. These walls are made of materials that resist fire. They are designed to withstand fire for several hours. Fire walls are weakened by openings such as doorways. Therefore, fire doors at openings help to strengthen the fire wall when resisting fire. Fire doors often are designed to close automatically in case of fire. Nationally recognized testing laboratories study the reliability of these doors.

Stairwells

During evacuation, stairwells (made of masonry construction) provide a fire-resistant path for escape. Fire codes often require stairwells to withstand a fire for at least two hours. Stairwells may be equipped with fans to reduce smoke during evacuation.

Access Control

During an emergency, electronically controlled doors should be connected to the life and safety system to permit escape. From the security perspective, this presents a problem because an alarm condition may provide an opportunity for an offender to enter or exit with ease. To deal with such a vulnerability, CCTV and security officers can be applied to select locations.

Building codes mandate the use of exit devices that enable quick escape during emergencies. A door locked from the outside may be easily unlocked from the inside to allow theft or unauthorized passage. Therefore, the door needs to be secured from both sides while permitting quick escape in case of an emergency. Often, the solution is a controlled exit device (see

Figure 12–5). One type of controlled exit device stays locked for a fixed time, usually 15 seconds, after being pushed, while sounding an alarm. The delay provides time for security to respond. In a true emergency, such a device is unlocked immediately through a tie-in with the building's fire protection system.

The Las Vegas MGM Grand Hotel fire in 1985 provides a graphic example of security (locked exit doors) being one of the major reasons for the large loss of life. All the exit doors to the stairwell had a controlled exit device (panic hardware). However, once the occupants were in the stairwell, smoke was encountered. Unfortunately, the doors were locked on the stairwell side to ensure security for each floor. A person had to exit the building on the first floor to regain access. With heavy smoke rising in the stairwell, and no access to one of the floors, the occupants were trapped and died.[6]

Fire-Resistive Buildings

The report by the National Commission on Fire Prevention and Control, "America Burning," pointed to a major weakness in building design and construction. That weakness is the architects and builders. Frequently, these professionals think in terms of dollars without seriously considering fire protection. Quite often, after a building has been constructed and insur-

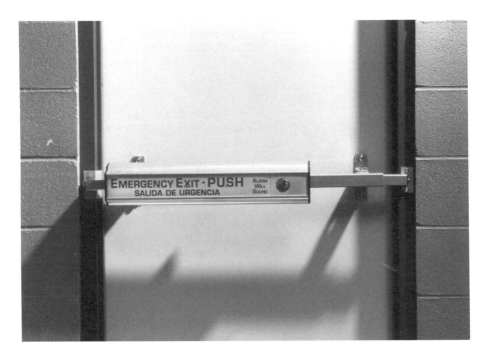

Figure 12–5   Emergency exit. Courtesy: Sargent & Greenleaf, Inc.

ance practitioners have decided on a premium, fire hazards are exposed. If a person stops to think about the tons of combustible materials transported into a building during construction and as it becomes operational, he or she may be hesitant to enter. Wood in construction and furnishings, cloth and fibers in curtains and carpets, paper, cleaning fluids, and other combustibles are hazardous. But reinforced concrete or protected steel construction and fire-resistive roofs, floors, ceilings, walls, doors, windows, carpets, furniture, and so on, all help to produce greater fire protection.

Training and Fire Brigades

With the threat of fire, employee training is of tremendous importance (see Figure 12–6). Of top priority during a fire should be to safeguard lives, and then the securing of valuable assets during orderly evacuation. If specific employees are responsible for fire suppression, thorough training is required. This is especially true when local public fire fighting capabilities

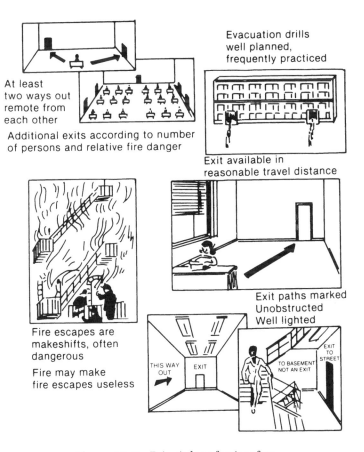

Figure 12–6   Principles of exit safety.

are incompatible with the type of fire that may develop at an industrial plant. In this case, a private fire department at the industrial site is appropriate.

Integrating Fire and Security Systems

There are many horror stories of state-of-the-art, integrated fire and security systems that do not operate as originally touted. As confusion and disappointment mounts, each manufacturer may blame the other. And, fire authorities may refuse to issue an acceptance of the fire alarm portion of the system. Unfortunately for the loss prevention manager, he or she must explain why the corporation is spending so much money for a system that does not operate properly. Here are some guidelines to improve decisions:

1. Listen to the salesperson claim that he/she can integrate fire and security systems. Then conduct research of such success and speak with end-users.
2. Hire engineers with verified skills in security and fire alarm systems. Have them prepare specifications and a budget.
3. Contact the local fire department for their input.
4. Develop goals of how the integrated system is to operate and put it in writing as part of the contract.
5. If possible use a single manufacturer for both systems; otherwise seek a written contract between the manufacturers for integration of their products.
6. Seek precise information on maintenance and warranties.
7. Develop the fire alarm system as the first priority because of the need to deal with the fire authority having jurisdiction and codes and standards. This approach is in light of the limited codes and standards in the security industry which leads to abuses in systems application, design, and installation.
8. The *National Fire Alarm Code*, adopted by the NFPA, describes the minimum acceptable requirements for all fire alarm systems.[7]

When integrated systems operate as intended, they become a life and safety system worthy of the investment, as shown by the following scenario: A fire smolders in a utility closet of a 50-story building. Smoke enters a hallway and triggers a smoke detector on the ceiling. The temperature climbs and then activates an overhead sprinkler system. At a security desk on the first floor, several alarms ring and the officer views a computer screen that reads: "Smoke detector activated—19th floor; sprinkler system activated—19th floor." The officer calls the fire department. The building's computer-controlled public address system automatically instructs employees on the 18th, 19th, and 20th floors to enter the fire-protected stairwell and calmly evacuate the building. Those on other floors are notified that a fire has been detected and are told to wait outside the nearest stairwell for further instructions. Electronically controlled doors are unlocked for emergency escape; however, CCTV focuses on areas requiring increased protection and security officers are dispatched. When firefighters arrive, they put out what is left of the flames.[8]

What do you think can improve fire suppression in the United States?

OTHER DISASTERS

Planning and training are two key strategies to reduce losses when disasters strike. Employees need to know what to do to protect lives and assets.

Other disasters can be accidents, bomb threats and explosions, strikes, civil disturbances, sabotage, utility failures, building collapses, windstorms (tornado and hurricane), floods, blizzards, and earthquakes. These disasters can be either constructed or natural occurrences; for instance, a fire can be caused by human error or by lightning.

Constructed Disasters

Accidents

An accident at, for example, a manufacturing plant has the potential for serious injury, death, and production slowdown. Thousands of lives, hundreds of thousands of injuries, and billions of dollars of losses are sustained each year because of accidents. Prevention is a key strategy. The seriousness of this problem is pointed out in Chapter 13.

Bomb Threats and Explosions

In the World Trade Center bombing in New York City in 1993, 6 people were killed, more than 1000 were injured, and the damage exceeded a half-billion dollars. Two years later, 168 people were killed and many injured in a bombing in Oklahoma City at the Alfred P. Murrah federal building. The front of the building was actually ripped away by the blast. In light of these and other incidents, bomb threats and the possibility of bombings are taken more seriously today. Even the commonly circulated statistic that 98 percent of bomb threats are hoaxes makes decision makers more concerned than ever about the other 2 percent. "Over the past 10 years, the number of actual and attempted bombings in the US has quadrupled to more than

3,000 annually."[9] Accurate statistics are difficult to gather on bomb threats, attempts, and actual bombings. Organizations may not report threats. Police agencies may "play down incidents" to prevent copycat threats and bombings.[10]

Here are basic strategies for protection against bomb threats and explosions:

1. Seek management support and prepare a plan and procedures.
2. Ensure that employees know what to ask if a bomb threat is made over the telephone (see Figure 12–7).
3. Establish criteria and procedures for evacuation. Post routes. The evacuation decision can be especially difficult for management because of safety concerns versus the thousands of dollars in productivity lost due to evacuation of large numbers of employees.

Date of Threat: _____

Time: _____ Number of minutes on telephone: ___

Exact words of caller: _____

_____

_____

_____

_____

_____

Ask the caller these questions: _____

When will the bomb explode? _____

Where is bomb? _____

What type of bomb? _____

What does it look like? _____

Why did you place bomb? _____

_____

Description of caller's voice: Age: _____ Accent: _____

Sex: _____ Background noise: _____

Tone of voice: _____

Additional comments: _____

_____

Employee receiving call: _____ Telephone number: _____

Figure 12–7   Smith Corporation bomb threat form.

4. Recruit and train *all* employees to observe and report suspicious behavior, items, or vehicles. And, something suspicious never should be approached or touched.
5. Control parking and access according to the unique characteristics and requirements of the facility.
6. Control and verify outsiders (e.g., service personnel) prior to access.
7. Screen mail. Route deliveries to a specific location for screening, rather than permitting direct access to employees (see Figure 12–8).
8. Maintain unpredictable patrols to avoid patterns that can be studied by offenders.
9. Inspect the exterior and interior of buildings.
10. Ensure that emergency plans, response teams (e.g., fire brigades), and public safety agencies are coordinated for action. What are the qualifications, experience, and response time of the nearest bomb squad?

Strikes

The direct and indirect costs of a strike are astronomical. Major losses include productivity, profits, employees and customers who never return, vandalism, additional loss prevention services, and legal fees. *The best defense for a strike is early preparation.* If possible, a company that antici-

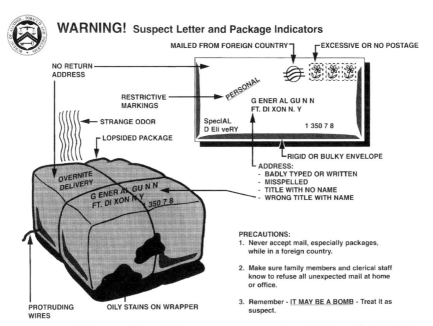

Figure 12–8   Suspect letter and package indicators.

pates a strike should build up inventory and oversupply customers. When a labor contract is almost ready to run out, trouble can be expected. Management should contact local law enforcement agencies to ensure that peace is maintained and property protected. Security is likely to focus on perimeter protection for the facility, the protection of key executives and their families, and evidence gathering. Both public and private police will be working together in most instances.

Both striking workers and a company have certain legal rights. The *National Labor Relations Board* (NLRB) controls relations between management and labor.

It is essential that management and loss prevention personnel be familiar with labor laws to avert charges of unfair labor practices. Surveillance and investigation of union activities is a violation of the National Labor Relations Act, which makes it an unfair labor practice to interfere with, restrain, or coerce employees in the exercise of the rights to self-organization, assist labor organizations, and to bargain collectively through representatives. One type of surveillance, photographing activities of striking workers, is unlawful, unless there is a legitimate purpose, such as gathering evidence for the prosecution of criminal acts (e.g., assault or destruction of property). In one case, a security service company took 60,000 pictures and collected thousands of hours of videotape that were used in court against strikers, who ended up owing $64 million in fines.[11]

Care must be exercised when instituting loss prevention strategies during management-labor tension. Precautions (e.g., additional officers, CCTV) to protect company property may be construed as interference with union activities. For example, courts have declared illegal the observance by officers of who is going in and out of union meetings. Also, it has been held that even "creating the impression" of surveillance (e.g., management implying that surveillance is taking place) is illegal. The NLRB found that aiming CCTV on a company building in which a union meeting was held created the impression of surveillance. Undercover investigations that conduct labor surveillance are illegal.

Civil Disturbances

Demonstrations and precipitating incidents have evolved into destructive riots. Demonstrations are common as groups display their views. A typical precipitating incident is a public police arrest of a minority group member for a minor charge. Sometimes, all it takes for a crowd to go into a contagious frenzy is a rock thrown into the crowd. Whatever the cause of civil disturbances, deaths, injuries, and extensive property damage can result. The public police may not be able to contain rioters, and the private sector must be prepared for the worst. Summer months and high temperatures, when people gather out of doors, may precede a civil disturbance. Rumors also are dangerous. The social and political climate can be analyzed for possible predicting indicators.

Sabotage

Production can be deliberately hindered by a destructive act such as cutting electrical wires in a plant. The threat of sabotage can come from both internal and external sources.

Utility Failure

Electrical breakdowns are known to produce not only production obstacles but serious threats to loss prevention measures. Without a source of electric power, alarms, CCTV, access control, electrically activated extinguishing systems, electric fire pumps, and other systems are useless. Secondary power sources such as generators should be in place.

Building Collapse

Good building maintenance and periodic inspections can ensure the integrity of a building. Weight distribution on floors of multistory buildings must be carefully studied when heavy machinery, heavy stock, or any other weighty objects are placed in buildings.

Natural Disasters

Windstorms

Tornadoes (called *cyclones* in some regions) are extremely violent and destructive, often occurring without warning. Hurricanes (called *typhoons* in the eastern Pacific Ocean) usually afford more warning time than tornadoes. The Atlantic and Gulf coasts are more susceptible to hurricanes, whereas tornadoes occur in many parts of the United States. Loss prevention efforts should concentrate on studying local climate conditions and then preparing contingency plans. The following measures are useful:

1. Design buildings for maximum wind velocity expected.
2. Closely follow weather reports.
3. Close down production when necessary.
4. Establish a safe, low-level area for employees.
5. Instruct employees to stay away from windows.
6. Open doors and windows on the side of the building away from the storm. This will help to equalize pressure and prevent building collapse.
7. Acquire emergency power sources.
8. Set up a communications system.
9. Anchor and protect company property from being damaged or blown away.
10. Cooperate with local officials.
11. Take steps to hinder looting.

Floods

Lowlands along bodies of water are subject to flooding. Dams and dikes have reduced this problem, but it is still a threat to many locales. Some practical remedies are these:

1. Work with the U.S. Army Corps of Engineers, which provides assistance to those areas subject to frequent flooding.
2. Work with local officials for employee safety and to hinder looting.
3. Provide a safe place for valuable assets.
4. Exit from the flood area in time to avoid being marooned. Secure adequate gasoline for vehicles.
5. If a team remains at the plant site, ensure adequate supplies, such as food, blankets, a boat, life preservers, rope, communications equipment, first-aid kit, sandbags, pumps, and so on.
6. At the plant, take precautions before the flood. Store valuable records, equipment, tools, and chemicals above the expected flood level. Shut off utilities. Heavily grease machines and other equipment subject to water damage.

Blizzards

Blizzards are snowstorms accompanied by high winds and very cold temperatures. Sufficient warning usually is obtained from weather forecasts. Injuries and deaths occur because people do not reach proper shelter. If a blizzard is forecast, employees should be sent home. Preplanning is essential if employees have a chance of being stranded at work. Food, bedding, a heat supply, radios, communications equipment, and televisions will aid those stranded.

Earthquakes

Violent motions in the ground caused by an earthquake can be very damaging. Stringent building codes and adequate building design in suspect areas (e.g., California) are vital for reduced losses. Building collapse, damage to bridges, and falling debris are major causes of injuries and deaths. If indoors, one should take cover in a basement or under reinforced floors or doorways. If outdoors, one should watch out for falling objects and electrical wires.

What do you think is the most serious potential disaster facing your community or organization? What protection methods do you recommend?

Emergency Planning and Disaster Recovery

Emergency planning focuses on preparation that increases the chances that people and an organization will survive a disaster. *Disaster recovery* aims to place an organization in the position it was prior to a disaster.

No one plan can be applied to all organizations to prepare and recover from a disaster. Unique needs must be met. A high-rise building, for example, should select and train individuals and teams from each floor to assist with emergencies and evacuation. Similar planning is required for a hospital, plus staff sleeping and food arrangements are needed so patient care is not interrupted. A retail chain with stores in the path of a hurricane would establish a command post, track the hurricane, and render aid so affected stores can be operational as soon as possible.

The list that follows provides a foundation for emergency planning and disaster recovery:

1. As with other threats requiring attention, seek management support from the top and competent leaders.
2. Prepare policies and procedures, a command structure, and lines of authority.
3. Rely on checklists during planning and recovery.
4. Focus on the prevention of injury and death, the protection of assets, and the continuation of business.
5. Store vital records at two locations.
6. Plan for disasters that are likely to occur but also consider the unexpected. Study similar businesses, climate, geography, insurance and risk management reports, among other sources. Rate the likelihood of risks.
7. Consider the impact of each potential disaster on the company's financial condition, sales, and legal and regulatory requirements.
8. Identify all the organizations that might be involved in a disaster: police, fire service, emergency medical service, utilities, and so forth. Hold a meeting and develop a master plan.
9. Plan a command post with a common communication channel.
10. Plan for disruption of essential services: electricity, telephone, computer, water, and sanitation.
11. Plan for shortages of food, water, and medical services.
12. Consider that there may be denial of access to the building by government agencies because of unsafe conditions.
13. Conduct annual training and unannounced drills. Note weaknesses and improve performance.
14. Ensure that employees know how to operate equipment such as fire extinguishers.
15. Compile a list of employee skills (e.g., first aid) that may be useful.

16. Consider employee problems such as injury, family and home needs, and transportation.
17. Ensure that emergency procedures and equipment are in compliance with the Americans with Disabilities Act of 1990.
18. Work with insurers to help the business manage risks and survive.
19. Research the possibility of moving the business to an alternative site during recovery.
20. Locate recovery service companies.
21. List critical tasks that must be performed for business recovery and consider personnel and equipment requirements.
22. Prepare a directory of people and organizations helpful during emergencies and recovery.
23. Put in writing the emergency and disaster recovery plans and review it annually for improvements.

Federal Emergency Management Agency

The central point of contact within the federal government for a wide range of emergency management activities is the *Federal Emergency Management Agency*, or FEMA (FEMA, National Emergency Training Center, Emmitsburg, MD 21727-8998; Tel.: 301-447-1000; FEMA, DC; Tel.: 202-566-1600). This agency is involved in planning and preparedness activities while providing financial and technical support for a full range of emergencies from local disasters to nuclear war. FEMA extends through all levels of government and the private sector. Among FEMA's activities are

* Coordinating civil emergency preparedness for nuclear accidents or attack.
* Ensuring continuity of government and coordinating mobilization of resources during national security emergencies.
* Supporting state and local governments before, during, and after disasters.
* Reducing the nation's losses from fire through the U.S. Fire Administration.
* Coordinating federal aid for presidentially declared disasters and emergencies.
* Providing training and education at all levels of government.
* Administering national flood insurance.
* Operating the National Defense Executive Reserve program for recruiting and training a group of senior executives from the private sector to enter government service in the event of a national emergency.

CASE PROBLEMS

12A. As a loss prevention manager at company headquarters, your superior tells you to design a fire protection program for a new window and door manufacturing plant. A lot of wood cutting with electric circular saws will take place at this plant. Workers then will assemble the windows and doors using electric drills. A large stock of wood products will be stored in the plant. What will you recommend to the architects who will design the building? What are your fire prevention plans? What are your fire suppression plans?

12B. As a loss prevention manager at an office building containing 800 employees, your boss requests that you prepare criteria for evacuation of the building in case of a bomb threat. List criteria for management to consider and estimate the cost of a two-hour evacuation if the average employee earns $25,000 annually.

12C. As a corporate loss prevention manager, you have been assigned the task of designing a protection plan against windstorms for manufacturing plants located along the coast of Florida and those located in Kansas. What general plans do you have in mind?

NOTES

1. Michael J. Karter, Jr., "NFPA's Latest Fire Loss Figures," *NFPA Journal* (September–October 1996): 53–55.
2. Gordon P. McKinnon, ed., *Fire Protection Handbook*, 14th ed. (Boston: National Fire Protection Association, 1976), p. ix.
3. See Sandra L. Breisch, "Is Your Workplace Fireproof?" *Safety and Health* (July 1989): 40–44.
4. U.S. Department of Commerce, U.S. Fire Administration, *Fire in the United States* (Washington, DC: U.S. Government Printing Office, 1978), p. 54.
5. Percy Bugbee, *Principles of Fire Protection* (Boston: National Fire Protection Association, 1978), p. 170.
6. Wayne D. Moore, "Balancing Life Safety and Security Needs," *Security Technology and Design* (January–February 1997): 69–70.
7. Wayne D. Moore, "The Art of Integrating Fire and Security Systems," *Security Technology and Design* (March 1994): 61–62.
8. Gregory A. Gilbert, "The Vital Signs of Life Safety," *Security Management* (January 1997): 32–37.
9. Mark M. Warrington, "Bomb Threat Exploding," *Security* (February 1997): 56.
10. David H. Estenson, "Should Bomb Blasts Be Kept Quiet?" *Security Management* (November 1995): 120.
11. Brenda P. Sunoo, "Managing Strikes, Minimizing Loss," *Personnel Journal* (January 1995): 58.

13

Safety

OBJECTIVES

After studying this chapter the reader will be able to

1.   Explain why safety is important;
2.   Discuss the history of safety legislation and workers' compensation;
3.   Explain OSHA's development, objectives, jurisdiction, standards, record keeping requirements, and inspections;
4.   Describe at least four strategies for improving safety in the workplace.

What is meant by *safety*, *accident*, and *injury*? Safety is a major loss prevention measure to reduce the likelihood of accidents and injuries. When accidents and injuries occur, both losses and a drain on profits inevitably result. Webster's *New Collegiate Dictionary* defines *safety* as "the condition of being safe from undergoing or causing hurt, injury, or loss" and "to protect against failure, breakage, or accident." *Accident* is "an unfortunate event resulting from carelessness, unawareness, ignorance, or a combination of causes." *Injury* is "hurt, damage, or loss sustained."

ACCIDENT STATISTICS AND COSTS

Since the earlier part of this century, great strides have been made to increase safety in the workplace. Safer machines, improved supervision, and training all have helped to prevent accidents. If one were to compare the industrial fatality rate that existed in 1910 to the present workforce in the United States, over 1.3 million workers would lose their lives each year from industrial accidents. In the past, a manual worker's welfare was of minimal concern to management; the loss of life or limb was "part of the job" and "a normal business risk." In the construction of tall buildings, it was expected that one life would be lost for each floor. A 20-story building would yield 20 lost lives. During tunnel construction, two worker deaths per mile was the norm. Coal mining experienced exceedingly high death rates.[1]

The National Safety Council reported the following (U.S.) workplace statistics for 1995 as 5300 unintentional deaths and 3.6 million disabling injuries. Work-related accidents cost $119.4 billion in 1995; this included wage loss, medical expense, health insurance administration cost, and fire loss.[2]

Confined Area Entry

Hazards that are not easily seen, smelled, or felt can be deadly risks to people who work in confined areas. For instance, storage tanks may reduce oxygen or leak combustible or toxic gases. The cardinal rule for entry into a confined area is, "Never trust your senses." A harmless-looking situation may indeed be a potential threat. Some of the deadliest gases and vapors have no odor. *Before entry, the following safety strategies are recommended: proper training, equipment to identify hazards, and an entry permit issued by a safety specialist.*

For example, in the petroleum industry, a storage tank may have been rinsed and vented for several days. When checked with gas detection equipment, no flammable gases were measured. But, after workers removed loose rust, scale, and sediment, the percentage of flammable gas rose and ignited.

As another example, two employees of a fertilizer company descended into an old 35-foot well to repair a pump. The well was covered with a concrete slab and entry was made through a covered manhole. About 6 feet below the opening was a plank platform. When the first worker dropped to the platform, he was immediately overcome and fell unconscious into the water below. His partner sought help quickly. When two helpers entered the well, they, too, fell unconscious to the water below. A passerby, in an attempt to save the drowning men, jumped into the water and drowned also. By this time the fire department had arrived. The fire chief, wearing a self-contained breathing apparatus, went to rescue the victims. On the platform he removed his face mask to give instructions to those above and was overcome. Subsequent tests revealed that the well atmosphere contained a lethal concentration of hydrogen sulfide. Five men died from pulmonary paralysis.[3]

Direct and indirect losses are costly; for example, the death of a worker in a manufacturing plant immediately creates a tremendous direct loss to family and friends. Direct losses also involve an immediate loss of productivity, medical costs (e.g., first aid, hospitalization), and insurance administration. Indirect costs include continued grief by family and friends, continued loss of productivity, profit loss, selection and training of a new employee, overtime for lost production, and possible litigation. In addition, internal and external relations may suffer. The lowering of employee morale can result from the belief that management is incompetent or does not care.

Rumors frequently follow. In the eyes of the community, the company may appear to have failed.

Hazards

A *hazard* can be defined as a dangerous condition, behavior, or object that can cause an accident, injury, or death. A list of common hazards follow:

Nonuse of safety devices on machinery	Poor supervision
Noncompliance with safety policies and procedures	Dangerous storage of toxic or flammable substances
Electrical malfunctions	Fire
Poorly supported ladders and scaffolding	Inadequate fire fighting equipment
Blocked aisles, exits, and stairways	Inadequate fire prevention measures
Overloaded inventory storage bins	Insufficient lighting
Inadequate training	Poor ventilation
Excessive noise	Horseplay; running

HISTORY OF SAFETY LEGISLATION

In 18th century England, as the Industrial Revolution progressed, a number of statutes governing working conditions were passed. One of the first statutes for safety resulted from a serious outbreak of fever at cotton mills near Manchester in 1784. Because child labor was involved, widespread attention added to public concern and government pressure to improve the dangerous and unsanitary conditions in factories. A few years later, additional legislation dealt with hours, conditions of labor, prevention of injury, and government inspectors. In 1842, the *Mines Act* provided for punitive compensation for preventable injuries caused by unguarded mining machinery. Subsequent to this law, a series of mining accidents caused more laws to be passed for miner safety. During this time "strong evidence" pointed to incompetent management and the neglect of safety rules. Laws relating to factory safety also were expanded. More and more trades were brought under the scope of the law.

In the United States, textile factories increased in number between 1820 and 1840. Massachusetts, first of the United States to follow England's example, passed laws in 1876 and 1877 that related to working children and inspection of factories. Important features pertained to dangerous machinery and necessary safety guards. As years went on, some industries increasingly realized that hazards were potentially harmful to workers, production, and profits. Consequently, more and more industrialists became safety conscious. However, serious hazards still existed in the workplace through the 20th century.[4]

Workers' Compensation

Increasing concern for workers led to *workers' compensation laws*. In essence, these laws require employers to compensate injured employees. England passed such laws in 1897, and the United States followed in 1902, when Maryland passed this country's first workers' compensation law, although, essentially, the Maryland workers' compensation law (1902) was so restrictive that it was almost useless. In 1911, Wisconsin passed the first effective workers' compensation law. Seven other states passed similar legislation during that year. Amid controversy between businesspeople and groups interested in the welfare of laborers, the Supreme Court upheld the constitutionality of these laws in 1916. Businesspeople argued that they could never bear such compensation costs nor could they control accidents; they predicted that the cost of goods would rise considerably. Those who favored workers' compensation laws believed that these laws would provide the impetus for greater safety, because business owners and managers would want to control losses.

Workers' compensation laws provided insurance companies with a new opportunity. As states enacted these laws, business owners became concerned about their ability to pay for workers' compensation. Therefore, insurance companies sold casualty insurance policies to businesses that needed the security from a possible workers' compensation burden. *A concurrent benefit of such insurance was that insurance companies were willing to reduce premiums if a company instituted accident prevention measures.* To remain competitive, insurance companies provided safety specialists who would survey a business and recommend prevention strategies (e.g., safeguards on machines). Businesspeople became increasingly interested in safety; insurance companies developed safety expertise.

Today, all states have workers' compensation laws. These laws vary from state to state, but each requires the reporting of injures that are compensable. Most employers are insured for workers' compensation judgments by private insurance companies. Other employers are self-insured (insurance provided by the employer and not purchased through a private insurance company; it is regulated by a state insurance commissioner) or place this insurance with state insurance funds. When an employee is injured, medical benefits usually are granted, and benefits for wages lost are granted when an employee is incapacitated and cannot work.

The workers' compensation system of today has its problems. Because dealings with the insurance industry are frequently adversary in nature, injured employees often believe that the system helps them only when they obtain the services of an attorney. Insurers, on the other hand, claim that they must protect their interests and that fraud (i.e., worker malingering) is a very serious problem.

Are workers' compensation laws necessary today? Support your viewpoint.

The Development of OSHA

With the advent of improved safety conditions, accidents and injuries declined until the 1950s. In the late 1950s, rates leveled off until the late 1960s, when accidents and injuries began to increase. This upward turn caused the federal government to become increasingly concerned about safety. Several safety-related laws were passed during the 1960s, but none was as monumental as OSHA. OSHA stands for the *Occupational Safety and Health Administration*, a federal agency, under the U.S. Department of Labor, established to administer the law on safety and health resulting from the William Steiger Occupational Safety and Health Act of 1970. This federal legislation was signed into law by the then president, Richard Nixon, and became effective on April 28, 1971. The basic purpose of the OSHA legislation was to provide a safe working environment for employees engaged in a variety of occupations (U.S. Department of Labor, OSHA, PO Box 37535, Washington, DC 20213; Tel.: 202-219-6091).

The OSHA act was significant because it was the first national safety legislation applying to every business connected with interstate commerce. "The need for such legislation was clear. Between 1969 and 1973 [in the United States] more persons were killed at work than in the Vietnam war."[5]

OSHA is administered by the Secretary of Labor via 10 regional offices. The secretary has the authority and responsibility to establish occupational safety and health standards. Workplace inspections can result in citations issued to employers who violate standards.

The National Institute for Occupational Safety and Health (NIOSH) performs numerous functions that aid OSHA and those striving for worker safety. These functions relate to research, the development of criteria and standards for occupational safety and health, training OSHA personnel and others (e.g., employers and employees), and providing publications dealing with both toxic substances and strategies on how to prevent occupational injuries and illnesses. NIOSH is under the U.S. Department of Health and Human Services.

Objectives of OSHA

The OSHA act of 1970 states that it is "to assure so far as possible every working man and woman in the Nation safe and healthful working conditions and to preserve our human resources." Objectives of OSHA are as follows:

1. Encourage employers and employees to reduce hazards in the workplace and to implement new or improve existing safety and health programs;
2. Establish separate but dependent responsibilities and rights for employers and employees for the achievement of better safety and health conditions;
3. Establish reporting and recordkeeping procedures to monitor job-related injuries and illnesses;
4. Provide for research, establish training programs, and develop mandatory job safety and health standards and enforce them effectively; and
5. Encourage the States to assume the fullest responsibility for establishing and administering their own occupational safety and health programs, which must be at least as effective as the Federal program.[6]

The Act's Jurisdiction

OSHA rules extend to all employers and their employees in the 50 states, the District of Columbia, Puerto Rico, and other U.S. possessions. An employer is anyone who maintains employees and engages in a business affecting commerce. This broad coverage involves a multitude of fields: manufacturing, construction, agriculture, warehousing, retailing, longshoring, education, and so on. The act does not cover self-employed persons, family-owned and operated farms, and workplaces protected by other federal agencies. Although federal agencies are not covered by OSHA, agencies are required to maintain a safe working environment equal to those groups under OSHA's jurisdiction. State and local government employees are excluded from OSHA.

OSHA Standards

OSHA promulgates legally enforceable standards to protect employees in the workplace. *Since OSHA standards are constantly being updated and reviewed, it is the employer's responsibility to keep up-to-date.* One of the best sources for standards and changes is the *Federal Register*. It is available at many public libraries or it can be ordered, for a fee, from the Superintendent of Documents, U.S. Government Printing Office, Washington, DC 20402; Tel.: 202-512-1800. Another source of up-to-date information is the OSHA Subscription Service. This service is available from the Superintendent of Documents.

There are actually thousands of OSHA standards. Some pertain to specific industries and workers, whereas others are general and practiced by most industries. Examples include safety requirements for machines, equipment, and employees, such as requiring face shields or safety glasses during the use of certain machines; unobstructed aisles and exits in the workplace; prevention of electrical hazards; adequate fire protection; adequate lunchrooms, lavatories, and drinking water; and monitoring of employee exposure to chemical or toxic hazards.

The following standards demonstrate OSHA's concern for worker safety and health.

Subpart 1—Personal Protective Equipment

1910.132 General requirements.

(a) Application. Protective equipment, including personal protective equipment for eyes, face, head, and extremities, protective clothing, respiratory devices, and protective shields and barriers, shall be provided, used, and maintained in a sanitary and reliable condition wherever it is necessary by reason of hazards of processes or environment, chemical hazards, radiological hazards, or mechanical irritants encountered in a manner capable of causing injury or impairment in the function of any part of the body through absorption, inhalation or physical contact.[7]

Subpart K—Medical and First Aid

1910.151 Medical services and first aid.

(a) The employer shall ensure the ready availability of medical personnel for advice and consultation of matters of plant health.

(b) In the absence of an infirmary, clinic, or hospital in near proximity to the workplace which is used for the treatment of all injured employees, a person or persons shall be adequately trained to render first aid. First aid supplies approved by the consulting physician shall be readily available.

(c) Where the eyes or body of any person may be exposed to injurious corrosive materials, suitable facilities for quick drenching or flushing of the eyes and body shall be provided within the work area for immediate emergency use.[8]

OSHA Hazard Communication Standard

This standard was established because more than 30 million workers could be exposed to one or more chemical hazards; and over 650,000 hazardous chemical products exist, with hundreds of new ones being introduced annually. Also known as a *right-to-know law*, this standard requires all employers who have employees that may be exposed to hazardous substances on the job to inform them about such substances and how to deal with them. Employers are required to write and implement a hazard communication program, conduct a chemical inventory, ensure that a *Material Safety Data Sheet* (MSDS) is available for each chemical, label chemical containers, and train employees on the safe use of chemicals (e.g., protective equipment, procedures).[9]

OSHA Bloodborne Pathogens Standard

This standard limits exposure to blood and other potentially infectious materials, which could lead to disease or death. The standard covers all employees facing potential exposure. Employers are required to establish an exposure control plan covering safety procedures, protective equipment, and the control of waste. The Hepatitis B vaccination is to be made available to all employees who have occupational exposure to blood. Post-exposure evaluation and follow-up is to be made available to all employees who have had an exposure incident, including laboratory tests at no cost to the employee. Exposure records must be confidential and kept for the duration of employment plus 30 years. Training is required on all aspects of this standard and the training records must be maintained for three years.[10]

OSHA Record Keeping and Reporting

Before the development of OSHA's centralized record keeping system, workplace statistics on injuries and illnesses were kept by some states and private organizations. No uniform, standardized system existed. Today, with the help of OSHA's comprehensive statistics, it is easier to pinpoint serious hazards and work toward improvements.

Although OSHA record keeping by an employer may appear burdensome, the task does not require much time or energy. In fact, the records actually can help employers reduce losses by revealing hazards. The employer is responsible for keeping the records up to date and available to OSHA inspectors. These records are not to be sent to OSHA (except Form 2005), but remain at the workplace for five years beyond the year of recording.

The records for employers are described as follows:

OSHA No. 200, Log and Summary of Occupational Injuries and Illnesses: Each recordable occupational injury and illness must be logged on this form within six working days from the time the employer learns of it. If the log is prepared at a central location by automatic data processing equipment, a copy current to within 45 calendar days must be present at all times in the establishment. A substitute for the OSHA No. 200 is acceptable if it is as detailed, easily readable and understandable as the OSHA No. 200.

OSHA No. 101, Supplementary Record of Occupational Injuries and Illnesses. The form OSHA No. 101 contains much more detail about each injury or illness. It also must be completed within six working days from the time the employer learns of the work-related injury or illness. A substitute for the OSHA No. 101 (such as insurance or workers' compensation forms) may be used if it contains all required information.

Annual Survey. Employers selected to participate in the annual statistical survey receive in the mail, soon after the close of the year, form OSHA No. 2005 for this purpose. Each employer selected must complete this form using form No. 200 as the source of information.[11]

How does OSHA define occupational injury and illness?

An *occupational injury* is any injury such as a cut, fracture, sprain, or amputation which results from a work-related accident or from exposure involving a single incident in the work environment. An *occupational illness* is any abnormal condition or disorder, other than one resulting from an occupational injury, caused by exposure to environmental factors associated with employment.[12]

When does OSHA require occupational injuries and illnesses to be recorded? Death must be recorded regardless of the length of time between injury and death and regardless of the length of the illness. One or more lost workdays for an employee, restriction of work or motion, loss of consciousness, transfer to another job, or medical treatment other than first aid must be recorded. If an on-the-job accident occurs that results in the death of an employee or the hospitalization of five or more employees, *all* employers must (by law) report the accident, in detail, to the nearest OSHA office within 48 hours.[13]

Additional OSHA Employer Responsibilities

An employer is required to post specific OSHA-related material for employee review. The OSHA poster Job Safety and Health Protection informs employees about their rights and responsibilities and must be displayed in an appropriate location for employees. Copies of the OSHA act and relevant rules and regulations must be available if requested by employees. A summary of petitions for variances also must be posted—an employer is allowed to petition OSHA for a *variance*, that is, an opportunity to do something contrary to the usual method of a standard or regulation if the employer cannot comply right away or if the employer can show that his or her method is equal to the OSHA method. The employer also is required to display copies of citations for violations of standards and the summary of injuries and illnesses (see OSHA Form 200).[14]

OSHA Inspections

An important priority of OSHA compliance inspectors was to view the workplace as it functions on a typical day. To attain this goal and to prevent an employer from altering typical workplace characteristics by concealing unsafe conditions, inspections frequently were made unannounced. However, only a few years after this practice began, it was challenged in the courts. In 1975, the president of a utility installation company, who posted a copy of the Bill of Rights on his office wall, sued while claiming that the Fourth Amendment restricts warrantless searches. The federal appellate court upheld the employer's contention. The case was appealed, and in May 1978 the Supreme Court, in *Marshall* v. *Barlow*, ruled that the Fourth Amendment protection against unreasonable searches protects commercial establishments as well as private homes. Therefore, OSHA inspectors must obtain a warrant before making an inspection, unless employers consent. Such a warrant is to be based on administrative probable cause: the inspector is required to show a judicial officer that the inspection is part of OSHA's general administrative plan to enforce safety and health laws, or upon evidence of a violation.[15]

When an inspection takes place, the employer and even employee representatives may join the inspector. The inspector is obligated to show credentials that contain a photograph and serial number. The number can be verified via the nearest OSHA office. Typically, machinery, equipment, and other workplace characteristics are examined. The inspector can interview the employer and employees in public or in private. Any interference with the inspector's duties can result in stiff penalties. The employer is wise to document the inspection and comments by the inspector through note taking. This information may become useful if a disagreement or a dispute of a citation or penalty evolves.

Because millions of workplaces are subject to inspections, OSHA has established priorities. Obviously, workplaces with serious accidents and injuries will be subject to inspections. A high-priority inspection will result from a report of an accident that causes the death of an employee or the hospitalization of five or more employees. Other inspections might result from employee complaints, belonging to a hazardous industry, or merely routine inspections.

The National Federation of Independent Businesses' (NFIB) publication *Mandate* recommends the following strategies "when the OSHA inspector shows up at your door":

1.   The method for dealing with an OSHA inspector should be worked out with an attorney as soon as possible.
2.   Find out if the inspector is from the state or federal OSHA. Get his name and credentials.

3.   Ask the inspector why he is at your business. Was there an employee complaint? Is he responding to a workplace injury? Is this a random search?

4.   In the event the inspector has a warrant, find out what judge issued it and when. Note the specific workplace areas mentioned on the warrant.

5.   Contact your attorney.[16]

A violation of an OSHA standard may cause the issuance of a citation and then a penalty. Severe violations can result in civil and criminal penalties. Citations inform both the employer and employees about characteristics of the violation and the time span for correction. Citations must be posted for employees.

OSHA: Criticism and Controversy

Through the years since its inception, OSHA has been the target of considerable criticism and controversy. Most of the OSHA battles have taken place on Capitol Hill, when different interest groups pressure legislators to either maintain and expand OSHA or to reduce or eliminate it. The forces in favor of OSHA are primarily OSHA itself, the AFL-CIO labor organization, and select legislators. Those opposed to OSHA consist mainly of businesspeople, business organizations, and select legislators. Some say the controversy essentially is between "big labor" and "big business."

The main arguments against OSHA are the following:

1.   "Regulatory overkill" is a major theme of those against OSHA. Many business organizations believe that OSHA has gone beyond what is necessary for fostering a safe and healthy workplace. Businesspeople and employers often rate OSHA as the prime example of excessive government regulation; they state that the agency's overzealous inspectors afflict employers with rules.

2.   OSHA is not cost effective. It provides limited benefits.

3.   The costs of OSHA, reduced productivity, lost jobs, and higher prices for goods add to inflation and are a threat to companies' competitive position.

4.   OSHA and other government bureaucrats, who are appointed rather than elected and thus are not accountable to the people, are making decisions that businesspeople should be making for themselves.

5.   OSHA has had an impact on the labor-management process that has compounded labor troubles. Many unions have become involved in worker safety and employees' rights under OSHA to the point where productivity is hindered.

6.   Numerous employers have become paranoid due to adverse publicity and labor disputes arising from unnecessary OSHA citations.

The major arguments in favor of OSHA are these:

1. OSHA is essential to reinforce a safe and healthy workplace for employees.
2. Many deaths and injuries have been prevented because of OSHA.
3. In today's technologically complex business world, employees need protection that only government regulation can provide.
4. Employers who oppose OSHA are too interested in the costs of safety and health, and productivity and profits, and not concerned enough about employees.
5. There are employers who have a favorable attitude toward OSHA and benefit from its existence. These employers actively work with OSHA in a joint effort to prevent and reduce safety and health problems. To these businesspeople, OSHA compliance is cost effective.

Are you for or against OSHA? Support your viewpoint.

OSHA's Role in Loss Prevention

Because safety is a major portion of a comprehensive loss prevention program, OSHA can help to strengthen strategies for preventing and reducing losses. If management is not very interested in workplace safety and health and perceives OSHA as a nuisance and expense, then the loss prevention program will suffer. However, with management enthusiasm and support, loss prevention personnel can use OSHA to improve safety. This positive attitude will enable OSHA to serve as a source of knowledge and guidance; losses inevitably will decrease.

Why have OSHA responsibilities consistently been placed by management with the loss prevention and security function? The role of OSHA compliance within the loss prevention and security sphere evolved because of the law enforcement and penalty nature of OSHA. Furthermore, the mutual preventive goals of security, fire protection, and safety have helped to hasten the inevitable subsumption of these three functions under the field of loss prevention.

Assistance with Problems

Multiple sources provide assistance for employers concerned about workplace safety or health problems. The following sources of help aid employers:

1. Many insurance companies provide personnel who visit, inspect, and recommend strategies for preventing and eliminating hazards at client workplaces.
2. Trade associations and employer groups have become more conscious about safety and health.
3. Trade unions and employee groups are often interested in coordinated activities for preventing and eliminating hazards.
4. The *National Safety Council* has an extensive information service (Address: 1121 Spring Lake Dr., Itasca, IL 60143; Tel.: 1-800-621-7615).
5. Local doctors may be willing to provide information on a consulting basis about workplace medical matters. The Red Cross is a source of first-aid training. An employer who is not able to locate a local chapter should write to the American National Red Cross, National Headquarters, Safety Programs, 8111 Gatehouse Rd., Falls Church, VA 22042; Tel.: 703-206-7090.
6. Libraries contain a wealth of information on safety and health matters.
7. Colleges and universities may have educational programs in the field of occupational safety and health. By contacting the relevant departments, educators often provide useful information.
8. Free on-site consultation is offered in many states through agreements between OSHA and either a state or private contractor. These consultants do not write citations but expect cooperation or OSHA will be contacted. Enforcement action is rare, especially because the employer requested the consultant and showed a concern for safety and health.

SAFETY STRATEGIES

The *OSHA Handbook for Small Businesses* states seven basic elements for "Developing a Profitable Strategy for Handling Occupational Safety and Health":

1. The top manager assumes the leadership role through personal concern, clear policies, and by setting a good example.
2. Responsibility for safety and health activities is clearly assigned. After appropriate policies have been established, the top manager delegates authority for the accident prevention program, assigns specific duties, and includes all employees in the program.
3. Accident causes are identified and either eliminated or controlled. This includes identifying unique workplace hazards and instituting procedures and devices for prevention.
4. Safety and health training is implemented and all employees instructed on workplace materials and equipment, the use of safety devices, and the need to report workplace injuries and

illnesses. The training pays particular attention to new employees.

5.   A reporting and recordkeeping system is maintained. The OSHA system is helpful for collecting facts and determining causes. These records and others are necessary for not only OSHA but also workers' compensation and insurance audits.

6.   A medical and first-aid system is established according to OSHA requirements. For instance, selected employees are trained in first aid. Equipment for emergency use, such as an emergency shower in the workplace in the event an employee makes contact with a harmful substance, is provided.

7.   Continued involvement by all employees in safety and health strategies is planned for. Safety and health in the workplace is ensured through employee involvement programs (e.g., incentive programs for prolonged non-accident periods).[17]

Socialization

Training is a prime strategy for accident prevention. The objective of training is to change the behavior of the employee. He or she should think and act in a safe manner. Safety videos and lectures by specialists are useless unless employees are motivated to continually act in a safe manner. Even if familiar with safety procedures and other relevant information, this does not signify that an employee will "practice what is preached." A method for stimulating the employee to act safely and to use safety knowledge is necessary. This objective is accomplished through incentive programs.

Safety and Health Committee

A safety and health committee can be an important part of an effective loss prevention program. When employees jointly communicate about and work toward increased safety and health, consciousness raising is a result, and employees develop a greater awareness of associated problems and solutions. Safety training is reinforced through committee activity.

The safety and health committee should meet at least every month. Management support and attendance at the meeting will strengthen the committee's prime objective, which is safety. Other staff members, such as department heads, loss prevention practitioners, safety specialists, line employees, and employee representatives, can add numerous perspectives to topics of concern. Participatory management can generate varied ideas from those who work in the actual job environment.

The functions of the committee often are aimed at recognizing hazards and developing countermeasures. At meetings, topics to discuss can include past accidents and illnesses, OSHA standards and inspections, and cases of accidents, illnesses, and remedies that occurred at similar facilities.

Incentive Programs

Incentive programs motivate employees to work safely. An article in *Occupational Hazards* exemplifies several kinds of safety incentive programs:

1. When a particular company has no accidents for a specific time period (e.g., a week or so) the coffee vending machines are open to all employees.
2. Every time a manufacturing plant reaches a million hours in its ascent to 7,500,000 workerhours without a lost-time accident, every employee receives a gift. The gifts have included blankets, picnic sets, and umbrellas. This company spent $100,000 on the incentive program during one year.
3. Safety bingo was initiated at a plant. Numbers are drawn every workday for a week and posted on a sign in the employee parking lot. If an employee completes a row, $25 is awarded. If the whole card is filled, $1000 is won. When lost-time accidents occur, the game is halted until a month later.
4. Companies often set safety goals for individual departments, which facilitate a competitive spirit to win prizes.
5. Safety, rewarded by merit pay increases for employees, will also reduce accidents. Employees who perform unsafe acts or resist safety equipment or other features of the safety program lose eligibility to participate in incentive programs for specific periods.[18]

What are the results of such incentive programs? Safety incentives provide a powerful, cost-effective management tool to prevent accidents. Enthusiasm and safety awareness increase. Employees are more vigilant about other workers' safety. Peer pressure increases, which reduces discipline problems for supervisors and management. Incentive programs provide fun in the workplace, which results in higher morale. As accidents decline, so do insurance premiums for workers' compensation. Money is saved. Fewer accidents mean fewer production interruptions and greater profits. It is feasible to use incentives for a comprehensive loss prevention effort involving not only safety but also crime and fire prevention.

Investigations

After an accident, an investigation is vital to prevent future accidents; the cause of an accident can be pinpointed so that corrections can follow. Established procedures important for well-planned accident investigations include the following:

1. Respond quickly to reinforce that loss prevention personnel are "on the job." This will also show employees that management cares.
2. Find out who was involved, where did it occur, when did it happen, who was injured, and what was damaged.

3.   Try to pinpoint the cause. Investigate possible direct and indirect causes. Study equipment, work procedures, and the employees involved.
4.   Estimate injuries and direct and indirect costs.
5.   Use a standard accident report that fits management's requirements and aids the investigative inquiry.
6.   Maintain an open mind, remaining aware that some employees attempt fraudulent workers' compensation claims by staging an accident or by providing false information.
7.   If necessary, complete appropriate forms (e.g., workers' compensation, OSHA).
8.   Prepare a presentation for the safety and health committee concerning the accident. Solicit feedback from the committee to solve problems.
9.   Follow up on corrective action to ensure safety.

One of the most difficult questions to answer during an accident investigation is the *cause*; often considerable controversy is generated. Opinions vary, but facts are necessary.

Harry Nash, Machinist, Is Injured Again

As Harry Nash was cutting a piece of metal on a band saw, he accidentally cut off his thumb. Workers in the surrounding area rushed to his aid. The foreman and the loss prevention manager coordinated efforts to get him and his thumb to the hospital as quickly as possible. After Harry was in the care of doctors, the foreman and the loss prevention manager began an investigation. A look at Harry's record showed that he had been working for the company for eight years. During the first year he slipped on some oil on the workplace floor and was hospitalized for three weeks with a sprained back. The third year showed that he accidentally drilled into his finger with a drill press. The report stated that Harry did not receive any training from a now-retired foreman, who should have instructed Harry on drill-press safety techniques. By the fifth year Harry had had another accident. While carrying some metal rods, he fell and broke his ankle because he forgot about climbing one step to enter a newly constructed adjoining building.

Even though Harry had had no training in operating the band saw, the loss prevention manager and the foreman believed that Harry was accident prone. The foreman, angry about Harry spoiling the department's safety record and incentive gifts, wanted Harry fired. The loss prevention manager was undecided about the matter.

Later, a meeting of several high-ranking employees, including the foreman and the loss prevention manager, decided to assign Harry to a clerical position in the shipping department. Harry eventually collected workers' compensation for his lost thumb.

There are two primary causes of accidents: unsafe conditions and unsafe acts by people. Frequently, unsafe conditions (e.g., unguarded moving parts, poor lighting) are known, but corrections are not made because of inaction or costs. Unsafe acts by people can result from ignorance, poor training, negligence, drugs, fatigue, emotional upset, poor attitude, and high production demands. Other circumstances also can cause accidents. One of the oldest and most controversial theories of accident causation is the *accident-proneness theory.* This theory suggests that people who repeatedly have accidents are accident prone. Many experts agree that about 20 percent of the people have most of the accidents, whereas the remaining 80 percent have virtually no accidents. However, because an individual's susceptibility to accidents varies from person to person, there is no profile of characteristics that can positively identify accident-prone employees.

Additional Safety Measures

Other safety measures are to display safety posters, create a safety-by-objectives program, and recognize employees with excessive accident records and reassign or retrain those workers. Safety posters or signs are effective if certain guidelines are used. Research indicates that if the safety message is in negative terms (e.g., "Don't let this happen to you," followed by a picture of a person with a physical injury) it causes fear, resentment, and sometimes anger. Posters with positive messages (e.g., "Let's all pitch in for safety") produce better results. Posters and signs are more potent when they are located in appropriate places, are not too numerous, and have attractive colors (see Figure 13–1).

Figure 13–1 Safety signs.

A safety-by-objectives program is a derivative of management by objectives. In a manufacturing plant, department heads formulate safety objectives for their departments. Management makes sure that objectives are neither too high nor too low. Incentives are used to motivate employees. After a year, the objectives are studied to see if the objectives were reached. Future objectives are modified or increased.

When certain employees are having excessive accidents, management must act to prevent future losses. Quick reassignment is not always appropriate. A thorough investigation of the individual and the work environment is vital. Remember that accidents can result either from the individual (e.g., personal problems) or the environment (e.g., poor safety equipment or inadequate training). After a careful study of the total situation, management must act to correct any deficiencies, which may include improved training, additional safety equipment, or reassignment.

CASE PROBLEMS

13A. As a loss prevention practitioner for a large corporation, a local college professor asks you to lecture on the pros and cons of OSHA. What will your comments be to a class of safety management students?

13B. If you were a company loss prevention manager, how would you react to an OSHA inspection? What conditions in your company do you think would influence your reaction?

13C. In reference to the case describing Harry Nash, do you feel that the loss prevention manager and the foreman were justified in labeling Harry as accident prone? Support your answer.

NOTES

1. C. Richard Anderson, *OSHA and Accident Control Through Training* (New York: Industrial Press, 1975), pp. 5–6.
2. *Accident Facts, 1996 ed.*, National Safety Council (1121 Spring Lake Dr., Itasca, IL 60143), p. 48.
3. See *A Primer on Confined Area Entry*, Bio Marine, Inc., 456 Creamery Way, Exton, PA 19341; Tel.: 610-524-8800. Also Michael Chacanaca, "Specialty—Confined-Space Rescues," *Emergency* (February 1996): 61–65.
4. John V. Grimaldi and Rollin H. Simmonds, *Safety Management* (Homewood, IL: Richard D. Irwin, 1975), pp. 33–43.
5. Joseph B. Mason, "OSHA: Problems and Prospects," *California Management Review* 19, no. 1 (Fall 1976): 21.
6. U.S. Department of Labor, OSHA, *All About OSHA* (Washington, DC: U.S. Government Printing Office, 1995), p. 2.

7. Office of the Federal Register, National Archives and Records Administration, *Code of Federal Regulations* (Washington, DC: U.S. Government Printing Office, July 1, 1988), p. 359.
8. Ibid., p. 375.
9. U.S. Department of Labor, *Hazard Communication Standard*, Fact Sheet No. OSHA 93-26 (1993).
10. U.S. Department of Labor, *Bloodborne Pathogens Final Standards: Summary of Key Provisions,* Fact Sheet No. OSHA 92-46 (1992).
11. U.S. Department of Labor, *All About OSHA*, pp. 13–14.
12. Ibid., p. 12.
13. Ibid., p. 13.
14. Ibid., p. 15.
15. Ibid., pp. 17–18. Also Mark S. Dreux, "When OSHA Knocks, Should an Employer Demand a Warrant?" *Occupational Hazards* (April 1995): 53.
16. National Federation of Independent Business, "Standing up to OSHA," *NFIB Mandate* (150 West 20th Avenue, San Mateo, CA 94403), no date, p. 5.
17. U.S. Department of Labor, OSHA, *OSHA Handbook for Small Businesses* (Washington, DC: U.S. Government Printing Office, 1979), pp. 2–12.
18. John C. Bruening, "Incentives Strengthen Safety Awareness," *Occupational Hazards* (November 1989): 49–52. Also S. L. Smith, "Reaping the Rewards of Safety Incentives," *Occupational Hazards* (January 1996): 99–102.

14

Risk Management and Insurance

OBJECTIVES

After studying this chapter the reader will be able to

1. Define risk management;
2. Explain the role of the risk manager and the tools of risk management;
3. Describe the insurance industry;
4. Discuss crime insurance, bonds, fire insurance, and property and liability insurance;
5. Elaborate on insurance claims.

Risk is exposure to possible loss. Crime, fire, or accident are by no means the only kinds of risk that confront businesses. The wise businessperson is knowledgeable about all possible risks. Business interruption, for example, results from crime, fire, accident, flood, tornado, and the like. Another risk is liability. A customer might become injured on the premises after falling or be harmed in some way when using a product manufactured by a business.

RISK MANAGEMENT

The most productive way of handling unavoidable risks is to manage them as well as possible. Hence, the term risk management has evolved. *Risk management* makes the most efficient before-the-loss arrangement for an after-the-loss continuation of a business. Insurance is a major risk management tool.

Risk management and loss prevention are naturally intertwined. Loss prevention is another tool for risk managers to make their job easier. Insurance is made more affordable through loss prevention methods. Additional risk management tools are described in succeeding pages.

Both loss prevention and risk management originated in the insurance industry. Fire insurance companies, soon after the Civil War, formed the

National Board of Fire Underwriters, which was instrumental in reducing loss of life and property through prevention measures. Today, loss prevention has spread throughout the insurance industry and into the business community. Risk management is also an old practice. The modern history of risk management is said by many insurance experts to have begun in 1931, with the establishment of the insurance section of the American Management Association. The insurance section holds conferences and workshops for those in the insurance and risk management field.

The Role of the Risk Manager

Traditionally, businesses purchased insurance through outside insurance brokers. Generally, a broker brings together a buyer and a seller. Insurance brokers are especially helpful when a company seeking insurance has no proprietary risk manager to analyze risks and plan insurance coverage. Not all businesses can afford the services of a broker or a proprietary risk manager; however, risk management tools are applicable to all businesspeople.

The risk manager's job varies with the company served. He or she may be responsible for insurance only; or for security, safety, and insurance; or for fire protection, safety, and insurance. *One important consideration in the implementation of a risk management (or loss prevention) program is that the program must be explained in financial terms to top executives.* Is the program cost effective? Financial benefits and financial protection are primary expectations of top executives that the risk manager must consider during decision making.

Among the many activities of the risk manager are to develop specifications for insurance coverage wanted, meet with insurance company representatives, study various policies, and decide on the most appropriate coverage at the best possible price. Coverage may be required by law or contract such as workers' compensation insurance and vehicle liability insurance. Plant and equipment should be reappraised periodically to maintain adequate insurance coverage. Also, the changing value of buildings and other assets, as well as replacement costs, must be considered in the face of depreciation and inflation.[1]

It is of tremendous importance that the expectations of insurance coverage be clearly understood. The risk manager's job could be in jeopardy if false impressions are communicated to top executives, who believe a loss is covered when it is not. Certain things may be excluded from a specific policy that might require special policies or endorsements. Insurance policies state what incidents are covered and to what degree. Incidents not covered are also stated. An understanding of stipulations concerning insurance claims, when to report a loss, to whom, and supporting documentation are essential in order not to invalidate a claim.

During this planning process, loss prevention measures are appraised in an effort to reduce insurance costs. Because premium reductions through loss prevention are a strong motivating force, risk managers may view strategies, such as security officers, as a necessary annoyance.

Deductibles are another risk management tool to cut insurance expenses. There are several forms of deductibles, but generally the policyholder pays for small losses up to a specified amount (e.g., $100, $1000), while the insurance carrier pays for losses above the specified amount, less the deductible.

A major concern for the risk manager in the planning process is *what amount of risk is to be assumed by the business beyond that covered by insurance and loss prevention strategies.* A delicate balance should be maintained between excessive protection and excessive exposure.[2]

Within the planning process and before a final decision is made on risk countermeasures, the practitioner should consider five additional tools for dealing with risk: risk avoidance, risk transfer, risk abatement, risk spreading, and risk assumption.

- *Risk avoidance.* This approach asks whether or not to avoid the risk. For example, the production of a proposed product is canceled because the danger inherent in the manufacturing process creates a risk that outweighs potential profits. Or, a bank avoids opening a branch in a locality that is subject to yearly flooding.
- *Risk transfer.* Risk can be transferred to insurance. The risk manager works with an insurance company to tailor a coverage program for the risk. This approach should not be used in lieu of loss prevention measures but rather to support them. *Insurance should be last in a series of defenses.* Another method of transferring risk is to lease equipment rather than owning it. This would transfer the risk of obsolescence.
- *Risk abatement.* In abatement, essentially a risk is decreased through a loss prevention measure. Risks are not eliminated, but the severity of loss is reduced. Losses from fire, for example, are reduced by alarms and sprinklers.
- *Risk spreading.* Potential losses are reduced by spreading the risk among multiple locations. A large retail store can scatter cash register locations to minimize risks associated with operation. In another example, vital records can be duplicated and stored at a remote, secure location.
- *Risk assumption.* In the assumption approach, a company makes itself liable for losses. One path is when no action is taken and no insurance is obtained. This may result because the chance for loss is minute. Another path, self-insurance, provides for periodic payments to a reserve fund in case of loss. Risk assumption may be the only choice for a company if insurance cannot be obtained. With risk assumption, prevention strategies become essential.

> What do you think are the most difficult aspects of a risk manager's job?

INSURANCE

Insurance is the transfer of risk (exposure to possible loss) from one party (the insured) to another party (the insurer), in which the insurer is obligated to indemnify (compensate) the insured for economic loss caused from an unexpected event during a period of time for which the insured makes a premium payment to the insurer. The essence of insurance is the sharing of risks; insurance permits the insured to substitute a small cost (the premium) for a large loss under an arrangement whereby the fortunate many who escape loss will indirectly assist in the compensation of the unfortunate few who experience loss. For an insurance company to function properly, a large number of policyholders is required. This creates a "shared risk."

The technical aspects of the insurance industry involve the skills of statisticians, economists, financial analysts, engineers, attorneys, physicians, and of course, risk managers and loss prevention specialists, among others. Insurance companies must carefully set rates, meticulously draft contracts, establish underwriting guidelines (i.e., accepting or rejecting risks for an insurance company), and invest funds prudently.

Insurance rates are dependent on two primary variables: the frequency of claims and the cost of each claim. When insurance companies periodically review rates, the "loss experience" of the immediate past is studied.

The insurance industry is subject to two powerful forms of control: competition among insurance companies and government regulation. Competition enables the consumer to compare rates and coverage for the best possible buy. Government regulatory authorities in each state or jurisdiction have a responsibility to the public to assure the solvency of each insurance company so policyholders will be indemnified when appropriate. Furthermore, rates should be neither excessive nor unfairly discriminatory.

The business of insurance in the United States is divided into two broad categories: life and health insurance and property and casualty insurance. Altogether the insurance industry provides 2.2 million jobs and has responsibility for assets that at the end of 1995 were valued at more than $2.9 trillion. About 6000 insurance companies are domiciled in the United States. Some of these companies sell all lines of insurance; many specialize in one or more kinds.[3]

Because types of insurance are numerous, varied, and confusing, the *Insurance Services Office* (ISO), a trade association of insurers, introduced a new commercial lines program in the late 1980s. Although many insurance companies do not use ISO contracts, what we are seeing are continued efforts at standardization.[4]

Crime Insurance and Bonds

Two basic kinds of protection against crime losses are fidelity and surety bonds and burglary, robbery, and theft insurance. The first covers losses caused by dishonesty or incapacitation from persons entrusted with money or other property who violate this trust. The second form of protection covers theft by persons who are not in a position of trust.

What are the differences between insurance and a bond? A *bond* is a legal instrument whereby one party (the surety) agrees to indemnify another party (the obligee) if the obligee incurs a loss from the person bonded (the principal or obligor). Although a bond may seem like insurance, there are differences between them. Generally, a bonding contract involves three parties, whereas an insurance contract involves two. With a bond, the surety has the legal right to attempt collection from the principal after indemnifying the obligee; collection would be absurd by an insurer against an insured party unless fraud was evident. Another difference is that insurance is easier to cancel than a bond. The insured can cancel insurance by simply notifying the insurer or by nonpayment of premium. Breach of the insurance contract by the insured, or nonpayment of premium, is the insurer's frequent reason for cancellation and also a legal defense by the insurer to avoid liability. On the other hand, with a bond, the surety is liable to the beneficiary even though breach of contract or fraud occurred by the principal.

Fidelity Bonds

Generally, a fidelity bond requires that an employee(s) be investigated by the bonding company to limit the risk of dishonesty for the insured. If the bonded employee violates the trust, the insurer (bonding company) indemnifies the employer for the amount of the policy.

Fidelity bonds may be of two kinds: (1) those in which an individual is specifically bonded, by name or by position, and (2) "blanket bonds," which cover a whole category of employees.

Surety Bonds

A surety bond essentially is an agreement providing for compensation if there is a failure to perform specified acts within a certain period of time. One of the more common surety bonds is called a contract construction bond. It guarantees that the contractor(s) involved in construction will complete the work that is stipulated in the construction contract, free from debts or encumbrances.

Several types of surety bonds are used in the judiciary system. A fiduciary bond ensures that persons appointed by the court to supervise the property of others will be trustworthy. A litigation bond ensures specific conduct by defendants and plaintiffs.

Burglary, Robbery, and Theft Insurance

Understanding the definitions for *burglary*, *robbery*, and *theft* is important when studying insurance contracts. In reference to businesses, a valid burglary insurance claim requires the unlawful taking of property from a closed business that was entered by force. In the absence of visible marks showing forced entry, a burglary policy is inapplicable. Robbery is the unlawful taking of property from another by force or threat of force. Without force or threat of force, robbery has not occurred. Theft is a broad, catchall term that includes all crimes of stealing, plus burglary and robbery.

Insurance for losses from these crimes varies from limited, specific coverage to comprehensive coverage. A sampling of policies follows.

A *safe burglary policy* covers loss of assets taken by forced entry of a safe or vault. Associated damage to property also is covered. Proof of forced entry is required for indemnification. If the victim is forced to open a container, he or she needs a separate robbery policy for coverage. Property stolen from areas outside of the container also would require separate coverage.

The *mercantile open stock* (MOS) *burglary policy* covers stock from a merchant's shelves as well as property contained in a safe. This policy also covers loss (or damage) of merchandise and equipment and robbery of an after-hours security officer.

A *storekeeper's burglary and robbery policy* is a package policy applicable to small business retailers. It covers seven perils: (1) burglary of a safe; (2) MOS burglary; (3) damage to money, securities, merchandise, furnishings, and equipment caused by a robbery or burglary; (4) theft of money or securities from a bank night depository or a residence; (5) robbery outside the premises; (6) robbery inside the premises; and (7) kidnapping to force access to the premises.

One popular form of crime insurance for businesses is known as a *3-D policy* (comprehensive dishonesty, destruction, and disappearance). This broad-coverage policy contains five parts: (1) an employee dishonesty bond; (2) robbery, burglary, or disappearance of money, securities, or property from the premises; (3) the disappearance of money, securities, or property off the premises (e.g., money being transferred); (4) check forgery; and (5) the counterfeiting of securities. Of the five parts of coverage, a company can select any or all, plus the amount of coverage for each one.

Crime insurance against computer fraud is another option especially important today because of widespread use of computers. This insurance covers losses due to theft through fraudulent transfer by computers of money and securities or other property.

Despite the availability of insurance, crime against property is one of the most underinsured perils. Estimates are that less than 10 percent of loss to property from ordinary crime is insured. Risk assumption remains the often-used tool to handle the crime peril.

Federal Crime Insurance

The *Federal Crime Insurance Program*, established by Congress, began operation in 1971 to counter the difficulty of obtaining adequate burglary and robbery insurance, particularly in urban areas. The program was discontinued in 1995. Private insurers and their agents administered the coverage, and the federal government, through the *Federal Insurance Administration*, was the bearer of the risk.

Kidnapping and Extortion Insurance

Another form of crime insurance covers losses from a ransom paid in a kidnapping or through extortion. During the 1970s, an upsurge in domestic and international kidnappings and terrorism created a need for this form of insurance. U.S. banks and corporations with overseas executives are especially interested in this coverage. These policies cover executives, their families, ransom money during delivery to extortionists, and corporate negligence during negotiations, among other areas of coverage.

You Be the Judge[*] 1

Cliff Hawkins, the newest member of Conway Excavation's repair crew, pulled his rolling tool chest to a stop and extended his hand to his new supervisor.

"Well," said Dave Greco, smiling and shaking Hawkins's hand, "it looks like you brought everything but the kitchen sink."

"A good mechanic can't do much without a good set of tools," replied Hawkins, patting the chest gently. "It took me five years and almost $3000 to build up this set. Which reminds me"—he glanced around the garage—"if you expect me to leave these tools here, you'd better have some kind of security."

"You've got nothing to worry about," replied Greco. "We lock up at night, and nothing has ever been stolen yet."

But there's a first time for everything. A short time after Hawkins started working for Conway Excavation, the garage was broken into. Hawkins's tools were stolen.

"I thought you said my tools would be safe here," Hawkins fumed when he faced Greco.

"I never said that," Greco corrected him. "I said this garage had never been broken into. And it hadn't."

"Yeah, well I hope this company is prepared to reimburse me," Hawkins said.

Greco sat up in his chair, surprised. "Reimburse you?" he echoed. "No way! You knew our security wasn't very extensive, but you chose to leave your tools here anyway."

continued

"I had to leave my tools here," Hawkins said angrily.

Greco shrugged. "Still, they were your tools and their loss isn't this company's responsibility."

"We'll see about that," Hawkins said as he stormed out of the office.

Hawkins went to court to try to force Conway Excavation to reimburse him for his stolen tools. Did Hawkins get his money?

Make your decision; then turn to the end of the chapter for the court's decision.

* Reprinted with permission from *Security Management—Plant and Property Protection,* a publication of Bureau of Business Practice, Inc., 24 Rope Ferry Road, Waterford, CT 06386.

Fire Insurance

Historically, the fire policy was one of the first kinds of insurance developed. For many years, it has played a significant role in assisting society against the fire peril. Prior to 1873, fire insurance contracts were not standardized. Each insurer developed its own contract. Omissions in coverage, misinterpretations, and conflicts between insurer and insured resulted in considerable problems. These individualized contracts and resultant ambiguities caused the state of Massachusetts, in 1873, to establish a standard contract. Seven years later, the standard contract became mandatory for all insurance companies in the state. Today, except for minor variations in certain states, the wording of fire insurance contracts is very similar. But, in recent years, these standard fire policies have diminished in importance as broad coverage policies have increased in number.

An understanding of insurance rating procedures provides risk managers and loss prevention managers with the knowledge to propose investments in fire protection that can show a return. Factors that influence fire insurance rates include the ability of the community's fire alarm, fire department, and water system to minimize property damage once a fire begins. Class 1 communities have the greatest suppression ability, whereas Class 10 have the least. Strategies such as convincing the community to take steps to improve its grade and installing sprinkler systems can produce a return on investment.[5]

Contract Components

A fire insurance contract consists of the declaration page, the insuring agreement, the conditions, and a "form" (also called amendments or endorsements). The declaration page shows the insured's name, location of property covered, amount of insurance, and premium costs. The insuring agreement summarizes what is agreed on by the insurer and insured, and what each agrees to do. Conditions include such topics as perils excluded and voiding of the policy due to fraud. A form, the most common being the general property form, is added to the contract because the basic fire policy does not describe in detail the property covered nor does it accurately define conditions, limitations, and exclusions. The form helps to tailor coverage for specific needs, covers additional perils, details the coverage, and reduces the chance of misunderstandings.

Property and Liability Insurance

The following discussion of business property insurance, liability insurance, and workers' compensation insurance intends to provide a broad overview of the varieties of property and liability insurance.

Business Property Insurance

The *general property form* (GPF), an addition to the standard fire policy, provides coverage for owned real property, owned personal property, and nonowned personal property. Owned real property includes the building(s) listed in the declaration page of the insurance contract plus extensions, fixtures, and equipment. Owned personal property consists of personal property owned by the insured and customary to the occupancy. Nonowned personal property (1) represents permanent alterations made to a leased building by the insured and (2) personal property of others in the insured's control. Repair services especially have this coverage. The GPF has other kinds of property coverage that can include personal property of employees, valuable papers and records, property away from the premises for repair, and outdoor foliage. The perils insured against in the GPF include fire and lightning and extended-coverage perils such as windstorm, hail, riot, and explosion. Endorsements for other perils such as sprinkler leakage also are available.

The *special multiperil policy* (SMP) is a popular, comprehensive policy often recommended as a good buy for businesses and institutions. The SMP coverage is broad: property, liability, crime, and boiler/machinery. Of these four, only the first two are mandatory for the basic SMP. The SMP also permits a full range of indirect loss coverage.

Another important kind of insurance is business interruption insurance. It indemnifies the insured for profits and fixed expenses lost because of damage to property from an insured peril.

As a risk manager, list five guidelines you would consider prior to purchasing insurance for your employer.

Liability Insurance

Legal liability for harm caused to others is one of the most serious risks. Negligence can result in a substantial court judgment against the responsible party. There are several kinds of exposures in the liability area. Relevant factors are the functions performed, relationships involved, and care for others required, such as the employee-employer relationship, a contract situation, consumers of manufactured products, and professional acts.

In many jurisdictions the law views the failure to obtain liability insurance against the consequences of negligence as irresponsible financial behavior. Mandatory liability insurance for automobile operators in all states is a familiar example.

Several kinds of business liability insurance are available. The *comprehensive general liability* (CGL) policy covers bodily injury and property damage resulting from conditions on the premises (e.g., customer slipping on wet floor); business operations (e.g., losses when working at a customer's home); product liability (e.g., faulty product); completed operations (e.g., losses after working on equipment at a customer's home); and operations of independent contractors (e.g., negligence by a contractor hired by a business).

Workers' Compensation Insurance

Coverage includes loss of income and medical and rehabilitation expenses that result from work-related accidents and occupational diseases. An employer can obtain the coverage required by law through three possible avenues: (1) commercial insurance companies, (2) a state fund or a federal agency, and (3) self-insurance (risk assumption). Although self-insurers commonly post a bond, it is one of the most frequently used methods of coverage.[6]

Claims

When an insured party incurs a loss, a claim is made to the insurer to cover the loss as stipulated in the insurance contract. For an insurance company, the settling of losses and adjusting differences between itself and the policyholder is known as *claims management*. Care is necessary by the insurer because underpayments can lead to lost customers, yet overpayments can lead to bankruptcy.

An insurance company investigation of a claim commonly includes (1) a determination that there has been a loss, (2) a determination that the insured has not invalidated the insurance contract, (3) an evaluation of the proof of loss, and (4) an estimate of the amount of loss. An example of item (2) occurs when the insured has not fulfilled obligations under the insurance contract, such as not protecting property from further damage after a fire or not adequately maintaining loss prevention measures. Furthermore,

The Cost of Risk Survey Shows Risk Management Produces a Return on Investment[7]

For the last few years, the Cost of Risk Survey has shown that risk is a manageable and controllable expense and that risk managers can contribute to the bottom line. This survey is conducted jointly by the Risk and Insurance Management Society, Inc. (see note 1) and Tillinghast-Towers Perrin (695 East Main St., Stamford, CT 06901; Tel.: 203-326-5400). The survey covers over 700 organizations across 26 industries. The Cost of Risk Survey has been used to analyze various elements of the cost of risk, and it can be used to set a benchmark of an organization's costs against peer companies. Recent survey results showed, for example, that the cost of risk per $1000 of revenue was $6.07 for retailers and $19.27 for the health care industry. Also, workers' compensation and liability costs decreased for survey respondents. The decline in the former was attributed to safety programs, managed care, less reliance on traditional insurance, and legislative reform. A decline in the latter was attributed to the competitive insurance market, heightened awareness of loss prevention, and litigation control. The survey results were not positive with all risks; a string of natural catastrophes led to record property losses.

most insurance contracts specify that the insured party must give immediate notice of loss. The purpose of that is to give the insurer an opportunity to study the loss before evidence to support the claim has been damaged. Failure to provide immediate notice may render the insurance invalid. The insured usually has 60 to 90 days to produce proof of loss. Accounting records, bills, and so on that might help in establishing the loss are expected to be provided by the insured.

Before a settlement is reached, the insurer checks the coverage, the claim is investigated, and loss reports and claim papers are prepared. Then, the insurance company claims department studies the loss, the policy is interpreted and applied to the loss, and a payment is approved or disapproved.

You Be the Judge* 2

A vice president had been embezzling money from the Michigan Mining Corporation for several years, but Security Director Steve Douglas had finally caught him. It was something of a Pyrrhic victory, however—the culprit was nabbed, but the company was out $135,000. Luckily, MMC had comprehensive business insurance that Douglas was sure would cover most of the loss.

The security director looked over the two policies, but they were poorly written and very confusing, so he called Lester Blank, the agent who handled the policies.

continued

"I limped through the policies," Douglas explained, "and I think I get the gist of them. MMC's covered for $100,000, right?"

"Wrong," Blank said. "The second policy replaced the first. You're only covered for $50,000."

Douglas was stunned, but he recovered quickly. "Now, wait a minute," he said. "I may not have caught every mixed-up word in these policies, but the second one says we can collect on the first one for up to a year after its expiration date, provided the loss occurred during the time the first policy was in effect."

"But the total limit is still $50,000," insisted the insurance agent. "You'll find a clause to that effect in the second policy, if you read carefully."

"If I read carefully!" Douglas cried. "This second policy is so full of spelling and clerical errors that it's anybody's guess what it means. One look at this piece of slipshod writing and any court will side with us."

So MMC went to court, claiming that because the policy was so complicated and poorly written, it should be interpreted in the company's favor.

Did the court agree with MMC?

Make your decision; then turn to the end of the chapter for the court's decision.

* Reprinted with permission from *Security Management—Plant and Property Protection,* a publication of Bureau of Business Practice, Inc., 24 Rope Ferry Road, Waterford, CT 06386.

Insurance companies employ different classifications of adjusters to settle claims. An insurance agent (i.e., salesperson) may serve as an adjuster for small claims up to a certain amount. A company adjuster is more experienced about claims and handles larger losses.

From the insurance industry's perspective, the work of an adjuster is demanding. A high priority is to satisfy claimants in order to retain customers. At the same time the interests and assets of the insurance company must be protected. Some claimants make honest mistakes in estimating losses. They may place a value on destroyed property that is above the market value. Exaggerations are common. Confusion may arise when claimants have not carefully read their insurance policy. Consequently, a process of education and negotiation often takes place between the adjuster and the claimant. Once the claimant signs the proof of loss papers or cashes the settlement check, this signifies that the claimant is satisfied and that further rights to pursue the claim are waived. In a certain number of claims, an agreement is not reached initially. The policy states the terms for settling claims. Typically, arbitration results. Each party appoints a disinterested party to act as arbitrator. The two arbitrators then select a third disinterested party. Agreements between two of the three arbitrators are binding. In liability cases, the court takes the place of arbitrators.

Dishonest claimants are a serious problem for the insurance industry, and for society. Insurance fraud is pervasive and costly. The United States Chamber of Commerce estimates that 10 percent of all insurance claims are in some way fraudulent. The actual figure without a doubt is much higher. Policyholders are the ultimate group that pays for these crimes through increased premiums.

Arson is unfortunately a popular way of defrauding insurance companies. Generally, a property owner sets a fire to collect on an insurance policy. A professional arsonist may be recruited. Arson is difficult to prove because the fire destroys evidence. However, law enforcement agencies and the insurance industry have increased efforts to combat arson through additional arson investigators, improved training, better detection equipment, and computers that search data for patterns of those who defraud insurance companies.

Insurance and Related Service Organizations[8]

- American Insurance Services Group, Inc.
  85 John St.
  New York, NY 10038
  212-669-0400

A subsidiary of the American Insurance Association (see Chapter 12), the group provides a variety of services: a national clearinghouse on bodily injury claims; a database on fire, burglary and theft; and technical services.

- Coalition Against Insurance Fraud
  1511 K St., NW, Suite 622
  Washington, DC 20005
  202-393-7330

This is an alliance of consumer, law enforcement, and insurance industry groups dedicated to reducing insurance fraud through public education.

- Insurance Committee for Arson Control
  3601 Vincennes Rd.
  PO Box 68700
  Indianapolis, IN 46268
  317-876-6226

This is an all-industry coalition and liaison with government to control arson.

- Insurance Cost Containment Service
  230 West Monroe St., Suite 310
  Chicago, IL 60606
  312-368-0700

This firm assists insurance companies with property claims adjustment and arson and fraud claims investigation.

continued

- International Association of Special Investigation Units
  IASIU, c/o John McHale
  CIGNA
  1601 Chestnut St., TLP-20
  Philadelphia, PA 19192
  215-761-2657

The association was organized to counter fraud; it represents over 3000 insurance companies.

- National Insurance Crime Bureau
  10330 S. Roberts Rd.
  Palos Hills, IL 60465
  708-430-2430

This group represents the merger of anticrime groups dedicated to combating insurance-related crimes through information, investigative, and training services.

Claims for Crime Losses

The information that follows describes claims for crime losses. A loss prevention practitioner may be confronted with important decisions in a claim in an attempt to minimize losses for his or her employer. Although crime claims are emphasized here, several points are applicable to other types of claims.

When a person or business takes out an insurance policy to cover valuables, the insurance agent frequently does not require proof that the valuables exist. But when a claim is filed, the insurer becomes very interested in not only evidence to prove that the valuables were stolen, but also evidence that the valuables in fact existed. Without proof, indemnification may become difficult. To avoid this problem, several steps are useful. First, the insured should prepare an inventory of all valuables. Accounting records and receipts are good sources for the inventory list. The list includes the item name, serial number, date it was purchased, price, and a receipt. Photographs of valuables are also useful. Copies of the documentation package should be given to the insurance company and to an attorney. Two other copies should be located in two separate safe places. Periodic updating is necessary.

After a burglary the policyholder contacts the insurer immediately and also the local police. An insurance representative asks for the policy number, the policyholder's name, and business name and location. A police report ordinarily is required by the insurer; documentation requirements depend on the circumstances and the insurer. Signs of forced entry are usually a burglary policy stipulation.

Payment from an insurance company for a loss can be delayed for many reasons. Incomplete forms or missing documentation often are cited. In addition to many telephone calls to the insurer by the insured, two other alternatives are available to the insured to facilitate prompt payment: the insured can ask the insurer to make a partial payment or settle for less. The insurer may delay payment to a business tight on cash in anticipation of a request for a better deal for the insurer. Careful claim preparation by the insured will hinder this ploy.

Another point of consideration is that insurance policies typically cover actual loss, not replacement cost. Depreciation of equipment over two years will have a definite impact on what the insurer will pay the insured after a loss.

Bonding Claims

Numerous insurance companies have found the fidelity bond business to be generally unprofitable. To compound the situation, businesspeople have attempted to use fidelity bond claims to cover losses from mysterious disappearance and general inventory shortages, rather than for its intended purpose—coverage for internal theft. For these reasons, when a claim takes place, the insurer and insured have a tendency to enter negotiations as adversaries. The strength of the loss prevention practitioner's case will definitely affect the settlement. Care must be exercised throughout the interaction with the insurer so as not to in any way invalidate the contract. Furthermore, the burden of proof for losses rests entirely on the insured.

Depending on the type of bond, the employee ordinarily completes an application for bonding and undergoes an investigation prior to bonding. Before 1970, the insurer investigated applicants and notified the insured of any criminal history of the applicant that would bar coverage. Because of economy measures and the difficulty in checking into a person's background, a shift has been made by many insurers to the insured for verifying the applicant's past. Bonds stipulate that past dishonesty by the employee justifies an exclusion from bonding from the day the information is discovered. If a loss occurs and the insurer can prove that this information was known to the insured company but not reported to the insurer, the bond is likely to be invalid.

Another way to invalidate a bond is through restitution by the employee to the employer without notifying the insurer. In many cases, the employee is eager to pay back what was stolen initially, but only makes a few payments before absconding. Thereafter, if a claim is made, the bond is useless.

In reference to the burden of proof, the loss prevention practitioner should have considerable expertise when dealing with the insurer on behalf of his or her employer Confusion often arises from the "exclusionary clause" of the fidelity bond policy. This clause essentially states that the bond does not cover losses that are dependent on proof from inventory records or a profit and loss computation. Prior to 1970, these records were not even allowed to establish the extent of losses even though employees had confessed. But, in the early 1970s, courts began to be more flexible in limiting the exclusionary clause and thus allowing inventory records and associated computations to establish the amount of the loss when independent proof also has been introduced to establish that there has been loss due to employee theft.

A confession is of prime importance to bonding claims. A guilty verdict by a criminal court or a favorable labor arbitration ruling are additional assets for the claimant.

As a risk manager, list three guidelines for successful claims preparation.

CASE PROBLEM

14A. As a loss prevention manager, you will soon explain to top management personnel why they should provide support and funds to initiate a risk management program by hiring a risk manager. You have formulated four areas to answer for top management:
   a. How a risk manager can help to perpetuate the business;
   b. Why the hiring of a risk manager would be cost effective;
   c. How five risk management tools are applied;
   d. How the risk manager and loss prevention manager will work together, and what each will do for the company.

THE DECISION FOR "YOU BE THE JUDGE 1"

Hawkins got reimbursed for the stolen tools. The court held that, when Hawkins left his tools in the work area overnight with the knowledge and consent of his employer, his employer accepted temporary custody of the property. This situation is known as a *bailment*, and in such a situation the party accepting custody of the property usually is responsible for its care and safekeeping. Under the laws of the state in which this case was tried, Conway Excavation might have escaped liability for the theft of Hawkins's tools if it had taken more extensive steps to make the garage secure. Instead, it had to pay him some $3000.

This case is based on *Harper* v. *Brown & Root* 398 Sa2d 94. The names in this case have been changed to protect the privacy of those involved.

THE DECISION FOR "YOU BE THE JUDGE 2"

The court disagreed with MMC, concluding that, although the policy was complicated and full of errors, it was not ambiguous in spelling out the limits of its liability—$50,000. MMC would have to absorb the rest of the loss itself. Security Director Douglas *could have saved his company a lot of money if he had taken the time to read the insurance policy when it was first issued.* That's the time to ask questions and demand clarification. If you can't understand the policy, find someone who can—the insurance agent or your company's attorney are two of the best people to ask. After the company puts in a claim, it may be too late to clear up the ambiguities.

This case is based on *Davenport Peters* v. *Royal Globe Ins.*, 490 FSupp 286. The names in this case have been changed to protect the privacy of those involved.

NOTES

1. See Robert M. Bieber, "The Making of a Risk Manager—Part One," *Risk Management* (September 1987): 23–30. For additional information contact the Risk and Insurance Management Society (655 Third Ave., New York, NY 10017; Tel.: 212-286-9292).
2. See Luther T. Griffith, "10 Survival Skills for Managing Corporate Risks in the Future," *Risk Management* (January 1989): 16–20.
3. Insurance Information Institute, *Fact Book 1997* (100 William St., New York, NY 10038; Tel.: 212-669-9200), p. 5. This is an excellent booklet containing insurance industry statistics, types of losses, and directories for information.
4. C. Arthur Williams, Jr., et al. *Risk Management and Insurance,* 7th ed. (New York: McGraw-Hill, 1995), p. 537.
5. Ibid., pp. 341–345.
6. See Phillip L. Polakoff and Paul F. O'Rourke, "Workers' Compensation—Managing the Cost Crunch," *Risk Management* (March 1988): 52–53.
7. "Cost of Risk," *Risk Management Advisor* (April 1997): 7. Also "1995 Cost of Risk Preview," *Risk Management* (January 1996): 50.
8. Insurance Information Institute, *Fact Book 1997*, pp. 127–140.

SPECIALIZED PROBLEMS IN LOSS PREVENTION

15

Retail Loss Prevention

OBJECTIVES

After studying this chapter the reader will be able to

1. Discuss the problem of shrinkage;
2. List personnel problems in retailing and countermeasures;
3. List and explain at least four internal loss prevention strategies for retailers;
4. List the types of losses at the checkout counters and countermeasures;
5. Discuss the shoplifting problem and countermeasures;
6. Elaborate on robbery and burglary countermeasures.

Numerous factors can be attributed to an unsuccessful retail business. Poor management, unwise store location, noncompetitive marketing (selling) techniques, and consumer dissatisfaction with merchandise can all hinder profits.

Another important factor that can make or break a retail business is the quality of the loss prevention program. With a very small profit margin in many retail businesses, loss prevention is a necessity for survival. Vulnerability to employee theft, shoplifting, burglary, robbery, fire, and poor safety can cause extensive losses.

SHRINKAGE

The term *shrinkage* is used by retailers to mean inventory losses from internal theft, shoplifting, damage, and paperwork errors. Security management performance in retailing often depends on the level of shrinkage, and this figure must be kept as low as possible. Shrinkage is gauged after an inventory, and an accurate inventory is vital.[1] Shrinkage of, say, 8 percent of annual sales is conducive to business failure. A more comfortable percentage generally is between 1 and 3 percent. According to the National Retail Security Survey, in 1995, U.S. retail revenues were about $1.40 trillion, with shrinkage at about $27 billion, or 1.87 percent. In 1990, the figures were $1.27 trillion, $22.7 billion, and 1.79 percent, respectively. The 1995 survey showed retailers lost $10.4 billion from employees and $9.7 billion from shoplifters.[2] Therefore, it is important to have a repertoire of strategies to lower shrinkage and increase the chances for business survival.

Personnel Problems in Retailing

Because retail loss prevention is highly dependent on the efforts of all employees, it is important to discuss the realities of personnel problems in retailing:

1. Many part-time or temporary employees;
2. Inexperienced workers (e.g., usually young people at their first jobs);
3. Employees dissatisfied with working conditions (e.g., low wages and long hours);
4. High rate of turnover.

Loss can become a by-product of each of these personnel factors. For instance, some part-time employees may be working during holiday seasons to make extra money and also may be stealing to support gift expenses. An inexperienced worker may unknowingly undercharge customers for merchandise. A dissatisfied employee may perform a variety of vindictive activities. A high rate of turnover creates additional training expenses and, moreover, many inexperienced employees.

Losses caused by part-time or temporary workers can be reduced by cost-effective screening, adequate socialization, and by good methods for accountability of inventory. Another possible measure would be to assign part-time and temporary workers to be supervised by and work with regular employees. Additionally, these types of workers could be barred from performing certain tasks and entering specific areas.

Although the potential exists for losses from part-time and temporary employees, potential losses from full-time regular employees must not be underestimated.

Screening

The quality of job applicant screening is dependent on numerous factors. In a small store, the owner may interview the applicant; record pertinent information, such as the address, telephone number, and social security number; and ask for a few references. In large multistore organizations, however, employment procedures commonly are more structured and controlled.

The intensity of screening also depends on the type of employee sought. A management trainee would likely receive screening that is different from that given a salesperson. The depth of the interview and scope of the background check should be greater for higher level positions.

A screening process should include verification of the application. Telephone checks with previous employers not only reveal personality characteristics but also the correctness of the application information. At least two telephone checks are a wise investment. A check via letter is time consuming but less expensive, and people tend to be more frank on the telephone as opposed to a letter where they have to put the information in writing.

Unfortunately, many of these screening measures are not performed. Research indicates that most small business retailers do not perform background investigations of their employees.[3]

Socialization

Various training programs can be instituted to assist in adequately socializing an employee toward business objectives. Training can reduce employee mistakes, raise productivity, create customer satisfaction, and reduce turnover. A loss prevention training program can reinforce attitudes that result in decreased losses.

Some retail businesses require employees to sign a statement that they understand the loss prevention program. This procedure reinforces loss prevention programming.

Executives must adhere to company policies and procedures. If employees observe executives violating policies and procedures this behavior will have a negative impact on the organization. As models of appropriate work attitudes and behavior, executives should *set a good example* and *practice what is preached.*

INTERNAL LOSS PREVENTION STRATEGIES

Theft is a major factor in internal losses. There are numerous targets for internal theft: merchandise, damaged items, cash, repair service, office supplies and tools, parts, time, samples for customers, food and beverages, personal property.

It is difficult to obtain accurate statistics about what percentage of shrinkage is attributed to either employee theft or shoplifting. Some retail employees portray deceiving statistics when this question arises. A mail survey of 254 retail merchants in the state of Mississippi found that employers have no systematic method for determining either the total amount of shrinkage or the proportion of total shrinkage emerging from various sources.[4] The authors conclude that employers greatly underestimate the extent of employee theft.

Although internal theft is a major part of the internal loss problem, there are other categories of internal losses:

1.   Accidents;
2.   Fire;
3.   Unproductive employees;
4.   Unintentional and intentional mistakes;
5.   Excessive absenteeism and lateness.

Strategies used by companies to address the problem of internal loss include motivation and morale programs, employee discounts, shopping services, undercover investigations, and insurance.

- *Motivation, morale, and rewards.* Attempts must be made by management to help employees feel as if they are an integral part of the business organization. Praise for an employee's accomplishment can go a long way in improving morale. Other methods of increasing morale and motivation are clean working conditions, participative management, and a company sports team. Contest and reward programs also reinforce improved morale and motivation. The employee with the best loss prevention idea of the month could be rewarded with $50 and recognition in a company newspaper.
- *Employee discounts.* Employee discounts usually range between 15 and 25 percent. An identification card is often issued so employees can shop at various branches of a large retail chain. These discounts are an obvious benefit to employee morale even though the discount is sometimes abused by purchases for relatives and friends. Also, some retail businesses have loose accountability of discount cards, and former employees continue to use the cards.
- *Shopping service.* A *shopping service* is a business that assists retail loss prevention efforts by supplying investigators who pose as customers to test cashiers and other retail employees for honesty, accuracy, and demeanor. One common test of salesclerks involves two shoppers who enter a store separately, acting as customers. One buys an item, pays for it with the exact amount of money needed, and leaves, while the second shopper, pretending to be a customer, observes whether the salesclerk rings up the sale or pockets the money. Theft of cash is not the only source of loss; "research indicates that a large amount of business revenues are lost due to the curt or even abrasive behavior of some sales personnel."[5]
- *Undercover investigations.* Investigations can be used as a last resort when other controls fail. By penetrating employee informal organizations, investigators are able to obtain considerable information that may expose collusion and weaknesses in controls.
- *Insurance.* Some retailers rely solely on insurance as a bulwark against losses. This is a mistake. Insurance should be an integral part of a comprehensive loss prevention program. Loss prevention procedures, policies, services, and devices are primary measures that are backed up by insurance on failure.

As well as liability from crimes, fires, and accidents, retailers may be held liable for a variety of occurrences such as customer injury while using an item purchased or customer sickness after eating food. The more frequent kinds of insurance that retailers rely on are as follows:

1. Fire insurance includes losses due to fire, smoke, and water.
2. Liability insurance protects against customer accidents in a store, items purchased that may have resulted in injury, and false arrest.
3. Crime insurance assists in reducing losses from burglary, robbery, and other crimes.
4. Bonding insurance protects against dishonest employees.
5. *Self-insurance* is provided by the company itself, as when a large retail firm with several stores pools the amount of premiums normally paid to an insurance company in case of a loss at any store.
6. Workers' compensation insurance provides for possible payment of medical and salary expenses to an injured employee.
7. Plate glass insurance is used to reduce losses from breakage of large plate glass windows at stores.
8. Sprinkler leakage insurance protects against water damage.
9. Insurance protects goods in transit.

Preventing Losses at the Checkout Counters

Checkout counters are locations in a retail business that accommodate customer payments, refunds, and service. According to research by Arthur Young and Company for the *International Mass Retail Association*, the checkout counter is the point most vulnerable to employee theft.[6]

Although most cashiers are honest and bar codes and scanning technology prevent losses, the following activities hinder profits:

1. Stealing money from the register;
2. Failing to punch in the sale and then stealing the money (this is especially tempting when no customer change is required);
3. Failing to punch in the sale, leaving the cash register drawer open for the customer's change, and then stealing the money;
4. Overcharging customers, keeping a mental record, and stealing the money at a later time;
5. Presenting the customer with the wrong change;
6. Accepting bad checks, bad charge cards, and counterfeit money;
7. Making pricing mistakes;
8. Undercharging for relatives and friends;
9. Failing to notice an altered price tag;
10. Failing to notice shoplifted items secreted in legitimate purchases.

Cashier Socialization of Procedures

The quality of training will have a direct bearing on accountability at cash registers. Procedural training can include, but is not limited to, the following:

1. Assign each cashier to a particular register.
2. Have each transaction recorded separately and the cash drawer closed afterward.

3.   Establish a system for giving receipts to customers.
4.   Train cashiers to meticulously count change.
5.   Show cashiers how to spot irregularities (e.g., altered price tags).
6.   Encourage cashiers to seek supervision when appropriate (e.g., to check price of item, question about customer credit).

Accountability of Voids

Voids are used to eradicate and record mistakes by cashiers at cash registers. Theft occurs when, for instance, a cashier voids a legitimate no-mistake sale and pockets the money. Fraudulent voids can be prevented by limiting void keys to supervisors who must sign and complete a short void form. Appropriate records can provide feedback to cashiers with excessive voids. Technological changes have altered methods of completing voids and auditing them.

Point-of-Sale Accounting Systems

Retailers are increasingly making use of point-of-sale (POS) accounting systems and bar-code technology to produce vital business information. Merchandise contains a bar code that is read by a scanner during inventory or at the checkout counters. This stored information provides a perpetual inventory, helpful to ascertain what is in stock and to assist with reorders of merchandise. In addition to shrinkage figures, POS systems can also be designed to produce a variety of loss prevention reports, exposing cashiers who repeatedly have cash shortages, voids, bad checks, and so forth. Ratios are also helpful to spot losses. Examples include cash to charge sales and sales to refunds.[7]

CCTV

Closed-circuit television can be used in both the overt and covert manners. CCTV can be integrated with POS systems to give a loss prevention practitioner an opportunity to view a cash register total and compare it with the merchandise sold. System capabilities enable the register total to appear on the TV monitor with the date and time. Furthermore, "exceptions" (e.g., voids) noted by the POS system can also trigger CCTV and a recording for later reference.

In Chapter 7, video technology is explained, including video multiplex, digital recording, security video at the desktop computer, and remote monitoring. Figure 15–1 shows a remote monitoring system that transmits audio and images over phone lines, provides alarm verification, hard disk storage, and prints images.

Refunds and Repair Service

Losses may be sustained by the retailer during refund and repair service activities. Such losses can be attributed to activities of employees, customers, or both.

Figure 15–1 Remote monitoring system. Courtesy: TeleSite USA, Inc.

In loosely controlled businesses, employees have an opportunity to retain a customer receipt (or hope that the customer leaves one) and use it to substantiate a fraudulent customer refund (merchandise supposedly returned for money). With the receipt used to support the phony refund slip, the employee is "covered" and can pocket the cash.

Some offenders enter retail stores and search for sales receipts, then look for merchandise that matches the receipt's price, and attempt to get a refund for cash. Especially bold offenders might enter a store, pick up an item, and then go directly to the refund desk and demand a cash refund without a receipt. Another ploy is to use a stolen credit card to purchase merchandise and then obtain a refund at another branch store. In other instances, collusion may take place between employees and customers. Employees simply issue refunds to family and friends.

Refund fraud is minimized through well-controlled supervision and accountability. A supervisor should account for returned merchandise before it is returned to the sales floor and sign and date the sales receipt after writing *refund*. Some retailers guarantee money (e.g., $5) to customers if the customer does not receive a receipt.

Losses involving repair services for customers can also drain profits. Employees sometimes fix their own items using company time and parts.

Repair employees have been known to steal all the parts necessary to construct an entire product.

Loss from repair operations is prevented via supervision of repair work orders. Close accountability of parts is essential, also.

International Perspective: Refund Fraud in Australia[8]

The refund fraud problem in Australia provides an illustration of how a few universally applied preventive procedures can reduce this growing multimillion dollar problem in that country. "Unfortunately, most retail outlets are their own worst enemy; their refund policies are so weak, outdated and customer friendly that they cater [to] the criminal." This crime is easy money and such a soft target that it brings a wide range of types of offenders: major and minor criminals, drug addicts, the unemployed, and first offenders. Basically, the offender lies about the origin of the property to obtain cash or other property. The majority of the items result from shoplifting or other forms of theft. Bold offenders are confident enough to walk out of a retail store with an exposed item as if they just paid for it. Teams of offenders rely on busy, overworked staff members to distract during their crimes. More sophisticated offenders use copiers, computers, and printers to create receipts or duplicate bar codes to purchase items at a lower price. To deal with this problem, and other retail crimes, almost every large police department in Australia has a retail crime unit. Although the refund fraud problem will not be eliminated, as in the United States, a few simple procedures will reduce it: proof of purchase, identification of the customer, and a refund form to record information.

BAD CHECKS AND CREDIT CARD LOSSES

Due to technological innovation and an aim toward expediency, *debit card* transactions are gaining momentum. This system operates with the assistance of a centralized computer, which contains individual financial records. When a customer purchases merchandise, the cost is fed into a computer (via a terminal at the store) and payment is transferred from the customer's account (savings) to the store's account. *Chip cards* are also being introduced, which is a migration from magnetic stripe credit cards. Chip cards contain a tiny computer enabling several features, such as being loaded with money in advance. Because these systems will require additional years before dominating retail transactions, millions of customers will continue to make purchases with personal checks. Therefore, personal checks and a variety of other types of checks will continue to be a source of losses for retailers.

Checks: Types and Irregularities

Checks are categorized by the Small Business Administration as follows:[9]

1. *Personal check.* Issued as a blank form by banks, the personal check is written and signed by the person offering it. Most of the time, a bad personal check happens when the check is not backed up by sufficient funds. Usually, customer negligence, in personal bookkeeping, causes this problem; the situation is often quickly rectified. Some customers knowingly write bad personal checks. At other times, lost or stolen personal checks are used, or bad checks are written on accounts that are either closed or never existed.
2. *Two-party check.* A two-party check is issued by one person to a second person, who endorses it so that it may be cashed by a third person. This kind is most susceptible to fraud because the maker (the first party) can stop payment at the bank.
3. *Payroll check.* An employer issues a check to an employee for services performed. Employer and employee names are usually on this check. Often, various types of information (e.g., names) are printed by a check writing machine. Sometimes offenders establish a phony company and print bogus payroll checks. An attempt is made to cash them with merchants who, if they called the "company" for verification, would be reassured that the person presenting the check is an employee.
4. *Government check.* Issued by many agencies of the government, these checks cover salaries, tax refunds, benefits, and so on. Government checks frequently are stolen from mailboxes and signatures forged for endorsement.
5. *Traveler's check.* Traveler's checks are sold with a preprinted amount to travelers who do not want to carry large amounts of cash. The traveler signs the checks at the time of purchase and should countersign them only in the presence of the person who cashes them. Offenders often forge the countersignature on stolen or lost travelers checks.
6. *Money order.* A money order, usually bought to send in the mail, can be passed as a check. Most stores should not accept money orders in face-to-face transactions.

A check is nothing more than a piece of paper until the money is collected. It may be worthless. Characteristics of bad checks include an inappropriate date, written figures that differ from numeric figures on the same check, and smeared ink. Of about 61 billion checks written each year, about 1.3 million are fraudulent. The FBI estimates losses at $12 to $15 billion to businesses each year.[10] The problem is growing worse because of newer color copier machines, scanners, computers, and laser printers.

Prevention of Bad Checks

Among the kinds of checks just described, personal checks create the greatest problem for retailers. Several methods can be used to reduce the problem. One method is for the retailer to refrain from accepting checks. This approach would eliminate the problem, but customer convenience will suffer and sales will be lost. More practical alternatives, which are prevention oriented, follow.

- *Policies, procedures, and training.* When employees know what is expected of them, they can act to cut losses. Guidelines include carefully examining checks, not accepting checks over a certain amount, seeking supervisory approval for checks written over a certain amount, prohibiting checks from out of state, and never providing cash for a check.
- *Proper identification.* Proper identification is a key factor in reducing the bad check problem. Retail employees should scrutinize customer identification for irregularities. Many employees look at identification cards but do not see irregularities. *Concentration is necessary to match (or not to match) the customer with the identification presented.* Many retailers require two types of identification before a check is accepted. A driver's license, vehicle registration, or credit card is usually acceptable. Many other types of identification (e.g., social security cards, birth certificates, insurance cards) are easier to obtain, forge, and hold for a period of time without detection.
- *Malfunctions in the identification system.* No identification system is totally foolproof. For instance, an offender may review old government records for the name of a child who died and whose birth year approximates the offender's. Thereafter, a birth certificate is obtained or forged and then a driver's license, checking account, credit cards, and so on. In 1978, a study by the FBI found that valid California licenses had been issued in the names of almost 1000 people who had been dead for years.[11] Some steps have been taken to reduce this problem. A federal task force, in 1974, suggested that restrictions be placed on the issuance of birth certificates to unauthorized persons.[12] Today, most locales restrict the issuance of birth certificates; however, offenders continue to develop new identities.
- *Records.* Careful record keeping is a practical measure to reduce bad checks. A system of recording the names of customers who have passed bad checks and a record of employees who accept many bad checks is advisable. Retailers often have systems listing customers who regularly cash checks. When a customer cashes the first check, appropriate information is entered into the system. Thereafter, customer convenience is facilitated. Referrals are made to this system when needed.

- *Check clearing service.* On-line check clearing services maintain a database of customers who pass bad checks. Retailers subscribe to such a service to make decisions on whether to accept checks from customers. These services also cover checks that bounce even though the service cleared the customer, provided the retailer followed guidelines established by the service.
- *Photo identification and fingerprint systems.* A photo ID system records a picture of the check passer, the check, and the identification presented. The customer simply stands in front of the camera at the checkout. These pictures have been used to prosecute persons passing bad checks. The photo identification system primarily is a deterrent. A retailer should analyze the cost versus benefits of such a system in light of losses due to bad checks. The system can be costly and ineffective. One retail store had a wall in the loss prevention office that was completely covered with photos of bad-check passers. The number of photos was in the hundreds, which made identification difficult. (If the FBI's ten most wanted list were increased to 100, identification, likewise, would be more difficult.) The bad-check problem in this store was out of control. Another strategy requires the customer's fingerprint. Shoppers who cash checks are asked to leave a fingerprint using invisible ink on a sticker attached to the check. If a check for a large amount bounces because it was stolen or forged, police can use the fingerprint to catch the offender by running it through the FBI's computer system.

Recovery from Bad Checks

A retailer's recovery from a bad check depends on the circumstances. Many times a customer with bad record keeping practices will quickly cover the bad check after being notified. If difficulties arise for the retailer, alternative action may be necessary with the assistance of the justice system. Procedures depend on the state. Usually, a retailer must send the check writer a registered letter requiring payment within 5 to 15 days. If the letter is not effective, the retailer can sign a warrant against the person who wrote the bad check.

In one jurisdiction, a "bad-check brigade" has been formed. A magistrate coordinates the warrants, which are distributed to constables (part-time law enforcers) who are paid $10 for each warrant served. Each week the brigade takes numerous offenders to jail. Offenders found guilty of issuing a bad check (in South Carolina) can be jailed for up to 30 days and fined up to $200.

Retailers should check with public police about local practices. Some jurisdictions require collection through civil procedures. Another strategy, especially for large retailers, is to contract collection work to specialized firms.

If a retailer receives a check returned from a bank stating that there is "no account" or "account closed," then fraud may have been perpetuated. The police should be notified. An altered or forged U.S. government check should be reported to the U.S. Secret Service.

Credit

Credit is basically a method used to increase sales volume. This strategy may fail, however, and a loss will be sustained on customer nonpayment.

Several kinds of credit are used by retailers. *Open account credit* allows a customer to receive items and pay at a later date. *Installment credit* permits customers to spread payments over a long period of time. *Revolving credit* allows a customer to purchase items up to a specified limit. This line of credit remains open as long as the limit is not exceeded. Monthly payments depend on the unpaid balance. Many large retailers issue their own credit cards to customers.

Because of the increasing popularity of Visa and Mastercard, few retailers are refraining from participating in this type of bank-issued credit. Moreover, by subscribing, retailers can avoid the costs of maintaining a credit department, investigating the financial background of potential credit customers, collection costs, and taking a loss due to nonpayment. Some retailers maintain that their own credit program, without the use of credit cards, is worth the expense. Other retailers use their own credit program and credit cards in addition to bank credit cards.

Three major groups are involved in credit card usage: *card issuers* (banks, oil companies, retail businesses, travel, and entertainment groups), *acceptors* (merchants), and *users.* All of these groups are susceptible to losses due to fraud. Worldwide, bank card fraud losses to Visa and Mastercard alone have increased from $110 million in 1980 to about $1.63 billion in 1995.[13] Lost or stolen cards can cause monetary loss to users. Acceptors who are careless may become financially responsible for fraud under certain circumstances and could even be placed at a competitive disadvantage if no longer authorized to accept the issuer's card.

The theft of credit cards from the postal system, for example, creates enormous losses. However, the fastest growing type of bank card fraud is illegal counterfeiting of Visa and Mastercards. New technology has aided offenders in producing, from scratch, exact replicas of existing cards with security features such as the magnetic stripe and hologram (e.g., the Visa dove on the card that looks three dimensional). The next generation of cards, "smart cards," will contain computer chips to store more information on the holder, plus a PIN will be required. Naturally, like today and throughout history, offenders will follow technological changes in an effort to defeat security.[14]

Techniques to counter a multitude of criminal methods against issuers, acceptors, and users of credit cards involve lengthy training. The following information emphasizes acceptor (retailer) preventive measures.

Acceptors (retailers) are wise to check credit cards for the following characteristics:

1. The card has expired or is not yet valid.
2. Alteration of the card is obvious.
3. Signatures on the card and charge slip are significantly different.

Of particular importance for the retailer is to ensure that credit cards are subject to electronic authorization (swiped through the magnetic reader). This helps to ensure that accounts are valid and purchases are within credit limits.

Mail and phone order businesses are particularly vulnerable to fraud because the customer, the credit card, and a signature are not present for the transaction. Offenders obtain card numbers from many sources (e.g., discarded credit card receipts), establish a mail drop, and then place fraudulent orders.

Counterfeiting

Counterfeiting is the unlawful duplication of something valuable to deceive. Counterfeit items can include money, coupons, credit cards, clothes, jewelry, and so forth. Here, the emphasis is counterfeit money. This federal offense is investigated by the U.S. Secret Service, a branch of the U.S. Treasury Department.

Persons who recognize that they have counterfeit money will not be reimbursed when they give it to the Secret Service. Because of this potential loss, many people knowingly pass the bogus money to others. The extended chain of custody from the counterfeiter to authorities causes great difficulty during investigations.

Counterfeiting is a growing problem because of the newer color copier machines, scanners, computers, and laser printers that are in widespread use. The U.S. government has countered the problem through a security thread embedded in the paper running vertically to the left of the Federal Reserve seal on all notes above $1. Microprinting also appears on the rim of the portrait.

The best method to reduce this type of loss is through the ability to recognize counterfeit money. In comparing the suspect money with genuine money, one should look for the red and blue fibers scattered throughout the bill. These fibers are curved, about a quarter inch, hair thin, and difficult to produce on bogus bills. Also, look for the security thread and microprinting. Another technique is to watch for $1 bills that have counterfeit higher denomination numbers glued over the lower denomination numbers. Also, compare suspect coins with genuine coins.

What do you think is the most serious vulnerability at the checkout counters? Support your answer and include countermeasures.

SHOPLIFTING

Shoplifting is a multibillion dollar problem, as noted at the beginning of this chapter. To deal with this serious problem, loss prevention practitioners should have an understanding of the kinds of shoplifters, motivational factors, shoplifting techniques, and countermeasures.

Kinds of Shoplifters:
Understanding Motivational Factors

Amateur

The amateur shoplifter, often referred to as a *snitch*, represents the majority of shoplifters. This person generally steals on impulse while often possessing the money to pay for the item. Individuals in this category represent numerous demographic variables (e.g., sex, age, social class, ethnicity, and race). The distinguishing difference between the amateur and the professional thief is that the former shoplifts for personal use, whereas the latter shoplifts to sell the goods for a profit.

Juvenile or Student

On the whole, juveniles usually take merchandise that they can use, such as clothing and recreational items. Frequently working in groups, their action is often motivated by peer pressure or a search for excitement.

Housewife

The housewife is another major kind of shoplifter. Various motivational factors may relate to unemployed husbands and other domestic problems that causes pressure to "stretch the budget." Rationalizations include unreasonably high retail prices, deceptive advertising, and a belief that retailers are making a huge profit. Many times the shoplifting housewife has the cash to pay for the stolen item.

Easy-Access Shoplifter

The easy-access shoplifter is neither a retail company employee nor a customer. Because of their work, they have easy access to retail merchandise and are familiar with basic retail operations and loss prevention programs. Delivery personnel, salespeople, repair personnel, and public inspectors make up this category. Even public police and fire personnel have been known to represent this group, especially during emergency situations. The motivation is obvious: to get something for nothing. The extent of this problem is difficult to ascertain, but it does contribute to the shoplifting problem.

Drunk or Vagrant

Fairly easy to detect, the drunk or vagrant shoplifter usually shoplifts liquor, food, and clothing for personal use or shoplifts other merchandise to sell for cash. These persons often are under the influence of alcohol and have a previous alcohol-related arrest record.

Addict

The addict shoplifter is extremely dangerous because of the illegal drug dependence problem and accompanying desperation. This person generally peddles stolen loot to a "fence," who pays less than one-third the value of the merchandise. The addict may also "grab and run."

Professional

The professional or "booster" accounts for a small percentage of those caught shoplifting. (This low figure could be the result of the professional's skill in avoiding apprehension.) The motive is profit or resale through the shoplifting of watches, rings, cameras, electronic gear, clothing, and other expensive items. The professional may utilize a *booster box* (a box that looks wrapped and tied, but really contains a secret entrance), hooks on inside clothing, or extra long pockets. A criminal record is typical, as are ties to the underworld organization (e.g., fences) that will supply bail money and attorney assistance.

Kleptomaniac

Kleptomania is a rare, persistent, neurotic impulse to steal. The kleptomaniac usually shoplifts without considering the value or personal use of the item, and seemingly wants to get caught. This type of shoplifter usually has a criminal record from previous apprehensions and may have been caught several times at the same retail store. According to one observer, "The criminal prosecution of a kleptomaniac may present the district attorney with a problem when it becomes necessary to rebut the defense of insanity. Moreover, it appears that kleptomaniacs as a group are the least likely to be deterred by criminal prosecution."[15] Another relates, "One man, whose wife had such a compulsion, made an arrangement with the stores frequented by his wife, whereby they would send him the bills for the things that his wife took."[16]

Shoplifting Techniques

Techniques of shoplifting are numerous. Professional shoplifters are skilled practitioners; some employ special devices to assist in their stealing. The amateur shoplifter, although crude in technique, represents the majority of shoplifters and causes huge losses to retail companies.

The following list presents only a few of the many shoplifting techniques:

1. Shoplifters may work alone or in a group.
2. A person may simply shoplift an item and conceal it in his or her clothing.
3. A person may "palm" a small item and conceal it in a glove.
4. Shoplifters often go into a fitting room with several garments and either conceal an item or wear it and leave the store.
5. An offender may ask to see more items than a clerk can control or send the clerk to the stockroom for other items; while the counter is unattended, items are stolen.
6. A self-service counter can provide an opportunity for a shoplifter to pull out and examine several items while returning only half of them.
7. Merchandise often is taken to a deserted location (e.g., restroom, elevator, stockroom, janitor's supply room, and so on) and then concealed.
8. A shoplifter may simply grab an item and quickly leave the store.
9. A shoplifter may drop an expensive piece of jewelry into a drink or food.
10. Shoplifters arrive at a store early or late to take advantage of any lax situation.
11. Offenders have been known to pick up an item and walk directly to a salesperson to try to get a refund without a receipt.
12. Disguised as a priest (or other professional), the shoplifter may have an advantage when stealing.
13. Some bold offenders have been known to impersonate salespeople while shoplifting and even to collect money from customers.
14. Price tags are often switched to attain merchandise at a lower price; sometimes the desired price will be written on the price tag.
15. Shoplifters are aided by large shopping bags, lunch boxes, knitting bags, suitcases, flight bags, camera cases, musical instrument cases, and newspapers.
16. Dummy packages, bags, or boxes ("booster box") are used, which appear to be sealed and tied but contain false bottoms and openings to conceal items.

17. Hollowed-out books are used by shoplifters.
18. Stolen merchandise is often concealed within legitimate purchases.
19. Expensive items are placed in inexpensive containers.
20. Shoplifters sometimes slide items off counters and into some type of container or clothing.
21. Sometimes shoplifters wear fake bandages or false plastic casts.
22. Professional shoplifters are known to carry store supplies (e.g., bag, box, stapler, price tickets, or colored tape) to assist in stealing.
23. A shoplifter may remove a staple and receipt from the bag of a recent purchase, open the bag, deposit stolen items, and then reseal the bag with the receipt.
24. Baby carriages and wheelchairs have been utilized in various ways to steal.
25. Shoplifters sometimes wear oversized clothing, clothing with hooks or special belts on the inside, large pockets, socks with pockets, or slit pockets that permit access to inner clothing.
26. Sometimes items are hidden in a store for subsequent pickup by an accomplice.
27. Various contrived diversions (e.g., appearing to be drunk, dropping and breaking an item, faking a heart attack, fainting, choking, pretending to have an epileptic seizure or labor pains, setting a fire or smoke bomb, breaking a glass, or having someone call in a bomb threat) have been used to give an accomplice a chance to shoplift.
28. Teenagers sometimes converge on a particular retail department, cause a disturbance, and then shoplift.
29. Adult shoplifters have been known to use children to aid them.
30. Sometimes "blind" accomplices with "guide" dogs are used to distract and confuse sales personnel eager to assist the disadvantaged.
31. "Crotchwalking" is a method whereby a woman wearing a dress conceals an item between her legs and then departs.

Prevention and Reduction of Shoplifting Through People

People are the first and primary asset for reducing shoplifting opportunities. The proper utilization of people is the test of success or failure in preventing shoplifting. Management, salespeople, store detectives, uniformed officers, and fitting-room personnel can all provide assistance. *Good training is very important.*

* *Management.* Management has the responsibility for planning, implementing, and monitoring antishoplifting programs. The quality of leadership and the ability to motivate people are of paramount importance.

The loss prevention manager and other retail executives must cooperate when formulating policies and procedures that do not hamper sales.

- *Salespeople.* An antishoplifting program increases a shoplifter's anxiety. One method to accomplish this is by having salespeople approach all customers and say, for instance, "May I help you?" This approach informs the potential shoplifter that he or she has been noticed by salespeople and possibly by loss prevention personnel. Obviously, the anxiety level will be raised. Sometimes salespeople annoy honest customers by hounding them with persistent offers of assistance. This can hinder sales. A moderate approach is appropriate. For those who have been store detectives, there are few activities as annoying as a salesperson who unknowingly interferes with a potential apprehension of a shoplifter. To avoid this problem, policies and procedures must be formulated and communicated to appropriate employees. One solution may be to have the store detective signal salespeople, for example, by carrying a certain colored bag. The colored bag would signify to salespeople that they should ignore the potential shoplifter.

- *Store detectives. A good store detective must have the ability to observe without being observed, remember precisely what happened during the offense, know criminal law and self-defense, effectively interview, testify in court, and recover stolen items.* Store detectives must blend in with the shopping crowd and look like shoppers. This can be done by dressing like the average shopper, carrying a package or two, and even a bag of popcorn. The detective can also wear a pair of special glasses with small mirrors on the sides to facilitate seeing behind. The antiquated term "floor walker" for *store detective* should be limited to historical discussions. This will help to professionalize the image of this important role in loss prevention.

- *Uniformed officers.* The differences between a uniformed officer and a store detective are obvious. Store detectives usually covertly watch and finally apprehend shoplifters. Officers, on the other hand, watch shoppers in an overt manner, and only the foolish shoplifter would steal in the presence of an officer. The physical presence of an officer, for example, at a doorway to a store, will remind shoppers of the presence of a loss prevention program, increase the anxiety of a potential shoplifter, and thus deter shoplifting. A well-planned antishoplifting program must not lose sight of the systems approach to loss prevention. As one writer reports:

> The store had four security guards or personnel. These people were also looked upon as "jokes." The security personnel were primarily concerned with catching shoplifting customers. Most of their time was spent behind two-way mirrors with binoculars observing shoppers. So in reality while the security personnel caught a customer concealing a pair of pants in her purse, an employee was

smuggling four pairs of Levi's out the front door. Security was concerned with shoppers on the floor while all employee thefts usually occurred in stockrooms.[17]

- *Fitting-room personnel.* Employees who supervise merchandise passing in and out of fitting rooms play a vital role in reducing the shoplifting problem. Many stores place a limit on the number of items that can be brought into a fitting room.

Training

Employees must realize the economic impact of shoplifting and other crimes. They must understand that, if crime is not prevented, then the retail store may go out of business and jobs will be lost. Thus, everyone should play a role in reducing the crime problem.

At frequent training sessions, employees should become familiar with various crimes such as shoplifting and associated techniques. A knowledge of basic criminal law may help to avert lawsuits. Training sessions can include discussions of company policies and procedures. Simulated shoplifting incidents can give employees an opportunity to make mistakes and learn. Shoplifting equipment (e.g., booster box, specially designed clothing with hooks) can be demonstrated. A store newsletter can be used as an additional educational tool.

Allocation of Personnel

Research results have produced a mixture of times and locations when there appeared to be a high incidence of shoplifting in retail stores. Holiday seasons show an increase in shoplifting. Many observers believe that noon to 2 P.M. and 6 P.M. to 8 P.M. are the high incident hours for shoplifting. However, these high incident hours can vary. Shoplifters are known to take advantage of shift changes. There seems to be a general consensus that the majority of shoplifting takes place on the main floor of retail stores. The crowds and numerous exits make the main floor a favorite target.

Each retail store is unique, so loss prevention managers should determine the times and locations when shoplifting is most prevalent. With these research results, a more efficient allocation of personnel is possible. Because the research results probably will be based on analyzing apprehensions, these statistics must be used cautiously. There is the possibility that another time and location may represent the true extent of shoplifting, but this information may not be attainable because of the absence of apprehensions.

Reward Program

A reward program can effectively motivate employees into assisting retail stores in countering shoplifting. Research results have shown that many customers are heavily absorbed in their shopping activities and do not notice many shoplifting incidents. Customers who do witness shoplifters stealing may not report the offense to retail employees because of fear of a countersuit and court appearance. Research results point out that the more populous the customer's hometown, the less likely he or she is to report shoplifting. This would suggest that there is less reporting in urban areas. The cost benefit is minimal for customer reporting of shoplifting.

Retail personnel, especially salespeople, must receive increased cost benefits for reporting shoplifters. Reward programs could include, for instance, a gift certificate worth 50 percent of the item shoplifted. (These programs can also be used to reduce employee theft.)

Managers must carefully plan a reward program to minimize adverse consequences such as excessive complaints, false charges, and conflicts with public police agencies. A multistore retail company can institute an experimental reward program at one store to study the advantages and disadvantages of various plans.

Community Involvement

Because most retail stores are small in size and have limited budgets, a pooling of personnel, money, and material would reap large dividends in thwarting shoplifting. A group of retailers could share an antishoplifting unit that contains store detectives, uniformed officers, and fitting-room personnel. This unit could circulate through the member stores while remaining alert to special needs. The retailers could have weekly meetings to foster greater cooperation.

Education programs are broad in scope. They include antishoplifting signs in stores and training sessions for retail employees. Community education programs include media campaigns and discussions at educational institutions and other appropriate locations.

Community education programs are especially important because research results have shown that students have underestimated the economic consequences (e.g., higher prices) of shoplifting. Many students are not aware of the seriousness of the offense.

Prevention and Reduction of Shoplifting Through Devices

Devices are the second major asset of an effective antishoplifting program. However, *devices are only as good as the people operating them.* A retail company can spend millions of dollars on antishoplifting devices, but if personnel are not knowledgeable about the maintenance, operation, limitations, and advantages of these devices, then their usefulness will be stymied.

Physical Design

Physical design includes architectural design and store layout (e.g., merchandise displays). One objective of physical design, in terms of the present discussion, is to create "defensible space."[18] This term is used to describe a series of physical design characteristics that prevent crime (see Chapter 8). The concept has been used in residential design; however, many associated topics can be applied to other structures such as retail stores. For instance, increased visibility of customers by retail personnel can be facilitated by designing an employee lounge that is raised above the sales floor and has a large glass window. Also, barriers can be constructed that direct customer traffic toward highly visible locations.

Traditionally, loss prevention devices have been installed after building construction. Because of increased expenses (e.g., tearing walls, drilling holes) due to installation, many devices are now planned within the original building design. Meetings between architects and loss prevention managers are beneficial in this regard.

Stores should be attractive so that customers will buy more items, and therefore, devices must not become too threatening or hostile. A balance between attractiveness and loss prevention is essential.

Store layout can provide additional loss prevention features. Cashier locations that are raised a few inches increase visibility. Counters containing merchandise should be set up to let employees at cash registers observe activities down the aisles. Adequate lighting is essential. Merchandise or other store features that are more than a few feet in height will be an aid to shoplifters. Eight-foot paneling would be more appropriate along the store's perimeter walls.

The proper utilization of turnstiles, corrals, and other barriers can limit the circulation of shoplifters and funnel customer traffic to select locations (e.g., toward cash registers). Usable exits can be limited, and restrooms locked so that customers need to ask for the restroom key.

Other methods to hinder stealing include locking display cabinets, displaying only one of a pair, using dummy displays (e.g., empty cosmetic boxes), arranging displays neatly and in a particular pattern to allow for quick recognition of a disruption in their order, having hangers pointing in alternate directions on racks to prevent "grab and run" tactics, and placing small items closer to cash registers.

Electronic Article Surveillance

The electronic article surveillance (EAS) system is an innovative and effective method of thwarting shoplifting and employee theft. This device watches merchandise instead of people. Generally, electronic tags are placed on merchandise and removed by a salesperson when appropriate. If a person leaves a designated area with the tagged merchandise, a sensor at an exit activates an alarm.

This device has been on the market since the late 1960s. Because these plastic tags tended to be large (about 3 or 4 inches) and difficult to attach to many goods, they were used on high-priced merchandise such as coats.

However, improved technology has permitted manufacturers to develop devices the size of price tags, at a lower cost. The newer device is small, with an adhesive back to allow it to stick to merchandise. Several new types include low-cost (pennies) disposable labels and higher-cost ($1 to $2) reusable tags.

Three major kinds of EAS are on the market, using similar technology today as when these systems were introduced in the 1960s. The primary difference among the systems is their frequency signal. The *radio frequency* type contains a tiny circuit. If the cashier does not remove or deactivate it and the customer walks between a radio transmitter and a sensor, then the circuit in the label or tag picks up the signal and an alarm is triggered. The cashier removes or deactivates this device from the label by covering it with a piece of metal. Its weaknesses are that shoplifters can cover the labels with aluminum foil and the tags cannot be used on metal objects. A similar system uses *high-frequency microwaves* but can be thwarted by covering the tag with one's body. A third kind, *electronmagnetic*, used mainly in libraries, employs a metal strip that interferes with a magnetic field at an exit.[19]

Each company contends that its system is best. None is without problems nor is any foolproof. False alarms or failure of the cashier to deactivate or remove the tag has led to retailers being sued for false arrest. Another problem results from employees who carry an EAS tag on their person and activate the system as a pretext to stop and search suspicious customers. High-quality training and caution and politeness when approaching customers will prevent litigation. Many state that the bigger problem of employee theft is not alleviated by EAS. Others view the tags and labels as too expensive to be justified as both price tags and EAS for low-cost merchandise. Many tag only high-shrinkage items. Despite these disadvantages plus initial costs and maintenance, this device can be cost effective and is popular. In fact, such systems are being used in certain industries to watch inventories. Prisoners and patients also are being monitored with such technology.

Innovations have further enhanced EAS technology. Integrated systems use programmable CCTV technology to target an alarm location or "walk a beat" (see Figure 15–2). Inktags attached to items leak an indelible dye when forcibly removed and, thus, ruin merchandise for the shoplifter (see Figure 15–3). Another type of tag sends out an audible alarm when tampering occurs. *Source tagging* is growing in popularity and involves the manufacturer placing a hidden EAS tag into the product during manufacturing, to be deactivated at the POS. This saves the retailer the labor of tagging and untagging merchandise.

Alarms

In addition to EAS, technological breakthroughs have produced a variety of alarms that can protect merchandise from theft. *Loop alarms* consist of a

Figure 15–2 CCTV, camera domes, and EAS (white portals at exit), work as an integrated system. Courtesy: Sensormatic, Inc.

cable that forms a close electrical circuit that begins and ends at a battery-operated alarm device. This cable usually is attached through appliance handles and openings. When the electrical circuit is disrupted by someone cutting or breaking it, the alarm sounds. *Cable alarms* also use a cable that runs from the merchandise to an alarm unit. This alarm differs in that a pad attached to the end of the cable is placed on the merchandise. Each item has its own cable pad setup, which is connected to an alarm unit. Cable alarms are useful when merchandise does not have openings or handles. Retailers also use heavy nonalarmed cables that are also woven through expensive items such as leather coats. This cable usually has a locking device.

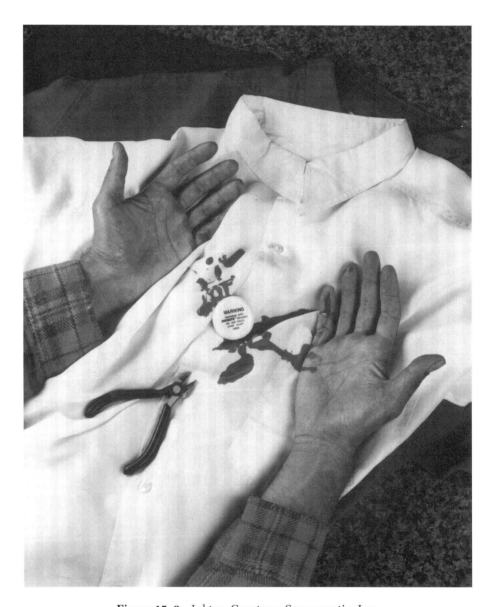

Figure 15–3 Inktag. Courtesy: Sensormatic, Inc.

Wafer alarms are sensing devices that react to negative pressure. This device, about the size of a large coin, is placed under the protected item; if a thief removes the item, an alarm sounds.

Oil paintings on canvas can be protected by a *seismic geophone* that detects the vibrations of touch. *Ribbon alarms* can be placed on or under the cushions of antique furniture. They react to the pressure of a person sitting.

Display cases are often locked and sometimes alarmed. Depending on the expense of the items on display, some display cases are equipped with sophisticated alarms that sound if a salesperson leaves the display area.

Plug alarms allow expensive appliances to be plugged into alarmed outlets. When the plug is removed by a thief, the alarm is activated. Hotels and motels use this device for television sets.

Closed-Circuit Television

Closed-circuit television has become a popular antishoplifting device. Cameras with remote control and zoom lenses can be strategically located within a store and moved automatically at preset patterns. Sometimes, systems contain both real and dummy cameras, although too many dummy cameras can cause these fake deterrents to become a farce. Comprehensive systems allow personnel actually to follow people through a store. Close communications between the monitoring station and personnel throughout the store are necessary. Since CCTV primarily is a deterrent, people should be made aware of it through signs. Chapter 7 covers CCTV and recording capabilities, which in shoplifting cases can be used as evidence.

Mirrors

The primary mirrors used to curb the shoplifting problem are see-through mirrors and wide-angle convex mirrors. These mirrors are relatively inexpensive and provide personnel with advantages that aid in the surveillance of shoplifters.

Observation booths usually are equipped with see-through mirrors; their location is above the sales floor at various places within a store. Personnel often use binoculars while watching customers (and employees) from these vantage points. A good communication system is necessary to summon aid because, when the observer leaves the booth, the shoplifter's actions are not being watched. If the shoplifter returns the item before being apprehended, the retail store may be faced with a lawsuit.

Wide-angle convex mirrors have been placed extensively throughout small and large retail stores to facilitate greater visibility and reduce blind spots around corners. Convex mirrors and regular mirrors can be located along walls, ceilings, at support columns, above merchandise displays, and at any point to create greater visibility and thus deter theft.

In one case, a juvenile was shoplifting record albums by sliding them into the bottom of a bag that had been stapled closed with a receipt attached. The incident occurred while the store was closing and over 20 retail personnel attentively watched the shoplifter in action from the other side of a 7-foot-high partition that had a convex mirror placed above it. The situation was interesting because the record department had been cleared of retail employees and the juvenile rushed around the department selecting albums while nervously watching for people he did not know were watching him via the mirror.

Additional Devices and Measures

Fake deterrents are debatable loss prevention methods. A dummy camera or a periodic, fake loudspeaker statement (e.g., "dispatch security to main floor") may prevent shoplifting, but the level of effectiveness is difficult to measure. Obviously, a retail store with 20 dummy cameras and a small loss prevention staff will suffer great losses when the fake deterrents are discovered and become a joke to shoplifters. Many stores combine fake and real methods.

The acquisition of store supplies can be an aid to shoplifters. Salespersons must carefully control and keep hidden the store's shopping bags, boxes, string, colored tape, and price tags. Retail personnel can reduce this problem through vigilance.

Shopping bags that are folded at the top and stapled closed, with the receipt attached, will hinder shoplifters. Colored tape is used on large items that cannot fit into bags. A receipt is placed under the tape to verify payment. Many stores change the color of the tape every day. Self-destructing price tags that tear when removed create difficulty when someone attempts to switch price tags. All unused price tags should remain in safe locations inaccessible to shoppers.

Confronting the Shoplifter

Detection and Apprehension

Most shoplifters exhibit the following activities and characteristics before, during, and after a theft: extreme sensitivity to those around them, surveillance of the sales floor, nervousness and anxiety, and walking repeatedly to certain areas. Other characteristics that invite suspicion are a group of juveniles or a person wearing excessive clothing on a warm day.

Two *prerequisites to an apprehension* are *make sure to have seen the shoplifter conceal the store's merchandise,* and *never lose sight of the shoplifter.* The observer must be positive that he or she saw the item removed from a rack, because the customer could have brought the item into the store. If a customer wears a store item out of the store or alters or switches a price tag, one must make sure an eyewitness account is available. Some shoplifters panic on being observed and "ditch" the concealed merchandise or give it to an accomplice. Some people conceal merchandise, return it to the counter unnoticed, and hope to be apprehended in order to sue to collect damages. Retail personnel who witness a shoplifting incident must be positive that they can identify both the store's item and testify that it was not purchased by the subject who intended to steal it. To help prove intent, the offender should be permitted to pass the last cash register and exit the store.

Juveniles are handled differently from adults. Police and parents usually are called. A loss prevention practitioner should be familiar with local procedures regarding juveniles.

Many security personnel who work alone prefer to work on the sales floor instead of from an observation booth. A disruption of eye contact occurs if a store detective witnesses a shoplifting incident and must travel from the booth to the floor. A team approach with a communications system is vital.

If a retail employee is not certain about a shoplifting incident, no apprehension should take place. In this situation, some practitioners recommend the "ghosting technique," which involves a salesperson carrying a duplicate of the shoplifted item as he or she walks close to the suspect. No words are spoken, but the message is obvious, if a theft has taken place. This technique has advantages for prevention, but it may permanently frighten customers from the store.

When retail personnel positively witness a shoplifting incident, loss prevention personnel must be notified for apprehension purposes. The detector (e.g., salesperson) should assist as an eyewitness. Additional personnel can stand by in case the subject becomes violent. Only a reasonable degree of force can be used to control the subject. *It is best to avoid a physical confrontation because the subject may be armed and the liability potential is significant. If the suspect flees, obtain a description and call police.* Immediately on approaching the subject, loss prevention personnel identify themselves by displaying identification or a badge. Personnel must never threaten the subject. *To reduce the problems associated with error, it is wise not to accuse the subject of stealing; the subject can be asked, "Would you mind answering a few questions about an item?" The next step is to quickly ask the subject to accompany personnel to the loss prevention office.* This perhaps is the most crucial point of the confrontation. At all times, careful observation of the subject is important because the merchandise may be "ditched" or escape may be attempted. If the subject escapes, again, avoid a physical confrontation and call police.

Detention and Arrest

After entering the loss prevention office, the subject usually is asked to produce some type of identification as well as the concealed merchandise. If the subject does not comply with these requests, the loss prevention officer should call the public police.

After receiving the merchandise, a receipt should be requested to reduce the possibility of error. Usually, a shoplifter will state some type of excuse in an attempt to cover up not having a receipt.

Many jurisdictions have adopted the retailer's privilege of detaining shoplifters. *The difference between an arrest and detention is that the former requires the arrester to turn the suspect over to the public police, whereas the latter does not. Conditions for detention involve probable cause (reasonable grounds to justify legal action, such as an eyewitness account) and a reasonable time span, for detention, to accomplish questioning and documentation.* Many shoplifting statutes protect the retailer's right to detain, provided legal action was conducted in a reasonable manner. If an arrest is made, the crime charged by the retailer should be shoplifting, not larceny, to retain the right to detain under the shoplifting statute. For both detention and arrest, probable cause is necessary, and the suspect's freedom is restricted. The detention of a person can evolve into an arrest. Many attorneys argue that any type of restricted movement placed on the suspect is equal to an arrest. The ultimate decision may rest with a jury in a lawsuit.

Loss prevention personnel—or any store personnel—should refrain from touching the subject. If force is used to exercise legal action, it must be reasonable. When a shoplifter is controlled after a struggle, it would be unreasonable to strike the offender. Deadly force is restricted to life-threatening situations. *Unreasonable force can lead to prosecution difficulties, as well as criminal and civil action.*

Subsequent to proper detention or arrest, shoplifting statutes generally do not stipulate how merchandise is to be located and recovered from the shoplifter. Some states permit a search, whereas others forbid it. A shoplifter can be requested to empty his or her pockets and belongings to produce the stolen items. The public police should be called for obstinate shoplifters, and the police should conduct the search.

If the subject complies voluntarily, an arrest has not been made unless specified. *The loss prevention officer should ask the offender to sign a civil release form, which is vital before releasing the subject. It provides some protection against civil liability and also becomes a record of the incident.* The form contains, in addition to basic information (e.g., name, date), a voluntary confession of the store's items stolen, the value, and a statement that retail personnel did not use force or coercion and that the cooperation is voluntary. Although a release may state that the subject agrees not to sue, the retail personnel still can be sued. The release has psychological value in that the subject may believe that a suit is impossible and not seek legal advice, although a claim possibly can be made that the subject signed while under duress. If the shoplifter is obstinate or violent, an arrest is appropriate; handcuffing may be necessary. With this situation, the public police must be summoned; they usually will act in an advisory capacity and transport the prisoner to jail. A decision to call the police and prosecute makes obtaining a signature on the form less important. A criminal conviction perhaps is the best protection against civil liability. If the retailer intends to release the shoplifter without calling public police, then the civil release form is vital for some protection against litigation.

The courts have yet to require private police to state to a suspect the *Miranda* rights (civil liberties) prior to questioning, as public police are required to do. Courts have held that any involuntary confession, gained by public or private police, is inadmissible in court. To strengthen their case, many loss prevention practitioners recite the *Miranda* rights and request that subjects sign a waiver-of-rights form if willing to confess.

When apprehended shoplifters are uncooperative and an arrest is appropriate, the stolen merchandise and the eyewitness to the shoplifting incident will be the primary evidence that will aid in the prosecution. The interviewer must not coerce the shoplifter into a confession by prolonged questioning or tricky tactics. This forceful approach can easily destroy a case.

Throughout the confrontation, at least two retail employees should be present. One employee must be of the same sex as the shoplifter. Problems inevitably develop if no witnesses are present or if two male employees forcibly retrieve an item from within the clothing of a woman. A witness can prevent charges related to brutality, coercion, a bribe, and sexual assault. Insurance companies write coverage protecting retailers against liability for false arrest, malicious prosecution, willful detention or imprisonment, libel, slander, and defamation of character.

Prosecution

The deterrent effect of prosecution is debatable. However, many retailers favor the prosecution of all shoplifters, believing that *shoplifters will avoid a "tough" store that has a reputation for prosecutions.*

Retailers should institute policies that are cost effective. Prevention appears to be less costly than a strict apprehension program.

When a shoplifter is arrested and about to be prosecuted, the witness or loss prevention practitioner probably will be asked to sign a complaint or warrant, the legal document containing the facts making up the essential elements of the crime. The loss prevention practitioner should read it before signing and maintain and safeguard all relevant records and forms. Public police, prosecutors, judges, and juries will be interested in facts. In most cases, especially minor cases, the defendant pleads guilty in a lower court, pays a fine, and a trial is avoided. For serious cases, a preliminary hearing may be necessary to give the judge an opportunity to review evidence and to decide on the necessity for a trial. Most defendants waive their rights to a hearing and a trial in exchange for a plea-bargaining opportunity. Some defendants choose to go to trial and retain an attorney. Security personnel facing a criminal trial must have an excellent case, or else an acquittal is likely to lead to a lawsuit.

The testimony of the eyewitness as to the shoplifting incident often is the main evidence of a shoplifting case. CCTV systems provide visual evidence to strengthen cases.

The responsibility for preserving physical evidence for court appearance is part of the loss prevention practitioner's job. Accurate records are necessary. The evidence should be properly labeled and secured in a box or plastic bag. Two problems exist related to the preservation of physical evidence. First, millions of dollars of confiscated merchandise are not returned to the sales floor at hundreds of retail stores. Court congestion and delays can extend to months and years until the merchandise is out of date. Second, perishable items can deteriorate. A package of eight-month-old chicken breasts would present obvious resale problems when released after no longer needed as court evidence.

A solution to these problems involves photographing the stolen and recovered merchandise. Local requirements will vary concerning this procedure. A witness to the photographs can assist in strengthening the case. Color photos that contain a ruler marked with measurements will also aid in the effectiveness of this evidence.

If the prosecution of shoplifters becomes expensive and time consuming, if repeat offenders are not deterred, if the justice system becomes a "revolving door" (i.e., in for prosecution, out to commit another crime), and if cases are not successful, then antishoplifting strategies must be changed.

Civil Recovery

Almost every state has a civil recovery law that holds shoplifters liable for paying damages to businesses. Some states even extend these laws to employee theft. Civil recovery laws vary and may allow retailers, for example, to request three times the actual damages. These civil demand statutes aim to recover attorney's fees, court costs, and even the cost of security. Essentially, the expense of theft is passed on to thieves.

To recover damages a retailer sends a shoplifter a demand letter and a copy of the state's civil recovery law. Guidance can be obtained from a state retail association or an attorney. If there is no response, a second letter is sent stating that nonpayment may result in civil court action. With no response after a second letter, a retailer will have to decide whether to pursue the case in small claims court and whether a favorable judgment for damages can be collected.

Loss prevention personnel at some businesses may attempt civil recovery while the accused shoplifter is still in custody because the chance for recovery diminishes once the suspect leaves the store. The problem with this approach is that the shoplifting case may be based on faulty evidence. And, in some states, a guilty verdict may be necessary before civil action is sought. Other states permit simultaneous criminal and civil actions. In addition to the possibility of having a weak case against a suspected shoplifter, civil demand following an apprehension may result in legal action against the retailer for false imprisonment, extortion, and intentional or negligent infliction of emotion distress. The law of the respective state should be carefully studied as a foundation for store policies.[20]

A retailer may want to establish an in-house recovery program or contract with a service firm (this is the trend) that usually charges 30 percent of any money collected. Outside firms save the retailer the time and expense of operating a civil recovery program.

> If you were a retailer, what steps would you take to deal with the
> shoplifting problem?

ROBBERY AND BURGLARY

Robbery is the taking of something from an individual by force or threat of
force. *Burglary* is unlawful entry into a structure to commit a felony or theft.
    Loss prevention specialists repeatedly call for retailers to prevent *bur-
glary* by (1) *hardening the target*, (2) *creating a time delay*, and (3) *reducing
the loot*. Hardening the target pertains to security devices such as locks and
alarms. The reasoning behind creation of a time delay is to increase the time
necessary to commit the crime and, thereby, frustrate the offender. The
offender may abort the offense or the delay may provide additional time for
police apprehension. When the loot is reduced, losses are minimized. Some
people may mistakenly favor all three of these measures for *robbery*. In
Table 15–1, a robbery/burglary matrix illustrates some problems when all
three strategies are incorrectly applied to robbery.

Robbery Countermeasures

According to the FBI, in 1995, there were 580,545 robberies, a decrease of
6.2 percent over 1994 and representing the lowest total since 1989. The total
loss for 1995 is estimated at $507 million. The major targets of robbery are
distributed as follows: street and highway, 54 percent; commercial and
financial, 21 percent; and residential, 11 percent.[21]

Table 15–1   Robbery/Burglary Matrix

	Robbery	*Burglary*
Harden the target	Yes[a]	Yes
Create time delay	No[b]	Yes
Reduce loot	Yes	Yes

[a] For instance, a retail business hardened for robbery may
include an alarm and hidden cameras; however, if the robber
becomes trapped due to a metal gate that has blocked the only
exit (for example), then violence and a hostage situation may
develop.

[b] Once a robbery is in progress, for safety's sake a time delay can
be dangerous. The exception would be if there were no
threatening situation (unlikely in a robbery); then a time delay
might aid in immediate apprehension. Police agencies favor
robber–police confrontations outside of the crime scene, away
from innocent bystanders.

Employee Socialization of Procedures

- *Opening.* The daily opening of a store is often referred to as the "opening routine." This can be a dangerous time because a "routine" can aid a robber who carefully studies a target. Therefore, a varied opening procedure reduces the chances for robbery. A typical procedure is for one employee to go inside the store while another waits outside; the person returns within 5 minutes and signals that the "coast is clear." If the employee does not signal correctly or fails to appear, the police are called. The signal should be changed periodically to limit routine. Retailers in urban areas frequently open stores in the presence of security people or with a group of three to five employees. Many have permits for handguns.
- *Closing.* Closing procedures should include positioning a trusted store employee either inside or outside of the store with easy access to a telephone. Various signaling procedures also are advisable.
- *Cash handling and transportation.* The POS should be located at the front of the store to enhance visibility by those passing by. A self-locking gate or Dutch-door prevents access to the register by nonemployees. The cash drawer should require a key or code for access. Reducing the "loot" available will reduce the loss. Cashiers should possess only the amount of money needed for transactions; accumulating cash is not advisable. When cash and other valuables (e.g., checks and credit receipts) accumulate, a pickup system is necessary. Usually retail managers walk to each cash register for collections while performing associated accountability procedures. Then, the money is taken to the store money room. Two retail employees often participate in this operation. After the money is accounted for in the money room, a retail employee (or two) takes the money to a bank or an armored car pickup takes place. Procedures vary. Persons handling and transporting cash must be known by employees. If an employee transports money to a bank, use of a money bag is not advisable. It is better to use an innocuous paper bag. Local police sometimes are available as escorts to banks.

Whatever procedures are employed to protect people and money, there is always the possibility that a former employee has provided such information to offenders. Therefore, *periodically change procedures and signals.*

Security Manager Looks Bad

A retail executive from headquarters came to a chain store, displayed a company badge on his impressive suit, and systematically collected, with the usual money box, over $2000 from eight cash registers before leaving the store after the unauthorized collection. The purpose was to test security.

In the event of robbery, employees should have been trained to act in the following ways:

1. Concentrate on *safety*; don't try to be a hero; accommodate the robber's requests as well as possible.
2. If safety permits, activate alarm and camera; give the robber bait money.
3. Concentrate on details: description of the robber(s), license tag, type of vehicle, if any, and direction of travel.
4. After the robber leaves, telephone the police immediately.

Devices and Services

- *Alarms.* Robbery alarms are activated by the retail employee. A button or foot device signals a silent alarm to authorities. Another type of alarm is activated when money is removed from a money clip within the cash register drawer. The employee must try to prevent the robber from noticing the silent alarm activation by hand or foot movement.
- *CCTV.* A recording of a robbery is helpful in identifying and prosecuting robbers.
- *Safes.* A *drop safe* permits a deposit into the safe without opening it; only management can open the safe. Certain sections of a *time delay safe* cannot be entered until preset times. *Dual-key locks* on safes require a key from two people, such as a retail employee and an armored car officer. Care must be exercised when designing safe access because a robber may become impatient and resort to violence; warning signs to deter robbers provide some protection.
- *Bait money.* Bait money, also known as *marked money,* has had the banks of issue, denominations, series years, and serial letters and numbers recorded by the retailer. This record should be kept in a safe place. Prosecution of the robber is strengthened if he or she is found with this money. Retail employees should carefully include the bait money with the loot.
- *Security officers.* Armed, rather than unarmed, officers should be used to prevent robbery. Another method is to hire off-duty police officers.
- *Armored car service.* An armored car service can increase safety for retail employees while providing security for the transportation of money.

Burglary Countermeasures

According to the FBI, in 1995, there were 2,594,995 burglaries, a 4.3 percent decrease over 1994 and representing the lowest total in the past two decades. The total loss for 1995 is estimated at $3.3 billion. Two-thirds of burglaries were residential; the remainder were at nonresidential locations.[22]

Employee socialization and physical defense are two strategies that can be used to reduce burglaries. Earlier chapters contain expanded information on these topics.

Employee Socialization

Employee socialization can involve the following:

1. Surveying possible burglar entry points;
2. Leaving lights on (inside and outside);
3. Overturning cash register money trays on top of opened cash register drawers, at closing;
4. Rechecking doors and windows at closing;
5. Rechecking alarms;
6. Notifying public police immediately after mistakenly activating an alarm;
7. Cooperating with public police as thoroughly as possible;
8. Preserving the crime scene to protect any evidence upon discovering a burglary.

Physical Defense

The burglar's most frequent method of intrusion is by forcing open a door or window. Thus, good construction is vital. This is associated with hardening the target. Additional target-hardening methods are alarms, locks, fences, lighting, and safes.

If you were a retailer, which problem do you think would be more serious, robbery or burglary? Why?

Shopping Mall Strategies

The size of a retail operation has a direct bearing on the extent of its loss prevention program. A small, one-owner retail store obviously will require a different program from that of a shopping mall. A mall's loss prevention program would include not only countermeasures for crime, fire, and accident but also methods for numerous merchant needs, crowd control, parking lot problems (e.g., traffic, dead batteries, keys locked in autos), and lost people and merchandise. The size and complexity of malls compound loss problems.

A shopping mall's loss prevention program should be centralized and headed by an executive who responds to overall needs. Monthly meetings with merchants will facilitate cooperation and the sharing of problems, ideas, and resources. These meetings can provide an opportunity for a short training program. Special sales and events require further preparation. For malls experiencing many crime incidents, the establishment of a police sub-station is helpful.

CASE PROBLEMS

15A. A group of eight merchants who own retail stores at a small shopping center have hired you as a loss prevention consultant. These people are interested in reduced losses and increased profits. Their loss problems are employee theft, losses at the checkout counters, shoplifting, robbery, and burglary. As a loss prevention consultant, what is your plan? Don't forget, you must earn your fee, satisfy the merchants to develop a good reputation, and produce effective loss prevention measures that will reduce losses and increase profits.

15B. As a regional loss prevention manager for a retail chain, you are growing increasingly suspicious of one of the stores in your region. The store manager and employees constantly state that the high shrinkage of 4 percent at the store is due to shoplifters. The manager argues that very little shrinkage results from damaged merchandise or employee theft. EAS and CCTV systems are functioning at the store, but no security personnel are employed; a variety of nonsecurity employees maintain and operate these systems. What questions would you ask the store manager on an upcoming visit? What action would you take?

NOTES

1. For a discussion of how shrinkage is formulated and its importance for loss prevention practitioners, see Michael Levy and Barton A. Weitz, *Retail Management* (Homewood, IL: Irwin Pub., 1992), p. 591. And Philip Purpura, *Retail Security and Shrinkage Protection* (Boston: Butterworth–Heinemann, 1993), pp. 103–109.
2. "Retail Shrink Up; Losses Top $27 Billion," *Security* (January 1997): 20.
3. U.S. Department of Justice, *Security and the Small Business Retailer* (Washington, DC: U.S. Government Printing Office, 1978), p. 71.
4. Joseph F. Hair, Jr., et al., "Employee Theft: Views from Two Sides," Retailing Abstracts, *Journal of Retailing* 53, no. 5 (Summer 1977): 94.
5. U.S. Department of Justice, *Security and the Small Business Retailer*, p. 69.
6. *An Ounce of Prevention, 1988–89 Edition*, (Arthur Young & Co., 277 Park Ave., New York, NY 10172), p. 8.
7. Philip Purpura, *Modern Security and Loss Prevention Management* (Boston: Butterworth–Heinemann, 1989), p. 240.
8. Michael A. Freauf, "Refund Fraud: Australian Police Unit Cracks Down," *Law and Order* (February 1996): 92–95.

9. Leonard Kolodny, Small Business Administration, *Outwitting Bad Check Passers* (Washington, DC: U.S. Government Printing Office, June 1976), p. 3.
10. Michelle Vachon, "Check Fraud Booming, Thanks to Technology," Scripps Howard News Service (March 30, 1997).
11. "Criminal Use of Fraudulent Driver's Licenses," *The New York Times* (April 1, 1979).
12. Jan L. Horn, "Indiana's Document Security Lamination System," *FBI Law Enforcement Bulletin* 48, no. 10 (October 1979): 22.
13. Keith Slotter, "Plastic Payments, Trends in Credit Card Fraud," *FBI Law Enforcement Bulletin* (June 1997): 2.
14. Ibid., pp. 1–7.
15. A. James Fisher, *Security for Business and Industry* (Englewood Cliffs, NJ: Prentice-Hall, 1979), p. 175.
16. Loren E. Edwards, *Shoplifting and Shrinkage Protection* (Springfield, IL: Charles C Thomas Publishing Co., 1958), p. 52.
17. David L. Altheide et al., "The Social Meanings of Employee Theft," *Crime at the Top* (New York: J. B. Lippincott Co., 1978), p. 115.
18. See U.S. Department of Justice, Oscar Newman, *Design Guidelines for Creating Defensible Space* (Washington, DC: U.S. Government Printing Office, 1976).
19. Robert DiLonardo, "Electronic Article Surveillance: What's Up?" *Security Technology and Design* (October 1996): 50–57.
20. Michael Gips, "Shoplifter Shakedown?" *Security* (January 1997): 10.
21. U.S. Department of Justice, *Crime in the United States, 1995 Uniform Crime Reports* (Washington, DC: U.S. Government Printing Office, 1996), pp. 26–27.
22. Ibid., pp. 38–39.

16

Loss Prevention at Select Facilities

OBJECTIVES

After studying this chapter the reader will be able to discuss loss problems and countermeasures for

1. Computer facilities;
2. Nuclear facilities;
3. Businesses under a Department of Defense contract.

Even though universal characteristics can be found among the variety of loss prevention programs in existence, the unique requirements of businesses, institutions, and other concerns call for specially designed strategies. Of facilities that experience specific loss problems, computer, nuclear, and Department of Defense facilities have very special needs.

COMPUTER FACILITIES

As we know, computers are in widespread use and computers have become the accounting book of the business world. Coupled with increasing usage and dependence, losses are inevitable. Three characteristics of computers should be understood:

1. Computers are operated by people; a computer does not operate independently but relies on human action.
2. Computers do exactly what they are told and therefore are subject to various human behaviors and motivations.
3. Basically, a computer is composed of hardware and software; hardware consists of electronic components and electromechanical devices designed to follow a programmed sequence of instructions, and software essentially is a program, created by computer programmers, that instructs the computer.

Operation of a computer can be divided into five main functions:

1. *Input.* Information is fed into the computer.
2. *Programming.* Precise operating instructions are fed into the computer by the programmer.
3. *Processing.* The computer processing unit, the memory bank, processes information.
4. *Output.* The computer provides data, the results of processing.
5. *Communication.* Output data is transmitted between computers or between computers and remote terminals by such methods as telephone or teleprinter.

Electronic data processing (EDP) has become known as *information technology* (IT) to emphasize the importance of information as compared with the computer itself and to recognize the synergy between computers and communications. The IT acronym is INFOTEC. The acronym INFOSEC, for information security, connotes the protection of information prepared for, transmitted by, processed by, stored in, or output from information technological apparatus.[1]

Three primary threats to computer operations are error, crime, and disasters. The news media has convinced society that crime is the greatest threat to computers. However, crime is not the most serious threat. According to the U.S. Department of Justice, organizations that use computers generally lose far more from accidental loss caused by errors and omissions than that from intentionally caused losses.[2] A percentage breakdown of losses is as follows: errors, accidents, and omissions, 50 to 60 percent; dishonest employees, 10 percent; disgruntled employees, 10 percent; fire, 15 percent; and hackers, 3 percent.[3] Even viruses (computer programs containing devastating instructions) represent an extremely small percentage of *total* computer losses.[4] More recent research supports these trends.[5]

Losses from Errors

Personnel errors involving computer operations are varied. One common error is to feed incorrect data into a computer. Other errors result when an overenthusiastic employee devises a faster way to obtain specific data from a computer that differs from standard procedures; during the shortcut, precise computer programs are altered, and inaccurate data is produced during subsequent computer operations. If vital business decisions are based on inaccurate data, the damage can be enormous. Other examples are seen when inexperienced employees accidentally delete files, update the wrong records, or unknowingly supply outsiders with sensitive information.

Methods to hinder errors and other losses include recruiting and employing appropriately qualified individuals, good training, establishing

and communicating procedural rules that are enforced, requiring accountability of those active with computer operations, and designing computer
programs that cross-check and notify the operator and management of errors
and irregularities.

Losses from Criminal Acts

The United Nations Commission on Crime and Criminal Justice surveyed
3000 computer sites in Canada, Europe, and the United States and found
that 72 percent of the respondents reported a security incident during the
preceeding 12 months, with 43 percent reporting the incident was criminal
in nature. The researchers found that the greatest security threat came from
employees or others with access to the computers. External breaches from
hackers also were noted, with this problem expected to increase. The fastest
growing computer-related crime was theft of information.[6]

A survey of 1200 readers (10% response) by *InfoSecurity News*
revealed a variety of breaches, as shown in Table 16–1. The top INFOSEC
defenses were virus protection (90%), computer access control (80%), and
network security (77%).

A national study of corporate security directors and computer security
found the following:

* 98.5 percent of the respondents had been victims of computer-related
  crime.
* The type of crime most frequently increasing was theft of information.
* Most computer crimes were committed by full-time employees, followed by part-time or "outsource" employees.

Table 16–1   Breaches experienced

*In the past 12 months, which of the following
security breaches have you experienced?*

Virus infection	68%
Abuse of access privileges by employee	40
Attempted unauthorized system access by outsider	27
Theft or destruction of computing resources	24
Destruction of data	17
Hacking of phone/PBX/voice-mail	14
Leakage of proprietary information	12
Successful unauthorized system access by outsider	8

Note: Only discovered intrusions are reported.
Source: Davis S. Bernstein, "Industry Survey," *InfoSecurity News* (May
    1997): 20–27.

- Corporate security directors feel that law enforcement agencies do not recognize the magnitude of the problem and have not devoted enough attention to it.
- Data encryption shows a relationship to reduced theft of information in corporations; however, these tools need to be changed periodically because hackers are challenged to crack these codes.
- Although firewalls do provide security, hackers look at them as a puzzle, rather than an obstacle.
- Operations security, such as monitoring users and creating audit trails, also led to decreased theft.
- Computer crime is a multi-billion dollar problem.[7]

Computer crimes take many different forms. The following discussion features the way crimes occur in each of the previously mentioned five main functions of computer operations. False information can be fed into a computer (input) or key information can be omitted or removed. For example, the offender inserts fraudulent data creating phony suppliers and invoices. Checks are produced (output) for payment, which the offender converts to cash. In another example, the perpetrator manipulates the system (input) to provide additional pay (output) in his or her salary. Or, payroll checks are generated for nonexistent employees and cashed by the offender. Other examples could include causing the system to generate cash-value documents such as stocks and savings certificates, which can be converted to cash; submitting fraudulent expenses not incurred; or stealing cash receipts and removing related input documents. In reference to program abuses, a programmer, for instance, can alter a program to add a few pennies to the cost of purchased items, and then through the input of fictitious suppliers, generate checks for personal use. Another ploy is to take money from one set of accounts and transfer it to others, generate checks, and cash them. Programs and program files are subject to theft, destruction, and sale to competitors. The central processing unit is susceptible to wiretapping, whereby proprietary information (e.g., product designs, sensitive processes, marketing plans) is stolen and held for ransom, blackmail, or sold to an outsider. Output (e.g., checks, mailing lists) also is subject to theft, destruction, and sale to competitors. During communications, the final of the five main functions of the operation of a computer, data can be electronically intercepted (i.e., by wiretap) and then altered or stolen. Large amounts of money are transferred between banks via computers; these transfers of money are susceptible to theft through a sophisticated wiretap. Many computer crimes occur by utilizing a combination of operational functions (e.g., altering both input data and the program). Several of the fraudulent techniques just mentioned also can take place in manual (bookkeeping) systems.

Fraud and embezzlement are common and costly computer-assisted crimes. Theft of information is a growing problem as companies resort to illegal means to overcome competitors. Property theft via computers costs millions of dollars per year as merchandise is transferred illegally into other accounts without the offender ever touching the items. Numerous computer facilities have been victims of theft of computer time. A typical case is an operator who uses his or her employer's computer to provide an outside service for a profit. The computer and its components also are subject to theft. Today's laptop computers are especially vulnerable. A thief in England happened to steal a laptop from a military officer's automobile; the computer's memory contained detailed plans for England's participation in the Gulf War. Two other threats, vandalism and sabotage, can cause extensive losses. Disgruntled employees, as well as individuals with political motivations, have created chaos at computer facilities. Physical damage to a computer facility and erasure of data are costly. In one case, a business went bankrupt after an employee programmed the computer to erase all accounts receivable data several months after leaving the job. Computer personnel have clogged systems with worthless information and overloaded computers with so many time-consuming requests that others were unable to use it. Arson and bomb threats are other menaces. Both disabled power sources and air-conditioning/heating units have rendered computer operations inoperable. Computers have been shot at, blown up, and held hostage. Considerable losses are possible from business interruption and replacement of equipment and data.

Hackers

Hackers strive for access to computer systems by using a computer and modem connected to communication lines. Once they figure secret commands and gain access, an assortment of crimes may follow. They can steal, alter, or destroy data; eavesdrop; add calls to someone's bill; steal facsimile documents being transmitted; and so forth.

Telephone companies are particularly vulnerable to hackers because switches that route calls are mostly electronic, meaning that they are essentially big computers. The increased computerization of the telephone network is creating serious threats because a hacker can disable telephone service. Hackers have been known to tie up the telephones of people they did not like or add several custom-calling features to create large bills for their enemies. Adding long distance calls to someone's bill is a growing threat. Businesses and individuals know they have a serious problem when their telephone bill arrives in a box rather than an envelope.

Viruses

A *virus* is a destructive computer program that attaches itself to other programs to alter them or destroy data. It can also reproduce itself. A virus is attached to normal software, which becomes its "Trojan horse." The virus spreads when people exchange software via electronic means or by trading disks. Because the virus remains dormant, people are unaware of its existence until, at a predetermined time, the virus activates itself.

Research has shown a strong relationship between virus introduction and theft of information or assets.[8] *Like an offender setting a fire to destroy evidence, a computer criminal may introduce a virus into a computer to destroy any evidence of his or her presence and to make it difficult to detect and investigate the crime.* Investigators should look for a virus when a computer crime occurs and, conversely, look for criminal activity when a virus is found.

Viruses also may be introduced following layoffs and firings, which necessitates denying these people access to company computers once the bad news surfaces. Major motivating factors behind viruses are revenge, impeding business, harassing employees, and playing with the system.

Defenses against viruses include *policies and procedures* that, for example, prohibit employees from using their own programs on the company system. A second defense is to *inspect incoming software* by using a free-standing personal computer.[9] A third defense is *scanner software* that searches for viruses. No defense is guaranteed. For instance, certain viruses can fool scanners by hiding themselves by changing their appearance in each infected file. Specially designed scanners counter this threat; however, virus writers are always busy attempting to circumvent defenses.[10]

Strategies to Combat Computer Crime

Years ago, as computer systems were developing, data were obtained at the computer site. Today, however, technology has produced management information systems that transmit data over telephone lines and via microwave and satellite to remote consoles and teletypes located around the world. With such systems, the user is capable of having access to the computer from distant points. For instance, an executive may communicate with a company computer while at home. Remote terminals, telecommunications equipment, and communications lines are subject to unauthorized access to steal sensitive data or to create fraudulent transactions. Consequently, remote access creates difficult loss prevention problems. Furthermore, many access control methods are not easy to apply at remote locations. Experts recommend not using multiaccess systems for the storage of sensitive data.

Because our topic here focuses on communications security, two subtopics are *technical security* and *emanations security.* The former is concerned with defenses against the unauthorized interception of data communication through "bugs" and wiretaps. The latter defends against the interception of electromagnetic emanations (which may result in the capture of data) from computer equipment. (See Chapter 18 for more on these topics.)

These security strategies to combat computer crime follow: access controls, encryption, input/output controls, and auditing.

Access Controls

The control of traffic into, out of, and within a computer facility is a prime method to combat losses. Naturally, only authorized personnel should have access. The access control principles explained earlier are applicable to computer facilities. Automatic access control systems are popular in combination with limited entrances, the double-door entry concept, visual verification, badge identification systems, and access control according to time, place, and specific personnel. Additionally, the installation of magnetometers at entrances will detect metal objects (e.g., guns, or magnets that can destroy data files).

Access controls are required not only for the computer facility but also for the computer itself. This includes protection against unauthorized remote access. Older techniques involve machine-readable magnetically or electrically coded cards or badges by which personnel can identify themselves to the computer. However, these can be transferred among individuals or stolen. Newer technology, such as biometric access control systems (see Chapter 7), enable identification by fingerprints, voice, and so forth.

Access to sensitive data must be safeguarded on the premises and from remote locations, even by legitimate computer users. *Passwords* or *codes* are identification procedures that release data only after the proper code is entered into the computer. The code should be changed periodically because it can be revealed to others. Alarms to signal attempts at unauthorized access to sensitive information should be incorporated into computer software.

Another defense against unauthorized access is the *silent answer/callback modem.* When a call into a computer is attempted, the user's access code is requested. If the code is verified, the modem hangs up, calls the user on the officially listed number, and the log-in procedures begin. Hackers have defeated this defense by call forwarding. There is also the problem of interception by offenders who monitor mobile radiotelephone and cellular radio frequencies with scanners.

Firewalls are software and hardware controls that permit system access only to users who are registered with a computer. Attempts to gain access are challenged by the use of passwords. These challenges are "layers" that data must go through before reaching its destination. A firewall sits between a company's internal computer network and outside communications. Firewall products offer a range of features such as file or virus checking, log and activity reports, encryption, security and authentication schemes, and monitoring and alarm mechanisms for suspicious events or network intruders. From the security manager's perspective, putting up a firewall is similar in certain respects to implementing physical security—assess the vulnerability, determine need, and after understanding the technology, decide on a proper level of protection. Magazines such as *Data Communications, InfoSecurity News,* and *Network World* periodically test and rate firewalls.[11]

Encryption

Many practitioners in the computer field consider encryption the best protection measure for data within a computer or while it is being transmitted. *Encryption* consists of hardware or software that scrambles (encrypts) data, rendering it unintelligible to an unauthorized person intercepting it. The coding procedure involves rules or mathematical steps, called an *algorithm*, that converts plain data into coded data. This transformation of data is accomplished through what is called a *key*, which is a sequence of numbers or characters or both. The key is used in both transmitting and receiving equipment. Key security is vital because it is loaded into both ends of the data link. Furthermore, encryption tools should be changed periodically because breaches have become something of a game. Developers of encryption systems are finding that their estimates of how long it would take to crack the codes are too long. Rapidly evolving technology has shortened the life of promising encryption systems. Another point is noted by computer expert John M. Carroll, who adds that, when you become mesmerized by the wonder of some promising crypto device, ask yourself one question: "How much do I trust the person who sold me this gadget?" He extends this question to the international level by claiming that it would be unlikely for any country, even an ally, to provide an encryption system to another without retaining the keys.[12]

Controversy has developed over whether the U.S. government should have the power to tap into every telephone, fax, and computer transmission by controlling keys. From the law enforcement perspective, such control is necessary to investigate criminals and spies. Opponents claim violations of privacy and damage to the ability of American businesses to compete internationally. Without tight controls over encryption systems, the U.S. government also fears that criminals will use such systems to send and receive secret communications, making investigations very difficult. Although the issues remain, businesses will need encryption systems for sensitive information and the growing use of electronic mail, which, without encryption, is like sending a postcard. One computer security expert quipped that no legislation can stop the spread of encryption systems and there are hundreds of foreign encryption products.[13]

What are your views of government control of encryption systems and keys?

Input/Output Controls

When information (e.g., expenditures, merchandise received) is entered into a computer (input) and when output (e.g., checks, confidential reports) is produced, controls obviously are necessary to maintain accuracy and deter manipulations. The following controls are recommended:

1. Save original input records for a certain period to enable comparisons to output documents.
2. Prenumber standard forms. Maintain accountability. Ensure that all appropriate data are fed into the computer.
3. Require documentation of all changes in input and output data.
4. Ensure that employees report all discrepancies to both supervisors and loss prevention personnel.
5. Establish computer programs that detect and report unusual data.
6. Spot check input data against source documents; for example, compare the number of items and costs on several prenumbered receiving documents with computer data on the same merchandise.
7. Compare physical inventories with inventories from computer data.
8. Provide reports of computer data to employees who produced source (input) documents to reveal discrepancies.
9. Limit the number of sensitive reports produced by the computer. Maintain accountability of each report.
10. Apply appropriate controls used in manual operations to computer operations.

Auditing

Examining and checking a system or operation often uncovers deviations. This essentially is the reason for auditing. The loss prevention practitioner should audit basic defenses such as perimeter security and logging of personnel. For more complex auditing of the computer operation, a combination accountant-programmer-computer analyst is a wise investment. Auditing can be performed by an internal group, external group, or a combination of both. Irregularly scheduled audits throw offenders and potential offenders off guard.

There is a booming business for computer-trained auditors who consult. The millions of dollars that these consulting companies earn each year results from uncovering loopholes in computer operations, deviations, and crimes.

Internet Security

As organizations increasingly embrace Internet technology as an avenue to conduct global business, many may not be prepared to protect against losses. A disruption of business can result from hacking, by insiders and outsiders; a virus that invades the system and crashes the software; a malicious influx of e-mail messages that clog the network; a power outage; or excessive traffic

continued

causing delays. Furthermore, the Internet is not a secure computing environment. E-mail is not private, and it may be read by a hacker. When a message is sent, it is tagged with the user name, password, and server identification. Hackers can tag along and obtain identification information then use the ID information to commit crimes in another's name. Changing passwords frequently and not giving it out over the Internet prevents losses. Any software downloaded from the Internet could contain a virus. And, it is wise to assume that information on the Internet, unless clearly designated as in the public domain, is copyright protected.[14]

Internet security includes firewalls. A shift should take place from static firewalls (that do not adapt to ever-changing policies and viruses) to intelligent firewalls (that dynamically change). Scanning software is another strategy as discussed earlier. An organization's *computer emergency response team* (CERT) provides another defense. It involves a team approach against intrusions and captures statistics on attacks. The concept began at Carnegie Mellon University, in Pittsburgh, which acts as a clearinghouse for Internet security incidents. Another avenue for security strategies is the *National Computer Security Association* (NCSA) (10 South Courthouse Avenue, Carlisle, PA 17013; Tel.: 717-258-1816). The NCSA conducts research and publishes guidelines addressing Internet security. For further information, contact NCSA at www.ncsa.com/webcert/sgl_site.html [15]

Defense Against Losses from Fire and Other Disasters

Fire Protection

Fires at computer facilities usually are caused by fires in adjacent facilities and electrical problems. Numerous wires and electrical components and accumulations of paper provide combustibles for fire. Because important records are maintained at computer centers, one fire can create financial ruin for a business. In addition, expensive equipment can be destroyed. But, with adequate fire prevention and fire suppression measures, losses can be minimized.

Fire prevention entails the enforcement of no smoking rules, the proper disposal of trash, preventive maintenance, good employee socialization, and audits of prevention measures. Furnishings that are flammable should be removed or treated with sprays to hinder flammability. Under-floor areas, where many electrical wires are located, need to be cleaned and checked periodically.

Fire suppression is aided by smoke sensors. Ionization detectors are most efficient because they detect the earliest stages of smoke or flame. Carbon monoxide (CO) gas detectors can save lives because people have been overcome by CO before other detectors provided warnings of fire. Detectors normally are placed on ceilings, under raised floors, in air ducts, and within equipment. The detectors should be connected to separate power supplies since electricity and air-conditioning units are often turned off during a fire. This will prevent electrocution of an employee if water is sprayed on burning equipment, reduce damage to the computer, and avoid an air-conditioning unit blowing fire and smoke to other parts of a building. Emergency lighting is important in conjunction with these strategies.

A primary method of fire suppression for computer facilities is a sprinkler system, which may be required by local codes. However, sprinklers are controversial because of the potential danger to people due to electrocution and likely equipment damage. Such systems may be activated by accident or by a small fire that could have been extinguished with a portable extinguisher. To reduce the impact of a sprinkler system, consider a dry pipe system with a shutoff valve nearby, noncombustible construction materials, a one-hour fire resistance rating surrounding the computer room, and noncombustible water-resistant covers for computer equipment.

Halon 1301 (Freon) was popular as an extinguishing agent for computer rooms; however, it is banned because it harms the ozone layer. Carbon dioxide extinguishing systems were another earlier alternative to water, but these systems should be avoided because they smother a fire by cutting off oxygen, an obvious danger to humans.

Portable fire extinguishers are helpful to suppress small fires. If portable carbon dioxide extinguishers are used, careful planning (e.g., evacuation) and caution are important because of the danger to humans.

Prevention of Disasters

Human-made or natural disasters have the potential for producing considerable disruption and damage to computer centers. Through careful site location, construction, and design, the impact of disasters can be reduced. *Contingency plans are a key loss prevention measure.*[16] An auxiliary power supply (i.e., a generator) will provide power in case the main source of electricity fails. A backup air-conditioning/heating unit will ensure that the proper temperature is maintained so that valuable equipment is not harmed. Backup computers and the protection of records are essential considerations for the continuation of both computer operations and the organization. Mutual assistance agreements enable two or more separate computer centers to rely on each other in case of an emergency. Associated problems may entail system incompatibility, program differences, and computer time requirements. To ensure reliability, a computer specialist should conduct an initial study and then periodic evaluations. Special computer safes protect computer media from fire, theft, and adverse environmental conditions. A second copy of data stored at another secure location also will avert losses. Off-site data need to be updated repeatedly.

Additional Safeguards

The following suggestions can afford additional security for a computer facility or operation:

1. Carefully plan computer facilities.
2. If possible, locate the computer(s) in a separate structure to avoid the spread of fire from an adjacent building or room.
3. Study local police and fire protection capabilities and response time.
4. Limit entrances and establish perimeter security.
5. Make sure the person in charge of computer loss prevention has a computer background.
6. Carefully select and socialize personnel.
7. Control the turnover of personnel through both good human relations and personnel administration practices.
8. To impede collusion, limit contact among computer operators, programmers, auditors, and maintenance technicians.
9. If possible, make sure that programmers have no access to computers.
10. Institute a "two-key" system: two people required to fulfill computer activity; for example, one person writes a program, a second checks it.
11. Rotate personnel. Insist that they take vacations.
12. Maintain records of any program changes.
13. Design programs that reveal unauthorized use or program alterations.
14. Include a statement of ownership in each program.
15. Audit programs prior to and during usage.
16. Control the issuance of programs and other software. Store them in secure containers and have a librarian log users.
17. Audit the use of computer time.
18. Control the disposal of waste and stored data (e.g., printouts) that may contain sensitive information; use shredders.
19. Avoid the placement of system components near windows or doors since they can be viewed from outside via binoculars, telescopes, and cameras.
20. Store select sensitive information in traditional containers (e.g., a safe) rather than in computers.
21. When possible, disconnect computers from outside communication networks.

NUCLEAR FACILITIES

Supporters of nuclear energy favor it as a safe way to reduce America's dependence on imported oil. Detractors frantically testify about dangers from unsafe conditions and radiation. The debate will continue for years.

Public utilities and government have developed guidelines for maintaining a safe and secure environment. The American nuclear industry and its 110 commercial reactors are responsible for fully implementing the requirements for protecting the public health and safety as prescribed by the U.S. Nuclear Regulatory Commission (NRC). But the NRC has been criticized over the years for not fulfilling its mandate and overlooking serious safety problems to keep plants on-line. Also, whistle blowers have come forward.[17] Despite the criticism, an enormous amount of effort in terms of money, personnel, and equipment is expended to reduce the chances of accidents and losses. Moreover, the nuclear industry has a responsibility to the community, stockholders, and customers.

Nuclear Security

The NRC, in conjunction with other federal agencies, develops physical security criteria or standards for nuclear operations. These standards involve defenses against both internal and external threats. A possible internal threat is someone on the inside, with or without cooperation from others, who commits sabotage or theft of special nuclear materials (SNM). SNM can be used to manufacture a nuclear weapon. An external threat could be posed by several people who are dedicated to their objectives, well trained in military skills, and possess weaponry and explosives. An insider may be part of this threat. Nuclear security programs typically are designed to protect against radiological sabotage and the theft or diversion of SNM. Radiological sabotage of nuclear materials, during shipment or at the plant site, can endanger the public by exposure to radiation. Theft or diversion of SNM could be used for extortion, terrorism, publicity, or financial gain.

The NRC regulates the nuclear industry by licensing companies to build and operate nuclear reactors and to use nuclear materials. Rules and standards must be followed by licensees to ensure safety and security. A proposed program must be technically adequate before legal permission is granted to the licensee to operate. NRC inspections are conducted periodically to ensure compliance; corrective action often results. NRC security regulations stipulate which security levels must be maintained at nuclear plants. Physical security criteria assist licensees prior to submitting, for approval, a physical security plan (PSP). The PSP guards against two key threats—sabotage and theft—among others. NRC criteria stress *redundancy* (i.e., duplication) and *in-depth protection*. Examples are two barriers and two intrusion alarm systems. Through a combination of defenses, an adversary probably would be detected and reported as quickly as possible; a strong response would follow.

Separate monitoring systems operate at nuclear plants. Three specific monitoring systems are security, fire, and safety. The trend in other industries to integrate these systems into one computer-controlled system has not caught on in nuclear facilities. The security system is similar to a proprietary central station. Sophisticated and redundant equipment features (e.g., additional communications paths) provide safeguards against malfunctions. A modern, well-designed computer system can be connected to perimeter intrusion alarms, access controls, CCTV, duress alarms, and communications equipment. A record keeping function is essential, especially to comply with stringent NRC record keeping regulations.

Title 10, Code of Federal Regulations, Part 73, explains elements of an acceptable nuclear security program. It includes physical security organization, supervision, training, physical barriers, intrusion detection, access requirements, communications, testing and maintenance, and armed response requirements. Following the World Trade Center bombing, the NRC ordered all nuclear power plants to install barriers against vehicle bombs.

A double fence frequently is constructed along nuclear plant perimeters. Both microwave and e-field intrusion detection systems are common at the same site. Sophisticated and expensive CCTV cameras enable viewing during adverse weather conditions. NRC regulations necessitate minimum lighting levels, which usually are exceeded. Access controls can be very complex and effective. Special-purpose detection devices (e.g., X-ray, weapons, explosive), strategically placed, are integrated with other systems.

SNM need protection as an integral part of the security program. Accountability and frequent inventories will reduce the possibility of losses while increasing the chances of recovery in the event of a loss.

Portal of the Future[18]

Because the U.S. Department of Energy (DOE) maintains sites that support nuclear weapons production, it plays a lead role in designing security portals that search incoming and outgoing vehicles. Searching trucks and cars is labor intensive and time consuming, and when technology makes the task easier, the ideas spread to such locations as nuclear plants. DOE ideas include the following. A *fiber optic weight-in-motion system* enables operators to weigh vehicles as they are moving up to 5 mph. Security personnel can weigh a vehicle before and after it enters a site to note discrepancies. An *undervehicle scanning system* provides video of the bottom of vehicles and photographs the license plate. An *enclosed space detection system* detects vibrations from a heartbeat from a person hiding in an enclosed space. This system uses seismic geophones or microwaves to detect the shock waves created by a beating heart. Other systems detect explosives and small radiation levels. Such technology can be applied to not only tighten security at sites containing nuclear materials but also at prisons, borders, military posts, and other high-security locations.

Protection Force

NRC regulations require an armed response force present at a nuclear facility at all times (see Figure 16–1). Criteria established by NRC reinforce adequate selection, training, weapons, and equipment. Sufficient power is expected from the response force to counter an adversary. This entails the use of deadly force in self-defense or in the defense of others. Local law enforcement assistance is to be called in the event of an attack. However, because of a response time delay from local authorities, the primary armed defense is expected from the on-site nuclear security force. The licensee has an obligation to convince the NRC licensing staff that the security measures are capable of detecting and delaying an attack until the response force intervenes.

Nuclear security officers spend most of their time ensuring plant protection. Certain areas need to be regularly inspected, CCTV monitors and alarms require attention, and employees and visitors are scrutinized and searched at access points.

> NRC regulations require an armed response force to be present at a nuclear facility at all times.

Figure 16–1 Security officers at a nuclear generating plant. Courtesy of Wackenhut Corporation. Photo by Ed Burns.

Transportation of Fuel and Waste

Nuclear fuel is produced at locations away from plant sites and must be transported to the plant by truck or train. Likewise, the highly radioactive spent fuel rods removed from the reactor core and contaminated clothing and equipment must be carried to distant disposal sites. The NRC studies and approves (or rejects) transportation plans by utilities. Security is extensive and mandates a heavily armed escort and devices that foil would-be hijackers. Shipments are transported on large flatbed trucks. In the event of an attack, truck drivers are capable of quickly activating antihijacking equipment that would disable the truck and prevent it from being stolen. The characteristics of these security plans are kept as secret as possible.

Fire and Safety

Fire records indicate that the most vulnerable period for fire damage in the probable lifetime of a large reactor system, such as found at nuclear power plants, exists during the construction stage.[19] Because the construction of a reactor normally requires building a containment structure first, there are limited exits for evacuation and limited access for fire suppression. The chances for fire are reduced through fire prevention measures. For instance, the use of metal rather than wood scaffolding and stairways limits combustible materials.

Automatic sprinklers are a major component of fire suppression systems at nuclear facilities. With radiation a potential hazard for personnel, sprinklers are an attractive choice to obviate the need for firefighters entering dangerous areas. If the water becomes contaminated, it must be collected and disposed of properly. This is aided by waterproofed floors and a drainage system. Smoke confinement is another problem. A well-planned, comprehensive fire protection program will increase safety.

DEPARTMENT OF DEFENSE REQUIRED SECURITY

U.S. technology and industry are vital to our nation's defense. Businesses under contract with the Department of Defense (DOD) must protect government classified information. The Defense Investigative Service (DIS), established in 1972, is responsible for our nation's National Industrial Security Program (NISP). *Industrial security* is the integration of information, personnel, and physical security principles applied to the protection of classified information within industry.[20]

The DIS is a separate agency of the DOD under the direction, authority, and control of the Assistant Secretary of Defense. It is a law enforcement, personnel security investigative, and industrial security agency. DIS is assigned the administration of four programs: the Personnel Security Investigations Program; the Arms, Ammunition, and Explosives Program; the Key Asset Protection Program; and the DOD portion of the NISP. The Personnel Security Investigations Program is designed to elicit information pertinent to individuals assigned to or affiliated with the DOD who require a security clearance, sensitive position, or seek entry into the Armed Forces. The Arms, Ammunition, and Explosives Program provides for the protection of conventional arms, ammunition, and explosives in the custody of or produced by contractors associated with the DOD. The Key Asset Protection Program promotes the security of those facilities that provide critical industrial production and services, thereby ensuring emergency mobilization preparedness capability. The following discussion emphasizes the NISP.

The DIS industrial security representative (ISR) provides advice and assistance to the DOD contractor community with respect to the implementation of the NISP. The ISR assists company management and the facility security office (FSO). Responsibilities of the security program are numerous: perimeter defenses, visitor and pass control through a badge and accountability system, internal investigations, fire protection, emergency plans, classified material protection and destruction, and audits. Over the years, *emphasis has shifted from physical security to a more balanced approach involving personnel security.* According to Thomas J. O'Brien, "Every loss [of classified information] could be traced to cleared, authorized individuals abusing the trust placed in them or otherwise acting negligently in handling classified information."[21]

Personnel investigations involving DIS special agent fieldwork consist of a search of investigative files maintained by federal agencies, contact with local law enforcement agencies, checks of credit bureau records, and interviews with friends, coworkers, and neighbors.

The Personnel Investigations Center (PIC) controls and manages the 800,000 plus personnel security investigations initiated by DOD components annually and includes over 160,000 high level investigations. The center also maintains approximately 2.9 million records of closed investigations.

A facility security clearance (FCL) is an administrative determination that, from a national security standpoint, a facility is eligible for access to classified information at the same or lower classification category as the clearance being granted. There are 12,000 such facilities (e.g., plants, contractors, universities). The FCL may be granted at the confidential, secret, or top secret level.

The *National Industrial Security Program Operating Manual* (NISPOM)[22] provides a foundation for DIS work with defense industries to maintain security. The manual covers a variety of topics such as access control systems, network security, training, safeguarding classified information, and personnel clearances. The NISPOM replaces the DOD *Industrial Security Manual for Safeguarding Classified Information.*

The *Department of Defense Security Institute* (DODSI) (8000 Jefferson Davis Hwy., Richmond, VA 23297; Tel.: 804-279-4759) is the principal security training, research, and education awareness facility for the DOD. The DODSI graduates over 15,000 students annually through a variety of on-site and independent study courses for U.S. government employees, contractor employees, and representatives of selected foreign governments. It hosts worldwide conferences and seminars and publishes proceedings of such forums.[23]

CASE PROBLEMS

16A. Select two types of facilities explained in this chapter, and describe why the ones you chose are unique in terms of loss problems and prevention strategies.

16B. Choose two types of facilities from this chapter. For each, establish a priority list of the five most important measures to counter losses. Explain the reasoning behind each ranked list.

16C. Select two facilities mentioned in this chapter. (1) Refer to additional sources to gather further information, and (2) explain why you would prefer to work in one over the other. Maintain a bibliography.

16D. Of the locations discussed in this chapter, which do you think is the most demanding for a security manager? Justify your answer.

NOTES

1. John M. Carroll, *Computer Security*, 3rd ed. (Boston: Butterworth–Heinemann, 1996), p. 3.
2. U.S. Department of Justice, *Computer Crime* (Washington, DC: U.S. Government Printing Office, 1979), p. 3.
3. Carl B. Jackson, "Making Time for DP Risk Analysis," *Security World* (March 1986): 69.
4. "$555 Million Loss; Service Theft Up," *Security* (May 1989): 52.
5. Carroll, *Computer Security*, p. 10.
6. UN Commission on Crime and Criminal Justice, *United Nations Manual on the Prevention and Control of Computer-Related Crime* (New York: United Nations, 1995).
7. David L. Carter and Andra J. Katz, "Computer Crime: An Emerging Challenge for Law Enforcement," *FBI Law Enforcement Bulletin* (December 1996): 1–8.
8. Ibid., pp. 1–8.
9. Carroll, *Computer Security*, pp. 444–445.
10. Ian Whalley, "Virus Defenses for the Future," *Security Management* (November 1996): 60–64.
11. Amy Thompson, "Smoking out the Facts on Firewalls," *Security Management* (January 1997): 25–30.
12. Carroll, *Computer Security*, p. 249.

13. Vic Sussman, "Policing Cyberspace," *US News and World Report* (January 23, 1995): 55–60.
14. Anthony Martinez, "What Risk Managers Should Know About the Internet," *Risk Management* (November 1996): 43–46. And Ronald Lander and James E. Roughton, "The Security Professional in Cyberspace," *Security Management* (January 1996): 38–44.
15. Ibid. And Peter S. Tippett, "Top Ten Internet Security Issues," *NCSA News* (October 1996): 4.
16. Bill Zalud, "Here's How to Survive a Disaster," *Security* (May 1989): 48–50.
17. Eric Pooley, "Nuclear Warriors," *Time* (March 4, 1996): 46–54.
18. "Oak Ridge's Portal of Future Putting Emphasis on Security," *Security Concepts* (October 1996): 7.
19. Gordon P. McKinnon, ed., *Fire Protection Handbook*, 14th ed. (Boston: National Fire Protection Association, 1977), pp. 4–66.
20. Defense Investigative Service, *Introduction to the Defense Investigative Service National Industrial Security Program* (Alexandria, VA: DIS, n.d.).
21. Thomas J. O'Brien, "The Changing Face of DOD Security," *Security Management* (July 1988): 62.
22. Department of Defense, *National Industrial Security Program Operating Manual, DOD 5220.22-M* (Washington, DC: DOD, January 1995).
23. Department of Defense Security Institute, *Info. Guide* (Richmond, VA: DODSI, 1997), pp. v, 86.

17

Loss Prevention at Select Institutions

OBJECTIVES

After studying this chapter the reader will be able to discuss loss problems and countermeasures for

1. Educational institutions;
2. Health-care institutions;
3. Banks and financial institutions;
4. Government institutions.

These four kinds of institutions serve as examples for a discussion of planning programs for institutional loss prevention: educational, health-care, bank and financial, and government.

EDUCATIONAL INSTITUTIONS

Two major kinds of educational systems are emphasized here: school districts and higher education campuses. A big difference between school districts and college and university campuses is that, in the former, students normally go home at night and buildings often are empty. On campuses, instructional buildings may be empty at night, but students live on the premises in dormitories. Exceptions are community and technical colleges whose students commute. School districts and campuses both schedule evening and weekend activities such as evening classes, sports events, and meetings. A major factor for those who plan and implement loss prevention programs for these institutions is that the protective measures must cater to the needs and characteristics of the particular institution.

Problems and Losses at Educational Institutions

Today, many educational institutions are faced with financial crises. And, losses from crimes, fires, and accidents make matters worse. Therefore, cost-effective loss prevention measures are especially vital.

Theft of educational property is a recurring problem. Burglary, larceny, and internal theft cause the disappearance of computers, books, and laboratory, audiovisual, and sports equipment. Drug abuse and distribution are common at educational institutions. *Vandalism*, the deliberate destruction of property, is a particularly annoying expense to school districts, more so than at colleges and universities. Damage includes broken windows, destroyed educational equipment, graffiti, and ruining of entire buildings. Crimes against people are among the most serious offenses. Inner city schools are plagued by assaults against teachers and students, robberies, rapes, and occasional murders. Youth gangs are known to participate in many crimes.

There has been a long held belief that campuses of higher education are a sanctuary immune to crime. However, this is not so. Large wooded campuses create criminal opportunities, as do colleges with public streets going through their campuses. Well-publicized crimes and security-negligence lawsuits, drug abuse, and "date rape" awareness all have brought campus security and safety issues into the open.[1] As with the rest of society in the United States and elsewhere, vulnerability also exists on campuses. Registration, when students pay tuition, presents robbery temptations. Numerous property crimes occur in dormitories. Sports events require traffic, parking, and crowd control. When controversial speakers or VIPs appear on the premises, extra security is required. Student activism is another potential threat. The 1960s and 1970s were decades of major student unrest, when riots and building "takeovers" occurred, and these courses of action are not going to disappear. Computer facilities need protection against manipulation and attack. Bomb threats, fires, and arson are troublesome.

Countermeasures

Several strategies are useful for school districts and colleges and universities. Typical measures are identification cards, access controls, emergency telephones, intrusion alarms, patrols, lighting, and CCTV.

The following list describes additional measures for the protection of school districts and institutions of higher education:

1. Lock doors and windows.
2. Consider an automatic access control system.
3. Provide secure locations for valuables. If possible, bolt portable equipment to stationary surfaces.

4. Mark expensive items to deter theft and fencing and to aid in criminal apprehension and return of stolen property. Contact local police for assistance for what is known as *operation identification*.
5. Maintain accountability, and conduct inventories of equipment and valuables.
6. Install electronic article surveillance systems in libraries to reduce book thefts.
7. Stagger custodial shifts to ensure round-the-clock presence in buildings.
8. Use unarmed students to supplement security forces, especially for special events; provide good training.
9. Conduct drug abuse education and prevention programs. Contact local alcohol and drug abuse agencies for aid.

If it is possible to contribute loss prevention advice before the construction of a new or renovated school, the following suggestions are cost effective:

1. Design buildings with "defensible space" in mind (e.g., surveillance opportunities through windows and unobscured walkways to promote safety).
2. Avoid planting high shrubbery that provides hiding places and hinders visibility.
3. Do not plant trees close to buildings.
4. Avoid unnecessary exterior fixtures.
5. Limit roof access by eliminating low overhanging roofs.
6. Lock roof doors and hatches.
7. Install flexible internal gates in halls to impede access to specific areas.
8. Avoid suspended ceilings in restrooms and locker rooms.
9. Use self-closing faucets; ensure proper drainage in case of flooding.
10. Use vandal-resistant construction materials, especially glass made of unbreakable substances.
11. Install stainless steel mirrors rather than glass in restrooms.
12. Install emergency lighting.

School Districts

A comprehensive school district loss prevention program must involve the community: students, teachers and administrators, parents, public safety agencies, civic groups, and businesses. Good ideas evolve from a concerted effort. Public police, for instance, may be willing to use unoccupied schools to write reports. A mobile home may be donated by local business people so that a person can live rent-free on the school premises while watching for suspicious activity. Neighbors adjacent to schools may be willing to observe the premises.

Educational leaders should be at the forefront of preventive measures. One idea is for a certain amount of money from the district budget to be set aside to cover vandalism costs for a year. If any money remains at the end of the year, the students would decide on its use. This approach creates peer pressure while educating students about vandalism costs. Older students can be employed, with the aid of videos, to teach younger students about the adverse effects of vandalism and other crimes. Local police often are willing to help. To deal with graffiti, loss prevention practitioners can designate specific walls for students' artistic abilities. The walls could be repainted every year for new student artwork.

If school districts provide individual attention to problem students, the benefits will probably outweigh the expenses. A combined counseling and education approach might reduce student hostility and funnel student time into constructive activities rather than crime. Traditional suspension from school often sends troublesome students to the streets where more trouble is likely. On the other hand, if students remain at the school in an appropriate program, improved results are probable.

One of the most serious problems facing schools is violence. From the Civil War to the present, 567,000 Americans have died in combat; but since 1920, over 1 million American civilians have been killed by firearms. Among teenagers 15 to 19 years old, the problem of gun violence is alarming: one of every four deaths is attributable to firearms.[2] The National Institute of Justice found that one in five inner city students surveyed (one in three males) had been shot at, stabbed, or otherwise injured with a weapon at or in transit to or from school in the past few years.[3] Violent crimes committed by juveniles peak at the close of the schoolday and decline through the evening; this contrasts with adults, whose violent crime increases from early morning through midnight.[4] Students are not the only victims of violence. School employees, volunteers, and innocent bystanders also are victims.

According to the National Center for Injury Prevention and Control, Centers for Disease Control and Prevention, CCTV, metal detectors, and locker searches have little effect beyond the immediate environment of the school building; school officials should work closely with other agencies in their communities to develop a comprehensive approach to prevent violence and crime.[5] *If school security planners argue for more security personnel and hardware to curb school crime, they may be faced with others who see broader solutions to the problem.* And, whatever strategies are implemented, they should be subject to research and evaluation to produce the best possible solutions and utilization of resources.

As part of a broader violence prevention program that included curriculums, peer mediation, and crisis intervention teams, the New York City school system instituted a metal detector program. Sixteen schools were chosen. A mobile staff of 120 began using handheld metal detectors to conduct unannounced lobby searches of students at the start of the day. In addition to removing more than 2000 weapons at the schools, weapon-related incidents decreased in 13 of the 15 schools, attendance improved, and students expressed an increased sense of security.[6]

The National Institute of Justice evaluated two middle school violence prevention programs:

- *Project STOP* (Schools Teaching Options for Peace), a traditional conflict resolution program that included a curriculum and peer mediation.
- *The Safe Harbor Program*, which included a 20-session curriculum, a counseling component, and a schoolwide antiviolence campaign.

The effects of both programs on attitudes were positive and strong. Students who participated in the STOP program tended to use reasoning more frequently to resolve conflicts than students who had no exposure. The Safe Harbor participants were less likely to advocate retaliation in response to conflict than students with no exposure.[7]

Colleges and Universities

In response to increasing crime on college campuses and the need for more accurate statistics, Congress passed the *Student-Right-to-Know and Campus Security Act of 1990.* This legislation requires crime awareness and prevention measures at colleges and reporting campus crime to the FBI *Uniform Crime Reports* program, while making these statistics available to students and the general public. Such data enables comparisons among colleges and universities. However, one study found that 32 percent of campus police agencies surveyed stated that they did not provide accurate crime figures. The research explained that administrators sometimes encourage victimized students to not report crimes to campus police or to report the crime to local police.[8] FBI crime data has been criticized over the years because it represents crimes *reported* to police, and many crimes are never reported or recorded, as shown by victimization studies.[9]

Research of campus law enforcement agencies (serving U.S. four-year colleges and universities with 2500 or more students) by the U.S. Department of Justice, with assistance from the *International Association of Campus Law Enforcement Administrators* (638 Prospect Ave., Hartford, CT 06105; Tel.: 860-586-7517), found the following:

1. Each agency received an average of 7 reports of serious violent crimes and 250 reports of property crimes in 1994. (Research by *Security* magazine found the following risks on campuses, in descending order: theft and burglary, unauthorized access, computer security, vandalism, alcohol or drug abuse, privacy, and staff theft or fraud.[10])

2. The 680 campus law enforcement agencies surveyed included 20,067 full-time employees, with 10,651 sworn (with general arrest powers) and 9,416 nonsworn officers; most sworn officers were armed.

3. About a fourth of all campuses used some contract personnel.

4. Campus law enforcement operating expenditures averaged $109 per student.

5. All agencies reported they provided routine patrol services and most performed traffic duties.

6. About 80 percent were responsible for locking and unlocking campus buildings and for central alarm monitoring.

7. About 77 percent had emergency phones that connect directly to campus police and 66 percent had an emergency 911 telephone system.

8. Eighty-five percent operated a crime prevention unit, 66 percent had a date rape prevention program, and 60 percent had a stranger rape prevention program.

9. About half operated programs against alcohol and drug abuse.[11]

10. It should be noted that many colleges have an enrollment of under 2500 students and two-year colleges were not represented in this research.

Research by Bonnie S. Fisher and John J. Sloan produced guidelines that should be considered when evaluating programs designed to reduce campus crime. Some of their major points follow:

- A comprehensive evaluation requires (1) identifying the individual departments or groups on campus that will be involved and assigning safety and security responsibilities to them; (2) detailing their role in reducing crime and fear; and (3) describing what specific policies they will implement.

- A comprehensive approach includes security, faculty members, staff members, students, and public law enforcement personnel.

- Campus administrators should conduct surveys of the campus community to understand the nature and extent of crime and fear, perceptions of the effectiveness of security, and participation in crime prevention programs and whether participants adopted any of the preventive measures. Until evaluations become an integral part of responding to campus crime, administrators will continue to make poor decisions on security strategies.

- Research has confirmed that crime on campuses is influenced by poor lighting, excessive foliage, blocked views, and difficulty of escape by victims. (As we can see, crime prevention through environmental design, or CPTED, as discussed earlier in the text, has universal application.)

- Location measures (e.g., proximity to urban areas with high unemployment) are predictors of high campus crime rates.[12]

An illustration of how the last problem can be countered is seen at Yale University, New Haven, CT, which has invested in its surrounding community in an effort to reduce crime. One Yale strategy is to offer employees up to $20,000 to purchase a home in New Haven. The response was greater than anticipated. Another strategy included a multimillion dollar project to redevelop deteriorating blocks. On campus, 200 emergency blue light telephones and additional lighting were added, plus a student escort and shuttle bus service. A police substation in a commercial area near the campus also was added. These efforts were intensified following the murder of a Yale student on the edge of campus.[13]

Numerous campuses have implemented the strategy of many public police agencies; namely, community policing. *Community policing* aims to control crime through a partnership of police and citizens, and it strives to become a dominant philosophy throughout a police department. This partnership strives to develop a higher level of trust and cooperation. Rather than police reacting to the same problem over and over again, a unique, proactive approach is employed for problem solving. For a campus, preventive strategies are designed in cooperation with various campus departments, community service agencies, and other groups.[14]

What do you view as the top three strategies to prevent violence at school districts? How would you answer this same question for colleges and universities?

Fire Protection at Educational Institutions

The *National Fire Protection Association Code for Safety to Life from Fire in Buildings and Structures*, concisely referred to as the *NFPA Life Safety Code*, defines *educational occupancies* "as including all buildings used for gatherings of groups of six or more persons for purposes of instruction, such as schools, universities, colleges, and academies."[15] The principal fire hazards endangering life in places of public assembly are (1) overcrowding; (2) blocking, impairing, or locking exits; (3) storing combustibles in dangerous locations; (4) using an open flame without proper precautions; and (5) using combustible decorations.[16] Furthermore, hazards of educational buildings vary with construction characteristics and with the age group of students. Younger students, for example, require protection different from that for older students. The NFPA Life Safety Code specifies that kindergarten and first grade rooms should be on the floor of exit discharge so that stairs do not endanger these students. Building codes also specify similar guidelines. Because junior and senior high schools contain laboratories, shops, and home economics rooms, these facilities should have construction with a fire-resistance rating of one hour. School kitchens require similar protection. Distance to exits must not exceed 150 feet unless the building has an automatic extinguishing system specified by the Life Safety Code; with the system, the distance may be increased to 200 feet. A fire alarm system is required for all educational buildings. Most schools conduct fire drills for pupils. The Life Safety Code and many good building codes provide numerous standards for increasing fire safety.

For colleges and universities, the Life Safety Code is applied depending on building characteristics and use. If buildings are windowless, the Life Safety Code requirements for special structures are applicable. This would include automatic extinguishing systems, venting systems for smoke, and emergency lighting and power. Because many campus buildings are multistory, specific safeguards are necessary. Fire drills are often impractical in a college setting because of a wide variety of class schedules, so students and faculty members should be informed about emergency procedures.

HEALTH-CARE INSTITUTIONS

Hospitals, nursing homes, and other health-care institutions possess specific crime, fire, and safety weaknesses that require countermeasures. A large inventory of consumable items are located within health-care buildings: food, medical supplies, linens, and drugs. Thousands of meals and prescriptions are served each day in many of these locations. Assorted crimes are possible (e.g., theft, kickbacks to purchasers, fraud). Drugs are susceptible to not only internal theft but also robbery. Expensive medical and office equipment and patient and employee belongings are other tempting targets for offenders. Moreover, the safety of people must be a high priority. There is a never-ending flow of employees (doctors, nurses, assorted specialists, nonprofessional support personnel, volunteers), patients, visitors, salespeople, and repair technicians. A large number of female employees need protection, especially during night-time shift changes. Patients are particularly vulnerable at all times because of their limited physical capabilities. What makes protection difficult is that these institutions remain open 24 hours a day.

Precise crime statistics for health-care institutions are difficult to obtain because many crimes go unreported. Estimates on losses per bed per year range from $1200 to $2300.[17] Certain industry executives agree that 3 percent of any operating budget is a fairly accurate measure of crime loss.[18] Total crime losses in this industry are estimated at $5.5 billion annually.[19]

Emergency plans and special equipment are necessary in case of fire, explosion, accidents, bomb threats, and strikes. Flammable medical gases and oxygen support combustion, which necessitates safety precautions.

Accumulations of trash as well as safety in the operating rooms are additional considerations.

The protection of patient information also requires attention. Sometimes personal medical data is obtained in devious ways for use in litigation or insurance matters. Privacy is destroyed by these incidents.

Strategies for Health-Care Institutions

Accountability and Inventory Control

Because much of the inventory in health-care institutions can be used by employees at home or sold to others, accountability and inventory control can minimize shrinkage. A perpetual inventory of all items is the best method, but it is not practical. An alternative is a good periodic inventory of everything, and a perpetual inventory of select high-shrinkage items (e.g., food, linens, soap).

Imaginative preventive techniques should be applied where possible. For example, Russell L. Colling, in *Hospital Security*, explains that, when a hospital supervisor entered newer linen into the system, a date of six months earlier was recorded so that employees would think the newer linen was old and used.[20] Linen and other property permanently imprinted with the name of the institution will aid shrinkage-control efforts. Disposable items (e.g., paper towels) are less expensive but also subject to pilferage. Soiled-linen chutes are convenient hiding places for stolen goods. Offenders often wrap stolen merchandise in dirty linen for later recovery. Daily inspection of soiled linens and trash collection and disposal systems ensure that these theft techniques are impeded.

Auditing

When accounting and other safeguards are checked for deviations, loss prevention programs are strengthened. Do accounting records conform to management expectations? Are patients being properly billed? How accurate are accounts receivable and accounts payable records? In the food service operation, how careful are the controls over the ordering of foods and food preparation and distribution? The food service area is a prime location for theft. Every loss prevention measure should be audited to make sure it is functioning as designed.

Applicant Screening

Losses are caused by both professional and nonprofessional staff members. Stethoscopes, blood pressure testers, and other equipment and supplies may accompany doctors from a hospital to his or her private practice. Likewise, nurses have access to a broad spectrum of items. Low-skilled health-care workers, many of whom are transient, create additional problems.

Several measures can be instituted to obtain good employees. A good employment application and background investigation are wise choices. The time and effort expended on applicant screening will help to avert the hiring of quacks as well as drug and sex offenders who are attracted to health-care facilities.

Access Controls

When entrances are limited, unauthorized entry is hindered. Uniformed officers should be stationed at each entrance. Of course, emergency exits are a necessity for safety; but alarms on these doors will deter usage. Identification badges worn by employees assist in recognition by other employees. Outside individuals on the premises for any extended period of time (e.g., contractors or technicians) should be issued ID badges.

The control of visitors must be handled with compassion and empathy. Visitors wanting to see an ill family member are often emotionally upset. Furthermore, recovery of the patient can be aided by visits from loved ones. These factors must be stressed in health-care training programs. Many locations issue visitor passes to avoid overcrowding in patients' rooms and to inhibit a variety of problems such as the deviant man who dresses like a doctor to "examine" female patients.

Patrols, CCTV

Surveillance of interior and exterior areas, through the use of patrols and CCTV, deters crime. Good lighting is an integral aspect of this effort. Large medical centers have a command center for communications and CCTV observation. More intense vigilance usually is needed at night, but assorted crimes are possible at any time; to name a few, surreptitious entry, theft, vandalism, and disorderly conduct. Automobiles may be broken into in parking lots to obtain valuables. Doctor's automobiles are particularly vulnerable, especially if medical bags are left behind. Aggressive patrolling and surveillance are required during shift changes; women are escorted to their vehicles to foil attempts at purse snatching, assault, or rape. During slow periods when traffic is limited, uniformed officers should resume patrolling while checking for safety hazards.

Some locations have chosen sports jackets or blazers for loss prevention personnel to create a "nonpolice image." But most facilities seem to favor uniforms to provide a "police image" to reinforce crime deterrence and to signify that the location is protected.

The arming of personnel is controversial. Some medical institutions issue revolvers to all officers, whereas other locations issue them only to those assigned to external areas. "Indoor bullets" are used for added safety and to impede liability in case an unfortunate incident arises. These bullets are composed of a subvelocity load, have a range of about 35 feet, and will crumble on striking a hard surface beyond 35 feet.[21]

Emergency Room

At least one officer must be stationed in the emergency room at all times. Depending on the crime rate, officers may have to be armed, equipped with bullet-resistant vests, and prepared to frisk people, confiscate weapons, and make arrests. Signs prohibiting weapons should be posted as well as notices of metal detectors. Disturbances occur here regularly in busy hospitals. Verbal arguments, assaults, and destruction of property may be caused by belligerent patients, visitors who are intoxicated, and rival gangs. Disturbances recurrently are the result of long waiting periods before treatment. Medical personnel can reduce a portion of disturbances if they adequately explain the reasons for delays. Emergency treatment areas should be sealed off if necessary and panic buttons available.

Newborn Nursery

Infant abduction is a particularly disturbing problem for parents, employees, and police. The *National Center for Missing and Exploited Children* (NCMEC) (2101 Wilson Blvd., Suite 550, Arlington, VA 22201; Tel.: 1-800-843-5678) in 1983 created a database on infant abduction that led to the creation of guidelines for hospitals. Such offenders often impersonate medical staff and "case" the nursery prior to the crime. Countermeasures include taking footprints of infants, requiring photo ID cards of all employees and volunteers, restricting visitors, CCTV, and installing an electronic surveillance system that detects infant bracelets. If an abduction occurs, immediately notify the police, the FBI, and the NCMEC; conduct a search; check exit points; and begin a thorough investigation. Such "target hardening" at hospitals can displace kidnapping to areas outside the hospital and to the home of the infant. Parents should protect the infant by, for example, not placing pretty bows outside the home to signify a birth. Security personnel can prepare a brochure on protection at home.

"Target hardening" can displace crime. Can you think of other examples, besides the one just given, where enhanced security caused crime patterns to shift?

Pharmacy Protection and Robbery

A small percentage of the population is addicted to drugs and will do anything to obtain them. There have been instances where medical personnel have withheld drugs from a patient for their own use or sale. One technique is to substitute flour for medication. Hospital administrators are reluctant to report these acts for fear of lawsuits. Another technique is to write a phony prescription or alter an existing one. In one case, a hospital pharmacist diverted thousands of dollars of drugs to his retail drugstore. The maintenance of specific drugs (i.e., narcotics) is strictly regulated by the *Controlled Substance Act of 1970*, enforced by the Drug Enforcement Administration (DEA). All states regulate pharmacies, and in most states the pharmacy itself and the pharmacist must be licensed.

To curb pharmacy losses, these measures are recommended: (1) maintain strict accountability and inventory control; (2) protect blank, serial-numbered prescription slips; (3) set up a camera so that a picture can be taken of prescriptions and those who receive the slip; and (4) conduct undercover investigations.

For the protection of the pharmacy, cashiering operations, and the business office, the following measures will deter burglary, robbery, and other crimes: (1) intrusion and holdup alarms integrated with CCTV, (2) bullet-resistant glass, (3) electronically operated doors, (4) patrols, and (5) key control.

Health-Care Violence and OSHA Guidelines

According to the U.S. Bureau of Labor Statistics, health-care and social service workers have the highest incidence of assault injuries.[22] In addition to emergency rooms being a volatile environment, several other locations in the health-care industry are noted for potential violence. Children's hospitals, psychiatric units, and home health care are examples. To illustrate, in a children's hospital or pediatric unit, a child may require protection following abuse or to prevent kidnapping. If the child's parents are estranged, family strife may spill into the hospital. Protection methods include crisis intervention training for health-care employees, gathering information on the family at the preadmission stage, checking court papers showing parental rights or restraining orders, posting photos of persons to be barred from visiting the child, and even placing a false name on the nameplate of the patient's room.[23] Because of escalating crime at health-care facilities and several highly publicized cases—such as the case of a man who opened fire with a semiautomatic pistol in the emergency department at USC Hospital in Los Angeles and critically injured three doctors—government intervention has occurred. California and New Jersey are among states that have developed safety standards to prevent violence in the workplace. On the federal level, the Occupational Safety and Health Administration (OSHA) has released *Guidelines for Preventing Workplace Violence for Health Care and Social Service Workers.* According to OSHA, "all employers have a general duty to provide their employees with a workplace free from recognized hazards likely to cause death or serious physical harm" and "Employers can be cited for violating the General Duty

Clause if there is a recognized hazard of workplace violence in their establishments and they do nothing to prevent or abate it."[24] The OSHA guidelines are advisory in nature and focus on management commitment, work site analysis, hazard prevention and control (e.g., physical security), education and training, record keeping, and evaluation.[25]

Locker Rooms

Men and women who work in health-care institutions are accustomed to using separate locker rooms before, during, and after shifts. Locker rooms ordinarily are located in the basement or remote locations. CCTV and patrols can be applied to areas just outside locker rooms. Panic buttons that signal trouble are useful within locker rooms. Loss prevention personnel should conduct occasional locker inspections to deter assorted problems.

Mortuary

The mortuary has been the site for morbid crimes. People, including relatives of the deceased, have stolen jewelry directly from cadavers. Gold dental work has been extracted with a pocket knife. The rare sexual perversion called *necrophilia* (sexual activity with a corpse) is a possibility in the mortuary. Also, there are cases where the wrong body was taken away for burial. A complete inventory should be conducted of the personal property of the deceased soon after death. Witnesses and appropriate paperwork should be a part of this procedure.

Patient Property

A recurring puzzle sometimes accompanies patients prior to discharge: jewelry or other personal property is missing. In addition to theft, it is possible that the property is nonexistent, is at the patient's home, or has been misplaced. To avoid negative public relations, some health-care administrators quickly reimburse patients. But a few prevention measures are cost effective. The admitting form can contain a statement advising the patient to deposit valuables in a security envelope. These envelopes have the same serial numbers on both the envelope and the receipt. Valuables are inserted and the envelope is sealed in the presence of the patient. The patient and the clerk sign and date both the envelope and the receipt. An adequate safe is needed for these valuables.

Protection of Patient Information

Patient information requires protection. In one case, a private investigator telephoned a hospital pretending to be a physician who needed information to treat a patient. At another hospital, a medical clerk telephoned life insurance and diaper service salespeople immediately after the birth of babies. Privacy and confidentiality are subverted in such incidents. *Privacy* signifies that patients may not want certain information released for personal reasons. *Confidentiality* refers to the limitation on information revelation after a free flow of communications between the patient and medical staff members. Procedures should be implemented to obtain patient and physician approval before information is released to outsiders.

Today, electronic patient records are in need of greater protection. Sensitive information routinely is shared with noncaregivers, who use it legitimately for claim payments, research, and oversight. Transmission of patient information over public networks, like the Internet, or in electronic mail require protection.[26] Many of the computer protection methods (e.g., passwords, encryption) covered in the previous chapter are applicable here.

Cooperative Efforts

In urban areas where a concentration of health-care institutions are located, associations have formed to work toward mutual goals. Monthly meetings afford opportunities to share ideas and solutions to problems. Resources (e.g., training) are pooled, which results in lower costs.

At individual medical locations, cooperative efforts are facilitated by in-house surveys and feedback to individual departments. Loss prevention officers, equipped with a survey checklist, visit a department and conduct a survey. Deficiencies and recommendations are noted. Afterward, the officer and the loss prevention manager review the findings. Written recommendations are sent to the department and a copy is retained. This promotes good relations and also shows upper management the capabilities of loss prevention. If a surveyed department incurs losses, the retained documentation illustrates that prevention measures were advised.

Standards, Performance Measures, and Professionalism

The *Joint Commission on Accreditation of Healthcare Organizations* (JCAHO) (One Renaissance Blvd., Oakbrook Terrace, IL 60181; Tel.: 630-792-5005) is a dominant force in promoting standards in the health-care field that affect funding from government. JCAHO standard EC 1.4 addresses how hospitals should provide a secure environment for patients, staff, and visitors. Specific written plans for security are required for the "environment of care" (EC) standards as described here:

1. Establish, support, and maintain a security management program.
2. Address security concerns regarding patients, visitors, personnel, and property.
3. Provide for identification of patients, visitors, and staff.
4. Provide access control to security sensitive areas.
5. Provide vehicular and traffic control to the emergency service area.

6. Designate personnel who are responsible for the plan's development, implementation, and monitoring.
7. Describe methods for reporting and investigating all security incidents.
8. Provide for the annual evaluation of the plan.

Other standards focus on, for example, "staff knowledge of the plans" (EC 2.1), "implementation of the plans" (EC 2.3), and "life safety management" (EC 2.6). JCAHO is particularly interested in training employees and how they react to emergencies.[27]

Because measuring the preventive role of security is not an easy task, many security departments maintain extensive record keeping systems on a host of activities (e.g., logs of visitors, escorts, and parking notices issued). Such record keeping systems are "keys to survival." Another avenue that helps to measure security programs are *performance standards*, which are required by JCAHO and address both broad objectives (e.g., preventing crime) and specific outcomes (e.g., establishing response time to critical incidents). This avenue, also called *benchmarking*, gives the department a mark with which to measure performance. Here are examples:

> Standard: The security department will maintain 50 percent of officers certified by the IAHSS.
>
> Performance Measurement: Security personnel training records will be reviewed in January and July and reports will be presented to the director of security.
>
> Standard: All intrusion and panic alarm systems will be 100 percent operational and function as intended.
>
> Performance Measurement: These systems will be field tested (activated) the first week of each month and a report will be submitted to the director of security.[28]

The professionalism of those who protect health-care institutions is enhanced through the *International Association for Healthcare Security and Safety* (IAHSS) (PO Box 637, Lombard, IL 60148; Tel.: 630-953-0990). IAHSS was founded in 1968. It is a not-for-profit organization for hospital security and safety administrators and has over 1700 members worldwide. Two important purposes of this group are the development of standards for health-care security practices and training certification. For the various certifications, students study IAHSS manuals and JCAHO security standards.

Fire and Other Disasters

Because patients are physically weak or mentally impaired and unable to care for themselves during an emergency, fire protection problems are compounded. A multitude of fire codes and standards for health-care institutions emanate from local, state, and federal agencies. *The National Fire Protection Association 101, Life Safety Code,* and *NFPA 99, Standards for Health Care Facilities* provide a significant amount of information for these codes and standards.[29] Almost all states promote safety through minimum standards and health-care licensing requirements. The federal government, for example, adopted the Life Safety Code for Medicare and Medicaid regulations in health-care institutions.

JCAHO has worked closely with the federal government to provide adequate patient care and safety. Legislation has stated that hospitals must meet federal requirements for health and safety if they are accredited by JCAHO. All health-care locations are subjected to OSHA, except those that are federal. At times, overlapping regulations produce confusion between JCAHO and OSHA mandates.

Fire Protection

To prevent and suppress fires, the following methods can increase safety in a health-care environment:

1. Especially because health-care locations use a great deal of disposables, rubbish must be collected, stored, and eliminated properly. Fireproof receptacles are useful.
2. Flammable substances require safe storage, use, and disposal.
3. Electrical equipment and wiring should be inspected.
4. Operating and delivery rooms are subject to static electricity, which can spark a fire if close to anesthetics. These rooms should be tested for static electricity.
5. Because smoking is a recurring hazard, no smoking signs and sand urns will impede carelessness.
6. The person in charge of fire protection should make regular inspections.
7. A full-time fire marshal, fire engineer, or loss prevention manager should be in charge of fire protection. This individual coordinates training, evacuation plans, drills, equipment evaluation and purchasing, liaison with local fire agencies, plus other duties.
8. Common fire protection characteristics are ionized particle detectors, sprinklers, fire-resistive construction, adequate means to egress, exit markings and illumination, and emergency power. They are stressed in the Life Safety Code.
9. The early detection and suppression of fire plus fire-resistive construction will play major roles if patients cannot be moved and must be "defended in place."

Disasters

In addition to fire, a host of other disasters are an ever-present danger. Well-designed plans, training, and liaison with outside agencies will go a long way in reducing losses if disasters strike. JCAHO has requirements for disaster preparations.

An example of a disastrous situation is a strike by health-care workers. Associated losses are monumental: disruptions to patient care, loss of hospital income, intimidation of staff, property damage, and unfavorable publicity. Countermeasures can include formation of a strike planning committee, additional security, and enlisting the assistance of nonstriking employees and volunteers. If more than one union is at the location, management should strive for separate contract expiration dates. The preparation prior to the strike will have a definite bearing on management-union negotiations.

BANKS AND FINANCIAL INSTITUTIONS

There are thousands of financial depository institutions and branches in the United States. Money, securities, travelers checks, and other liquid assets make this industry attractive to internal and external culprits. *The range of offenses spans embezzlement and computer, credit, and loan frauds. These crimes result in greater losses while being more difficult to detect and solve than bank robbery and burglary.* Services that present particular loss problems are automated teller machines (ATM), after-hours depositories (AHD), and electronic fund transfer systems (EFTS). Personnel servicing ATMs and customers have been victimized by armed robbers. AHDs also present a robbery problem, such as when a retailer makes a deposit at the end of the business day. Banks have incurred losses from fraud during the transfer of funds. Sophisticated wiretaps on a bank's funds transfer line are an ominous reality.

Fraud and embezzlement are the more serious threats to banks and financial institutions. FBI statistics on bank fraud and embezzlement are based on reported offenses. Experts view these statistics as only the tip of the iceberg, because many crimes go unreported to avoid bad publicity.

The Bank Protection Act of 1968

An increase in crimes against banks and the lack of adequate countermeasures led Congress to enact the Bank Protection Act (BPA), which became effective in January 1969. It applies to all financial institutions chartered by the federal government, or that are members of the Federal Reserve System, or whose deposits are insured by either the Federal Deposit Insurance Corporation or the Federal Savings and Loan Insurance Corporation. The BPA establishes minimum standards to combat robbery, burglary, and larceny. Several federal agencies are responsible for the enforcement of these standards: the Comptroller of the Currency, the Federal Reserve System Board, the Federal Home Loan Board, and the Federal Deposit Insurance Corporation. During

1973, the BPA was amended to improve the minimum standards for security devices.

Even though the BPA was designed to counter losses from outsiders, a significant shortcoming of this legislation is that it does not establish standards for internal protection. For example, the savings and loan (S&L) scandal of the 1980s and 1990s, where bank executives approved risky loans to friends and so on (i.e., "the fox was guarding the hen house"), cost U.S. taxpayers billions of dollars (much more than bank robberies). Despite these drawbacks, the BPA was the first legislation reinforcing security for a large private commercial enterprise. It is impossible to ascertain the number of crimes that have been prevented because of the BPA.

Some of the original BPA minimum standards are summarized as follows:

1. The financial institution shall appoint an employee to be responsible for the planning and development of a security program that equals or exceeds BPA standards. This position also entails the installation, maintenance, and operation of security devices.
2. Security devices shall include a lighting system, tamper-resistant locks, alarm systems for robbery and burglary, and a photographic surveillance system that is silent and capable of reproducing images of offenders.
3. Walk-up or drive-in teller's windows should be protected by bullet-resistant glass and other features.
4. Vaults, safes, ATMs, and AHDs must meet certain specifications.
5. Procedures include a record of inspections, testing, and servicing of devices; currency to be kept at a minimum; "bait" money at each station; safe and cautious procedures during opening and closing of the premises; security training; and the filing of reports to a regulatory agency. (An excellent source for training and publications is the *American Bankers Association*, 1120 Connecticut Ave. NW, Washington, DC 20036; Tel.: 1-800-338-0626).

What are your views as to why the BPA of 1968 focused on external threats (e.g., robbery) rather than internal threats (e.g., white-collar crime, fraud)?

Congress revised the BPA in 1991, which resulted in a shift from security devices to administration and procedural aspects of security. A designated bank security officer reporting to the bank board of directors established more specific lines of authority and responsibility. An emphasis was also placed on a written security program and training. With Appendix A (physical security specifications) deleted from the original legislation, bank security officers are afforded more discretion in choosing "state-of-the-art" security; however, the possibility of liability for inadequate security remains.[30]

Other Legislation Affecting Banking

The *Bank Secrecy Act* was implemented in 1986 to establish reporting requirements for transactions of money to detect money laundering. In 1988, the *Anti-Drug Abuse Act* amended the Bank Secrecy Act and requires banks to report any "suspicious transactions" that may be associated with illegal drug trafficking. *The Antiterrorism and Effective Death Penalty Act of 1996* makes it a criminal offense for persons in the United States, other than those excepted by the government, to engage in financial transactions with countries that condone or encourage terrorism.

Because of so much reporting on financial transactions required by the federal government, some in the financial industry have questioned its value. To answer this question, the Internal Revenue Service, Criminal Investigation Division, reports that it initiated 954 investigations during fiscal years 1994, 1995, and 1996, as a result of such reporting; and this total does not include the number of reports from the financial industry that assisted ongoing investigations. An example of how reporting assists law enforcement is the case of a banker who alerted the IRS to suspicious currency deposits that resulted in a car dealership being charged with laundering drug money. The dealership allegedly sold vehicles for cash to drug dealers and the cash was divided into smaller amounts for deposit in banks to circumvent the $10,000 threshold for reporting by banks.[31]

Robbery

A common feature of many financial locations is the warmer, more personal atmosphere through the elimination of security barriers. Although this may please customers, robbery becomes a greater threat. When a robbery does take place at a bank, the teller is often the only one initially knowledgeable about the crime. The situation of a lone robber passing a holdup note to the teller is typical. In any robbery situation, the danger to life must not be taken lightly. The following suggestions can improve employee reaction:

1. Institute a training program.
2. During a robbery, act cautiously and do not take any chances.
3. Activate an alarm if possible without the robber noticing.

4. Provide the robber with bait money. Tear-gas or dye packs also are important. These devices look like packs of currency and emit tear gas and red smoke (that stains clothes and the money) when carried out of a bank. A radio transmitter activates the packet.
5. Study characteristics of the bandit, especially scars, shape of eyes, height, body structure, voice, speech patterns, and other permanent features.
6. Safely note the means of transportation, license number, and vehicle description.
7. Telephone the public police.

Kidnapping and Extortion

A common victim of a kidnapper or extortionist is the financial executive and his or her family. However, a bank teller is another likely victim. These crimes vary; two scenarios follow. An offender kidnaps a bank employee or family member while he or she is driving the family car or is at home. The kidnapped person is traded for cash. Another approach is when an extortionist calls a bank employee at work, claims to be holding a family member, and demands cash for a safe return of the kidnapped victim. The extortionist may even confront the bank employee personally. In these situations, violence is a potential hazard, even after cash is delivered.

A precise plan and employee training are essential prior to a confrontation. The following procedures should be observed by the person in contact with the kidnappers. Try to remain calm during the ordeal. If a hostage is involved, ask the caller to allow the hostage to come to the telephone to speak. Repeat demands to the caller to double-check any directions and procedures. Try to arrange for a person-to-person payoff and transfer of the hostage. If prepared, trace the call. After the call, record as much information as possible (e.g., date,, time, words spoken, background noises). Management should provide a standard form. Call the FBI and local police. If the hostage is brought to the bank or if the offender confronts a bank employee personally, notify other employees with a prearranged signal. Include "bait" money in any payoff.

Security at the residences of employees can prevent these criminal acts. Because most insurance companies feel that they are not liable for kidnap or extortion claims, unless otherwise agreed on, comprehensive plans and training are of the utmost importance.

Embezzlement and Fraud

There are numerous methods of embezzlement and fraud. Because computerization is a major characteristic of modern banking, loss susceptibility is compounded. The weaknesses of computer operations were illustrated in the previous chapter.

Several techniques of embezzlement are unique to the financial industry. An employee may tap a dormant account. This can be controlled by programming an alarm into the computer and requiring dual approval when a withdrawal is made from these accounts. Another form of embezzlement deals with the fractions of interest on depositors' saving accounts. There have been cases in which bank employees have programmed a computer to divert fractions of cents to a specific account to build a substantial amount. Loan officers are capable of approving loans to unqualified applicants for a bribe or embezzling funds by approving fictitious loans. Many of these misdeeds are foiled via good operating controls.

Check swindles, which are a common externally perpetrated fraud, may involve the forgery of stolen checks or the manufacture of fictitious checks.

Job applicant screening is a key countermeasure to prevent internal crimes. Bonding companies require specific screening procedures. Training, auditing, and follow-up of customer complaints are additional strategies.

Automatic Teller Machines

Crime has followed ATM self-service banking. Such crime is likely to increase as the number of ATMs also increases, and there is concern for safety and liability. Several state and local government bodies have passed ATM safety laws. These bills typically require surveillance cameras, adequate lighting, mirrors and low hedges to enhance visibility, and crime prevention tips to ATM card holders. As well as robbery, fraud is a problem. Although offenders watch for careless customers who do not protect their PIN numbers, a considerable amount of ATM fraud is committed by a family member or friend. Although "smart cards" containing information on the customer, and biometrics, will increase security, offenders, as usual, will be searching for methods to circumvent newer systems.

Crime Follows Technology

The security challenges facing the financial industry today are much different from what they were when the original BPA was enacted. Robberies still are a dangerous threat requiring traditional security measures. In terms of financial risk, the genuine issues involve check fraud, liability for failing to provide a safe environment for employees and customers, wire transfers and other electronic means of moving money, the emerging technology that banks will be using to permit customers access to their accounts, and a host of financial services through telebanking, the Internet, and other on-line computer services.[32]

GOVERNMENT INSTITUTIONS

In 1994, a Maryland trucker crashed a stolen plane on the White House lawn. One month later, an ex-con fired 29 rounds at the building. And then, in 1995, the devastating bombing occurred at the Alfred P. Murrah Federal Building in Oklahoma City. These incidents, especially the bombing, led President Clinton to direct the U.S. Department of Justice to assess the vulnerability of federal office buildings in the United States. Prior to the study and publication, *Vulnerability Assessment of Federal Facilities*, there were no governmentwide standards for security at federal facilities and no central database of the security in place at such facilities. Because of its expertise in court security, the U.S. Marshals Service coordinated the study that focused on the approximately 1330 federal office buildings housing about 750,000 federal civilian employees. One major result of the study was the development of 52 standards focusing on perimeter security, entry security, interior security, and security planning. Another result of the study was the division of federal buildings into five security levels, based on staffing size, use, and the need for public access. A Level I building has ten or fewer federal employees and is a "storefront" type of operation, such as a military recruiting office. A Level V building is critical to national security, such as the Pentagon. Recommended minimum security standards apply to each security level.[33]

The process of implementing the standards is being overseen by the Interagency Security Committee, established by presidential executive order, and the General Services Administration (GSA), the government's buildings manager. The GSA has approved thousands of security recommendations from building security committees, with a price tag of hundreds of millions of dollars.[34] State and local government institutions also are involved in security efforts to protect government buildings.

Do you think improved security at government buildings will increase protection? What types of crimes and what criminal methods do you think will follow the "target hardening" at government buildings?

As we know, military and nuclear weapons facilities are examples of government locations that have been involved in security programs for years. Another aspect of government with a history of security efforts is the criminal justice system. Jails and prisons have traditionally maintained tight security for obvious reasons. Police agencies, especially following the

Figure 17–1   Courthouse screening; walk-through metal detector, left; X-ray scanner, right. Courtesy of Wackenhut Corporation. Photo by Ed Burns.

unrest of the 1960s, have strengthened security in and around police buildings, including communications centers, evidence and weapons storage rooms, and crime labs. Following violence in the judicial system, courts have also increased security (see Figure 17–1). Because of the Sixth Amendment right of defendants to a public trial, court security is especially challenging. The U.S. Marshals Service has taken a leading role in developing court security methods. Each major component of the criminal justice system—police, courts, and corrections—is connected with organizations that promote either accreditation or performance measures containing security enhancements.[35]

CASE PROBLEMS

17A. Select two types of institutions explained in this chapter, and describe why the ones you chose are unique in terms of loss problems and prevention strategies.

17B. Choose two types of institutions from this chapter. For each, establish a priority list of the five most important measures to counter losses. Explain the reasoning behind each ranked list.

17C. Select two institutions mentioned in this chapter. (1) Refer to additional sources to gather further information, and (2) explain why you would prefer to work in one over the other. Maintain a bibliography.

17D. What do you think is the most demanding of the locations discussed in this chapter for a loss prevention manager? Justify your answer.

NOTES

1. Leigh Gaines, "People Power Battles Campus Crime," *Security* (August 1989): 44.
2. Office of Juvenile Justice and Delinquency Prevention, *Reducing Youth Gun Violence: An Overview of Programs and Initiatives* (Washington, DC: U.S. Department of Justice, May 1996), p. i.
3. National Institute of Justice, *Weapon-Related Victimization in Selected Inner-City High School Samples, Update* (Washington, DC: U.S. Department of Justice, January 1995), p. 1.
4. Hunter Hurst, "Juvenile Offenders and Victims," *Today's Youth* (Spring 1995): 1.
5. "School-Associated Deaths Top 50 Per Year in US," *Security Concepts* (July 1996): 2.
6. Office of Juvenile Justice and Delinquency Prevention, *Reducing Youth Gun Violence,* p. 35.
7. National Institute of Justice, *Evaluation of Violence Prevention Programs in Middle Schools* (Washington, DC: U.S. Department of Justice, September 1995), p. 1.
8. Gayle Cohen, "A False Sense of Security," *U. Magazine* (May 18–19, 1994).
9. Philip Purpura, *Criminal Justice: An Introduction* (Boston: Butterworth–Heinemann, 1997), pp. 32–36.
10. "O'Toole-Zalud Report," *Security* (January 1996): 62.
11. Brian A. Reaves and Andrew L. Goldberg, *Campus Law Enforcement Agencies, 1995* (Washington, DC: Bureau of Justice Statistics, December 1996), pp. iii–v.
12. Bonnie S. Fisher and John J. Sloan, "University Response to the Campus Security Act of 1990: Evaluating Programs Designed to Reduce Campus Crime," *Journal of Security Administration* 16 (1993): 67–77.
13. "How Yale Seeks to Reduce Crime by Investing in Surrounding Community," *Campus Security Report* (October 1994): 1–3.
14. Alan B. Jenkins, "Campus Community Oriented Policing and Problem Solving," *Campus Law Enforcement Journal* (March–April 1997): 25–31.
15. Gordon P. McKinnon, editor, *Fire Protection Handbook*, 14th ed. (Boston: National Fire Protection Association, 1977), pp. 8–22.
16. Percy Bugbee, *Principles of Fire Protection* (Boston: National Fire Protection Association, 1978), p. 41.
17. Lawrence J. Fennelly, editor, *Handbook of Loss Prevention and Crime Prevention*, 2nd ed. (Stoneham, MA: Butterworths Pub., 1989), p. 571.
18. U.S. Department of Commerce, *Crime in Service Industries* (Washington, DC: U.S. Government Printing Office, 1977), p. 66.
19. Skip Estrella, "Diagnosing Crime Trends," *Security Management* (May 1989): 80.

20. Russell L. Colling, *Hospital Security* (Boston: Butterworth–Heinemann, 1977), p. 345.
21. "Security Spotlight," *Security Management, Plant and Property Protection* (January 10, 1981): 3.
22. OSHA, *Guidelines for Preventing Workplace Violence for Health Care and Social Service Workers* (Washington, DC: U.S. Department of Labor, 1996), p. 1.
23. P. J. Cannon, "Children's Hospitals: Hotbeds of Emotion for Broken Families," *Access Control* (September 1996): 42–48.
24. OSHA, *Guidelines for Preventing Workplace Violence,* p. v.
25. Ibid., pp. 1–9.
26. "Pressure Needed to Improve Security and Privacy of Electronic Health," *Business and Facility Concepts* (April 1997): 21–22.
27. Bruce Morgan, "Developing a Security Management Plan," *FacilityCare* (February 1997): 10–11.
28. Russell L. Colling, *Security: Keeping The Health Care Environment Safe* (Oakbrook Terrace, IL: JCAHO, 1996), pp. 34–36.
29. Albert L. de Richemond, "Fires in Hospitals," *Speaking of Fire* (Winter 1996): 22–23.
30. Bill Clark, "Much Ado About Nothing?" *Security Management* (January 1993): 66–68.
31. Dennis Crawford, "Reports Really Do Help Law Enforcement," *Bank Security & Fraud Prevention* (March 1997): 9–10.
32. Edward McDonough and Linda Mikitarian, "Financial Institution Security," in Lawrence Fennelly, ed., *Handbook of Loss Prevention and Crime Prevention*, 3rd ed. (Boston: Butterworth–Heinemann, 1996), p. 454.
33. U.S. Department of Justice, *Vulnerability Assessment of Federal Facilities* (Washington, DC: U.S. Marshals Service, June 28, 1995).
34. "Federal Facility Update," *Security Management* (June 1996): 16.
35. Purpura, *Criminal Justice,* pp. 254–257.

18

Topics of Concern

OBJECTIVES

After studying this chapter the reader will be able to

1. List the methods by which an adversary might obtain sensitive information and list countermeasures;
2. Discuss communications security;
3. Describe the problem of terrorism and list countermeasures;
4. List strategies for executive protection;
5. Describe the problems and remedies associated with substance abuse;
6. Discuss the problem of violence in the workplace and what can be done about it.

This chapter concentrates on six topics of concern for loss prevention practitioners: (1) protection of sensitive information, (2) communications security, (3) terrorism, (4) executive protection, (5) substance abuse, and (6) workplace violence.

PROTECTION OF SENSITIVE INFORMATION

Sensitive information, defined to its broadest degree, is proprietary information that, if obtained by an unauthorized person, destroyed in a disaster, or lost, can cause harm to an organization. The information often is extremely valuable (e.g., a secret formula) and may represent the lifeblood of a company. Subsequent pages emphasize espionage and countermeasures. Previous sections of this book elaborate on security and fire protection for valuables. Also, we must not forget that information pertaining to the privacy of individuals requires protection. This would include credit, medical, educational, and other records protected under various laws.

Common types of sensitive information that might be obtained by a spy are the following: product design, financial reports, engineering data, tax records, secret formulas, marketing strategies, cost reduction methods, mailing lists, research data, client or customer information, trade secrets, personnel records, patent information, computer programs, oil or mineral exploration maps, loss prevention strategies, mergers, and contract information.

A *trade secret*, supposedly known only to certain individuals, is a secret process that is used to produce a salable product. It may involve a series of steps or special ingredients. A famous trade secret is the formula for Coca-Cola. The holder of a trade secret must take steps to maintain secrecy from competitors. If an employee were to reveal a trade secret to a competitor, the courts could issue an injunction, prohibiting the competitor from using the secret. Money damages might be awarded.

A *patent* provides protection for an invention or design. If the device is duplicated by a competitor, patent laws are likely to be violated and litigation would follow. Competitors often engineer around patents.

A *trademark* includes words, symbols, logos, designs, or slogans that identify products or services as coming from a common source. McDonald's® golden arches serve as an example.

Copyright provides protection for original works by giving the creator or publisher exclusive rights to the work. This type of protection covers books, magazines, musical scores, movies, and computer software programs.

Corporate Intelligence Gathering: Putting It in Perspective

Corporate intelligence involves gathering information about competitors. It ranges from the illegal activity of industrial espionage to the acceptable, universally applied, practice of utilizing salespeople to monitor public business practices of other companies. Corporate intelligence gathering makes good business sense, and this is why companies such as General Electric, Digital Equipment, and Gillette have established formal intelligence programs. Because of unethical and illegal behavior by certain people and firms when gathering intelligence, the whole specialization has earned a bad reputation. But, many avenues for gathering intelligence are legal. Let us first list the reasons for corporate intelligence gathering:

- Executives should take advantage of information that is publicly available to fulfill their fiduciary duty to shareholders. Because the Cordis Corporation, a pacemaker manufacturer, for example, was unsure of why its new line did not show improved sales, it asked its salespeople to check the tactics of the competition. The salespeople found that physicians were being offered cars and boats to stay with the competition. When Cordis increased educational support for doctors, added more salespeople, and matched the giveaways, sales increased.
- Competitive intelligence is a basis for strategic planning. One intelligence seminar director found a competitor using a "dirty trick" by enrolling in his course under an assumed name.

- It is necessary, in order to be successful against global competitors. The Japanese have "deployed armies of engineers and marketing specialists" to other countries. Likewise, U.S.-based firms have set up offices abroad to gather information.
- It can be useful for the introduction of a new product. Coors did extensive chemical analysis on Gallo's wine coolers and found that it could not compete on price.[1]

The *Society of Competitive Intelligence Professionals* (1700 Diagonal Rd., Suite 520, Alexandria, VA 22314; Tel.: 703-739-0696) views its vocation as an honorable profession with a code of ethics. A large part of the work focuses on research of public information and interviews with experts. The information explosion—computers, networks, data banks, and specialized publications—has enabled these professionals to find out almost anything they want about competitors.[2]

The following lists provide guidelines for information gathering. Ethical sources include

- Published material and public documents such as court records;
- Disclosures made by competitor's employees and obtained without subterfuge;
- Market surveys and consultant's reports;
- Financial reports and broker's research reports;
- Trade fairs, exhibits, and competitor's brochures;
- Analysis of a competitor's products;
- Legitimate employment interviews with people who worked for a competitor.

Arguably unethical sources include

- Camouflaged questioning and "drawing out" of a competitor's employees at a technical meeting;
- Direct observation under secret conditions;
- False job interviews with a competitor's employees (i.e., where there is no real intent to hire);
- Hiring a professional investigator to obtain a specific piece of information.

Illegal sources include

- Trespassing on a competitor's property;
- Bribing a competitor's supplier or employee;
- "Planting" your agent on the competitor's payroll;
- Eavesdropping on competitors;
- Theft of drawings, samples, documents, and similar property;
- Blackmail and extortion.[3]

Espionage Techniques

The techniques used by adversaries to acquire sensitive information are so varied that defenders must not fall into the trap of emphasizing certain countermeasures while leaving the "backdoor open." For example, a company may spend hundreds of thousands of dollars defending against electronic surveillance and wiretapping while not realizing that most of the loss of sensitive information from this company results from a few employees who are really spies for competitors.

Defenders against espionage must not fall into the trap of emphasizing certain countermeasures while leaving the "backdoor open."

Three patterns of illegally acquiring sensitive information, also referred to as *espionage* or *spying*, are internal, external, and a conspiracy that combines the two. An *internal attack* can be perpetrated by an employee who sells a secret formula to a competitor, for example. An *external attack* occurs when an outsider gains unauthorized access to the premises and steals product design data. The *combined conspiracy* is seen when an employee "just happens" to leave a secret mailing list on a desk and unlocks a rear door to aid an intruder.[4]

Various techniques are used by spies as seen in the nearby list. A spy might assemble trash, from a company and an executive's home, to "piece together" information. Spies may claim they are conducting a survey, as a "pretext" to acquire information. Several spies may each ask certain questions only, and then later, assemble the "big picture." A key employee might be tricked into being discovered in a compromising position (e.g., in bed with a prostitute), be photographed, and then blackmailed for information. A spy might frequent a tavern or conference populated by engineers to listen to conversations. A spy might attempt to gain employment at a target company. Sometimes, proposals for a merger, acquisition, or joint venture are used as a cover to obtain information. Salespeople, to make a sale, are known to supply excesses of information in an attempt to impress a customer. Sources of data leaks include company speeches, publications, trade meetings, disgruntled employees, and consultants. Wiretapping and planting electronic listening devices are other methods. "Reverse engineering" is a legal avenue to obtain a look at a competitor's product. The competitor simply purchases the product and dismantles it to understand the components. Patent applications, which are available to the public, can reveal valuable information. Some companies deliberately patent their failures to lead competitors astray.

The *Business Espionage Controls and Countermeasures Association* (BECCA, Inc., PO Box 260, Ft. Washington, MD 20749; Tel.: 301-292-6430) is a professional society whose aim is "to make life as difficult and dangerous as possible for the espionage practitioner." In their *Business Espionage Report*, which highlights methods used by spies, the association noted the interception of digital telephones, pagers, teleconferencing systems, and wireless telephone headsets.[5]

Even a home computer can become a listening device. A system with a voice-data modem on the computer and a duplex speaker can be accessed by activating the modem and speaker phone. For those communicating with others on the Internet and sharing ideas, this creates a database from which a "profile" can be established. Search programs are available that quickly sift through data to produce the profile, and because the writings were posted for thousands of people to read, it would be difficult to convince a court that it was private.[6]

A good spy does not get caught, and quite often the victimized firm does not discover that it has been subjected to espionage. If the discovery is made, the company typically keeps it secret to avoid adverse publicity.

Espionage is a pervasive problem. It may take place between small, highly competitive businesses in the same city, large multinational corporations, or countries. In the *Annual Report to Congress on Foreign Economic Collection and Industrial Espionage*, a report submitted by the president to Congress, it was noted that at least 12 countries actively target U.S. proprietary information and critical technologies, and another 26 countries are involved in related suspicious incidents.[7] The obvious objectives are self-improvement and superiority—a driving force behind all businesses and governments.

Research sponsored by the American Society for Industrial Security, published as *Trends in Intellectual Property Loss*, showed an increase in reported incidents of intellectual property loss, which costs billions of dollars each year. It was noted that insiders (e.g., employees, contractors) were involved in 74 percent of the reported incidents. Foreign nationals were identified in 21 percent of the incidents, with the top five being Chinese, Canadian, French, Indian, and Japanese. The research revealed that only 76 percent of reporting companies had a formal safeguarding proprietary information (SPI) program.[8]

Countermeasures

The first step in keeping sensitive information secure is to identify and classify it according to its value. The top-level executives in a business should perform this subjective job. If a company has a DOD contract, then strict DOD criteria would apply. Each classification has rules for marking, handling, transmitting, storing, and access. The higher the classification the greater are the controls. See Table 18–1 for sample classifications, explanations, and illustrations.

Here is a list of countermeasures:

1. *Prevention* is a key strategy to protect sensitive information, which can be stolen without anything being physically missing, and this valuable corporate asset often is not covered by insurance.
2. Establish formal SPI policies and procedures. Examples include security over passwords, maintaining a "clean desk" policy so important items are not left in the open when they should be in a locked container, and restricting the release of information on a "need-to-know" basis.
3. Provide training and awareness programs for employees, especially on methods used by spies, such as "pretext" interviews.
4. Reinforce SPI programs through new employee orientation, employee handbook, and performance evaluations.
5. Carefully screen employment applicants.
6. Use employee nondisclosure agreements and employee noncompete agreements.

Table 18–1   Classification Systems

	If Unauthorized Disclosure	*Illustrations*
Government Classification[a]		
Top Secret	"Exceptionally grave damage" to national security	Vital national defense plans, new weapons, sensitive intelligence operations
Secret	"Serious damage" to national security	Significant military plans or intelligence operations
Confidential	"Identifiable damage" to national security	Strength of forces, munitions performance characteristics
Corporation Classification		
Special Controls	Survival at stake	New process or product; secret formula or recipe
Company Confidential	Serious damage	Process, customer lists; depends on value to business
Private Confidential	Identifiable damage, or could cause problems	Personnel data, price quote

[a] Classified by the U.S. Department of Defense in *National Industrial Security Program Operating Manual* (Washington, DC: U.S. Government Printing Office, January 1995).

7. Implement physical security and access controls for people and property entering, leaving, and circulating within a facility (see Figure 18–1).
8. Secure sensitive items.
9. Review works written by employees prior to publication and their speeches, ensure protection during trade shows, and control media relations.
10. Control destruction of sensitive materials.
11. Maintain state-of-the-art computer security. Protect all forms of electronic communication—e-mail, network, faxes, telephone, etc.
12. Use technical surveillance countermeasures (TSCM).
13. Use internal and independent security audits to strengthen protection.[9]

Destruction of Sensitive Materials

Records and documents that are simply thrown into trash bins, when appropriate, enable spies to retrieve information. The total destruction of records will impede this espionage technique. Before pollution restrictions against burning, many firms placed unwanted records in incinerators. Today, *strip-cut shredders* (producing long strips of paper $^1/_4$-inch wide) are used by

Figure 18-1 Sen Trac ID® uses radio-frequency identification technology to provide hands-free access control and asset management to track people and products within a facility. Courtesy: Sensormatic.

many organizations. However, security is limited. This became painfully evident in 1979, when Iranian militants stormed the U.S. Embassy in Tehran and pieced together top secret documents that had been shredded by a strip-cut shredder. For increased security, *particle-cut shredders* (smaller pieces of paper) are the alternative. *Cross-cut shredders* offer even higher security and are suitable for DOD classified data. The highest level of security is offered by *disintegrators*. These devices produce confetti particles through the action of rotor and stationary knives. Disintegrators are growing in popularity because users can destroy magnetic tape, microfiche, floppy disks, printed circuit boards, and so forth. Since the Iranian disaster, the U.S. government requires classified data to be destroyed with either a cross-cut shredder or a disintegrator.[10]

COMMUNICATIONS SECURITY

Communications security involves defenses against interception. In providing a comprehensive approach to protecting sensitive information, subfields of communications security are listed here.

- *Line security* protects communications lines of computer systems, such as a central computer and remote terminals. Line security is effective over lines an organization controls; a wiretap can occur in many locations of a line. Cryptographic security defeats wiretapping.
- *Transmission security* involves communications procedures that afford minimal advantage to an adversary bent on intercepting data communications from computer systems, telephones, radio, and other systems.
- *Emanation security* prevents undesired signal data emanations (e.g., from computer equipment) transmitted without wires (e.g., electromagnetic or acoustic) that could be intercepted by an adversary. TEMPEST is the code word used by the National Security Agency for the science of eliminating undesired signal data emanations. "Shielding," discussed soon, is one strategy to reduce data emanations.
- *Technical security*, also called *technical surveillance countermeasures*, provides defenses against the interception of data communications from microphones, transmitters, or wiretaps.[11]

These methods of attack can be used together, which is one reason why communications security is a highly complex field. What follows here primarily is technical security; however, *we must not lose sight of the importance of a comprehensive approach to protecting sensitive information.* (The discussion of computer security in Chapter 16 also provides relevant protection strategies.)

Electronic Surveillance and Wiretapping

Electronic surveillance utilizes electronic devices to covertly listen to conversations, whereas *wiretapping* pertains to the interception of telephone communications. The prevalence of these often illegal activities probably is greater than one would expect. (The legality of such acts is supported by court orders.) Because detection is so difficult, the exact extent of electronic surveillance and wiretapping and what this theft of information costs businesses is impossible to gauge.

Electronic eavesdropping technology is highly developed to the point where countermeasures (debugging) have not kept up with the art of bugging. Consequently, only the most expertly trained and experienced specialist can counter this threat.

Surveillance equipment is easy to obtain. An electronically inclined person can simply enter a local electronics store and buy all the materials necessary to make a sophisticated bug. Prebuilt models are available by mail, or certain retailers will sell them if the buyer signs a statement not to use them for audio surveillance. Retail electronics stores sell FM transmitters or microphones that transmit sound without wires to an ordinary FM radio. Sound is broadcast over a radio several feet away after tuning to the right frequency. These FM transmitters are advertised to be used by public speakers who walk around as they talk and favor wireless microphones; the voice is transmitted and then broadcast over large speakers. They are also advertised to listen in on a baby from another room.

Miniaturization has greatly aided spying. With the advance of the microchip, transmitters are apt to be so small that these devices can be enmeshed in thick paper, as in a calendar, under a stamp, or within a nail in a wall. Bugs may be planted as a building is under construction, or a person may receive one hidden in a present or other item. Transmitters are capable of being operated by solar power (i.e., daylight) or local radio broadcast.

Bugging techniques are varied. Information from a microphone can be transmitted via a "wire run" or a radio transmitter. Bugs are concealed in a variety of objects or carried on a person. Transmitting devices can be remotely controlled with a radio signal for turning them on and off. This makes detection difficult. A device known as a carrier current transmitter is placed in wall plugs, light switches, or other electrically operated components. It obtains its power from the AC wire to which it is attached.

Telephones are especially vulnerable. A "tap" occurs when a telephone conversation is intercepted. Telephone lines are available in so many places that taps are difficult to detect. A tap can be direct or wireless. With a direct tap, a pair of wires is spliced to the telephone line and then connected to a tape recorder. An FM transmitter, similar to a room bug, is employed for a wireless tap. The transmitter is connected to the line and then a receiver and tape recorder are concealed nearby. Wireless taps (and room bugs) are spotted by using special equipment. Direct taps are difficult to locate. A check of the entire line is necessary. The wireless tap is safer for the spy because, with the direct tap, investigators can follow the wires to the culprit. *Because telephone traffic travels over space radio in several modes—for example, cellular, microwave, and satellite—the spy's job is made much easier and safer since no on-premises tap is required. What is required is the proper equipment for each mode.*

Another technique transforms the telephone into a listening device whether it is in use or not. A technique known as a "hookswitch bypass" short circuits (by changing wires) the telephone hookswitch (the switch that disconnects the microphone in the mouthpiece to the outside when a person hangs up) and transforms the ordinary telephone into a bug. This is easy to detect by hanging up the telephone, placing a radio nearby (for noise), tapping into the telephone line, and listening for the radio.

Many spies use a dual system. One bug is placed so that it will be found, which in many instances satisfies security and management. A second bug is more cleverly concealed.

When guarding against electronic surveillance and wiretapping, we must not forget about other methods of surveillance such as visual observation. If drawings or designs are on walls or in sight through windows, sensitive information can be lost. A spy, for example, stationed in another skyscraper a few blocks away might use a telescope to obtain secret data. Or, a window washer might appear at a window for surveillance. Another method is for a spy disguised as a janitor to be assigned to the particular site. Furthermore, a device (e.g., a camera with a pinhole lens) can be concealed in a wall or ceiling. All of these techniques by no means exhaust the skills of spies.[12]

Countermeasures

The physical characteristics of a building have a bearing on opportunities for audio surveillance. Some of these factors are poor access control designs, inadequate soundproofing, common or shared ducts, and space above false ceilings enabling access. Physical security methods and inspections of these weak areas will hinder penetrations.

With a broad-based knowledge of adverse construction characteristics and the many techniques of surveillance, the countermeasures expert is better prepared to defeat a spy. *Only the most expertly trained and experienced specialist can counter this threat.* Large companies are able to afford an in-house practitioner, whereas smaller firms have to recruit an outsider. Associated equipment is expensive.

In-house Expert

A candidate for in-house expert should have a background in electronics, especially transmission systems. Check education, training, and professional membership. Asking the applicant what periodicals he or she reads can help satisfy the interviewer that the applicant has necessary state-of-the-art knowledge of techniques and equipment. The person hired most likely will work unusual hours, as well as travel to specific sites. Sweeps commonly are made after hours to avoid suspicion, lowering morale, or disrupting daily business operations.

Consultant

If a countermeasure specialist is recruited from the outside, several questions are appropriate. What is the background of the consultant? Ask for copies of certificates of TSCM courses completed and a copy of the insurance policy for errors and omissions for TSCM services. What equipment is used? What techniques are employed for the cost? Are sweeps and meticulous physical inspections conducted for the quoted price? Watch for scare tactics. Is the consultant really a vendor trying to sell audio surveillance detection devices? Will the consultant protect confidentiality? The interviewer should request a review of past reports to clients. Were names deleted to protect confidentiality? These questions help to avoid hiring the unqualified "expert." One practitioner offered clients debugging services and used an expensive piece of equipment to conduct sweeps. After several years and hundreds of sweeps, he decided to have the equipment serviced. A service person discovered that the device was not working because it had no battery. The surprised "expert" never realized a battery was needed.

For a comprehensive countermeasures program, the competent consultant will be interested in sensitive information flow, storage, and retrieval. Extra cost will result from such an analysis, but it is often cost effective. *The employer should use an outside public telephone to contact the consultant in order not to alert a spy to impending countermeasures.*

Equipment

Detection equipment is expensive. A firm should purchase its own equipment only if it is cost effective and many sweeps will be conducted. According to one genuine TSCM specialist, a professional team will have at least $50,000 of equipment with, at a minimum, a spectrum analyzer capable of reading a minimum of 3 GHz, a wideband receiver, an electromagnetic field detector, an analyzer for receiving microwave transmittances, a telephone analyzer, and equipment to recognize laser transmittances.[13]

Some security personnel or executives plant a bug for the sole purpose of determining if the detection specialist and his or her equipment are effective. This "test" can be construed as a criminal offense. An alternative is specially designed test transmitters, commercially available, that have no microphone pickup and therefore can be used without liability. Another technique is to place a tape recorder with a microphone in a drawer.

A tool kit and standard forms are two additional aids for the countermeasures specialist. The tool kit consists of the common tools (e.g., screwdrivers, pliers, electrical tape) used by an electrician. Standard forms facilitate good record keeping and serve as a checklist. What was checked? What tests were performed? What were the readings? Where? When? Who performed the tests? Why were the tests conducted? Over a period of time, records can be used to make comparisons while helping to answer questions.

Another strategy to thwart listening devices is "shielding," also called *electronic soundproofing*. Basically, copper foil or screening and carbon filament are applied throughout a room to prevent acoustical or electromagnetic emanations from leaving. Although very expensive (over $100,000), several organizations employ this method to have at least one secure room or to protect information in computers.

Equipment is available on the market that *may* frustrate telephone taps and listening devices. Scramblers, attached to telephones, alter the voice as it travels through the line. But no device or system is foolproof. Often, simple countermeasures are useful. For instance, an executive can wait until everybody is present for an important meeting, and then relocate it to a previously undisclosed location. Conversants can operate a radio at high volume during sensitive conversations, and exercise caution during telephone and other conversations.

The collection of sensitive information does not stop with a bug or wiretapping. *Comprehensive defenses are necessary.* Information can be obtained with the assistance of a tape recorder, binoculars, telescope, camera, and telephoto lens. Laser-enhanced photography is another technological advance in the arsenal of the spy. Also, spies may access computer systems or facsimile or other transmissions.

Counterintelligence

Another avenue to protect sensitive information is *counterintelligence*, which is a broad term referring to activities that identify and counter threats by adversaries. The military and police agencies engage in counterintelligence activities. Examples include investigative and research units that collect and analyze intelligence on adversaries, internal awareness programs, and misinformation directed at adversaries. Although businesses have a different mission than the military and police, certain counterintelligence techniques, within legal guidelines, can be implemented by businesses.

Economic Espionage Act of 1996

Because intellectual property assets are often more valuable to businesses than tangible assets, Congress passed the Economic Espionage Act of 1996. This act makes it a federal crime for any person to convert a trade secret to his or her own benefit or the benefit of others with the intent or knowledge that the conversion will injure the owner of the trade secret. The penalties are up to ten years of imprisonment and a fine to $500,000. Corporations can be fined up to $5 million. If a foreign government benefits from such a crime, the penalties are even greater. The act defines *trade secret* broadly as information that the owner has taken "reasonable measures" to keep secret because of the economic value from it. The act raises two concerns for management:

- *Protecting trade secrets.* This would include a comprehensive SPI program (see the earlier discussion).
- *Hiring employees from competitors.* Employers may violate the act if they hire employees from other firms who may bring with them trade secrets.

Prevention includes a thorough interview of applicants, ascertaining whether the applicant signed contracts or agreements with others for the protection of sensitive information, and use of a company form that signifies that the new employee understands the act's legal requirements.[14]

The act also links the economic well-being of the nation to national security interests. And, it allows the FBI to investigate foreign intelligence services bent on acquiring sensitive information of U.S. companies. At some point, a company may have to decide whether to report a violation of the act to law enforcement authorities. The disadvantages are lost time and money, unwanted publicity, and the defendant's attorney may request secrets that may be revealed in court. Although the act offers some protection for proprietary information, this protection may depend on how a judge or attorneys in the case interpret the act. Discovery proceedings may result in information loss greater than the original loss. Also, the case may be lost in criminal and civil courts. Therefore, management must carefully weigh decisions on legal action. Another point to consider is that the act requires businesses to protect themselves from losses, which presents liability issues relevant to due diligence.[15] *Prevention is seen here, as with many other vulnerabilities, as the key avenue for protection.*

TERRORISM

There is general disagreement concerning how to define *terrorism*; many definitions exist.[16] This book defines *terrorism* as the use of aggressive strategies to produce fear, coercion, or violence for political, religious, or criminal ends. Terrorists often are highly trained and mobile. They are characterized by conducting surprise, violent attacks, usually to see maximum press coverage for their cause.

The numerous definitions of terrorism influence how it is measured and whether it is decreasing or increasing. Larry C. Johnson, who has a background with the U.S. Department of State and the CIA, argues that many government officials and private-sector experts view terrorism as increasing, which goes unchallenged because this view parallels public perception. He claims that careful analysis of CIA and FBI data shows terrorism, both domestic and international, is not on the rise and it was more deadly ten years ago. There were 665 international terrorist attacks in 1987 and 440 in 1995. The numbers are down because of toughening policies, sanctions against state-sponsored terrorism, increased FBI power to operate overseas with the CIA, and the breakup of the Soviet Union. He points to a decline in terrorism with a political agenda, as illustrated by the World Trade Center and Oklahoma City bombings, which were for revenge. Johnson notes that the availability of weapons of mass destruction could increase risk factors.[17]

A few major terrorist incidents can cause distorted perceptions of terrorism.

According to Stefan H. Leader, who works with the U.S. Department of Energy's security program, the lower numbers reflect narrow definitions of terrorism. Statistics gathered by Pinkerton Risk Assessment Services are based on a broader definition and show more incidents of terrorism than the Department of State. However, all sides agree that the business sector continues to be the leading target of terrorist attacks abroad.[18]

Countermeasures

When considering countermeasures against terrorism, first consider the methods used by terrorists, which go beyond bombings. The raw materials for both chemical and biological weapons can be purchased on the open or black markets. In 1991, a domestic extremist group manufactured the biological agent ricin and discussed using it against federal law enforcement officers. In 1995, a U.S. citizen illegally obtained three vials of bubonic plague from a Maryland firm before being arrested.[19] Terrorists might obtain or build a nuclear device or simply decide to wrap radioactive material around a conventional bomb. Ventilation systems of buildings are vulnerable avenues to disperse deadly substances. Product tampering is a form of terrorism that has resulted in deaths, injuries, fear, and serious economic harm to corporations.

The Internet is a source of information to build assorted weapons. Various groups publish manuals on tactics to be used to advance their cause. For example, some antiabortion activists have written a manual to close abortion clinics by squirting Superglue into the locks so the clinic cannot open, drilling holes in the low points of flat roofs, and placing a garden hose in mail slots at front doors.[20]

Strategies of terrorists include the postal system, telephone, e-mail, and computer systems. *CyberTerrorism* refers to the use of computer systems to commit terrorism. It is argued that the computer security and counterterrorism methods of today are no match against the CyberTerrorist, who may disrupt international financial transactions, enter air traffic control systems to cause aircraft crashes, or remotely alter the formulas of pharmaceutical firms to cause loss of life. Defenses include specialists who infiltrate and operate in the world of the CyberTerrorist.[21]

Here are some strategies against terrorism:

1. A British terrorism expert, Paul Wilkinson, stated, "Fighting terrorism is like a goalkeeper. You can make a hundred brilliant saves, but the only shot people remember is the one that gets past you."[22]
2. Government should increase intelligence efforts and infiltrate terrorist groups.
3. Maintain awareness of controversies that may increase exposure to terrorism.
4. Increase employee awareness of terrorism and terrorist methods and tricks.
5. Carefully consider leasing space in buildings occupied by multiple organizations.
6. Carefully plan access controls, glazing, other physical security, fire protection, and protection for utilities.
7. As enormous security expenditures "chase" terrorists away from their favorite targets, new targets will be attacked with innovative methods; security measures will "follow" the newer threats.

International Perspective:
How Is Terrorism Handled in Other Countries?

Several countries have had much more experience with terrorism than the United States because, up until the 1993 World Trade Center bombing and the 1995 Oklahoma City bombing, the United States has not been victimized like other countries. How have other countries fought terrorism?

During the 1970s, West Germany (before unification with East Germany) faced the Red Army Faction (RAF), which directed its terrorism toward "American imperialism." It carried out bombings, shooting, kidnappings, and bank robberies against U.S. and West German interests in West Germany. The West German government responded by passing laws that made it a crime to establish a terrorist organization. Police powers were also increased, such as providing police (with court approval) with the power to search entire apartment buildings for suspects. The police also could establish checkpoints on roads. They formed a crack antiterrorist unit and expanded their intelligence gathering. Initially, concessions were granted to the RAF when they took hostages; however, this prompted the RAF to take more hostages. The policy was reversed, deaths occurred, but hostage taking by the RAF declined. By the 1980s, the RAF threat was almost gone. In Italy, from the 1970s to the 1980s,

continued

the Red Brigade terrorists were known for "kneecapping," which is shooting victims in the legs to cripple them. The government responded by passing laws that made it a crime to promote violent overthrow of the government; increased police powers to stop, search, and detain suspects; and eased restrictions on wiretaps. One of the most successful tactics used by the government was to reduce the sentences of convicted terrorists if they volunteered information. Consequently, the Red Brigade began to collapse.[23]

The United Nations recommends the following to prevent and control terrorism:

1. Governments should exercise restraint, protect constitutional rights, and respect human rights.
2. Legislation should criminalize terrorism and prescribe severe penalties.
3. Government and the media should educate the public and keep it informed on ways to solve the problem.
4. Training is crucial for a professional police response.
5. Judicial groups and victims must be protected from reprisals, and the latter should receive compensation.
6. International cooperation should be promoted.[24]

EXECUTIVE PROTECTION

At home and abroad, businesses have become the target for kidnappings, extortion, assassinations, bombings, and sabotage. Terrorists use these methods to obtain money for their cause, to alter business or government policies, or to change public opinion. Organized crime groups also are participants in such criminal acts, but in contrast to terrorists, their objective almost always is money. Attacks against executives are common in Latin America, the Middle East, and Europe. But executives in the United States and other countries also have been subjected to terrorists. It appears that successful terrorist techniques employed in one country spread to other countries. This is likely to be one reason why companies are reluctant to release details of incidents or even to acknowledge terrorist occurrences. Coca-Cola, IT&T, Chase Manhattan, B. F. Goodrich, and other companies have experienced terrorist assaults in the past.

Planning

A key beginning for an executive protection program is to develop a crisis management plan and team. Considerable research and an awareness of many variables can improve the planning process. An interdisciplinary group, if cost effective, can greatly aid the program. The group could consist of top executives, the loss prevention manager, former federal agents, counterterrorism experts, political analysts, insurance specialists, and an attorney-negotiator.

The early stages of the plan, if not the preplanning stages, would be devoted to convincing upper management that executive protection is necessary. Resistance is sure to weaken upper management when terrorism incidents are exposed in the mass media. However, the loss prevention manager, in a well-prepared presentation to upper management, is the person responsible for explaining the cost effectiveness of executive protection. Subsequent budget allocations ideally will support protection efforts.

Early planning should clearly define areas of vulnerability and countermeasures. Which executives are possible targets? Where? When? Which are the indigenous terrorist groups? What are their methods? What are the social and political conditions in the particular country? What role has the specific government played in past terrorist incidents? Such questions require research and intelligence gathering as well as cooperative ties to government police agencies.

Planning consists of establishing policies and procedures in the event of a terrorist attack. Appropriate authority assigned to specific executives will help to coordinate both decision making and communications and could play a definite role in reducing losses. If a hostage were taken, precious time could be lost while the company coordinated a response team.

Education and Training

Depending on the extent of the executive protection program, many people can be brought into the education and training phase. Executives, their families, and loss prevention personnel (i.e., management, bodyguards, and uniformed officers) are top priorities. But chauffeurs, servants, gardeners, and office workers also should be knowledgeable about terrorist techniques and countermeasures that include prevention strategies, personal security, recognizing and reporting suspicious occurrences, the proper response to bomb threats or postal bombs, and skills such as defensive driving. Most in-house loss prevention personnel are not experts in dealing with executive protection. Therefore, a consultant may have to be recruited.

General Protection Strategies

Potential subjects of terrorists' interest should maintain a low profile and not broadcast their identity, affiliations, position, address, telephone number, net worth, or any information useful to enemies. Avoidance of publicity about future travel plans or social activities is wise. Those at risk should exercise care when communicating with others on the telephone or in restaurants and should dispose of sensitive information carefully.

Avoidance of Predictable Patterns

The famous Italian politician Aldo Moro, murdered in 1978, is a classic case of a creature of habit. Moro was extremely predictable. He would leave his home in the morning to attend mass at a nearby church. Shortly after 9:00 A.M. he was en route to his office. The route was the same each morning, even though plans existed for alternatives. Although Moro was guarded by five armed men, he met an unfortunate fate. An attack characterized by military precision enabled terrorists to block Moro's vehicle and a following police car. Then, on the narrow street, four gunmen hiding behind a hedge, opened fire. Eighty rounds hit the police car. Three policemen, Moro's driver, and a bodyguard were killed. Moro was dragged by his feet from the car. Almost two months later Moro was found dead in a car in Rome.

Recognition of Terrorist Tricks

A terrorist group may attempt to gain entry to an executive's residence or office under the pretext of repairing something or checking a utility meter. Repair people and government employees can be checked, before being admitted, by telephoning the employer. School authorities should be cautioned not to release an executive's child unless they telephone the executive's family to verify the caller.

Hiring bodyguards is a growth industry for the private sector. Bodyguards should be carefully screened and trained. Other employees (e.g., servants or gardeners) surrounding the executive likewise should be screened to hinder employment of those with evil motives.

Equipment appropriate for executive protection programs includes bullet-resistant vests and clothing, weapons, communications equipment, and armored vehicles. An executive personnel file should be stored in a secure location at the company's headquarters. If a kidnapping occurs, these data can be valuable. Appropriate for the file are vitae for the executive, family members, and associated employees; full names, past and present addresses and telephone numbers; photographs, fingerprints, voice tapes, and handwriting samples.

Protection at Home

A survey of the executive's home will uncover physical security weaknesses. Deficiencies are corrected through investing in access controls, proper illumination, intrusion alarms, CCTV, protective dogs, and uniformed officers. Burglary-resistant locks, doors, and windows hinder offenders. Consideration should be given to the response time of reinforcements. For a high-risk family, a "safe room" is an asset. This is a fortified room in the house that contains a strong door and other difficult-to-penetrate characteristics. A first-aid kit, rations, and a bathroom are useful amenities. A telephone, two-way radio, and panic button connected to an external monitoring station will assist those seeking help. If weapons are stored in the room, proper training for their use is necessary.

The following list provides some protection pointers for home and family:

1. Do not put a name on the mailbox or door of the home.
2. Have an unlisted telephone number.
3. Exercise caution when receiving unexpected packages.
4. Do not provide information to strangers.
5. Beware of unknown visitors or individuals loitering outside. Call for assistance.
6. Check windows for possible observation from outside by persons with or without binoculars. Install thick curtains.
7. Make sure windows and doors are secure at all times.
8. Educate children and adults about protection.
9. Instruct children not to let strangers in the home or to supply information to outsiders.
10. When children leave the house, be sure to ascertain where they are going and who will be with them.
11. Keep a record of the names and addresses of children's playmates.
12. Tell children to refuse rides from strangers even if the stranger says that the parents know about the pickup.
13. Provide an escort for children if necessary.
14. Teach children how to seek assistance.

Protection at the Office

As with the residential setting, physical security is important at the executive's office. A survey may reveal that modifications will strengthen executive protection. The following list offers additional ideas:

1. Office windows should be curtained and contain bullet-resistant materials.
2. Equip the desk in the office with a hidden alarm button.
3. Establish policies and procedures for incoming mail and packages.
4. Beware of access by trickery.
5. Monitor access to the office by several controls.
6. Escort visitors.
7. Access during non-working hours, by cleaning crew or maintenance people, should be monitored by uniformed officers and CCTV.
8. Educate and train employees.

Attacks While Traveling

History has shown that terrorists have a tendency to strike when executives (and politicians) are traveling. Loss prevention practitioners should consider the following countermeasures:

1. Avoid using conspicuous limousines.
2. Maintain regular maintenance for vehicles.

3. Keep the gas tank at least half full at all times.
4. Use an armored vehicle.
5. Install an alarm that foils intrusion or tampering.
6. A telephone or two-way radio will facilitate communications, especially in an emergency.
7. A remote-controlled electronic car starter will enable starting the car from a distance. This will help to activate a bomb, if one has been planted, before the driver and the executive come into range.
8. Consider installing a bomb-scan device inside the auto.
9. Headlight delay devices automatically turn headlights off one minute after ignition is stopped.
10. High-intensity lights, mounted on the rear of the vehicle, will inhibit pursuers.
11. Electronic "beepers" in vehicles will send a radio signal to those attempting to find the executive's auto in the event he or she has been hijacked in the vehicle.
12. Protect auto parking areas with physical security.
13. Avoid using assigned parking spaces.
14. Keep doors, gas cap, hood, and trunk locked.
15. Practice vehicle key control.
16. Avoid a personalized license plate or company logo on vehicle.
17. Inspect outside and inside of vehicle before entering.
18. The chauffeur should have duress signal if needed when picking up executive.
19. Do not stop for hitchhikers, stranded motorists, or accidents. It could be a trap. Use a telephone to summon aid, but keep on moving.
20. Screen and train the chauffeur and bodyguards. Include the executive and the family in training.
21. Evasive driver training is vital.
22. Have weapons in auto ready for use.
23. Maintain the secrecy of travel itineraries.
24. Be unpredictable.
25. Know routes thoroughly as well as alternative routes.
26. Use safety belts.
27. If being followed, use the telephone for assistance, continuously sound the horn or alarm, and do not stop.
28. For air travel, use commercial airlines instead of company aircraft. Unless the company institutes numerous security safeguards, the commercial means of air transportation may be safer.

Kidnap Insurance

Corporations obtain kidnap-ransom insurance policies for protection against the huge ransoms that they might be forced to pay in exchange for a kidnapped executive. Each year millions of dollars in premiums are paid to insurance companies for these policies. Of course, the insurance company requires certain protection standards to reduce the premium. Insurance companies are reluctant to admit writing these policies because terrorists may be attracted to the insured company executive. Moreover, these policies often contain a cancellation clause if the insured company discloses the existence of the policy.

Insurance should be considered one of the last strategies in a long line of defenses. Insurance acts as the "backup" loss prevention strategy.

If Abduction Occurs

After an abduction takes place, the value of planning and training becomes increasingly evident. Whoever receives the kidnapper's telephone call should express a willingness to cooperate. The recipient should ask to speak to the victim; this could provide an opportunity to detect a ruse. Asking questions about the hostage (e.g., birth date, mother's maiden name) of either the hostage or the kidnapper improves the chances of discovering a trick. Prearranged codes are effective. The recipient should notify appropriate authorities after the call. If a package or letter is received, the recipient should exercise caution, limit those who touch it, and contact authorities.

People who attempt to handle the kidnapping themselves can intensify the already dangerous situation. Loss prevention personnel and public law enforcement authorities (i.e., the FBI) are skilled in investigation, intelligence gathering, and negotiating. These professionals consider the safety of the hostage first, and the capture of the offenders second, although the reverse is frequently true in many foreign countries.

After an abduction, the company's policies for action should be instituted. These policies ordinarily answer such questions as who is to be notified, who is to inform the victim's family, what are the criteria for payment of the ransom, who will assemble the cash, and who will deliver it and how. Policies would further specify not disturbing the kidnapping site, whether or not to tap and record future calls, how to ensure absolute secrecy to outsiders, and use of a code word with the kidnappers to impede any person or group who may enter the picture for profit.

The crisis management team should be authorized to coordinate the company's response to the kidnapping. Because a terrorist act can take place at any time, the team members will have to be on call at all times.

Guidelines for the behavior of the hostage are as follows:

1. Do not struggle or become argumentative.
2. Try to remain calm.
3. Occupy your mind with all the incidents taking place.
4. Note direction of travel, length of time, speed, landmarks, noises, and odors.

5. Memorize the characteristics of the abductors (e.g., physical appearance, speech, or names).
6. Leave fingerprints, especially on glass.
7. Remember that an effort is being made to rescue you.
8. Do not escape unless the chances of success are in your favor.

The following organizations can supply assistance:

- FBI headquarters, Washington, DC (Tel.: 202-324-3000).
- U.S. Department of State Operations Center: primary point of contact between U.S. citizens and American embassies and consulates overseas (Tel.: 202-647-1512).
- U.S. Department of Transportation, toll-free travel advisory: 1-800-221-0673.

Do you think it is possible to provide foolproof executive protection? Why or why not?

SUBSTANCE ABUSE

Substance abuse refers to human abuse of any substance that can cause personal harm or harm to others. This problem is pervasive. Millions of people abuse substances.

Abuse by employees in particular adds another dimension to adverse effects; in addition to personal harm and harm to others, the added dimension is losses to an organization.

The following are ways in which an employee can be a substance abuser to the detriment of an organization:

1. The employee's performance can be altered by prescription or nonprescription drugs.
2. The employee obtains and uses illegal drugs at his or her work site.
3. The user sells illegal drugs to afford his or her habit.
4. The employee drinks alcohol or smokes marijuana before work, during breaks, and during lunch.
5. The employee sniffs glue or industrial or cleaning fluids to "get high."
6. An assembly-line worker abuses any type of substance to withstand a monotonous regimen.
7. An employee steals products or sensitive information to support a drug habit.

8. A machinist or machine operator operates dangerous equipment while intoxicated and causes an accident.
9. An employee slows production or makes a mistake due to substance abuse.
10. An employee frequently is absent because of the ill effects of alcohol or other drugs.

According to research by the U.S. Department of Health and Human Services, illicit drug use by American workers has declined by more than half since the mid-1980s.[25] However, as stated in Chapter 6, the cost of lost productivity from this problem is estimated at $34 billion annually.

No occupation is immune to substance abuse. Those afflicted are from the ranks of blue-collar workers, white-collar workers, supervisors, managers, and professionals.

Causes

One might ask why anyone would want to abuse substances. This is a difficult question to answer. Motives vary. A person may want to escape from a boring existence or overbearing problems or bolster self-confidence. Peer-group pressure is another cause. Curiosity and emotional immaturity are reasons why peer-group pressure is successful. A search for personal or spiritual insight also can be the reason for the choice of certain mind-altering substances. A truck driver or student, for example, may abuse stimulants to work longer hours and achieve certain goals.

Countermeasures

Unenlightened managers ordinarily ignore substance abuse in the workplace. As with so many areas of loss prevention, when an unfortunate event occurs (e.g., drug-related crime, production decline, or accident due to substance abuse), these managers panic and react emotionally. Experienced people may be fired unnecessarily, arrests threatened, and litigation becomes a possibility. In contrast, action should begin before the first sign of abuse.

Here is a list for action against substance abuse in the workplace:

1. Form a committee of specialists to pool ideas and resources.
2. Seek legal assistance from an employment law specialist.
3. Large corporations can afford to hire a substance abuse specialist. Outsourcing is another option. Also, contact the local government-supported alcohol and substance abuse agency.
4. Prepare policies that include input from a variety of employees. Policies should focus on the company's position on abuse of substances,

including alcohol; job performance and safety as it relates to substance abuse; drug deterrence such as urinalysis; the consequences of testing positive; the responsibility of employees to seek treatment for abuse problems; available assistance; and the importance of confidentiality.

5. Education and prevention programs can assist employees in understanding substance abuse, policies, and making informed decisions on life choices, health, and happiness.

6. Ensure that supervisors are properly trained to recognize and report substance abuse.

7. Drug testing must be well-planned. Questions include the following: What type of test? Who will do the testing? Cost? Who will be tested? What circumstances will necessitate a test? What controls will prevent cheating and ensure accuracy? Does the laboratory and its personnel comply with state or federal licensing and certification requirements? Are all legal issues considered?

Courts increasingly are holding companies accountable and liable for incidents resulting from employees who abuse substances, especially if the company has no workplace program to curb drug usage.

The following organizations provide assistance for preventing substance abuse:

- Drug-Free Workplace Helpline (Tel.: 1-800-843-4971).
- National Clearinghouse for Alcohol and Drug Information (Tel.: 1-800-729-6686).
- Drug Information, Treatment and Referral Hotline—Center for Substance Abuse Treatment (Tel.: 1-800-662-HELP).
- Employee Assistance Professionals Association (Tel.: 703-522- 6272).

Employee Assistance Programs (EAPs)

First introduced in the 1940s to curb the problem of alcohol abuse in the workplace, thousands of employee assistance programs (EAPs) exist today in the public and private sectors, where they incorporate a broad-based approach to such problems as substance abuse, depression, and marital and financial problems. These programs are characterized by voluntary participation by employees, referrals for serious cases, and confidentiality. The goal of EAPs is to help the employee so he or she can be retained, saving hiring and training costs.[26] According to the U.S. Department of Labor, employers generally find that for every dollar they invest in an EAP, they save from $5 to $16.[27]

Anti-Drug Abuse Act of 1988

The federal Anti-Drug Abuse Act, effective March 1989, is an attempt to create a drug-free workplace. The law requires federal contractors (of at least $25,000) and grantees to prepare and communicate policies banning illegal substances in the workplace and to create a drug awareness program and sanctions or rehabilitation for employees abusing substances. Federal contracts and grants are subject to suspension for noncompliance or excessive workplace drug convictions. The Federal Register is a source for additional information.

If management suspects substance abuse or the use of illegal drugs in the workplace, an undercover investigation can detect the magnitude of abuse. Drug testing may be necessary (see Chapter 6).

Alcoholism

Alcohol is the most abused drug in America. An *alcoholic* is defined as someone who cannot function on a daily basis without consuming an alcoholic beverage. The National Academy of Sciences has reported that the medical, social, and industrial costs of problem drinking may run as high as $60 billion a year, including at least $19.6 billion in lost productivity. After a five-year study, General Motors found that employees with alcohol-related problems drained 70 percent of the company sickness and accident benefits.[28]

Estimates of the number of alcoholics in the United States range between 9 and 15 million. These figures do not include the millions who are on the fringe of alcoholism. It is often a hidden disease, whereby the alcoholic hides the problem from family, friends, physicians, and himself or herself. Some major indicators are heartburn, nausea, insomnia, tremor, high blood pressure, morning cough, and liver enlargement. The alcoholic often blames factors other than alcohol for these conditions.

Today, many businesses are no longer hiding the problem. On the detection of alcoholism, a superior should notify management and obtain approval to proceed with the case. Public or private concerns that can correct the problem are contacted for information. Alcoholics Anonymous (AA), an organization for alcoholics and recovered alcoholics, run by people who have had a drinking problem, has had more success than most organizations. The employee is advised of "helping agencies," in addition to internal and external policies and procedures and what is expected of him or her by the employer regarding steps for recovery. Health insurance benefits and company disability income usually are applicable. Unless the employee takes heed of the supervisor's recommendations in seeking assistance, dismissal may occur because of poor job performance. The threat of job loss jolts many alcoholics into recognizing their serious situation and accepting treatment.

What do you think are the most successful countermeasures against substance abuse in society and in the workplace?

Types of Substances and Abuse

The explanation of four terms can assist the reader in understanding the human impact of various substance abuse categories.

- *Psychological dependence.* Users depend so much on the feeling of well-being from a substance that they feel compelled toward continued use. People can become psychologically dependent on a host of substances. Restlessness and irritability may result from deprivation of the desired substance.
- *Addiction.* Certain substances lead to physiological (or physical) addiction. This happens when the body has become so accustomed to a substance that the drugged state becomes "normal" to the body. Extreme physical discomfort results if the substance is not in the body.
- *Tolerance.* After repeated use of certain drugs, the body becomes so accustomed to the drug that increasing dosages are needed to reach the feeling of well-being afforded by earlier doses.
- *Withdrawal.* The person goes through physical and psychological upset as the body becomes used to the absence of the drug. Addicts ordinarily consume drugs to avoid pain, and possible death, from withdrawal. Symptoms vary from person to person and from substance to substance. An addict's life often revolves around obtaining the substance, by whatever means, to avoid withdrawal.

Five types of substances—narcotics, depressants, stimulants, hallucinogens, and inhalants—are discussed here.

Narcotics

Narcotics include opium, its derivatives, and their synthetic equivalents. Drugs in this category are heroin, morphine, codeine, and methadone, among others. Such drugs are used to relieve pain and induce sleep. The method of consumption is injection, oral, or inhalation. Both psychological and physiological dependence is typical, as well as a tolerance potential.

Heroin has been touted as the most serious illegally abused drug in the United States. The situation was particularly problematic during the 1960s and 1970s when heroin addicts committed an enormous amount of property crimes. Hundreds of thousands of addicts committed assorted crimes to obtain money to pay for their habit. Since then, many heroin addicts have been transformed into methadone addicts. The addict obtains methadone at a medically approved clinic. But many "street" addicts still prefer heroin and are prone to criminality. Because addicts often share unsanitized syringes, the AIDS virus unfortunately is transmitted among addicts, their sexual partners, and their infants. This has become a major health problem.

Depressants

Depressants fall into several categories: barbiturates include phenobarbital and secobarbital (Seconal); tranquilizers include Valium and Librium; non-barbiturate hypnotics include methaqualone (Quaalude); and miscellaneous depressant drugs include alcohol and chloroform. A depressant affects the central nervous system. Barbiturates ordinarily are prescribed for insomnia, whereas tranquilizers calm anxiety. Other depressants are used prior to surgery. Abuse of these drugs can lead to psychological and physiological dependence. Withdrawal is painful and can be fatal. Depressants have a tolerance potential. These drugs are taken orally or injected. They are obtained by a doctor's prescription or through illegal channels. Symptoms of depressant use are similar to that of alcohol use: drowsiness, slurred speech, disorientation, constricted pupils, irritability, and slow reflexes.

Stimulants

There are several types of stimulants; caffeine, amphetamines, and cocaine are the most common ones. These drugs affect the central nervous system and generally cause increased alertness soon after consumption, but restlessness and irritability are characteristic of long-term usage. There is a tolerance potential plus a susceptibility to dependence.

Caffeine is found in coffee, tea, cola drinks, and No-Doz. Increased alertness may be followed by insomnia, gastric irritation, and restlessness.

Amphetamines are widely used stimulants that are swallowed or injected. They are prescribed for narcolepsy (chronic sleepiness). Illegal amphetamines typically originate from legitimate sources. Abuse is characterized by anxiety, talkativeness, irritability, and dilated pupils.

Legally, cocaine is a narcotic, but physiologically it is a stimulant. It is expensive and the "high" is short-lived. The history of cocaine is interesting. It used to be an ingredient in Coca-Cola. Sigmund Freud experimented with it. The user inhales cocaine into the nose or injects it. Symptoms of abuse are similar to those of amphetamines plus damage to nasal membranes and the potential for hallucinations and hostile behavior.

Crack is a stimulant drug processed from cocaine hydrochloride by using baking soda and water and then heat to remove the hydrochloride.

The pebble-sized crystal remaining, called crack, is smoked in a variety of devices. Crack is popular because it is less expensive than cocaine and when smoked it is more rapidly absorbed than snorted cocaine.

Hallucinogens

Hallucinogens can produce a trance, fright, and irrational behavior. Examples are LSD, PCP, mescaline, and psilocybin.

Marijuana is categorized by itself. It is sometimes categorized as a hallucinogen, but its actions are different from LSD. Both marijuana and its derivative, hashish, are widely used. Because of widespread cultivation of hemp to produce rope prior to the Civil War, marijuana grows wild in almost every state. Because of so many users today, marijuana use is controversial. Many states have decriminalized (i.e., reduced the penalty) the offense. The effects of usage depend on the individual and the potency. There is no physiological dependence. Psychological dependence is possible. Research on tolerance is inconclusive. Millions of people smoke marijuana occasionally to feel relaxed and carefree.

LSD was popularized in the 1960s by the youth "counterculture." Use was touted as a consciousness-expanding experience. The effects vary greatly. There is no physiological dependence. Bizarre hallucinations, which can be either beautiful or terrifying, result from usage.

Inhalants

By inhaling volatile chemicals, intoxication can result. This can occur from one's own volition or by accident due to poor ventilation. The awareness of both causative factors should be understood by all employees.

Two types of volatile chemicals are volatile solvents and anesthetics. Volatile solvents include a variety of glues or liquid cements, cleaning fluid, paint thinner, and paint remover. Anesthetics are found in medical facilities for surgical purposes. Nitrous oxide (laughing gas) and ether are among the anesthetics.

Those who seek an altered state or "high" gather the substance or gas in a plastic bag and place it over the mouth and nose before breathing. Direct breathing from the container holding the substance is another method. Physiological dependence is nil, but a tolerance and psychological dependence may result. The effects are numerous and varied: intoxication, chemical odor on the person, drowsiness, stupor, and hallucinations.

WORKPLACE VIOLENCE

Two important questions on workplace violence are (1) how should it be defined and (2) how should it be measured? The definition of workplace violence affects not only how it is measured but also its cost. As the definition expanded from "one employee attacking another" to "any violence that occurs on the job" so too did the cost, from \$4.2 billion to \$36 billion.[29] According to the Bureau of Justice Statistics (BJS), in 1993, there were 121 million U.S. workers of which 1063 were murdered on the job, one-third of these victims were self-employed, only 59 of the 1063 were killed by coworkers or former coworkers, and the vast majority were men killed in robberies. Women are more likely to die as victims of violence than from any other type of work-related injury. A study by Northwestern National Life Insurance Company revealed that 25 percent of full-time U.S. workers were harassed, threatened, or attacked while on the job within the previous 12 months; 50 percent of those dealt directly with the public. This study estimated that about 2 million physical attacks on workers occur each year.[30] In putting the problem in perspective, the BJS noted the following rates per 1000 adults per year (incidents not necessarily in the workplace): accident 220, personal theft 61, assault 31, death (all causes) 11, robbery 6, death from cancer 3, and homicide 0.1.[31]

Obviously, incidents of workplace violence (e.g., homicides, assaults, rapes) occurred before increased attention focused on the problem in the early 1990s. What we have witnessed is a change in the way the problem is perceived and counted. This is beneficial for gauging increases and decreases in the problem and as a foundation for planning protection with scarce resources. The United States has been known to maintain good statistics on a number of problems and freely publicize trends. From an international perspective, others may view the United States as the most violent society, when we may be the best at gathering data.

> Do you think the United States is a violent society or do we just maintain good data gathering systems? Explain your viewpoint.

What follows is a list of strategies for dealing with violence in the workplace. *Organizations have a responsibility to protect people, as well as assets, otherwise litigation may result.* Several of the strategies here are applicable to other protection problems, which helps to justify security expenditures.

1. Establish a committee to plan violence prevention and to respond to such incidents. Include specialists in security, human resources, psychology, and law.
2. Consider OSHA guidelines to curb workplace violence (see Chapter 17 under health-care institutions).
3. Establish policies and procedures and communicate the problems of threats and violence to all employees.

4. Although human behavior cannot be accurately predicted, screen employment applicants. The ADA limits certain questions, however, these can be asked: "What was the most stressful situation you faced and how did you deal with it?" "What was the most serious incident you encountered in your work and how did you respond?"

5. Consider substance abuse testing as a strategy to prevent workplace violence. For years, BJS data has showed a relationship between violent crime and substance abuse.

6. Train managers and supervisors to recognize employees with problems and report them to the human resources department. Include training in conflict resolution and nonviolent response.

7. A history of violent behavior can help to predict its reoccurrence. The worker who becomes violent is usually male, between 25 and 45 years old, and has a history of interpersonal conflict. He tends to be a loner and may have a mental health history of paranoia or depression. He also may have a fascination with weapons.[32]

8. Managers and supervisors should be sensitive to disruptions in the workplace, such as firings. Substance abuse and domestic and financial problems also can affect the workplace; an EAP is especially helpful for such problems.

9. If a person becomes angry in the workplace, listen and show that you are interested in helping to resolve the problem. Do not get pulled into a verbal confrontation; do not argue. Acknowledge and validate the anger by showing empathy, not sympathy. Speak softly and slowly. Ensure that a witness is present. Maintain a safe distance, without being obvious, to provide an extra margin of safety. If a threat is made or if a weapon is shown, call the police.

10. Remember that outsiders (e.g., visitor, estranged spouse, robber) may be a source of violence and protection programs must be comprehensive.

11. If a violent incident occurs, a previously prepared crisis management plan becomes invaluable. Otherwise, a committee should be formed immediately after emergency first responders (i.e., police, EMS) complete their duties on the premises and affected employees and their families are assisted. At one major corporation, management was unprepared when the corporate security manager was shot. A committee was quickly formed to improve security and survey corporate plants. In addition to expenditures for physical security and training, an emphasis was placed on awareness, access controls, and alerts.[33]

CASE PROBLEMS

18A. As the security director for a corporation engaged in research, you see the need for a communications security consultant for improved protection. What criteria would you list to select such a specialist? What questions would you ask applicants during the selection process?

18B. As the security director for a corporation with plants in the United States and Europe, prepare a list of questions to answer as you plan protection against terrorism and establish an executive protection program.

18C. As a security manager you hear through the grapevine that several employees smoke marijuana during lunch when they go to their vehicles. What do you do?

18D. You are a security manager at a plant. One day, a former employee shows up at the front gate and demands to see his estranged wife. Plus, he wants to talk with the human resources manager about benefits. How do you handle this situation?

18E. Of the major topics in this chapter, which one would you select as a specialization and career? Why? How would you develop such a specialization and career?

NOTES

1. Gene Laczniak and Patrick E. Murphy, "The Ethics of Corporate Spying," *Ethics Journal* (Fall 1993): 1–4.
2. "Corporate Spying: Honorable Profession," Associated Press release (April 27, 1990).
3. Worth Wade, *Industrial Espionage and Mis-use of Trade Secrets* (Ardmore, PA: Advance House, 1965).
4. See Bill Zalud, "Spy Business," *Security* (January 1989): 53.
5. *Business Espionage Report* (November 1996): 3–5.
6. D. A. Nichter, "The Home Computer as a Listening Device," *Chain Link* (June 1996): 6.
7. "White House Reports on Espionage," *Infosecurity News* (September–October 1996): 14.
8. Richard Hefferman and Dan Swartwood, *Trends in Intellectual Property Loss* (Arlington, VA: ASIS, March 1996).
9. Ibid., pp. 17–32. The list of countermeasures was prepared with the assistance of this source, which emphasized survey results rather than an explanation of countermeasures.
10. Susan Thompson, "DOA: Destruction of (Almost) Anything," *Security Management* (May 1989): 77–79.
11. John M. Carroll, *Computer Security*, 3rd ed. (Boston: Butterworth–Heinemann, 1996), pp. 177–277.
12. See Glenn Whidden, "A Raid on Bugs," *Security Management* (June 1989): 85–88.
13. Correspondence (June 24, 1997) with Keith Flannigan, United Security Group (Tel.: 770-621-0023).
14. *Legal Alert Memo* (May 20, 1997), Childs & Duff, P.A., P.O. Box 11367, Columbia, SC 29211.

15. John A. Nolan, "Economic Espionage, Proprietary Information Protection: Difficult Times Ahead," *Security Technology and Design* (January–February 1997): 54–57.
16. See James M. Poland, *Understanding Terrorism* (Englewood Cliffs, NJ: Prentice-Hall, 1988), pp. 9–10.
17. Larry C. Johnson, "The Fall of Terrorism," *Security Management* (April 1997): 26–32.
18. Stefan H. Leader, "The Rise of Terrorism," *Security Management* (April 1997): 34–39.
19. FBI, *Terrorism in the US, 1995* (Washington, DC: U.S. Government Printing Office, 1997), p. 14.
20. "Pro-Life Terrorism: A How-To," *Harper's Magazine* (January 1995): 19.
21. Barry Collin, "The Future of CyberTerrorism," *Crime and Justice International* (March 1997): 14–18.
22. Leader, "The Rise of Terrorism," p. 39.
23. "Terrorism: How Have Other Countries Handled It? How Should We?" *The Bill of Rights in Action* (Fall 1995): 5–8.
24. United Nations, *Eighth United Nations Congress on the Prevention of Crime and the Treatment of Offenders* (July 1990), pp. 19–20.
25. "New Study Examines Drug Use by US Workers," *The Big Issue* (January–April 1996): 11.
26. John M. Ivancevich and William G. Glueck, *Foundations of Personnel*, 4th ed. (Homewood, IL: Richard D. Irwin, Inc., 1989), p. 813.
27. William Sessions, "The War in the Workplace," *Security Management* (August 1989): 102.
28. Earl Selby and Miriam Selby, "Business's Battle Against Booze," *Reader's Digest* (September 1981): 108.
29. Harvey S. Waxman, "Putting Workplace Violence in Perspective," *Security Management* (September 1995): 123. And "Work Violence: Cost Guess Rises as Definition Expands," *Security* (June 1995): 9.
30. T. Trombly, "An Epidemic of Workplace Violence," *Forum* (Winter 1995): 2.
31. "Workplace Violence: A Growing Exaggeration?" *Security* (January 1995): 9.
32. Waxman, "Putting Workplace Violence in Perspective," p. 124.
33. Philip Purpura, "When the Security Manager Gets Shot: A Corporate Response," *Security Journal* (July 1993): 150–157.

19

Your Future in Security and Loss Prevention

OBJECTIVES

After studying this chapter the reader will be able to

1. Discuss the effects of technology on loss prevention;
2. Elaborate on technology, research in the behavioral sciences, loss prevention, and civil liberties;
3. Discuss the directions of loss prevention education, research, and training;
4. List at least ten trends affecting security and loss prevention;
5. List at least ten employment opportunities in the security and loss prevention field and eight sources of employment information.

EFFECTS OF TECHNOLOGY ON LOSS PREVENTION

Computers and Loss Prevention

Future computer systems will perform an array of loss prevention activities beyond what is accomplished today. For example, if an intruder enters a building, not only will the computer pinpoint the entry location, via a series of sensors, and activate CCTV, but simultaneously will dispatch a robot to apprehend the intruder. After apprehension, the intruder will be carried to a central area where a private-sector investigator and public police will be waiting. Later, for prosecution purposes, a complete audiovisual record will be utilized.

The possibilities for computerized card access control are interesting. In fact, cards will become obsolete, for an individual will be able to stand in front of a sophisticated sensor and positive identification will be made by the analysis of a number of characteristics: bone structure, teeth, body odor, to name only a few. It would be especially difficult for an offender to duplicate several of these characteristics. The same sophisticated access control sensor could be placed at many locations to monitor personnel: parking lots, building entrances, elevators, high security locations, copying machines, lunchrooms, and restrooms. Obviously, with such a system, it would be possible to know exactly where a person was at every minute of every workday. If a fire developed or if sabotage occurred, the recorded location of everybody would aid loss prevention personnel. But, will employees appreciate computer records revealing how many times and for how long they visit the restroom or other locations? Suppose a computer system had the capability to record every conversation, every day, within a building. This could give management the opportunity to "weed out" those persons who were counterproductive to organizational goals. Also, because this computer would be capable of "recognizing" any conversations pertaining to losses, the loss prevention department could review these conversations and investigate vulnerabilities. With these possibilities in mind, one realizes the blessing and burden of technology. Are such intense measures worth sacrificing privacy? Certainly not. One must remain vigilant against "Big Brother" and protect individual privacy. *Countermeasures must strike a balance between preventing losses and protecting privacy. In the future, as today, the courts will be watching and ruling as technological innovations and loss prevention strategies are applied.*

Automatic Factory and Robots

Industrialized society is heading into the era of the *automatic factory* (AF):[1] computers will operate machines that transform raw materials into finished products without human input. Robots with self-contained minicomputers will be an essential part of the AF. Activities such as material handling, assembly, inspection, and quality control will be automated without direct human intervention. Human input will come from a computer control center, and maintenance will be performed periodically.

The future use of robots is promising. Eventually, they will mine deep under land and water for precious substances, repair vehicles in outer space, fight wars, and design and build other robots. They will operate 24 hours a day without a coffee break or vacation. Fringe benefits like hospitalization and pensions will be unnecessary for robots. Also, robots are immune to heat, cold, noise, radiation, and other hazards.

Loss prevention strategies within an AF would be quite different from those of today's plants. Imagine loss prevention for a plant operated by only three managers and six technicians. If internal pilfering occurred, the number of suspects would be narrowed to nine, excluding robots. Parking lots, frequently a source of crime, would be smaller. Fires and accidents, which are often caused by human error, would be reduced.

Will the AF become so automated that loss prevention practitioners will become obsolete? No, because losses are inevitable. Human beings are in charge of the AF, and a variety of losses are possible. Human error will not disappear. Crimes, fires, and accidents will take place. Internal and external threats will have to be prevented. Because computers are at the foundation of the AF, a loss prevention practitioner will need a strong computer background to perform activities such as audits on both computer programs and inventories. Alarms, sensors, and other devices will be tied into a computer system. And, moreover, the computer itself will need protection. Ultimately, people will need protection from computers and robots!

RESEARCH IN BEHAVIORAL SCIENCES AND LOSS PREVENTION

Research into the behavior of animals and humans is yielding results that are applicable to loss problems and countermeasures.[2] By understanding the sensory mechanisms and capabilities of animals one can prepare improved strategies while being alert to the use of such strategies against one's defenses. The olfactory capabilities of dogs and other animals are in widespread use as biological alarms for detecting drugs, people, and explosives. Dolphins are able to perform sentry duty in aquatic environments. This is helpful for facilities near seashores or in water. But dogs and dolphins are only a portion of the possibilities for the future. Other animals are capable of aiding loss prevention measures. A tiny mosquito can sense the presence of carbon dioxide. Rattlesnakes possess an infrared sensor. These animal systems are small in comparison to those made by humans and may even be more accurate. Studying these animals helps professionals improve existing systems. Also, research will produce knowledge about the capabilities of animals if they were to be used to circumvent loss prevention strategies. It is possible to surgically implant contraband (e.g., weapons, explosives) or a computer disk inside animals for smuggling purposes. What a herd could transport can be only imagined. In addition to transporting small items and messages, birds could hover over a facility for surveillance purposes with an appropriate device to transmit valuable information to distant humans.

Humans are not exempt from further study. Several areas of inquiry are worthwhile. Because humans involved in loss prevention will become increasingly dependent on machines (e.g., computers), what are the best possible designs for machines so that both humans and machines will yield optimum performance? This research, often referred to as *cybernetics* and *biocybernetics*, focuses on topics such as human factor problems, psychology, and physiology during human-machine interaction. Relevant questions for researchers include the following. What are the preferred speaking and listening rates during human-computer interaction? What is the most appropriate design for computer-generated hazardous signals? Where should specific controls be located on a machine? How can a computer be receptive to "brain waves" and pupillary dilation so that the computer will be more responsive to humans and improve performance?

Behavior Control

Today, electronic monitors can be attached to prisoners and patients to control their freedom. Technology is not far from perfecting telemetric sensors, which, when placed on the body or implanted under the skin, will maintain constant surveillance of a person. These sensors monitor such information as bodily characteristics (e.g., heart rate and respiration) and transmit the information to a control center. One device, called the *behavior transmitter-reinforcer*, is locked onto an individual's wrist. The device tracks the wearer's location, transmits information about his or her activities, and modifies behavior by reward and punishment.[3] Some see these devices as having great promise for solving correctional problems, ending the institutionalization of offenders, and reducing prison costs. Extended to loss prevention programs, these devices could be clamped on the wrists of employees who are caught pilfering. Then, the employee thief would be hindered from stealing again. In fact, all employees could wear such a device to eliminate losses due to crime. Retail stores also could use this device by clamping them on entering customers to reduce shoplifting. Naturally, such technology can get out of hand; unless it is controlled, it will do more harm than good.

CIVIL LIBERTIES

Technology versus civil liberties will be a recurring issue in the years to come. Were it not for the Bill of Rights of the U.S. Constitution, one can only speculate about what civil liberties, if any, U.S. citizens would have today. Whatever the reason for stifling the use of technology (e.g., environmental impact or invasion of privacy), technological research must not end. A continuation of the development of loss prevention strategies is essential for reduced losses. Loss prevention must keep pace with technological changes that alter the world, society, and industry. At the same time, new countermeasures to avert losses must not violate the rights of citizens.

> Can you describe a clash between technology and civil liberties? What were the issues and solutions?

EDUCATION

How relevant is a college education to the loss prevention careerist? A college degree will not guarantee a job or advancement opportunities. But, with a college degree, a person has improved chances for obtaining a favored position. If two equally experienced people are vying for the same loss prevention position and person A has a college degree while person B does not, person A probably will get the job. Of course, other characteristics within a person's background will improve job opportunities. *Education* and *experience* are top considerations. *Training* also is important. Two other characteristics are *personality* and *common sense*. As used here, personality pertains to one's ability to get along with others. Many consider this factor to be one-half of a person's job. *Common sense* is a subjective term that is used widely. It refers to an analysis of a situation that produces the "best" solution that most people would favor.

Loss Prevention Education: Today and Tomorrow

Although business degree programs are an excellent location for security and loss prevention courses, the criminal justice (CRJ) degree programs on hundreds of campuses in the United States today are the greatest driving force behind future security and loss prevention degree programs. During the late 1960s, many police science degree programs advanced to law enforcement and then CRJ degree programs. As CRJ programs developed, so did the spectrum of course offerings: from primarily narrow police courses, CRJ programs began offering courses relating to the entire justice system (i.e., police, courts, corrections). CRJ programs became interdisciplinary because the answers to complex problems were more forthcoming from a broader spectrum of study. Likewise, security and loss prevention degree programs will evolve into broader-based, interdisciplinary loss prevention programs and will include the study of business and computers.

Academic Research

The most practical question for loss prevention researchers to address is as follows: What strategies are best to prevent and reduce losses from crimes, fires, and accidents? Ongoing evaluative research will be instrumental in strengthening successful strategies while eliminating those that are less useful. Evaluative research used to measure public police crime prevention programs are useful as a base for studying private-sector crime prevention strategies. This base is suggested because of the limited evaluative research from private-sector loss prevention programs.

Additional directions for research are model training programs, determining the most appropriate courses for relevant degree programs, effective job applicant screening, model statutes for licensing and regulation of the security industry, model for regulatory bodies, criteria for the selection of services and devices, evaluation of services and devices, legal issues and liabilities, strategies to improve public-private sector cooperation, private justice system (whereby decisions for or against prosecution are made by management in the private sector), centralized data bank for the compiling of loss statistics, the feasibility of tax deductions for implementing loss prevention strategies by a variety of entities and residential settings, computer and communications security, and the use and effect of robots and other technological innovations.

An often unrealized area of research is the use of computers and computer-generated statistics to provide answers for loss prevention planning. Businesses normally produce a wide array of reports and statistics that never are seen by loss prevention managers. If a practitioner selects those reports and statistics relevant to loss prevention and programs a computer to generate helpful data, then decisions will be enhanced. Computers also can assist practitioners striving to obtain loss ratios or indicators that reveal deviations: sales volume to shrinkage, cash sales to charge sales, and product A sales to product B sales. Ratios or indicators would point to possible sources of trouble deserving investigation. Computer programs are useful to develop profiles of stores, manufacturing plants, warehouses, or truck routes most vulnerable to crimes, fires, and accidents. These data would assist in predicting problems and planning countermeasures. Profiles would include an array of characteristics such as profit potential, shrinkage, merchandise type, geographic location, personnel characteristics, and so on.

Many functions previously performed by government agencies are now being performed by the private sector. *Privatization* is the contracting out of government programs, either wholly or in part, to for-profit and not-for-profit organizations. An example is private prisons. Another example is private-sector police protection for residential areas not adequately protected by public police. This concept also is relevant to fire protection. The private-sector profit motive and competition may improve performance in combating crimes, fires, and accidents on a communitywide scale. Profit sharing, bonuses, and incentive programs are known to improve productivity in the private sector. Would a private-sector policing effort, in a community, be more effective than the present public police effort? What about a comprehensive (police, fire, emergency medical) private-sector effort? The implications and ramifications of these questions for research are enormous.

As well as college and university criminal justice and loss prevention programs sharing these research questions, other curricula, such as business, insurance, safety, architecture, and engineering degree programs are capable of providing valuable input. An interdisciplinary research effort would be most beneficial. Without adequate research, loss prevention practitioners will be hindered in their decision-making roles.

What directions for research can you suggest for the security and loss prevention field?

Training

The future direction of training largely depends on tomorrow's loss prevention strategies and technological innovations. Practitioners will need to know how to operate in an environment of new countermeasures and complex devices. But, even though loss prevention will change, many key topics taught in the training programs of today also will be taught tomorrow. Strategies against crimes, fires, and accidents will still be at the heart of training programs.

State involvement in training proprietary and service practitioners probably will increase for greater public safety. Uniformity in training will ensure that practitioners receive adequate information on basic topics such as laws of arrest, search and seizure, weapons, fire protection, and accident prevention. An interdisciplinary group would be the better choice to provide input for state-mandated training programs.

The training curriculum of tomorrow will continue to cater to the ever-increasing goal of professionalizing loss prevention personnel. The end product will be a thoroughly knowledgeable practitioner, able to provide a useful service to the community. Greater mutual respect will follow as public police and private-sector personnel share similar characteristics in education, training, salary, and professionalism.

Improved training helps to prevent costly liability suits; for example, from excessive force used by a uniformed officer. The quality of training, in terms of duration, intensity, and topics covered, is a prime consideration in such liability cases.

Programmed, *self-paced instruction* with the aid of computers very well may become common for loss prevention training. If the problems of turnover and constant hiring still are evident, then this method of training should be cost effective while freeing supervisory personnel for other tasks. Furthermore, new employees who learn quickly can move through the instructional program without having to wait for slower students. A varied training program may include not only programmed, self-paced instruction but also lectures, audiovisual productions, role playing, and demonstrations. *Distance learning* will increase in popularity as students learn from remote locations.

Additional information on education and training in the security field can be obtained from the *Academy of Security Educators and Trainers* (ASET) (Arcadia Manor, Rte. 2, Box 3644, Berryville, VA 22611; Tel.: 540-955-1129).

TRENDS AFFECTING SECURITY AND LOSS PREVENTION

As we enter the 21st century, there will be no shortage of vulnerabilities or threats facing businesses and institutions. The list that follows presents trends and challenges that will have an impact on the type of specialists required for security and loss prevention and thus employment opportunities:

1. The problems of crime, fire, and accidents will remain but increase in complexity.
2. Technology is both a blessing and a burden. For instance, computers make our lives easier, but they are subject to exploitation by offenders.
3. The *cycle of protection* will remain: as new technology is developed, offenders will exploit it, and security specialists and offenders will remain in constant competition—one group striving to protect; the other striving to circumvent defenses. Both sides will win "battles," but neither will win the "war."
4. Criminal organizations will become increasingly globalized. They have taken advantage of the information and technology revolution to as great, or a greater, degree than government and business.[4]
5. Top management in criminal organizations is becoming increasingly well-educated and trained. Criminals increasingly will have college degrees and experience in computers, engineering, money management, investments, and accounting. Likewise, security professionals require a similar background, and they are increasingly well-educated and trained in the latest technology. Security executives often possess a business background and see themselves as businesspersons specializing in security.
6. Public police, especially on the state and local levels, will continue to lag behind in technical expertise of high-tech criminals. Consequently, private security will continue to fill the void.
7. During the 21st century, computer viruses will be meaner and more intelligent.
8. Countless government agencies and private-sector services collect data about people, businesses, and organizations from around the world. The technology of our age has provided the capability to transmit information to and from remote points throughout the world—to a military outpost, mobile police vehicle, credit office, corporate office, home office, or wherever. The individuals or groups that have access to such information, legally or illegally, have great power.
9. Hackers will become more sophisticated and creative. As computers affect all areas of society, the vulnerability is almost endless: manipulating bank records from halfway around the world, changing criminal history files and creating new identities, and remotely altering manufacturing processes.
10. The protection of sensitive information (e.g., trade secrets) will become an even greater responsibility of security because of the information age. Survival of businesses depend on protection of sensitive information.

11. As we become a cashless society, offenders will be ready to gain illegally from system weaknesses.

12. The black market for weapons of mass destruction (e.g., nuclear, biological) will be a continuing threat.

13. Theft of computer components will continue to increase.

14. Counterfeiting will continue to be a huge business for organized criminals, especially in designer clothes, software, entertainment items, vehicle parts, and medical supplies. Counterfeiters have production facilities and distribution networks ready for new product lines.

15. Criminal entrepreneurs increasingly are knowledgeable of the operations of financial institutions and their areas of vulnerability. They will continue to infiltrate and manipulate financial institutions for their own purposes as this target becomes a top priority. Financial security professionals will continue to be challenged not only by external offenders but by internal ones as well.

16. Twenty-first century crime groups increasingly will own shares of multinational corporations and be involved in management decisions. This will create new challenges for security professionals.

17. Satellites increasingly will assist security through instantaneous communications throughout the world. People and assets will be more easily tracked. Such technology will assist in the investigations of kidnappings and hijackings.

18. Risk analysis will become more challenging for security executives because, with limited resources, priorities for protection will be established. Improved research methodologies for risk analyses must be sought for better decisions. Because all areas of vulnerability will not receive the same protection, documentation of risk analyses, research, and decisions will be extremely important.[5]

19. As more and more employees are displaced from smoke-stack industries during the information and technology age, frustration-induced crime may rise.

20. Downsizing or tight budgets may require security to assume additional duties (e.g., safety, fire protection, parking management), or specialize in new areas (e.g., information protection, computer security), or the security department itself may be eliminated or placed under another department (e.g., facilities management, health and safety).

21. We will see more outsourcing of security functions, partnering (i.e., forming alliances for mutual benefit), and use of technology to save recurring costs.

22. Corporate and institutional changes have had an impact on employee morale. The objectives of improving quality while downsizing and other workplace issues have taken their toll on loyalty among workers. Loyalty has been an asset to protection programs. Its deterrent value today must be questioned and studied. New innovative strategies are required.

23. Women, the elderly, and the disadvantaged will make up a greater portion of the workforce. Such groups present new challenges for security. Women and the elderly require protection not only in the workplace but also at home and while traveling. Cases of domestic violence, sexual harassment, and stalking are likely to occupy more of the security professional's time. Women and the elderly will be involved in more workplace crime. If increasing numbers of disadvantaged workers are employed, they may bring with them problems of gangs and illegal drugs.[6]

24. More research will focus on issues of minority group members and women in security positions. The majority of women in one study of women security managers felt they experienced relatively high levels of sex discrimination, sexual harassment, and on-the-job stress, plus they felt they were not paid the same as men for the same work. Despite these issues in this male-dominated vocation, the study showed three-fourths of the women surveyed were satisfied with their careers.[7]

25. Security must adapt to a multinational and multicultural workforce. As the workforce changes, security professionals must be aware of diversity and use it to the advantage of the business. Good communication can improve security, business, and even help develop new markets.

26. Global markets require security to be aware of each culture and related risks.

27. Twenty-first century police will spend most of their resources and time curbing violent crimes, while their efforts against property crimes will take a lower priority. Consequently, the private sector will fill the void.

28. In a speech to police leaders, Robert diGrazia, former police chief of Boston and St. Louis, said: "We are not letting the public in on our dirty little secret"; namely, "that there is little the police can do" about crime.[8]

29. More and more citizens and business people are realizing that the police have limited ability and resources to curb crime. Police are primarily "reactive"; that is, they respond to calls for service and investigate. They often are under great pressure to solve serious cases. Because of limited resources, police are not able to be more "proactive"; that is, prevent crimes before they occur. Again, the private sector will fill the void.

30. A panel of law enforcement specialists predicts that, in 2035, private security agencies will perform more than 50 percent of all law enforcement responsibilities.[9]

31. Three key factors to assist protection professionals today and in the future are a broad-based education (e.g., business, security, computers), the skill to show protection strategies have a return on investment, and flexibility to deal with rapid change.

32. Trends affecting the security and loss prevention profession point to employment opportunities in many organizations (both proprietary and contract) and government agencies and in many specialized areas.

What trends do you see in the security and loss prevention field?

EMPLOYMENT

Many employment opportunities can be found in the security and loss prevention field. The related field of criminal justice, which includes police, courts, corrections, probation, and parole, plus the growth of privatization, all provide opportunities and specialization for employment applicants. Chapter 2, "The Business of Security and Loss Prevention," lists facilities requiring protection (which includes any business, institution, or organization), security services and devices (a multibillion dollar industry), and specialists and consultants serving the industry. The security industry in the United States is a $100-billion-a-year business and growing.[10]

Entry-level security officer positions vary widely in pay, benefits, and training. Generally, these positions do not pay as well as public police. However, there are many opportunities for employment and advancement, many part-time positions, the hours offer some flexibility, and the duties are less risky than public policing. Supervisors in security have mastered the tasks of security officers, possess broader skills, and have good human relations qualities. Managers generally have more education, training, experience, and responsibilities than supervisors. They are involved in planning, budgeting, organizing, marketing, recruiting, directing, and controlling. Other careers in this field include sales of services and devices, self-employment (e.g., private investigations, consulting), and government security.

Research in 1996 on wages in security shows the average annual pay for unarmed security officers to be $17,154. Security directors average $67,617, often have a title of vice president, work in an urban area, are employed by a large corporation, possess a bachelor's degree (often a master's degree), and hold a certification (e.g., Certified Protection Professional, Certified Fraud Examiner).[11] Table 19–1 provides average annual income for security and loss prevention positions.

The broad yet specialized loss prevention field extends to the alarm and insurance industries. *The National Burglar and Fire Alarm Association* (7101 Wisconsin Ave., Suite 901, Bethesda, MD 20814; Tel.: 301-907-3202) published a pamphlet, *Alarm Security: A Business, a Public Service, a*

Table 19–1 Security and Loss Prevention Annual Compensation

Position	Average Cash Compensation
Security directors	$ 67,617
Computer security managers	55,539
Supervisors of investigations	49,916
Security managers	45,537
Fire protection managers	41,589
Investigators	37,762
Supervisors of guard operations	31,494
Security training managers	31,385
Store detectives	19,097
Security officers	17,154

Source: Abbott, Langer & Associates.

Career. This publication states that the alarm industry (over 6000 alarm companies in the United States) is

> growing steadily and has jobs available in almost any city, at almost any skill and education level, for men and women. . . . The industry needs more electronic engineers to design new equipment . . . more technicians to install and service alarm systems . . ., more sales persons and marketing experts, accountants, people to monitor alarm signals, secretaries, typists, receptionists, shop technicians, credit/collection and inventory control personnel. Some alarm companies even provide security officers or train and supervise guard dogs.

The *Insurance Information Institute* (see Chapter 14) published a pamphlet, *Careers in Property and Liability Insurance.* Some comments from this insurance publication follow:

> 700,000 men and women . . . work for about 2,900 insurance companies and thousands of agencies and brokerage firms countrywide. . . . Persons in this business . . . provide protection against financial loss from many causes. . . . An engineer clambers over the ruins of an earthquake-shattered building, looking for clues to construction methods that might help another building. . . . Safety experts . . . help . . . individuals, companies and communities find ways to prevent accidents and fires, to protect lives and property, and thus to keep insurance rates down. Insurance adjusters, often called claims investigators . . . hurry to scenes of accidents, fires and other disasters, determine if losses or damages are covered by claimants' policies, inspect damaged or destroyed property, and estimate costs of repair or replacement. . . . [T]he risk manager . . . determines . . . chances of loss . . . from such causes as fire, embezzlement and burglary.

By looking at only the alarm and insurance industries—two specialized fields that serve loss prevention efforts—we can see numerous employment opportunities. Because almost every firm, from pin manufacturer to jewelry store, needs a loss prevention program, the thousands of companies that provide either services or devices as well as the thousands of organizations that maintain their own proprietary programs will require millions of loss prevention employees.

Sources of Employment Information

- *Periodicals.* Within these sources, trends in employment and employment opportunities are common topics.
- *Professional associations.* Professional organizations serve members through educational programs, publications, and a variety of strategies aimed at increasing professionalism.
- *Trade conferences.* Trade conferences, which are advertised in trade publications, are attended by people with a common interest. By attending these conferences, a loss prevention practitioner or student can learn about a variety of topics. The latest technology and professional seminars are typical features. Trade conferences provide an opportunity to meet practitioners who may be knowledgeable about employment opportunities or are actively seeking qualified people.
- *Educational institutions.* Security and loss prevention and criminal justice degree programs are another source of employment information. Usually, these programs have bulletin boards, near faculty offices, that contain career opportunities. College or university placement services or faculty members are other valuable sources. Sometimes, these degree programs contain a specialized course that requires students to independently study both employment requirements and opportunities in the private and public sectors. These courses are capable of producing a wealth of employment information.
- *Libraries.* A wealth of information for a career search is available at libraries. Examples include periodicals, newspapers, telephone books, directories, books on career strategies, and on-line services.
- *Government buildings.* Public buildings often contain bulletin boards that specify employment news, especially near personnel offices. Government agencies frequently search for practitioners to maintain security and safety at government buildings and installations.
- *Newspapers.* By looking under "security" in classified sections, listings for many entry-level positions can be found. In large urban newspapers, more specialized positions are listed. For instance, the classified and business sections of *The New York Times* often contain pertinent management positions.

- *Public employment agencies.* Numbering close to 2000 in the United States, these agency offices operate in conjunction with the U.S. Employment Service of the Department of Labor. Personnel will provide employment information without cost and actually contact recruiters or employers. Local telephone books list the nearest offices.
- *Networking.* An informal network consists of people the applicant knows from past educational or employment experiences. It is a good idea for any professional to maintain contact, however slight, with peers. When employment-related problems develop and solutions are difficult to obtain, networking may be an avenue for answers. Likewise, this mutual assistance is applicable to employment searches.
- *On-line services.* The Internet is expanding into the largest database of employment listings in the world. There are several advantages: breadth of offerings, time is saved by reviewing opportunities open worldwide, it is more up to date than most publications, and you can respond electronically. Be aware that confidentiality is limited. Look for services that are free. The America's Job Bank (AJB) <http://www.ajb.dni.us> is a network of listings from over 1800 employment service offices throughout the country, and employers can list directly. Hundreds of thousands of opportunities are listed from all 50 states, plus other locations. The opportunities are primarily in the private sector and the service is free to employers and potential employees.[12]
- *Telephone books.* Both private and public entities, their addresses and telephone numbers, are abundant in telephone books. By looking up "security," "guards," "investigators," and "government offices," one can develop a list of possible employment opportunities.
- *Private employment agencies.* Almost all urban areas have private employment agencies that charge a fee. This source probably will be a last resort, and one should carefully study financial stipulations. At times, these agencies have fee-paid jobs, which means that the employer pays the fee.

Career Advice[13]

1. Read at least two good books on searching for employment and careers; both the novice and the experienced person will learn or be reminded of many excellent tips that will "polish" the career search and instill confidence.
2. Begin your search by first focusing on yourself—your abilities and background, your likes and dislikes, and your personality and people skills.
3. If you are new to the security and loss prevention field, aim to "get your foot in the door." As a college student, look for an intern position, work part-time, or do volunteer work. *Aim to graduate with experi-*

ence. As a retired government employee or if you are beginning a new career in security, market and transfer your accumulated skills and experience to this field.

4. Most people will enter new careers several times in their lives.

5. Searching for a career opportunity requires planning, patience, and perseverance. Rejections are a typical part of every search. A positive attitude will make or break your career.

6. When planning elective courses in college or when training opportunities arise, consider that employers want people with skills (e.g., writing, speaking, interviewing, computers).

7. Many students do not realize that a college education and some training programs teach the student *how to learn.* Although many bits of information studied and reproduced on examinations are forgotten months after being tested, the skills of how to study information, how to read a textbook or article, how to critically think and question, how to do research and solve problems, and how to prepare and present a report are skills for life that are repeated over and over in one's professional career. In our quickly changing information age, these skills are invaluable.

8. If you are fortunate enough to have a choice among positions, do not let salary be the only factor in your decision. Think about career potential and advancement, content of the work, free training, benefits, travel, and equipment.

9. Exercise due diligence on potential employers. For example, speak to present employees and check the organization's financial health.

10. Five key factors influencing an individual's chances for promotion are education, training, professional development and certification, experience, and personality.

11. Avoid quitting a job before you find another. Cultivate references, even in jobs you dislike (such jobs are a learning experience).

The employment situation in the security and loss prevention field reflects a bright future. Good luck on your career!

CASE PROBLEMS

19A. As a contract security supervisor with a major security service firm, you are faced with a major career decision. You have a bachelor's degree and have been with your present employer for a total of seven years, two years part-time while in college, and five years full-time since graduating. These years have been spent at a hospital where you would like to advance to site security manager, but you face competition from one other supervisor, who also has a bachelor's degree, the same certifications and training that you possess, and about the same years of experience. The present contract site security manager is a former detective who wants to retire to Arizona within the next year or two. You have repeatedly asked managers from the security service firm (i.e., your employer) about advancement opportunities, but nothing is available. Recently, you were offered the position of in-house security and safety training officer with a nearby, urban school district. The pay is $800 less annually than what you are earning now. However, you would receive additional insurance and retirement benefits and work only day shifts, Monday through Friday. You would be the only college-educated officer on the school district security force, which is primarily composed of contract officers. The director of security is the only other in-house security officer, a retired police officer with no college degree. What career choice do you make?

19B. As a regional security manager with a major retailer, you have 12 years of retail security experience. You earned bachelor's and master's degrees, a CPP, and you worked your way through various retail security positions to your present position. The territory you work covers nearly 100 stores in six southeastern states. You are on the road each day responding to security problems and wish you could spend more time with your spouse and two children. After eight years with the same company, and no chance for advancement, you decide to consider an offer as security director with a major retailer in the New York City area. The pay is $8000 more than what you are earning now, with similar benefits. You would have additional responsibilities, but you would travel much less. Your spouse and children do not want to move because of family and friends. What career choice do you make?

NOTES

1. See Daniel B. Dallas, editor-in-chief, "The Advent of the Automatic Factory," *Manufacturing Engineering* 85, no. 5 (November 1980): 66–75.
2. See U.S. Department of Commerce, *The Role of Behavioral Science in Physical Security* (Washington, DC: U.S. Government Printing Office, 1978).
3. Richard Quinney, *Criminology* (Boston: Little, Brown, 1975), p. 250.
4. See Richter H. Moore, "Private Security in the 21st Century: An Opinion," *Journal of Security Administration* 18, no. 1 (1995): 3–13.
5. Ira S. Somerson, "The Next Generation," *Security Management* (January 1995): 27–30.
6. "Here Comes the 21st Century: What Does It Hold for Security?" *Security Management Bulletin* (March 25, 1997): 4–7.

7. "Survey Studies Women in Security," *Security Management* (February 1996): 87–88.
8. Charles E. Silberman, *Criminal Violence, Criminal Justice* (New York: Vantage Books, 1978), p. 270.
9. William L. Tafoya, "The Future of Law Enforcement? A Chronology of Events," *C J International* 7 (May–June 1991): 4.
10. *Career* Opportunities in Security, pamphlet, n.d., American Society for Industrial Security (1625 Prince Street, Alexandria, VA 22314; Tel.: 703-519-6200).
11. *Compensation in the Security/Loss Prevention Field*, 9th ed., Abbott, Langer & Associates (548 First St., Crete, IL 60417; Tel.: 708-672-4200).
12. Mike Nevins, "America's Job Bank," *Government Technology* (March 1996): 34.
13. Philip P. Purpura, *Criminal Justice: An Introduction* (Boston: Butterworth–Heinemann, 1997), Chapter 15, "Your Future in the Criminal Justice System."

Index

References in *italics* indicate figures; those followed by "t" denote tables

AA. *See* Alcoholics Anonymous
Abduction, 435–436
Abuse, of drugs or alcohol. *See* Alcoholism; Substance abuse
Access controls
  for computer crime, 375
  in fire, 279–280
  at health-care institutions, 398
  for reducing internal threats
    description of, 135
    electronic card systems, 137–139, *140*
    employee identification system, 137
    employee traffic controls, 135–136
    movement of packages and property, 137
    for visitors, 136–137, 398
Accident-proneness theory, 309
Accidents. *See also* Hazards
  causes of, 309
  costs associated with, 294–295
  definition of, 293
  indirect effects of, 294
  OSHA role in prevention of. *See* Occupational Safety and Health Administration
  statistics, 293–294
Accountability
  of cashier operations, 250, 337
  definition of, 130–131, 246
  of documents, 249
  for evidence collection and presentation, 250
  at health-care institutions, 397
  informal nature of, 247
  internal theft reduction and, 130–131
  of inventory, 254–255
  schematic of, *252*

  of shipping, 253–254
  of voids, at checkout counters, 338
Accountant. *See* Certified public accountant
Accounting
  computerization of, 260
  definition of, 131, 245
  elements of, 246
  internal theft reduction and, 131
  as loss prevention strategy, 246–247
  loss sources in, 246
  point-of-sale, 338
Accounting statements, 247, *248*
ACFE. *See* Association of Certified Fraud Examiners
Addiction, 440
Administrative law
  agencies that enforce, 65
  compliance auditing, 65–66
  federal sentencing guidelines for violating, 66
AF. *See* Automatic factory
Affirmative action
  definition of, 102
  effect on applicant screening process, 102
Age Discrimination in Employment Act of 1967, 98
Agent of socialization, 116–117
AICPA. *See* American Institute of Certified Public Accountants
Alarm systems
  intrusion systems. *See* Intrusion alarm systems
  leasing of, 210
  purchasing considerations, 210
  for robbery deterrence, 365
  for shoplifting deterrence, 354–357
  signaling systems, 179, 183–185, 274
Alcoholic, definition of, 439
Alcoholics Anonymous, 439

Other Books from Butterworth-Heinemann

The Art of Successful Security Management by Dennis R. Dalton
1997   312pp   hc   0-7506-9729-6

Encyclopedia of Security Management: Techniques and Terminology
Edited by John J. Fay
1993   450pp   pb   0-7506-9660-5

Handbook of Loss Prevention and Crime Prevention, Third Edition
Edited by Lawrence J. Fennelly
1995   640pp   hc   0-7506-9703-2

Security Consulting, Second Edition by Charles A. Sennewald
1995   192pp   pb   0-7506-9643-5

The Ultimate Security Survey by James L. Schaub and Ken D. Biery, Jr.
1994   256pp   pb (with 3.5" disk)   0-7506-9577-3

Workplace Violence by Sandra L. Heskett
1996   210pp   hc   0-7506-9671-0

. . . .

Detailed information on these and all other BH-Security titles may be found in the BH-Security catalog(Item #800). To request a copy, call 1-800-366-2665. You can also visit our web site at: http://www.bh.com

These books are available from all good bookstores or in case of difficulty call: 1-800-366-2665 in the U.S. or +44-1865-310366 in Europe.

E-Mail Mailing List

An e-mail mailing list giving information on latest releases, special promotions/offers and other news relating to BH-Security titles is available. To subscribe, send an e-mail message to majordomo@world.std.com. Include in message body (not in subject line) subscribe bh-security